DECENTRING
&
DIVERSIFYING
SOUTHEAST ASIAN STUDIES

The **Institute of Southeast Asian Studies (ISEAS)** was established as an autonomous organization in 1968. It is a regional centre dedicated to the study of socio-political, security and economic trends and developments in Southeast Asia and its wider geostrategic and economic environment. The Institute's research programmes are the Regional Economic Studies (RES, including ASEAN and APEC), Regional Strategic and Political Studies (RSPS), and Regional Social and Cultural Studies (RSCS).

ISEAS Publishing, an established academic press, has issued more than 2,000 books and journals. It is the largest scholarly publisher of research about Southeast Asia from within the region. ISEAS Publishing works with many other academic and trade publishers and distributors to disseminate important research and analyses from and about Southeast Asia to the rest of the world.

DECENTRING
&
DIVERSIFYING
SOUTHEAST ASIAN STUDIES

PERSPECTIVES FROM THE REGION

EDITED BY

GOH BENG-LAN

ISEAS

INSTITUTE OF SOUTHEAST ASIAN STUDIES
Singapore

First published in Singapore in 2011 by
ISEAS Publishing
Institute of Southeast Asian Studies
30 Heng Mui Keng Terrace
Pasir Panjang
Singapore 119614

E-mail: publish@iseas.edu.sg
Website: <http://bookshop.iseas.edu.sg>

The responsibility for facts and opinions in this publication rests exclusively with the authors and their interpretations do not necessarily reflect the views or the policy of the publisher or its supporters.

ISEAS Library Cataloguing-in-Publication Data

Goh, Beng-Lan.
   Decentring and diversifying Southeast Asian studies : perspectives from the region.
   1.   Southeast Asia—Study and teaching.
   2.   Southeast Asia—Research.
   3.   Area Studies—Southeast Asia.
   I.   Title.
DS524 G61   2011

ISBN 978-981-4311-56-4 (soft cover)
ISBN 978-981-4311-57-1 (hard cover)
ISBN 978-981-4311-98-4 (e-book PDF)

Typeset by Superskill Graphics Pte Ltd
Printed in Singapore by

CONTENTS

PREFACE AND ACKNOWLEDGEMENTS

Current critical thinking on regions outside the West appears to have shifted from a preoccupation with the limitations of Western discourse to endeavours in fostering inter-referencing in Asian contexts as a means to decentre and diversify knowledge production (Chen 2010; Hillenbrand 2010). This book presents an instance of dialogue and elaborations among Southeast Asian scholars on their dilemmas and ethical recourse as they respond to the critique of area studies and new political-economic and cultural reconfigurations around them. It proposes that the contemplation of the future of Southeast Asian Studies by intellectuals in the region involves both epistemological and ethical questions: How can Southeast Asian intellectuals respond to current critical norms yet construct representations which are faithful to lived realities and meanings in the region and which can also challenge oppressive discourses at the official and oppositional levels? By insisting that theoretical distinctions are shaped by moral imperatives, this book hopes that it can help bring to an end the quarrel between insider-outsider or regional versus Eurocentric perspectives on Southeast Asia. The different interpretations between insider/regional or outsider/European perspectives may be more telling of distinct ethical-political imperatives in knowledge production than the ontology of Southeast Asia. Rather than being oppositional, these different perspectives may in fact complement each other.

This book is the product of the support of many individuals and institutions. It has its beginnings in a workshop in 2002, held with the aim of initiating an interdisciplinary and intergenerational dialogue amongst

Southeast Asian scholars in order to plan for a research-cum-retooling project for junior researchers from the region. The workshop was organized in my role as consultant to the Social Science Research Council (SSRC) of New York's Southeast Asia Programme. It was funded by both the SSRC and a Ford Foundation Seed Grant (No. 1005-0128). The venue for this workshop was provided by the Faculty of Arts and Social Sciences, National University of Singapore (NUS). From the SSRC, I want to thank particularly Mary McDonnell, Itty Abraham, Seteney Shami, and Craig Calhoun for their enthusiastic and steadfast support for this project. Without their wise counsel and the SSRC's provision of financial and logistical support, both the workshop and this book would not have been possible. At the National University of Singapore, I would like to thank Lily Kong, who was then dean of the faculty, for allowing us the use of NUS space, and also colleagues and students at the Southeast Asian Studies Programme for their kindness and assistance during the workshop.

The planning workshop eventually led to a two-year workshop series titled, "Local Scholarship and the Study of Southeast Asia: Bridging the Past and the Present", from 2004–05. This subsequent workshop series received funding support from a Toyota Foundation Initiative Fund (No. D03-P-003 28) and was jointly organized with my colleague, Reynaldo Ileto. I wish to thank Yumiko Himemoto and Reynaldo Ileto for making possible this subsequent workshop series. It brought twenty-five scholars comprising "junior" and "senior" Southeast Asian researchers to reflect on continuities and changes between past and present scholarship on and in Southeast Asia, with the aim of identifying agendas for the future. Insights gained from this subsequent workshop series have also helped shape ideas found in the introductory chapter.

Mainly, I wish to thank all the participants in the planning workshop and their contributions to this book. Although work commitments have prevented Kasian Tejapira, Diana Wong, and Liu Hong from participating in this book, their insights contributed as much to the success of the workshop. To all contributors of this book, my heartfelt thanks for their commitment and excellent chapters.

I also wish to thank NUS students who helped with logistics and served as rapporteurs during the planning workshop: Karen Chua Ee Hsuan, Haydon Leslie Cherry, Chew Kee Seng, and Vernie Oliverio. I want to thank Annie Karmel especially for her editorial assistance. This book has also benefited from Stephen Logan's skilful editing and I would like to thank him and his team at ISEAS.

Last, but not least, I am deeply indebted to four individuals who have provided invaluable intellectual support and help in refining the introductory chapter: Wendy Mee, Abidin Kusno, Tom Bender, and Joel S. Kahn. Wendy's input helped refined my early drafts. Abidin, Tom and Joel provided insightful comments which helped improve the coherency of arguments and Joel's fine sense of language further helped refine the presentation of the chapter.

This book invites colleagues in the field of Southeast Asian Studies to consider the importance of contextualizing debates on the future of the field. The way forward for Southeast Asian Studies in an increasingly self-conscious global age will require all practitioners to be open to, and learn from, the translations of ideas and practices across different geographical boundaries, especially between local and international/Western traditions.

References

Chen Kuan Hsing. *Asia as Method: Towards Deimperialization*. Durham, NC: Duke University Press, 2010.

Hillenbrand, Margaret. "Communitarianism or How to Build East Asian Theory". *Postcolonial Studies* 13, no. 4 (2010): 317–34.

Goh Beng-Lan
Singapore
March 2011

LIST OF CONTRIBUTORS

Wang Gungwu is University Professor at the National University of Singapore (NUS), Faculty of Arts and Social Sciences. His research interests focus on Chinese and Southeast Asian history. He recently edited *Nation-building: Five Southeast Asian Histories* (2005); and co-edited (2008 with Zheng Yongnian) *China and the New International Order*.

Taufik Abdullah is Chairman of the Social Commission, Indonesian Academy of Sciences (Akademi Ilmu Pengetahuan Indonesia) and AKADEMI JAKARTA (Arts and Culture). He was previously Director of the National Economic and Social Research Institute (LEKNAS) from 1974–78, and Head of the Indonesian Institute of Sciences (LIPI) from 2000–2002. His research focuses on Southeast Asian history, with special interests in Indonesian local history. His recently completed volume, *Indonesia: Towards Democracy*, was published by ISEAS.

Reynaldo Ileto is Professor of Southeast Asian Studies at the National University of Singapore. His research interests include religion and social movements in Southeast Asia, nationalism and revolution in the Philippines, Tagalog literature, and the politics of memory and knowledge production. The author of two prize-winning books, he recently wrote *Knowledge and Pacification: Essays on the U.S. Conquest and the Writing of Philippine History* (2011).

Wong Soak Koon is an independent researcher who has retired from the Universiti Sains Malaysia after thirty years of teaching literature at the School of Humanities. Her current research interests focus on contemporary Malaysian and Singaporean literature in English and Malay. Her recent works include "Exploring the Framing and Unframing of Malay-Muslim Identity in Select Malaysian Fiction" in *Writing a Nation: Essays in Malaysian Literature*, edited by Mohammad Quayum and Nur Faridah Manaf (International Islamic University, K.L. 2009), and "Nation and Belonging in Select Plays of Stella Kon" in *Sharing Borders: Studies in Contemporary Singaporean-Malaysian Literature, Vol. 1*, edited by Mohammad Quayum and Wong Phui Nam (National Library Board and National Arts Council, Singapore, 2009).

Paritta Chalermpow Koanantakool was Director of the Princess Maha Chakri Sirindhorn Anthropology Centre in Bangkok. Previously she has taught at the Faculty of Sociology and Anthropology, Thammasat University. Her research interests and publications are in the fields of shadow puppetry of southern Thailand, dance and dancers of central Thailand, and community-based museums.

Yunita Winarto is Professor of Anthropology at the Department of Anthropology, Faculty of Social and Political Sciences, University of Indonesia. She currently holds the Academy Professorship of Indonesia in Social Sciences and Humanities (KNAW-AIPI), at the University of Indonesia (2009–11). Her research interests focus on issues of human ecology and the dialectics of various domains of knowledge. She is the author of *Seeds of Knowledge: The Beginning of Integrated Pest Management in Java* (Yale University, Southeast Asia Council, 2004).

Melani Budianta is Professor of Literary Studies at the Faculty of Humanities, University of Indonesia. Her research focuses on gender and postcolonial issues. Her recent works include "Diverse Voices: Indonesian Literature and Nation-Building", in *Language, Nation and Development in Southeast Asia*, edited by Lee Hock Guan and Leo Suryadinata, (ISEAS, 2007), and "The Dragon Dance: Shifting Meaning of Chineseness in Indonesia", in *Asian and Pacific Cosmopolitans: Self and Subject in Motion*, edited by Katherine Robinson (Palgrave, 2007).

Patricio N. Abinales is Professor at the Centre for Southeast Asian Studies, Kyoto University. His current research is on the relationship between pestilence, diseases, and state formation in the Philippines. He co-wrote with Donna Amoroso, *State and Society in the Philippines* (2005), and his latest book

Orthodoxy and History in the Muslim Mindanao Narrative, 1898–2006, will be published by Ateneo de Manila University Press.

Goh Beng-Lan is Associate Professor and currently Head of the Southeast Asian Studies Department, National University of Singapore. Her research focuses on knowledge production, identity, and modernity in Southeast Asia. She is the author of *Modern Dreams: An Inquiry into Power, Cultural Production, and the Cityscape in Contemporary Urban Penang, Malaysia* (Cornell SEAP, 2002), and a co-editor of *Asia in Europe, Europe in Asia: Rethinking Academic, Social and Cultural Linkages* (International Institute for Asian Studies and Institute of Southeast Asian Studies, 2004).

Abidin Kusno is Associate Professor at the Institute of Asian Research, University of British Columbia. He is the author of *Behind the Postcolonial* (Routledge, 2000), *Gardu di Perkotaan Jawa* (Ombak Press, 2007), and *Appearances of Memory* (Duke University Press, 2010).

Fadjar I. Thufail is Research Fellow at the Max Planck Institute for Social Anthropology in Halle/Saale, Germany, and Research Associate at the Indonesian Institute of Sciences (LIPI). His interests include the anthropology of violence, the anthropology of the state, and legal anthropology. He is currently working on a project examining religious and political dimensions of social reconciliation in post-authoritarian Indonesia.

DISCIPLINES AND AREA STUDIES IN THE GLOBAL AGE
Southeast Asian Reflections

Goh Beng-Lan

In recent years the conceptual underpinnings and continued validity of area studies in a globalizing world have been severely questioned. Emanating from a critique of Orientalism, but also reflecting changing institutional politics in the American academe following the end of the Cold War, the attack on area studies has spread across the globe. This has resulted in growing pronouncements on the failure of area studies in producing a synthesis of knowledge that transcends disciplinary divides and power hierarchies between the Western and non-Western world. [1] The spread of this critique has led to a common view that area studies is in a state of "crisis". [2]

Ironically, however, this critique of area studies comes at a time when regional perspectives are gaining ground in defining regions based on local priorities. The critical agendas that propelled the attack on area studies in Euro-America appear to undermine such promising effort. As the crisis of area studies galvanized scholars to deliberate over its fate, some scholars in Asian Studies[3] have sought to find "afterlives" for area studies by pointing to regionally located scholarships as alternative sites from which Euro-American-centric visions could be denaturalized. [4] In the words of Miyoshi and Harootunian:

> The afterlife thus refers to the moment that has decentered the truths, practices, and even insitutions that belonged to a time that could still believe

in the identity of some conception of humanity and universality with a
Eurocentric endowment and to the acknowledgement that its "provinciality"
must now be suceeded by what Said called "a contrapuntal orientation in
history". (Miyoshi and Harootunian 2002, p. 14)

Yet the prospect of recentring knowledge production back to regions themselves
raises its own set of questions. For one thing, regional scholarships have always
existed alongside Euro-American social sciences. In fact, strident regional
scholarships were contesting the dominance of colonial scholarships during
the decolonization era in endeavours to map out national histories. These
local voices were often dismissed as "nationalist" if not "nativist" and have
remained under-examined and unnoticed, even by scholars located within the
regions themselves.[5] The unspoken politics of theory at the time, supposedly
speaking on behalf of some universal and objective standard, determined
which scholarship could be regarded as theory, and which relegated to more
subjective and parochial forms of knowledge.

Similarly, the quest for the afterlives of area studies is underpinned by
epistemological imperatives of a North American style of knowing, which
has strongly shaped post World War II discourses of area studies.[6] The
throwing back of area studies to local scholars comes at a time when the
epistemological rules of the day appear to be about a search for diversity
rather than similarity, an eschewing of western and nation state frameworks,
and a rejection of the possibility of any bounded geographical and identity
conceptions in the current world.

More poignantly, underpinning these imperatives is a vicious polarization
of opinions over disciplinarity in the context of epistemological challenges to
disciplinary foundations, and debates on the politics of knowledge production.
In this polarization where there is often no middle ground, disciplines are
either seen as immutable and to be strictly defended, or as oppressive and
to be dismantled. Equally, theoretical-political differences between the right
and left, and even amongst these groups themselves, are bitterly divided, and
growing more dogmatic in the face of postmodern challenges.[7] In such an
atmosphere, concepts and social categories become part of a social science
language game; they are hijacked, reified, and frozen by dogmatic ideological
and disciplinary purposes making alternative persuasions simply difficult or
misunderstood.

In this context, how might local scholars negotiate the difference in what
counts as "scholarship" in Southeast Asian and Euro-American settings, while
remaining true to their calling to prioritize local perspectives? Given the
global diffusion of Euro-American ideas in today's world, how are alternative

social scientific discourses possible? At the same time, what are the conditions and processes that enable alternative epistemologies and imaginings without falling into the traps of essentialism or chauvinism? If indeed the project of knowledge production has become polycentric, would the agendas and ideas from regional scholarships be accepted into dominant paradigms, even if they were to overthrow their fundamental disciplinary and epistemological (theoretical-political) premises? What are the grounds for equal comparative intellectual exchanges that will recognize epistemic dissent from regional practices and effect changes in existing canons of knowledge? Could different analytical and ethical imaginings emanating from diverse spatial and cultural settings help forge a new universal knowledge that does not explicitly or implicitly return us to Eurocentric legacies? Could regional remakings of Southeast Asian Studies within the context of power realignments in a post–Cold War era, in fact, overthrow assumptions about area studies being in a state of crisis?

This volume will explore these and other related questions in the changing parameters of Southeast Asian Studies, in which the crisis of area studies has revived controversies over the distinction between, and reconciliation of, "insider" versus "outsider" perspectives, so prevalent during the 1960s and 1970s.

Using intellectual biographies of eleven Southeast Asian scholars, which arose from a workshop on local dimensions of Southeast Asian Studies,[8] the contributors to this volume will explore how conceptualizations of Southeast Asia/Southeast Asian Studies from the region may be traced from the way regional practices in the humanities and social sciences (henceforth "human sciences") are *interconnected with, yet also distinct from*, Euro-American disciplinary and conceptual legacies. Building from these individual intellectual biographies, this volume identifies specific disciplinary and epistemological practices in local institutional settings, and explores their potential to help address fundamental questions and gaps surrounding knowledge production on Southeast Asia/Southeast Asian Studies as a means to engage with the crisis of area studies.

To fully appreciate how the intellectual biographies presented here provide us with alternative perspectives on the future of Southeast Asian Studies when compared with contemporary critiques of area studies, an exegesis of basic conceptual anxieties in the field and their intimate entwinement with questions of subject position (or where one stands/is located) is necessary. The individualized biographies offer us a glimpse into institutional, disciplinary, and theoretical evolution in parts of Southeast Asia, which are country-specific across different scholarship cohorts, reflecting a possible evolution of academic practices in particular country settings. Changing intellectual conditions, shared concerns, and continued scholarly commitment have brought different generations into dialogue on how to study, but importantly, also problematize, Southeast Asia as a region.

This introduction makes these arguments in three parts. Part I, "Subject Positionality, Agency, and the Search for Southeast Asian Perspectives", introduces the reader to both the breadth and specificities of key conceptual difficulties in the search for "local" Southeast Asian perspectives in the context of the strong "outside" influence of Euro-American styles of defining the region.

Part II, "Contexts, Connections, and Comparisons: The Intellectual Biographies", establishes the argument of this volume through the experiences and ideas raised by contributors, their different "national" and generational experiences, as well as "inter" disciplinary practices, and provides food for thinking about how insider/outsider differences may, in fact, be complementary to each other — they offer entwined, yet different, viewpoints on the region. Here discussions are divided under four subheadings in order to bring out changing human science practices within the region over time, that is: (i) "The Fluid Ecology Knowledge: Early Formations"; (ii) "Nation Building, the Cold War, and the Rise of American Social Sciences"; (iii) "The State, Public Intellectuals, and (Trans)National Grounds; Ethics and Politics of Knowledge"; and (iv) "Memories and the Return of the Real: Intellectual Predicaments and the War between Disciplines and Theory".

Finally, Part III, "Southeast Asian Studies in the Region: Late Beginnings, New Departures?" deals with the constraints and challenges encountered in doing Southeast Asian Studies within the region amidst disciplinary and theoretical shifts and wars in the human sciences more widely. It pins down epistemological differences arising from three conceptual frameworks which remain vital to Southeast Asian scholars, despite the dismissal of these frameworks in contemporary social theorizing. These differences are delineated in three subsections, that is, (i) "Challenges: East-West Binary Effects"; (ii) "Strategies: Resuscitating the Region"; and (iii) "Commitments: Nation and Redemption".

PART I
SUBJECT POSITIONALITY, AGENCY, AND THE SEARCH FOR SOUTHEAST ASIAN PERSPECTIVES
Background

In the development of Southeast Asia as a field of study, certain epistemological questions have repeatedly surfaced over the past fifty years.[9] Paramount among them is the issue of local contributions to building concepts that can better account for historical experiences specific to the region, which are at the same time interconnected with larger histories, given the experiences of migration, colonialism, foreign education, and other aspects of global interaction.

Scholars from the region have been engaging with these concerns since the 1950s.[10] During the late 1950s and throughout the 1960s, indigenous voices vigorously contested the dominance of colonial scholars in mapping out the field of Southeast Asian Studies. Forming part of the "indigenization" and "decolonization" intellectual movements in many Third World countries at the time, these local voices were often characterized by passionate and emotive writings about regionally embedded agencies and identities which were analysed within nation state frameworks. Often falling outside universal intellectual norms of impartiality and secular objectivity, they were sidelined as "Asia-centric" by academic discourses emerging from Southeast Asian Studies centres in the United States, Australia, and Europe. Tainted by the problem of atavism and essentialism, these scholarships were seen to be in the service of nationalist interests.

There was truth to these critiques and "Asia-centric" discourses have indeed served to justify domestic oppression, ethnic inequalities, and other self-serving purposes.[11] Yet a complete dismissal may be too hasty as there are important ethical dimensions to such scholarships. Rather than a wholesale dismissal of Asia-centric viewpoints, there is a need to understand and appreciate the local contexts from which they emanated at that point in time better — especially those of colonialism, decolonization, and the struggle to form new nation states.

Within these debates, the avant-garde views of John Smail (1961, 1993), a historian from the University of Wisconsin (Madison), provided a watershed in efforts to transcend the dichotomy between Asia-centric/Eurocentric views during the 1960s. As pointed out by Sears (1993, p. 9), Smail was a radical thinker for his time. He was critical of the newer racist ideals of primitive mentalities and post-war modernization in Euro-America, as well as the nationalist styles of scholarship amongst indigenous scholars in Southeast Asia. As a way of transcending nationalist and colonialist impulses on both sides of these debates, Smail proposed the idea of an "autonomous" history. "Autonomous" history, according to Smail, is one which is embedded in an objective, scientific, and universal rationality that looks beyond colonial and nationalist relations to focus on social structure and change among ordinary people rather than domestic elites. Smail was confident that all historians and social scientists would eventually take up "a single world culture or thought-world" (Smail 1993, p. 42).

While he was ahead of his time, with hindsight we can now say that Smail's ideal of a universal, but implicitly western thought-world amongst all historians, reflects the ethos of classical western liberalism which recognizes pluralism, yet endeavours to manage diversity within a unitary code. The postfoundational turn in the humanities and the social sciences has put Smail's approach in question.

Today, universalist models are no longer easily acccepted. Instead current progressive impulses demand forms of social analyses which are embeded in socio-historical contexts and which make power relationships in the course of knowledge production transparent. Alongside new geopolitical power realignments in a post–Cold War world, these theoretical transformations have severely disrupted the area studies paradigm (not to mention a variety of disciplines as well). Not only has it set off a crisis of area studies in Western settings, the search for new ideas to reform the field has led to debates on the role of regional voices in decentring knowledge production on area studies.

In Southeast Asian Studies, these debates have inevitably revived the insider/outsider dispute. Despite progressive sentiments, the current call for the participation of local voices appears to be double-edged. We are in a situation where views of local scholars are sought to "parochialize" or decentre Eurocentric conceptions, on the one hand, while fears of deviation from accepted universal/global norms of scientific values and ethics have also appeared, on the other.[12] Akin to older debates within the field, the newer search for "local/native" alterity is faced by the conundrum of should we abandon or retain the idea of a shared/single/western/universal scientific form of knowledge and truth. Underlying this dilemma is the fear that "local/native" knowledge may succumb to the subjective, fictive, and emotive, rather than conforming with the norm and ethical foundation of social scientific inquiry.

Caught in this limbo, we find a situation where the call for the inclusion of local/native voices is overwhelmingly supported, but this is accompanied by concern over the blight of "native blindness".[13] On the other hand, local scholars advocating "insider" imaginaries are overly defensive and go to great lengths to deny they have any advantage over outsiders to knowledge because of their birth, race, linguistic ease, nationality, and other criteria of regional membership (Abu and Tan 2003, pp. ix–xxv; Winichakul 2003, pp. 3–29). Such apprehension suggests that the invocation of the "insider/outsider" distinction is immediately suspect of partiality, racism, and/or ethno-cultural chauvinism.

Given this wariness, recent efforts to rethink Southeast Asia have tended to avoid the insider/outsider distinction, preferring instead to rely on disciplinary and epistemological efficacy to steer cutting edge thinking on the region. In this quest, many have taken the Orientalist critique to heart and turned to newer radical epistemes in order to ensure critical standards and revolutionary theory-making in the study of the region.

At least two significant trends can be observed in such revisionary theorizing.[14]

A Survey of Revisionist Trends

The first of these revisionary trends is manifest in the problem of disciplinary or newer anti-disciplinary frameworks which are believed to offer greater theoretical promise than an area studies approach held back by Orientalist legacies. There are two main proponents of this approach. The first is Victor King (2001; 2006), a leading British anthropologist of Southeast Asia, who calls for a return to disciplinary frameworks to produce cutting edge thinking on the region.[15] Using anthropological studies of the region as his point of reference, King repudiates Southeast Asian Studies as a distinct field of study, arguing that the region is predominantly studied as a specific locality/country rather than as a region per se. As such he opines that Southeast Asia is at best an empirical site for testing ideas in key disciplines active in defining the region, such as anthropology, history, and geography.

The other approach is advanced by Ariel Heryanto, a reputed, cultural literary scholar of Southeast Asia and a strong advocate of regional scholarship, who views cultural studies as the vehicle to take the study of the region forward. In a provocative essay titled, "Can there be Southeast Asians in Southeast Asian Studies?" Heryanto argues that a continued dominance of Western epistemology and the gate-keeping role of Western scholars make it difficult for Southeast Asian scholars to enter and achieve equal standing in redefined Southeast Asian Studies.[16] As a solution, Heryanto suggests that we turn to cultural studies — which he conflates with media and postmodern studies — to rebuild "new" Southeast Asian Studies to replace the "old" framework. Heryanto proffers that the radical analytical structures of cultural studies, characterized by a consciousness of "postmodernity" and critiques of "dominant paradigms" or "universalist theorization", will help dismantle the Orientalist and Cold War legacies of the "old" Southeast Asian Studies (2007, p. 102). Heryanto's turn to cultural studies could perhaps in part be understood as a reaction to the domination of positivist and empiricist approaches which tend to relegate culture as fluff or epiphenomenon in Southeast Asian Studies, particularly in the Australian academe where Heryanto is based.[17] However, Heryanto's faith in cultural studies is still in step with a wider Euro-American critique of area studies, whereby cultural and postcolonial studies have been proposed as radical replacements of area studies (Chow 2002; Harootunian 2002).

A second revisionist trend seeks instead to dismantle traditional categories and conceptions, particularly those of nation states, regions, and fixed notions of culture and identity. These studies are characterized by a preference for globally oriented approaches, with attention paid to external influences, the mobility of people, ideas, capital, and goods, the fluidity of identity politics, and the porosity of territorial borders, in attempts to revise understandings of the region. As a result, Southeast Asia has been increasingly studied via new frontiers such as the sea, "sub-regions" (King 2006, p. 25), "Zomia" (Van Schendel 2005, p. 282), and so on, or via fluid social practices of diasporas and transnational populations.[18] All in all, these developments have complicated and dislocated intact, coherent, and established conceptualizations of Southeast Asia, its peoples, culture, and societies.

There is a need to contextualize these revisionists arguments. It is evident that these approaches are propelled by specific critical agendas which reject the area studies paradigm for its Orientalist foundations and its irrelevance to a post–Cold War world shaped by global processes deemed no longer containable within any single set of spatial, temporal, and cultural boundaries. These intellectual politics, as we know, emanated from progressive Euro-American intellectual currents in the Orientalist critique of area studies/knowledge production. They are aimed at reforming Euro-American models of area studies which, among other things, had led to a return to disciplinary, or a call for anti-disciplinary paradigms, as well as concerted efforts to bring non-western societies (and "natives") back on to the global stage in social analyses (see Harutoonian 2000; 2002).

While these critical imperatives may be warranted, it would be a mistake to presume their universal relevance to other models. Although area studies paradigms outside Western settings are entwined with Euro-American models, they are embedded in different temporalities which may require different critical interventions in response to the politics of knowledge in a post–Cold War world. In considering a direct application of critical imperatives, originally aimed at rectifying Western scholastic traditions, to academic practices in Southeast Asia, at least two problems come to the fore. First, it would mean freezing Southeast Asian Studies in its Orientalist/Western origins, and missing out on the fact that alternative trajectories may have developed within the region which may require different forms of critical intervention. Second, it would bring about an unwitting reinstatement of Western universalism, albeit one shaped by progressive discourses, which places other ethical subjectivities that do not fully correlate with these critical logics at risk of erasure.

These predicaments aside, the claims of disciplinarity and anti/interdiscplinarity and a preoccupation with global or fluid/unbounded conceptions are not unproblematic. To begin with, assumptions about disciplinarity, anti-disciplinarity, and area studies being at odds with one another may be misplaced. This is because interrogations of disciplinary formation in the human sciences have revealed that disciplines have, in fact, already been constituted by dialectics between disciplinary and anti-/inter-interdisciplinary impulses (Anderson and Valente 2002, p. 2).[19] Hence, rather than pitting these different frameworks against one another, it may be beneficial to examine the history of interaction between disciplines/anti-disciplines and Southeast Asian Studies. Indeed precisely such an argument has been made by John Bowen (2000) who views Southeast Asian Studies as a distinct field of study which has brought about interactions between discipline/theory and place/empiricism and contributed to theory making.

Likewise, a preoccupation with global/fluid categories and conceptions faces a serious epistemological problem. Such conceptions have missed out on the fact that these unbounded sites, units of analyses, or meanings, do not merely shape human societies, but are themselves also products of time. This epistemological problem has been raised by Arif Dirlik, who has also warned that the deconstruction of reified categories, such as nation state, region, or bounded identities, if taken to an extreme, may be counterproductive to a better comprehension of the world around us (2005, p. 166). It may therefore be useful to develop theoretical perspectives which can consider the simultaneity and interaction of the global and the local, the inside and outside, the old and new, the centre and the periphery, the stable and the unstable, and so on, rather than seek to replace one by the other in the effort to redefine Southeast Asia.

We can surmise from the above that in exploring options to decentre colonial/imperial knowledge on Southeast Asia, there must be no foreclosures to alternative critical registers. This does not mean that there can be no shared assumptions about progressive politics and critical analyses. The issue is about understanding how critical dissent against knowledge/power hierarchies may take on different epistemological trajectories under different conditions within the region. It is crucial to this effort to develop analytical procedures, which can at once explicate alternative, epistemological imperatives relevant to regional academic practices, and recognize their coeval standing in the enterprise to decentre and pluralize knowledge about Southeast Asia.

To look for answers, we turn to debates beyond Southeast Asian Studies on the deconstruction of imperial/colonial knowledge, which grapple precisely with these questions.

Looking to Wider Debates

I shall begin with an important edited volume dealing specifically with the subject of area studies as a whole. This is the volume by David Szanton (2004) which provides refreshing insights into how area studies should be approached as a heterogeneous and dynamic intellectual movement by turning the critique of area studies on its head and questioning the politics that underpins it. Using contributions from American scholars working on various regions of the world, this volume stands out for emphasizing open engagements with, and learning from, different models of area studies and calling for multivalent conclusions on the area studies paradigm. Proposing that we look at area studies as having heterogenous genealogies, this volume prescribes "historicised" and "contextualised" approaches in order to better map the constitutions, directions, and contributions of area studies paradigms over time and across different locations (Szanton 2004, p. 3).

An important contribution in this volume is the essay by Timothy Mitchell, who questions the disciplinary assumptions that drive the critique of area studies. Mitchell argues that the future of area studies does not lie in turning against itself. Rather, crucial to its future is its capacity to question and dismantle disciplinary norms which subsume area studies and knowledge from non-Western settings to disciplinary cannons and categories. Mitchell points out that Euro-American theoretical and disciplinary discourses have continued to set the standard for global comparisons of disciplinary and area study developments, despite an age of theoretical deconstruction. He argues that unless the fundamental imbalance between area studies in the United States/the West and other regions is overturned, models outside the West will merely be "testing grounds for the universalization of western social sciences" (Mitchell 2004, p. 98). Mitchell challenges area studies to stop being "a servant of American social sciences" and instead strive to become "a place from which to rewrite the history of the social sciences, and to examine how their categories are implicated in a certain history of Europe, and, in the twentieth century, an unachieved American project of universal social science" (2004, p. 9). For Mitchell, the crisis of area studies is, therefore, really a crisis of Western human sciences. As he puts it:

> The question of the future of area studies is therefore a question about the future of the social science project rather than simply an issue of how best to learn about foreign parts. (p. 76)

Mitchell is not alone in his radical vision of area studies. Achille Mbembe — a scholar who works on Africa — is similarly concerned about the limits of Western social science categories and the need for regional knowledge to search for its own expressions. In his book *The Postcolony*, Mbembe advocates a "*different writing*" [his emphasis] from Western social sciences so as to better capture African subjectivities, which to his mind, originate from and remain interconnected to world history and Western social science, but do not fully correlate with Western theory, critical or otherwise (2001, p. 14). Mbembe argues that "African social formations do not necessarily converge toward a single point, trend, or cycle" (2001, p. 16). While Mbembe's treatment of Africa as a homogenous totality may be problematic, the point he is making about the need for the social sciences to learn from alternative narratives of real historical processes and develop a "*different writing*" to include them into scholastic discourse, is an important one (Mbembe 2001, pp. 14–15).

Similarly we can learn from Vinay Lal, author of *Empire of Knowledge,* who considers "dissenting perspectives on the politics of knowledge" as imperative, if we truly want to decentre, pluralize, and democratize modern knowledge structures (2002, p. 4). Lal shows how imperial knowledge has profoundly shaped modern definitions of time, space, ideas, and politics, silencing all alternative conceptions. He points out that current disciplinary (and anti-disciplinary) critiques of imperial knowledge, even of the most radical kind, are equally Western ultimately as they are largely derived from Western history. In such a scenario, Lal argues, colonial/imperial knowledge can only truly be decentred if we are not held hostage by modern knowledge structures, but strive to pluralize the analytical categories through which we view the world (2002, p. 4). He calls for the use of hermeneutical, dialectical, and dialogic approaches to bring competing "universalisms" into engagement in order to capture other ways of renewing and renegotiating definitions of time, space, and society better.

Yet dialectical and dialogical approaches do not in themselves provide guides on how epistemological agency is to be enabled. What kind of conditions and agency are needed to carve out locally relevant epistemologies? On these issues, I find the ideas of Walter Mignolo particularly useful. Mignolo is a scholar of Latin American history and literature who has written extensively on the coloniality of knowledge and political-ethical imperatives in decolonizing knowledge.

At the risk of simplifying Mignolo's complex ideas, I will draw on the part of his argument that deals with the links between epistemology, ethical agency, and the sensibilities of "the place of theorizing", to lay grounds for alternative thinking from and about Southeast Asia (2000, p. 191).

Mignolo's work begins with the premise of a doubled-edged modern world system since the end of the fifteenth century, whereby the experience of modernity is inevitably accompanied by a "darker" underside of coloniality (2000, p. 22). Modernity/coloniality are therefore simultaneous existences or two sides of the same coin, so to speak. Modernity/coloniality are each equally constituted by doubled movements of hegemonic and subaltern knowledge formations. At its "visible" side, modernity is represented by movements of "global designs" which circulate "planetarily" at particular local/national/ regional levels, on the one hand, and the "subalternization" of other forms of knowledge, on the other. On its underside, coloniality (which is experienced in both metropolitan and peripheral countries) is shaped by contestations over "local histories" between nationalist forces rearticulating "global designs", on the one hand, and subaltern resistance and struggle to emancipate subjugated knowledge, on the other (2000, pp. 64–65). Modernity/coloniality or global designs/subalternized imaginaries are not to be conceived in discrete terms, but rather as simultaneities or continua which contest one another at the global and national/local/regional levels (2000, p. 33).

It is from the simultaneity of hegemony and subaltern resistance that Mignolo constructs the capacity for ethical agency, using a concept of "border thinking". According to Mignolo, "border thinking" is an ethical agency emerging from dichotomous imaginaries of the hegemonic and the subalternized, but which also breaks away from both to form a new thinking (2000, p. 67). Importantly, this ethical theoretical agency is not historically given, but enacted and unfolds at both metropolitan and peripheral centres. This enacted subject positionality, or what Mignolo calls "locus of enunciation" is "an emerging discursive formation, as a form of articulation of subaltern rationality" (Mignolo 2000, p. 95). It arises from the development of a double-critique that enables one to become not only critical of hegemonic imaginaries, but also reflexive of one's own traditions. "Border thinking" is hence not neutral and, Mignolo argues, always foregrounded by "emotional sensibilities", arising from ethnic, national, cosmopolitan, sexual, class, and other forms of oppression (2000, p. 191). The capacity for ethical agency, Mignolo asserts, is not determined by any essentialist terms, but is formed and transformed through everyday experiences in the course of one's lifetime, whereby a political and ethical commitment is developed to emancipate subjugated knowledge associated with "the place of theorizing (*being from, coming from, and being at* [his emphasis])" (Mignolo 2000, p. 115).

Inevitably, Mignolo points out that "border thinking" will take different forms, depending on the "place of theorizing" from which subject position is enacted. For instance, he argues that the critique of colonial knowledge from the perspective of Western and colonial modernities in regions such as "Asia, Africa and the Americas/Caribbean" will likely be in conflict (2000, p. 11). Likewise, he opines that scholars born in the North/West or from the South/East, but writing and teaching in northern locations, may have different agendas than academics born or writing in the South/East, who often have to struggle against modern colonization as well as theoretical domination.[20] While such distinctions between North/West and South/East may be viewed with suspicion, Mignolo argues that there is a need for such lines to be drawn, not so much in terms of national identities, but rather on the basis of their "loci of enunciation" (1993, p. 122). He insists that it is precisely by making such distinctions that subalternized knowledge can be released to remap the cultures of scholarship. In fact, Mignolo views the crisis of "area studies" as a predicament of "old borders" (i.e., national or civilizational) and of distinctions between "hegemonic (discipline-based knowledges) and subaltern (area based knowledges)", whereby "border thinking" gives rise to new forms of what he calls "area-based disciplinary knowledges" which are "bringing together and erasing borders between knowing *about* and knowing *from*" [his emphases] (2000, p. 310).

By locating theoretical agency as a capacity for ethical action at the intersection of domination and subaltern resistance, Mignolo's approach provides a simultaneous recognition of the domination of authoritative knowledge, yet also the coeval standing of entwined but differentiated forms of knowledge. Such an approach enables us to talk about forms of *thinking from and about* Southeast Asia, which are different from, yet entwined and coeval with, current epistemological trajectories in the search for a new universalism of polycentric and multidirectional knowledge on the region.

Mignolo's approach is also useful in working towards a détente between the insider/outsider dispute in Southeast Asian Studies in at least two ways. First, it provides a way out of the anxiety about racial-cultural chauvinism associated with the insider/outsider divides by showing that racial, geo-cultural, and historical sensibilities do matter, and that recognizing their impact on intellectual formation does not have to be the same, nor should it be confused with racism and dogma. Rather, such a recognition enables us to capture analytically other forms of experience which arise in conjunction with, but also in differentiation from, dominant conceptual norms.

Furthermore, a subject position to *think from and about* the region does not have to exclude others not from or located in the region. Rather, both insiders and outsiders are capable of enacting such a positionality. What is only required is a scholarly commitment to the region, its places, and people and a responsibility to articulate regional idioms of experience in and on their own terms, without subsuming them under existing knowledge claims. It is precisely a recognition of this value of scholarly commitment to the region that led Thongchai Winichakul, a historian of Southeast Asia, to recover the disdained native/indigenous category, replacing it with a more inclusive group of "home scholars" (Winichakul 2003, p. 6). To Winichakul, "home scholar" is defined by commitment to the region and the stature and reception of one's scholarship within the field of study rather than by natural internal membership. In step with such an inclusionary effort, Vincente Rafael has also pointed out that commitment to a place of study amongst foreign scholars may often begin as chance encounters. But prolonged encounters often enabled these scholars to develop a "doubled identity" or an ability to identify with both Eurocentric and regional viewpoints (1999, p. 19). In fact there is now greater opportunity for foreign scholars to be based in Southeast Asia as they are increasingly recruited by regional universities and research institutions with ambition to become major players in the globalization of education. Singapore is a case in point, offering promise of an emergent scholarship by foreign scholars who are also based in and *thinking from* the region.[21]

Second, Mignolo's arguments are useful in addressing the antimony between insider/outsider perspectives on Southeast Asia by revealing their complementarity. If we treat insider/outsider differences as products of different "loci of enunciation", characterized by different sets of commitment to differentiated sensibilities of "the place of theorizing", then their quarrels may tell us more about divergent subject positions than about the ontology of Southeast Asia itself. Consequently, we can argue that the views of both regional and foreign scholars are equally subjective, dispelling the biased one-sided qualms about "native blindness". Accordingly, we must insist that neither side can claim accuracy or authority over the other. The way forward in the effort to reorganize knowledge about Southeast Asia is for each side to listen to, respect, and learn from the other.

Aims and Limitations of Regional Perspectives

This book is intended as a step towards the future of the dialogical and multidirectional human science of Southeast Asia by offering the thoughts and critiques of Southeast Asian scholars as they draw on their experiences both within and outside the region. It is a response to contradictions arising from both the critique of area studies/Southeast Asian Studies, as well as the regional political-economic configurations in the post–Cold War era. These transformations present tremendous challenges to Southeast Asian scholars studying the region in how they should respond, on the one hand, to rearticulations of area studies in a new global order where region and nation have come under scrutiny in new progressive scholastic discourse, and, on the other hand, what they make of the consolidation of national and regional powers and their new hegemonic ambitions. These ambitions are often articulated in a radical critique of western/imperial domination under new regional materialities in a world in transition.

This book is shaped by two convictions: First, that Southeast Asian scholars and the alternative, albeit emergent, models of area studies in the region must participate in the debates over the future of Southeast Asian Studies, so as to highlight interconnected yet also different sets of concerns and imperatives from regional practices and perspectives. This book is intended as a voice amongst many voices which are seeking to shape the future of Southeast Asian Studies.

Secondly, there is a need, at least in the short run, to create a platform to speak about Southeast Asian perspectives, despite their problematic nature, so that regional scholars sharing the same convictions can come together to discuss issues that may not be of concern to those outside of the region.[22] It is felt that a collective enterprise to build ethical imagining is necessary to counter regional imaginaries constructed in the service of conservative and sexist forces. These forces have grown increasingly sophisticated as stakes over a future world are ever more so fought out in terms of cultural and value differences.

The way contributors to this volume think and critique Southeast Asia may well come from their relation to the region as a place from which they come from, in which they live, or from which they speak. Inevitably, a rethinking of Southeast Asia from regional perspectives requires these scholars to navigate connections and tensions in disciplinary conventions, the socio-political environments of their embedments, as well as their personal agendas as researchers. This book is intended to be a reminder that as much as Southeast Asian Studies is for everyone, it is also for Southeast Asians themselves and that regional scholars have a responsibility to explicate lived realities and understandings of normative social science concepts within the region, rather than taking wider social theories emanating from the West/outside as the formulae for defining the region.

The time seems right for Southeast Asian voices to be taken seriously when foreign scholars appear to be in full support of facilitating scholarship by Southeast Asians, with some even advocating that the field should learn from new knowledge paradigms emerging from the region (Sears 2006; King 2006). As Thompson (2010) has recently pointed out, the world of Southeast

Asian Studies is now "large and diverse enough to have numerous, overlapping 'circles of esteem'"[23] which no longer refers only to American, European, or other international scholarship circles, but also to emerging intraregional networks of scholarship within the region itself.[24]

Such concerns and visions shaped the workshop (which led to a project on local dimensions to the rise of Southeast Asian scholarships), from which this volume springs. It was held in order to address some of the fundamental questions surrounding alternative knowledge production on the region, and to work towards détente in the insider-outsider dispute. Of the fourteen participants in this workshop, eleven are represented in this volume.[25]

Some qualifications about the representativeness of this book may be appropriate. First, lest it be misunderstood, this book cannot and *does not claim* that the microcosms of individualized scholastic practices presented in it are representative of all academic practices in Southeast Asia. Despite the individualized and unrepresentative nature of the intellectual biographies presented, there is still something which can be learnt from them. The intellectual conditions and concerns discussed are after all not isolated ones, but the products of interconnections between the domestic and global intellectual environments, as well as social-historical realities in different time periods in the region. The narratives presented provide a window on how scholars living in and/or thinking from the region make meaning out of the interplay between the world of disciplinary knowledge and the social-historical realities of academic and everyday life over time in the region.

Second, this book does not claim to provide an integrated totality of viewpoints from the region. Rather the perspectives offered here represent one of a diversity of views on the state-of-the-field in Southeast Asian Studies. Southeast Asian Studies have diverse genealogies both outside and inside the region and there will undoubtedly be criticisms of, and alternatives to, the arguments presented here from outside as well as within the region.

Third, there is no denying that the scholars represented in this book are privileged by their location in the relatively more developed Southeast Asian countries, which also makes the book's claims on ethical/progressive intervention suspect. Understandably, some will take issue with this book as merely representing situated and narrow elitist interests. Nevertheless, the complexities of the politics of knowledge in the twenty-first century, which have serious implications for human societies, do require us to make some difficult decisions to find some resolve, no matter what our class locations may be. Despite their privileged locations, many of the scholars represented here are "public intellectuals" and social activists, a common trend in a region where scholars are also often social-political actors in their own societies.

Finally, it has to be acknowledged that the book's claim of ethical/progressive intervention is not unproblematic. What is ethical/progressive is inevitably value laden. Any claim of the ethical/progressive is equally a claim to a higher moral ground which inexorably will also be contested. As the ethical/progressive is appropriated and used to signify different meanings by competing groups under different historical-political contexts, what are the grounds for us to distinguish between the ethical and the unethical? Does relativizing the ethical/progressive as value expressions of the particularities of place mean that there are no immanent, timeless, or universal virtues of ethics? How do we compare and reconcile the particular and the universal without subsuming one to the other?

There are no easy solutions to these questions.[26] Yet it is clear that ethical dilemmas over the interpretations of experiential and value differences are real and will continue to bedevil us as societies grow more complex. Intellectual dilemmas are equally both political and ethical ones as well. The ethical choices that we face and the decisions that we have to make may sometimes never be dialectically resolved. Despite difficulties, and for the lack of any better word, it still makes sense to hold on to the meaning of ethical/progressive, if such a term is closest to signifying the struggle for emancipation from all forms of suppression and domination and to recover subdued knowledge.

PART II
CONTEXTS, CONNECTIONS, AND COMPARISONS:
THE INTELLECTUAL BIOGRAPHIES

Profile of Contributors

The eleven scholars represented in this volume come from different generations and disciplinary backgrounds. Though a somewhat false divide, age-cohort was taken as a criterion for generational difference, with the justification that knowledge production is shaped both by personal experiences and social historical trajectory.

Contributors representing the "senior" generation of scholars are the illustrious Wang Gungwu, Taufik Abdullah, and Reynaldo Ileto while the middle generation is represented by Wong Soak Koon, Yunita Winarto, Melani Budianta, Paritta Chalermpow Koanantakool, Patricio Abinales, and myself. The "younger" generation is represented by Abidin Kusno and Fadjar Thufail.

The disciplinary backgrounds of contributors range from history, literary studies, anthropology, political science, to architectural history. However, as their intellectual biographies will show, all have developed cross- or interdisciplinary perspectives in the course of their engagement with, and thinking about, Southeast Asia.

Many of these scholars are "public intellectuals" who represent a distinctive regional phenomenon where many scholars are engaged in activism and write beyond the academic arena to reach a wider audience.

Only the countries of Malaysia, Singapore, Indonesia, Thailand, and the Philippines are represented here, with three of the contributors (Wang, Ileto, and Goh) currently based in Singapore. Inevitably, this participation is reflective of the structural gaps within the region, where academics from the mainland Southeast Asian countries of Laos, Cambodia, Vietnam, and Myanmar remain relatively isolated from their counterparts in other parts of the region.

All contributors, with the exception of Koanantakool,[27] who received both her undergraduate and graduate training in England, share the commonality of having been trained in both Western and local/regional institutions. With the exception of Abinales and Abidin, all contributors currently live and work at educational and research institutes in Southeast Asia. Abinales is attached to the Centre for Southeast Asian Studies in Kyoto University, Japan, while Abidin is at the Institute of Asian Research at the University of British Columbia, Canada.

While these eleven scholars have diverse disciplinary backgrounds and training paths, as well as different historical, geographical, and social locations, their individualized intellectual biographies, which stretch from the era of decolonization to the current (post–Cold War) period, provide us with a "microcosm" of academic experiences and intellectual concerns as a means to understanding continuities, differences, and boundary crossings in the human sciences as well as area studies, in the region over time.

This volume treats the eleven intellectual biographies as products of time and particular social and personal histories in order to identify commonalities and differences, as well as the particular historical experiences of the different Southeast Asian countries represented.

The scholars' narration of their intellectual trajectories during the workshop built a picture of local practices in the human and social sciences over time. It is clear that disciplinary and theoretical developments in western human sciences have had a tremendous influence on academic practices in the region. Yet the narratives presented also point to disciplinary practices, as well as epistemological concerns, over concepts such as the East-West binary, and region and nation, which *do not quite fit with, despite being inevitably connected to* Euro-American scholastic discourse.

Let us begin with the alternative disciplinary organization of the human sciences in the region as they emerged from the narratives.

The Fluid Ecology of Knowledge: Early Formations

The narration of their intellectual biographies enabled participants to paint an evolving picture of the human sciences as closely entangled with Western practices, yet strongly shaped by changing social conditions and local imperatives within the region. The picture of human science practices that emerged is one of fluid disciplinary practices during the formative years of regional academies from the 1940s to the 1960s towards increasingly established disciplinary boundaries and political-theoretical differences with the advent of a more systematic influence from the North American human sciences since the Cold War. These biographies also reveal a strong commitment to applied knowledge, in which ideas from the human sciences are used for socially and ethically informed practice. During the formative years, the project of applying knowledge in the pursuit of development appears to have been easier because local societies were united by the common goals of decolonization and nation building. Nevertheless, as academic practice began to exhibit disciplinary and ideological divisions in latter years, alongside growing social-political fragmentation of local societies, the imbrications of knowledge in social and moral practice became more complicated as they became caught in battles over the defence of disciplinary and ideological/ theoretical-political paradigms, and contesting ethical agendas between state and academic actors.

A picture of human science practices in the early period can be derived from the intellectual biographies of the three "senior" scholars: Wang Gungwu, Taufik Abdullah, and Reynaldo Ileto. Their narratives show that disciplinary divisions as we know them today were virtually non-existent in the 1940s, 1950s, and 1960s. While disciplines were already established in these early years, disciplinary conventions as we find them today were not yet strong. The narratives of the three "senior" scholars point to a formative era when disciplinary boundaries were hazy, when no identifiable scholarship styles, classical texts, or approaches could be associated with any one discipline, and when discipline-based institutions were rare.[28]

In these formative years of what Wang refers to as the "pre-Social Science" era, disciplinary divides meant very little. As pioneering students in local universities in these early years, all the "senior" scholars refer to their "multidisciplined" or even "undisciplined" training as they were exposed to a wide spectrum of theories and approaches which cut across the humanities and social sciences. Although all the three "senior" scholars are widely recognized as historians, their biographies reveal that they were not influenced by any single set of disciplinary ideas and approaches. Rather, all read widely across history, the social sciences, philosophy, and creative writings of their time. Their narratives reveal how borrowing from textual/literary studies, philosophy, area studies, music, the arts, and social sciences was a norm in the formative era. All three scholars were attuned to a variety of social scientific theories and methodologies beyond those found in history, the field of their training. Despite being widely revered as historians, they were well versed in structuralism, hermeneutics, phenomenology, and other interpretative and human-action oriented frameworks in the social sciences that were coming to the fore in the 1960s.

Looking back, Wang describes his educational background as "one-third plus social science and nearly two-thirds humanities". The combination of history and sinology, where he discovered Chinese sources and traditions of historiography, and his encounters with social scientific theories and methodologies as he later came to study the overseas Chinese in Southeast Asia, ultimately made Wang realize that he "could no longer claim ownership in any branch of knowledge that required the drawing of academic borders". As for Taufik, who was enrolled at the Department of History at University of Gajah Mada (UGM), Yogjakarta, Indonesia, studying history meant learning a variety of fields such as psychology, pedagogy, theology, ethnology, area studies, literature, linguistics, and so on. It was his broad educational background, which exposed him to sociology, literature, and textual criticism, that enabled Taufik to make his path-breaking constructions of Indonesian and Minangkabau social histories from local perspectives as he responded to the imperative of writing history "from within". For Ileto, who took up history after a "momentous" switch from engineering to the liberal arts, his undergraduate training exposed him to subjects from both the humanities and social sciences, ranging from philosophy, politics, English literature, art, music, Asian studies, communication arts, literature, and Chinese history. He developed a fondness for philosophy and literature during his undergraduate studies at the Ateneo de Manila University. This helped hone an "interdisciplinary" approach as he became ever aware of the need to give voice to local language worlds, or what he terms "the world of traditional Tagalog metrical romances" or *awit* and popular religious rituals, which would become the hallmark of his contributions to the study of Filipino history and revolution.

Institutional divisions between the humanities and social sciences during this "pre–social science" era also reflected the amorphous state of disciplinary practices. There were clearly no established practices, and institutional arrangements for the human sciences varied from university to university and country to country.

Wang, who did his undergraduate education at the National Central University in Nanjing, China (1947–48), and the University of Malaya (1949–54) when it was founded in Singapore, recalls how these universities were not interested in drawing clear boundaries between the humanities and social sciences. At the National Central University in Nanjing, where Wang studied at the Department of Foreign Language, the disciplines of history, literature, and philosophy were located in the Faculty of Arts. However, geography and psychology, which today are likely to be found in the humanities or social sciences, were located in the Faculty of Science, while economics was offered by the Faculty of Commerce. At the University of Malaya, where Wang joined the Faculty of Arts, English literature, history, geography, economics, and mathematics were considered arts subjects. In the case of University of Gajah Mada, Jogjakarta, Indonesia, where Taufik studied, history was located in the Faculty of Letters, Pedagogy, and Philosophy. History was a newly established discipline then. Taufik recalls how none of his lecturers had "a formal degree in history". At the Ateneo de Manila University in the Philippines where Ileto received a liberal arts education, divisions between the humanities and social sciences did not matter. At his faculty, both philosophical and social scientific traditions from continental Europe and America were taught simultaneously. Ileto attributes his "interdisciplinary" background to the teachers at this Catholic university, who were trained either in philosophy at Catholic universities in Europe, or in the social sciences at American universities.

Apart from ambiguous disciplinary practices, all the three "senior" scholars point to the absence of any single, dominant source of intellectual influence in the region. Ideas from the various colonial powers — Dutch, British, Spanish, and American — were prevalent, but so were other influences from France, Germany, Italy, and Russia, as well as, China, India, Japan, and the Philippines.

Ideological divides were not firm as recently as the late 1950s. No particular political-theoretical positions from the right or left, whether Marxist, socialist, liberal, or pro-capitalist, appear to have the upper hand, nor did any of the three "senior" scholars profess strong affiliation to any ideological position. Rather, their scholarship pursuits appear to be united by common "nationalistic" goals of wanting to get the colonial powers out of the various countries, or towards issues concerning the building of national communities in their individual societies. During this era of common political struggle, the project of developing autonomous local academic traditions appears to have been a little easier for the early generation of scholars. Describing this time as a "period of cultural innocence", Taufik attributes the non-divisive scenario to the fact that nationalist interests/ideologies were still not directly linked to concrete struggles over legitimate political power since the fight against colonial power was not yet over. However, independence and, eventually, the Vietnam War began to change things.

Nation Building, the Cold War, and the Rise of American Social Sciences

In contrast to the early fluid conditions, North American social sciences, characterized by sharp disciplinary divides and ideological divisions reflecting the Cold War, became systematically more influential in the region.[29] The advent of the Vietnam War (or American War to the Vietnamese) saw nationalist ideologies increasingly entangled with Cold War ideologies as Southeast Asian countries split into capitalist and communist blocks. The Association of Southeast Asian Nations (ASEAN), an anti-communist group on the American side of the Vietnam War, was created amidst rising anti-communist political rhetoric which saw anti-communist purges in the region.[30]

As the regional human sciences became implicated in nation building projects and Cold War ideologies, disciplinary divisions and ideological splits found in American human sciences became more prevalent. The narratives point to a distinct rise of disciplinary practices of American social sciences in various countries, even those which were ex-British colonies. Although British influence remained significant alongside rising American dominance, by the 1980s, universities in the former British colonies such as Malaysia were clearly teaching American-oriented social sciences. This shift is reflected in the intergenerational accounts of Wang, Wong Soak Koon, and Goh Beng Lan, all of whom did their undergraduate studies in Malaysia. In the case of Indonesia, the switch to an American system of education, as Yunita Winarto tells us, was linked in part to attempts to shake off the yoke of Dutch colonialism. Indonesia, as we know, had a Dutch system of a five-year *doktorandus* degree in Taufik's time. However by the 1970s, when Yunita was completing her undergraduate studies, Indonesian universities made a change to a four-year degree programme following the American system. Caught in this transition, Yunita ended up obtaining two undergraduate degrees in anthropology.

It is clear that America was gradually becoming a favourite place for Southeast Asians to pursue their graduate degrees from the 1960s onwards. In part this was due to scholarship programmes such as Fulbright. From amongst the senior scholars, Taufik and Ileto obtained scholarships for PhD studies at Cornell University, and became pioneering Southeast Asian students studying the region. This trend is repeated amongst the majority of other scholars represented here. From amongst the remaining eight scholars, all went to America for their graduate studies with three exceptions: Paritta Chalermpol Koanantakool who, in step with Wang's path, went to the United Kingdom; while Yunita and Goh received their PhD training in Australia.

Nevertheless, even as local scholarship began to take on an American social science style, it is clear that disciplinary and theoretical-political divides in Southeast Asian contexts remained inseparable from nation building projects, which themselves were shaped by political configurations, colonial experiences, and the contemporary locations in the capitalist globalization of Southeast Asia. Narratives presented in this volume suggest that the entrenchment of disciplinary and theoretical-political divides in social science practices during the Cold War occurred alongside strong contestations over social and moral agendas of national development within Southeast Asia. On the one hand, we find that the imperative of national survival amidst the threat of socialist revolution saw a pragmatic deployment of the social sciences for the economic and cultural agendas of various Southeast Asian nation states. On the other, we find the human sciences becoming an important site for the spread of revolutionary or alternative social and moral ideals to offset dominant state ideologies. These divergent pursuits have come to constitute Southeast Asian scholarship on the region, complete with both their virtues and problems.

It is tricky to evaluate these different normative practices in the human sciences. We all know that Southeast Asian scholarship has come under criticism for being co-opted by state agendas. There is no doubt that the threat of the erosion of independent and critical scholarship vis-à-vis the state is real. Yet there has also been little attention paid to how the consequences of colonialism, poverty, and social inequalities may have necessitated the deployment of the human sciences for development purposes in Southeast Asia. The intellectual narratives reveal that having to work with, or within, policies of the state, remains a reality as well as dilemma of academic life for all generations. With such realities, could we arrive at the unequivocal conclusion that working with the state is essentially bad while working against the state is inherently good? What are the yardsticks of ethical practices when one is called to think for the state, and when one is called to think for one's community/society? Could, in fact, both these calls be separated in all instances?

I do not presume to offer a resolution to these age-old moral dilemmas. Instead, I want to approach them indirectly by using the narratives presented in this volume to elucidate the conditions which have given rise to the different normative uses of the human sciences, and the ways through which their actions coped with, and made ethical meaning thereof, over time. Narratives represented here suggest that conditions and meanings of knowledge production in relation to state and society are complicated in each era. Let me begin by examining the deployment of social scientific research by and for state interests.

The State, Public Intellectuals, and (Trans)National Grounds: The Ethics and Politics of Knowledge

In the years of anti-colonial struggle and early independence, intellectual work was a decolonizing tool and the nation state was experienced as a source of promise to forge new communities. The deployment of the human sciences by the state and the elite for national development could be justifed for making scholarship more meaningful to the general population. Senior scholars such as Wang, unapologetically connect the human sciences to anti-colonial struggles and the project of building new nation states. There was an undisputed certainty about the use of the human sciences for national development as the soon-to-be or newly independent nations were faced with threats to national survival and the need to forge unity among their diverse populations.

Undoubtedly, the deployment of the social sciences, particularly those of the "harder" disciplines such as economics and political science, for developmental purposes persists today. An example is the case of the Berkeley-trained Indonesian economists during Soeharto's regime discussed by Melani Budianta. Popularly known as the "Berkeley-mafia", these U.S.-trained economists were chief advisors to Soeharto's New Order government in its policy of developmentalism in the 1970s and 1980s, which brought about great economic progress, but also deep social disparities and abuse of political power.[31] Given the growing authoritarian nature of the state in many Southeast Asian countries, the co-optation of social scientists by state agendas tended to be viewed negatively.

Experiences from all scholars represented here reveal encounters with state agendas. In the region the links between state and social scientific research materialized in a number of state-sponsored academic/research institutions. What are commonly known as "government think-tanks" in Southeast Asia are one example; public universities, another. In fact most established universities in the region are state funded. In spite of this the struggle to transform the human sciences into forms of knowing which might counterbalance the tyranny of state benevolence or domination has not disappeared. In one way or another, all scholars represented here talk about their efforts to bring to light subjugated types of knowledge in order to overturn monolithic conceptions of society and culture promulgated by the state.

Such struggles are particularly acute for those working in government "think tanks". The experiences of Fadjar Thufail, a member of the younger generation, who works with the Indonesian Institute of the Sciences (LIPI) — the prime state research body for both natural and human sciences — is one such case. As a social scientist who is also a civil servant, Fadjar struggles to juxtapose the demands of being a "good citizen" who fulfils what he calls the "'altruistic' role of the social science in leading the society towards development" on the one hand, and being a good researcher who is critical of the "objectivity" of scholarship, particularly its practical deployment for developmental purposes, on the other. Fadjar tells us that researchers at LIPI have to take up applied social research so as to direct government policies rather than only to fill knowledge gaps. Should a researcher privilege academic content and place less emphasis on the applied components of research, he/she could be penalized for low research achievement. Such constraints demand ingenuity on the part of researchers to carve strategies which can tailor research projects to meet state requirements without sacrificing theoretical rigour. Despite the limitations, Fadjar reminds us that LIPI researchers are perhaps some of the least obedient government researchers in Indonesia and, in fact, some LIPI researchers were renowned critics of the New Order Government at the time.

Yet there are instances where scholars see the virtue in joining state institutions in order to help transform things from the inside. Koanantakool saw this opportunity when she was elected to direct the Princess Maha Chakri Sirindhorn Anthropological Centre in Bangkok, a government agency with a mandate to document and promote anthropological research, as well as use anthropology to promote cultural diversity and peaceful coexistence in Thai society. Her move from a lecturer of anthropology in a university to being an administrator in a public institution allowed Koanantakool to engage in what she calls "building bridges". Her new job has forced Koanantakool to rethink the meaning of "public anthropology" as it unfolds in the Thai context, and how she could help reshape the manner and direction of anthropology's public engagement to bring about a balance between state and public interests. As she searched for answers, she soon realized that the model of "public anthropology" which emerged from the United States — a field to integrate anthropology into societal engagements and public policy advocacy — was not applicable to the Thai case. In Thailand, the insulation of the academic community from public issues had never happened, since Thai public intellectuals were already socially and publicly engaged. Rather, the problem faced by Thai anthropologists in public engagement is of another kind: that is, "culture", the subject of anthropological study, had long been the handmaiden of Thai national values. Before the discipline of anthropology was even established in Thailand during the 1970s, "culture" was being used by the state to signify nation, Buddhism, and monarchy from the 1940s. Culture is therefore a component of Thai bureaucratic practices whereby cultural sites, artefacts, and practices are defined by the state for its own purposes. In trying to rebalance the state of culture in the Thai context, two collaborative projects of research, capacity building, and knowledge sharing between researchers at the Sirindhorn Anthropological Institute and local communities have been established under Koanantakool's leadership. One is a project on community-based museums that supports indigenous museums run by local communities, which has not only contributed to a new "museology" within Thai anthropology, but also changed the way local communities have come to think about their own cultural heritage meanings and place within the Thai nation and society. The other is a more delicate project on what Koanantakool terms "cultural fluency", which aims at rectifying cultural ignorance and prejudices amongst Buddhist and Muslim communities in the highly volatile southern provinces of Thailand, which have been sites of escalating inter-ethnic and religious violence in recent years.

There are no simple solutions to the entwinement of state and social science research, nor are there easy ways to mitigate state policies. Yet the imperative of trying to influence government policy is clearly there even for those not directly working in government institutions. The attempt by Yunita to use the results of her "collaborative ethnography" project with Javanese farmers on local farming knowledge is a case in point. Using her appointment as University Professor in the Social Sciences and Humanities sponsored by the Royal Netherlands Academy of Arts and Sciences (KNAW), Yunita experimented with "collaborative ethnography" to encourage farmers to think of themselves as partners of social researchers and come up with their own solution to their farming woes. One result of these collaborative projects were two documentary films jointly produced by the farmers and researchers from Yunita's team. These documentaries were eventually used by the farmers themselves to lobby local authorities to concede to their farming preferences and needs, and, in the process, they won themselves some financial assistance.

The entwinement of the state and the human sciences is perhaps nowhere clearer than in the project of making national cultural subjectivities. One of the most important state concerns of postcolonial states has been with building nationalist histories. The complicity between knowledge production and politics was what led to the gradual loss of the era of "cultural innocence" of knowledge production referred to by Taufik. In the case of Indonesia, the first National History Seminar in Indonesia in 1957 was a watershed, marking the rise of and contestations over national history in Indonesia. Questions over differing philosophical and ideological approaches to national history began to emerge: Should national history be defined from the colonial, local, or regional perspectives, even though there was no consensus as to what constituted each of these perspectives?

Such contestations are not unique to Indonesia, but prevalent throughout the region. What is perhaps unique is that while disagreements abound over what constitutes "national", there appears to be a general commitment to the idea of "national" across all the cohorts, although this commitment is more complicated among the younger scholars, given theoretical pressures to repudiate "national". Among the senior scholars, for instance, allegiance to "national" is manifested in the intellectual anger of Taufik against a Java-centric national history of Indonesia which ignores contributions from nationalist movements in Aceh and West Sumatra. It was such erasures in Indonesia's nationalist narrative that motivated Taufik to eventually work on the Minangkabau community in West Sumatra. In the case of Ileto, the commitment to "national" is demonstrated by his six-month interlude participating in a Marcos-state sponsored *Tadhana* history project. Despite being a critic of the Marcos government, and having participated in the anti-martial law movement while studying in America, Ileto saw the *Tadhana* project as an instance of a general trend amongst intellectuals in the Philippines to attach themselves to educational and state institutes to construct history for revolutionary or nation building purposes. For Ileto, it was an opportunity to decolonize history and challenge the Catholic Church's emplotment of Philippines' history. Yet when he realized that the "basic scaffolding" of Philippine national history remained unquestioned and that the project was just another attempt by the state to recolonize history, he withdrew from the group.

Such departures from the state bring us to the oppositional role of the human sciences in Southeast Asian contexts. The narratives presented here indicate that the human sciences became a prime site of oppositional politics as Southeast Asia became a hotbed of Cold War ideological warfare. Alongside a systemic rise of an American brand of social sciences and its disciplinary and theoretical divisions, university campuses in the region quickly became sites for the inculcation of revolutionary ideas. In one way or another, scholars, particularly those educated during the Cold War era, talk about their exposure to emancipatory ideals from a variant of classical and newer leftist ideas ranging from socialist, but not necessarily Soviet-inspired Marxism, to Maoism, third-worldism, world-dependency theory, and so on. However, it is clear that the heavily secularist grounds upon which Cold War ideologies were fought out in American social sciences proved to be constraining when applied to Southeast Asian contexts.

If there is one thing the Cold War has made clear, it is that the complex sets of ideological struggles within scholastic discourses in the region are often inseparable from ethno-religious politics and are never fought over in secularist terms alone. Yet complex leftist ideological imaginaries within the region were often straitjacketed into Cold War ideological categories prevalent in American style social sciences which increasingly gained prevalence in the region. For senior scholars such as Wang, the beginnings of divisive Cold War politics manifested in differences between colonial-backed nationalists and communists, in how they understood decolonization and the ways to go about achieving Malaysian independence. This resulted in guerrilla warfare between the communists and the colonial/national state which lasted twelve years and became known as the Emergency era (1948–60). During the Vietnam (American) War in Southeast Asia, ideological struggles between leftist and conservative factions quickly became flattened by the Cold War ideological binary divide. However, these inevitably became intertwined with racial-religious ideologies in countries such as Indonesia and Thailand. In Indonesia, the anti-communist campaign sparked off by the 1965 military coup became an anti-atheist pogrom which deepened the polarization between *pribumi*/indigenous groups and the Chinese, as well as divisions within the Muslim community.

It was the turmoil and legacy from this violent era that led Yunita, an ethnic Chinese and a Catholic, to study anthropology, as she saw it as a field that could provide her with solutions to the ethno-religious conflict in her own society. In Thailand, the Cold War unfolded in the form of student massacres in 1972 and the "Octoberist" revolution of 1973, when student activists were accused, among other things, of being "communists" and "un-Thai", and "anti-monarchy".[32]

Even apolitical students studying abroad, such as Koanantakool, were affected by these events. Koanantakool not only became more politically conscious, having witnessed the sacrifice and idealism of her fellow students in Bangkok, but she also returned to a Thailand under an anti-communist military regime in which academic freedom was under threat. She recounts the great care she took to hide any books that could be associated with

Marxism/communism during her fieldwork in southern Thailand. Even her field of study, Thai puppetry, a field of the arts that is traditionally thought to be apolitical, turned out to be highly politicized as puppet performances became sites of political commentary on political actors in Bangkok. Similarly, in the Philippines, the Cold War ideological war was tied up with the politics of religion and nationalist revolution.

For Ileto who was educated at the height of the Vietnam War, the Cold War taught him to rethink the history of American intervention and the politics of resistance in the Philippines. His participation in the anti–Vietnam War protests in America made him aware of the Catholic Church's alignment with the right and how his Jesuit educational background had omitted accounts of revolution from nationalist and socialist traditions.

A decade or so later, Cold War politics and its associated theoretical-political divides in the human sciences had come to roost in university campuses in the Philippines during the generation of Patricio Abinales. By then, as Abinales tells us, left-wing struggles were not only threatened with annihilation by a powerful state, but also deeply fragmented by different strands of socialism such as Marxism, Stalinism, Maoism, and other leftist academic ideals. In particular, the flagship University of the Philippines (UP) in Manila became an "ideological combat zone" of leftist ideals as students, academics, and communist party cadres clashed over different types of socialist imaginaries. As a researcher in the Third World Studies Programme at UP's College of Arts and Sciences, Abinales was involved in this struggle. The institute, which promoted leftist, third world thinking, was established to counter Communist Party orthodoxies and Maoist anti-intellectualism. Caught in the fight among revolutionaries, Abinales began to work with the peripheral communities of the southern region of Mindanao, and his commitment to the leftist revolutionary ideals became profoundly unsettled after the ouster of Marcos in 1986. Instead of an anticipated battle between the state and leftist revolutionaries, the regime was replaced by people's power, comprising a diverse array of social classes with different interests. The new, allegedly democratic "People's Power" government proved again to be yet another brutal regime as communist party cadres were assassinated by elements associated with the military. Disillusioned, Abinales left to do a PhD at Cornell University and, thereafter, to Kyoto, where he is currently teaching. His experience of "exile" from the Philippines has made him critical of the extremes of both nationalism and revolution, which in his mind still dominate academic debates on the Philippines. Rather, Abinales now aspires to what he terms a " 'third way' of looking at progressive/radical writings, which is critical of both state and revolution" as he aspires to recover "subaltern" subjectivities missed out in existing debates on Philippine nationalism.

Abinales' disillusionment with leftist ideas is perhaps reflective of the wider struggle of socialists of his time. Marshall Berman (1999) has used the term "used Left" to describe this spirit of despair amongst leftists as socialist/revolutionary ideals gradually lost their appeal as a counter-ideology from the late 1980s onwards.

Reflecting the milieu of this time, the intellectual battles of subsequent generations were caught between strictly defended disciplinary and theoretical paradigms emanating from Western human sciences, as they pursued their graduate education overseas both in Western and non-Western locations.

Memories and the Return of the Real: Intellectual Predicaments and the War between Discipline and Theory

For many scholars, their intellectual sojourn during the 1980s exposed them to newer critical ideas emerging from the post-structuralist and postcolonial turns in the human sciences at a time when the West was beginning to deconstruct its own meta-narratives and hegemony. Many of the younger scholars found these newer critical approaches appealing, given their concerns with questions of racial and cultural inequities beyond previous critical, materialist currents. Yet the disjuncture between disciplinary and theoretical practices to which these scholars were directly exposed, and what they and their societies were living through, gradually drove them to rethink practices in the western human sciences rather than simply taking them as modus operandi for local academic practice.

Encounters with the rigidity of contemporary theoretical and disciplinary divides were often eye-opening and marked the beginning of a critical distance from Western disciplinary and theoretical politics by many of the scholars represented in this book. The experience of young anthropologist Fadjar is a useful analogy here. As a LIPI researcher trained to believe in the objectivity of the social sciences, his sojourn at Rutgers University for an MA degree enabled him to witness how paradigmatic differences within anthropology between positivistic human ecology and anti-positivistic postmodern/post-structuralist methods, became the grounds of a vicious political quarrel amongst academics there. This encounter made Fadjar conscious of how easily one could be labelled "postmodernist/post-structuralist" by colleagues, a phenomenon which had spilled over to Indonesian academe, as he discovered on his return home. His exposure to more reflexive thinking in the human sciences, and subsequent PhD training at Wisconsin-Madison in the United

States, consolidated Fadjar's departure from a belief in the practical role of social science, a practice which he deems to be prevalent in Southeast Asia after the Vietnam War. In Fadjar's view, it is the coming together of the state's need to use the human sciences to support social engineering and development, and a "new academic subjectivity" amongst Southeast Asian scholars to work towards development in response to the suffering from wars and conflicts within the region, that contributed to an indifference to the newer critical and reflexive approaches of the human sciences.

In other cases, the imperatives of new political hegemonies, coupled with resistance that took conservative, sexist, and racist forms occurring in the region, brought to light the disjuncture between theory and reality and led scholars to search for human science practices which could better respond to local imperatives. For some this meant that scholarship became inseparable from activism and social reform as they joined a growing community of scholars known as "public intellectuals" in the region. Melani Budianta's activist-cum-academic journey quickly began on her return from the United States when she discovered that the meaning of student activism had changed a hundred and eighty degrees just a decade after the New Order came to power. While student activists were protesting against the state in the 1970s, in the 1980s they had become the moral police for the state and Islamic orthodoxy. Melani tells us about an incident of a student outburst during one of her lectures because he suspected that her teachings on the Theatre of the Absurd contained ideas against Islam and the New Order's Pancasila principle of the belief in God. The looting and rape of Indonesian Chinese women in the chaos of the 1997 Reformasi era, which brought down Soeharto's thirty-two-year rule, was a transformative moment for Melani as it was for many other Indonesian scholars. It jolted them from their armchairs into social activism against these horrific acts of violence against women and children, and racism against the Chinese minority in Indonesia. In particular Melani found herself in a double bind as the realities that unfolded challenged the very foundations of her intellectual ideas. As a critical scholar she had always rejected all forms of racial, sexual, and cultural essentialism. Hence when she was beseeched by others to speak against these atrocities using her identity as a Chinese female academic, she was at first hesitant. Yet she was disturbed that the brutal rapes of Chinese women were symptomatic of "structured" acts of racism and othering all across conflict zones in Indonesia, which warranted action. Ultimately external circumstances pushed her to make a decision to join Indonesians from different ethno-religious, class, and political backgrounds to band together through interfaith and peace movements to protest against these criminal acts.

As their walls between theory and activism came down, others turned to writing in the vernacular and popular media in order to reach local audiences. Literary scholar Wong Soak Koon's journey is a case in point. While she was not quite shaken out of her complacency as a student of literature during the traumatic May 1969 racial riots, her return from PhD study in Berkeley to growing political and ethno-religious fissures in Malaysia finally pushed her into exploring the problematics of nation building in a plural society such as Malaysia. Just as she joined Aliran, a social reform movement, in 1987, the Malaysian state conducted a mass arrest of one hundred and nineteen social activists charged with racial and religious extremism in an operation called Operasi Lallang. The viciousness of the attack by the state pushed her into becoming a social activist through what she knew best, that is, writing. This propelled her to ask difficult questions about Malaysian identity, ethnic equality, and mutual respect. Her writings began to focus on the inconsistencies of the official narratives of the Malaysian nation state. Her renewed interest in challenging nationhood saw a switch from her previous focus on Euro-American literature to local writings, and she began also to write in Malay, the national language, in order to reach a local audience. In taking up contemporary Malaysian writers, Malay and non-Malay alike, Wong was able to interrogate the state's discourses of nation and become more reflexive about her own background and the instabilities of ethnicity and gender in Malaysian society.

As for Abidin Kusno, Fadjar, and myself, our concerns with the legacy of our nation state building projects and perplexity with new social phenomena in our societies, provided an impetus for us to rethink the disciplinary and theoretical paradigms in which we were trained. Abidin's narrative captures the struggle of an intellectual whose engagement with the country of his birth (Indonesia) is as much bound up with his disciplinary and theoretical pursuits as with personal questions about how he came to be and what he is. As a child of the New Order state, Abidin was born in the year when Soeharto came into power. He first studied architecture in Surabaya, but moved to work in Jakarta. For Abidin, Jakarta, the showcase of New Order power and vision, was at once a place of hope, terror, alienation, and inspiration. It was the deep contrast between the rich and the poor, which he encountered in the capital city, that made Abidin pursue a PhD in architectural history at the State University of New York in Binghamton, a university known for the Fernand Braudel Centre and its avant-garde brand of Marxist and post-Marxist scholarship. Trained in the art history department of Binghamton, where Euro-American paradigms and Eurocentric perspectives were being deconstructed and disciplinary boundaries challenged and crossed, Abidin became acutely aware of the need to rethink the location of the non-West vis-à-vis the trajectory of European experience. His search led him to interactions with renowned Indonesianists at the Centre of Southeast Asian Studies at nearby Cornell University, an important site of Indonesian studies in the United States. It was through ideas learnt, questions posed, and the different subjectivities of the scholars of Indonesia whom he encountered, that Abidin began to piece together his own political-theoretical location both as a student of a new art history that crosses disciplinary borders, and as an overseas-located subject of the New Order state. It was from such a position that Abidin produced a thesis which localized the Indonesian nation state through its shifting architectural and visual environments, from the colonial to the postcolonial eras. Fadjar's intellectual path, as we have learnt, was deeply shaped by his own struggle with his status as employee, subject of the Indonesian nation state, and social scientist. In my case, it was my sense of marginalization by Malaysian ethno-nationalism and my ultimate location as an academic in a Southeast Asian Studies department in Singapore that motivated my vexation and eventual exasperation with emancipatory ideals and disciplinary conventions emanating from Western social sciences.

This leads us conveniently to a final reason to speak about regional differences in human science practices, that is, the late start of the field of Southeast Asian Studies in the region, and its distinctions from Euro-American and other models of the field. Part III elaborates on the state-of-the field within the region.

PART III
SOUTHEAST ASIAN STUDIES IN THE REGION: LATE BEGINNINGS, NEW DEPARTURES?

Regional Practices

As the human sciences came to Southeast Asia late, so did the field of Southeast Asian Studies. When compared with the earlier origins of the field in Western Europe, the United States, China,[33] and Japan[34] before and immediately after World War II, Southeast Asian Studies first emerged within the region in the 1970s and only became widespread during the 1990s.[35] The first undergraduate programme in Southeast Asian Studies was established at the University Malaya in Malaysia in 1976.[36] Some two decades later, during the 1990s, we find the widespread establishment of Southeast Asian Studies degrees offered by departments in Singapore,[37] Indonesia,[38] Thailand,[39] Vietnam,[40] and the Philippines.[41] Given the lateness of its origins, it is not surprising that the study of Southeast Asia amongst local scholars is largely undertaken outside the framework of a distinct field of Southeast Asian Studies. It was only in the 1990s, at a time when area studies was experiencing a decline in Euro-America, that we see a flourishing of Southeast Asian Studies within the region, with more local scholars being located at Southeast Asian Studies departments and research institutes associated with this field of study.

It is important to note that this later spread and consolidation of Southeast Asian Studies as a distinct academic programme in the region came at a time of disciplinary and theoretical flux in the wider human sciences. These conditions provided a more conducive environment for interdisciplinary pursuits when compared with the experience of area studies in North America.[42] Another distinctive feature is the institutional autonomy of Southeast Asian Studies departments. Many of the Southeast Asian Studies departments offer both undergraduate and graduate degree programmes and have the ability to recruit their own staff. This trend departs from the North American model where area studies are often subordinated to traditional disciplinary departments for purposes of faculty appointment, promotion, and the admission of PhD students.[43] Having its own institutional autonomy has meant that the field of Southeast Asian Studies has more leeway to consolidate itself as a traditional disciplinary department would.

However, this does not mean that disciplinary turf wars between Southeast Asian Studies and other disciplines do not exist within Southeast Asian universities. My experience in Singapore offers an example. The National University of Singapore has become a growing centre for Southeast Asian Studies, with the establishment of the Southeast Asian Studies Programme[44] in 1991, to which I am affiliated, and, more recently, the Asia Research Institute, which has a significant focus on regional research. Yet the primacy of English at the National University of Singapore, as my chapter shows, also makes its model of area studies more susceptible to a dominantly North American model. The American influence, coupled with the increasing pressures of globalization to benchmark Singaporean academic practices against Western universities, has meant that Southeast Asian Studies in Singapore are perhaps more encumbered by disciplinary and theoretical polemics emanating from North American human sciences, when compared with its neighbouring countries. Soon after my move to the Southeast Asian Studies Programme at the National University of Singapore, I discovered just how easily "in-between" practices and ideas about area studies could be misunderstood and straitjacketed by positions deriving from the fight between disciplines and area studies, and between postcolonial and area studies perspectives, over the representation of non-Western societies. Teaching and researching in a Southeast Asian Studies programme has taught me to see how the postcolonial critique of area studies as an Orientalist paradigm and the dismissal of postcolonial ideas as nothing but narcissism by area studies specialists are both problematic. Trying to bring together these two warring paradigms made me realize that the only way in which Southeast Asian academic settings can benefit from the newer critical currents is for us to revise, complicate, and expand the disciplinary and theoretical registers of Western disciplinary and academic discourse. I became further convinced of this position when I realized how the expansion of postcolonial politics into the political sphere had increasingly debilitated progressive politics as the struggle for freedom from oppression became quickly associated with Western ideology and rejected. These experiences led me to conclude that Southeast Asian Studies in the region has an ethical obligation to forge its own directions rather than being tied to any particular sets of disciplinary or theoretical outlooks. One is called to develop pedagogic directions which are responsive to local social and material conditions, based on a recognition of different ethical imaginations emanating from the region in order to build bridges, not just within the academy, but also within the region and between the region and the rest of the world.

The overview of regional practices in the humanities, social sciences, and area studies in Southeast Asia provided above suggests that, while conditioned by Euro-American disciplinary and theoretical traditions, regional academic practices have diverged from them in significant ways. For Southeast Asian scholars, thinking about the local is inevitably a combination of their location in time, as well as their intellectual politics to resist domination and recover subjugated knowledge. In contrast to Euro-American settings, where area studies have lost their capacity to structure knowledge, Southeast Asian Studies has become an established reality in the region, being offered in an increasing number of institutions. If indeed the afterlife of area studies is, as declared, a moment when Eurocentric truths can be denaturalized, then there is a need to acknowledge the alternative "disciplinary" arrangements, as well as divergent epistemological concerns emanating from the region.

There are three main differences I want to discuss here. These are in the continued relevance of the East-West binary and the analytical frameworks of the region and nation state for understanding regional dynamics.

Challenges: East-West Binary Effects

With a new epoch of capitalist globalization posing radical changes to older imperial hierarchies, bounded territories, and unitary cultural identities, area studies scholars are increasingly challenged to reconsider non-Western transformations, which may no longer be adequately conceptualized in terms of differences between East and West, or unitary conceptions of national and regional identification.

The contributors to this book suggest that the rejection of the East-West binary may be somewhat premature when seen from the region. Despite changing geopolitical configurations, globalization has yet to fully erase the colonial legacy or the material disparities between the Western and non-Western worlds. In Southeast Asia, globalization may still be seen as a force which reproduces unequal power relations on a global scale. In fact, now more than ever, globalization is creating conditions for new forms of conflicts between Southeast Asia and the West. The inequalities between West and East (or North and South) are often evoked and rearticulated within nationalist and regional discourses, meaning the categories of West and East are still very much alive in the region.

The result is a situation where regional realities contrast academic efforts to debunk the East-West divide. While scholastic discourse is busy deconstructing the integrated totalities of these categories, within Southeast Asia the "West" is often portrayed and/or perceived as a coherent entity.[45] In fact, alternative modality imaginings of human existence, in both their progressive and conservative form, are often constructed from conceptions of East and West as opposing totalities.

The continuing power of this binary opposition can be observed both at the level of the state and below it. Nation states in the region have been known to actively construct various forms of cultural authenticity in order to reject Western civilization, secularism, and even modernity. In recent years, such claims have intensified, with some Southeast Asian states resorting to discourses such as "Asian Values", Islam, and Islamic law, as bulwarks against Western liberal democracy and universal human rights.[46] This trend may be regarded as sinister to the extent that official forms of East-West rhetoric resonate with ordinary people's experience of the legacy of colonialism and socio-economic inequality in their everyday lives. It is therefore not surprising that an anti-West stance is often adopted even by radical activists. Likewise a rhetoric of difference between East and West is also employed by conservative groups to discredit their progressive opponents for being Western lackies or dupes of Western discourse.

Clearly East-West imaginaries, no matter how problematic they may be, are major sites for the production of cultural difference in contemporary Southeast Asia. Therefore it is imperative not to dismiss their power, but to understand their social and political contexts and consequences. In particular there is a need for scholars to try to understand how the politics of East-West oppositions can place progressive agency in Southeast Asia in a perilous situation. This is because there is a danger that, on the one hand, academic discourse that contests Western/colonial power and espouses cultural/religious difference, may coincide with that of conservative powers and be easily rejected by outside critics motivated by political correctness in contemporary social theory, where all evocations of an East-West divide are rejected as "essentialist". On the other hand, critiques of the state, or other conservative forces in the region, can often be discredited for being colonized by the West and its liberal values. Melani's and Goh's chapters refer to such complexities between academic analyses and political agency in the struggles between Islam, democratization, and universal human rights in Southeast Asia. As citizens of predominantly Muslim countries, they point to the way in which anti-Western (or postcolonial) politics has been appropriated by the state and conservative groups and used in defence of patriarchal, exclusionary, and ethno-religious orthodoxy in Indonesia and Malaysia. This hijacking of postcolonial rhetoric by the state and conservative groups has potently weakened progressive agency, as well as made the academic project of theorizing local/regional difference much more difficult.

Melani shows how in Indonesia, the coming together of a pro-Western discourse of democratization and local politics, which led to political decentralization in Indonesia, had an underside: ironically it led to a return to patriarchy and the narrow forces of *putra-daerahism* or nativism. Despite this, Islamic conservative groups also joined the current anti-Western/global bandwagon to condemn progressive Muslims as dupes of Western interests.

Similarly in Malaysia, as my chapter shows, the imbrications of Malaysia's anti-Western rhetoric and the vicissitudes of global political Islam have led to a new Islamic conservatism that has increasingly gained the moral-political high ground. As Islamic orthodoxy expands into conflicts of jurisdiction between the country's civil and syariah courts over religious freedoms as provided for in the Malaysian Constitution, bitter contests between conservative and liberal/progressive groups (comprising both Muslims and non-Muslims) have broken out, further fracturing a society already deeply divided along racial and religious lines. That this is troubling, I argue, is because these opposing ideological positions have played to the tune of official nationalist discourses which pit Islamization against Western liberal democratization. Both sides to this dispute are uncompromising: orthodox groups vilify "liberals" as Western secularists, while "liberals/progressives" disparage Islamists as demagogues. What has made matters worse is that as radical activists-cum-academics intervene in this crisis, they often tout secularism, which is often immediately equated with Western liberalism in the Malaysian context, as the only workable democratic framework. Such progressive reactions have served only to fan further misunderstanding on the part of Islamists. The polarization of religious and human rights discourses in Malaysian society has made it difficult for any nuanced positions or analyses to be heard — perhaps not unlike the theoretical deadlock in the push within the social sciences to decentre Eurocentric knowledge and reconcile alternative subjectivities.

These examples point to the need to move beyond conventional social scientific conceptions of rights and human agency if we want to better understand and overcome the dispute between Islamic and Western views on human rights in the region. If following Western (post)liberal assumptions, we, as social scientists, insist that the politics of emancipation must involve a denunciation of racial-religious identifications, the result will be an impasse between the groups advocating Islamic orthodoxy and secular liberalism in Malaysian society. It is imperative that scholars of Southeast Asia find new ways of understanding how Southeast Asians work out resistance within the regimes of values and discourses they live under. [47] Islam is only one of the regimes encountered in Southeast Asia. We need to create spaces which can help create recognition and better define progressive ethics within the region in order to reveal their autonomous dimensions and interconnections with universal ethical values. Only when the fine distinctions of human existence/values which reflect local/regional aspirations, albeit their entwinement with larger world histories and human aspirations, are better identified and prevalently understood, will the deceptions of the ideological opposition between local/ national and West/outside become exposed and better challenged.

Strategies: Resuscitating the Region

In the wake of the attack on area studies, there has been a shift of focus in the study of regions from a concern with "external" influences such as capitalist globalization and a changing new world order. Unlike the older regionalism, in which regions were considered bounded, the new regionalism has focused on the porosity of territorial borders, the fluidity of identity politics, movements of people, and so on (for example, see Walters 2000). In contrast, local scholarship on Southeast Asia tends to depart from, and remains rooted in, a concern with the internal dynamics of change in the face of globalization.[48] To be sure, taking the region as a departure point needs qualification at a time when the concept of Southeast Asia has been condemned, or, at best, taken as a contingent entity in recent debates.[49]

While much of the criticism of regions as contrived geographical and cultural conceptions is warranted, critics often forget that the area study map of the Cold War has been adopted throughout much of the world, giving legitimacy to the regional boundaries demarcated on this map. New geopolitical realignment after the Cold War, alongside capitalist expansion into the Asia-Pacific region, has led to various forms of regionalization. Debates on the "Asianization" of Asian studies is an example (Dirlik 2005, p. 167). Likewise the current rise of China has led to a revitalization of Southeast Asian and East Asian regionalisms, ASEAN being a case in point. These movements, no matter how contrived or problematic they may be, are part and parcel of the lived reality of the constructed geography of Southeast Asia. Hence, while a territorially bounded concept of the region may be theoretically deconstructed, the lived reality of regional identity and geography cannot be ignored. Furthermore, this lived reality is consolidated by institutions such as ASEAN, not to mention various other seemingly apolitical forms of regional association in educational exchanges, sports events, and so on. On top of this, there is a flourishing of symbolic imaginaries of a regional identity found in popular culture and the mass media. The existence of regional structures, ideologies, and symbolisms has clearly generated sentiments and identifications about the region which cannot be wished away, no matter how manufactured they may be. Surely they deserve academic attention.

Similarly, in the wider critique of area studies, scholars have rarely questioned the agendas that propelled the prioritization of the global, and the repudiation of the local/region.[50] As pointed out earlier, the dismissal of regions over the global appears to stem from the progressive aim of putting non-western societies on par with western societies on a global stage (Harutoonian 2000; 2002). While this may have been liberating in Euro-American area studies, it is problematic elsewhere. To be sure, in a place such as Southeast Asia, external influences are difficult to ignore. As a diverse region long exposed to migration of people, colonization, international trade, and so on, the study of Southeast Asia has long been charted through global connections. It is in local sites that people create meaningful experiences. Globalization should never be taken to imply that regions/areas/localities have no significance.

Emerging trends in Southeast Asia suggest that regional synergies have been a reason to rethink Southeast Asian Studies from the perspective of regional locations and experiences. It is unmistakable that the field is being reclaimed by local scholars as a vehicle for local voices (see Abraham 2000; and Heryanto 2002). There are also new forces such as Asian funding institutions with their own stake in the future of the region. Many recent academic developments in the region are sponsored by Japanese Foundations (in particular, the Toyota, Japan, and Nippon Foundations), which appear to have overtaken the Ford Foundation in promoting Southeast Asian Studies within the region.[51] While these institutions may have their own agendas to influence the development of Southeast Asian Studies, it should be noted that many of their funded projects to develop cross-national expertise have led to the establishment of informal, independent networks of scholars.[52] For regional scholars, academic exchanges, such as the one from which this volume arises, have created opportunities for cultivating a body of knowledge on Southeast Asia in order to address some of the problems of knowledge production within the region. Melani's regional awakening came from her participation in networks such as the Asian Regional Network of New Alternatives (ARENA) (which has beginnings in the struggle of International Socialism) and the *Inter-Asia Cultural Studies*, a regional cultural studies journal. In fact, during the workshop on which this book was based, Melani Budianta lamented the fact that regional scholars are often very well informed about works by Western scholars, but know so little about works done by their Southeast Asian colleagues. She also noted the persistence amongst her students that knowledge is somehow located in the "West".[53] These sentiments explain why regional networking to share ideas and learn from one another remains vital in the thinking and critique of Southeast Asia.

Another reason to establish intraregional conversations is that the field of Southeast Asian Studies has become an established local reality. There is now an increasing number of regional researchers and academic institutions, and academic collaborations have become more common. Academic and student exchanges across nation state–based enterprises have provided grounds for rethinking Southeast Asia.[54] Collective synergies have, among other things, brought about the idea of *translation* across national borders to cultivate a body of knowledge out of the various vernacular languages. Efforts of translations across the various Southeast Asian/Asian national-borders have been undertaken in journals such as *Inter-Asia Cultural Studies* and, more recently, the online *Kyoto Review of Southeast Asia* based at Kyoto University, Japan. Such efforts can lessen dependency on global scholarship, which remains linguistically delineated and disseminated in the English language. They can also enable students to learn about local ideas besides those emanating from the West.

Hence the concept of "region" remains meaningful for local scholars, not only as a lived reality, but also as a conceptual tool which enables collective reflections on social formulations and existential meanings in Southeast Asia. While much of the criticism of the artificial origins and borders of the Southeast Asian region is valid, we must also remember that there are political, experiential, and epistemological grounds for the continued relevance of Southeast Asia as a region, and as a conceptual category in an era where knowledge production can no longer be determined by any single political-theoretical logic.

Finally, we turn to the delicate matter of resucisating the "national" in regional scholarship, against the push to repudiate and transcend "national" frameworks in contemporary social theory.

Commitments: Nation and Redemption

According to current academic convention, what counts as "good" scholarship often requires Southeast Asian scholars to exhibit "independence from nationalism",[55] move beyond "national narratives" (Antlov 2005, pp. xix–xxi), or search for "history at the interstices" or "history of the margins", away from national influences (Winichakul 2003, p. 10).

Against this trend, the framework of the nation state and nationalist narratives remain meaningful to local scholars. The framework of the "nation/national" remains a vital force that structures the prioritization of the local. The narratives in this book show how the structures of rule and regimes of knowledge of the nation state remain important forces within and against which scholars struggle to interpret their own lives and the societies around them. Indeed, the implicit presence of the nation state provided one of the few constant and common frameworks linking the contributors. Despite the particular histories of nation building across the region, the problematic of the nation emerges time and time again in the intellectual questions raised. Although everyone agreed on the need to contest the hegemony of official/state discourses of the national, the idea of transcending the national is not accepted by all. The differing intensities of concern about the importance of national legacies reflect differences in their countries' and personal histories.

Amongst the earlier generation, who began their intellectual work in the era of decolonization, the nation state was clearly experienced as a source of promise and as emblematic of a hope to forge a new form of community. For subsequent generations, the experience of the nation state was more complex. On the one hand, the nation state was a problem which needed to be deconstructed or re-evaluated in order to understand and expose its hegemonies and limitations. On the other, many remain committed to the idea of a "national" project, especially when considering the legacies of colonialism and the forces of capitalist globalization. As products of the various nation making projects and living in a world shaped by capitalist globalization, neo-imperial desire, and fluid boundaries, the younger generation appears to be more preoccupied with the crisis of the nation state project and the power of capitalist globalization in their societies. While they clearly endeavour to reject or undermine the rigidity and exclusions of state discourses on the national, it is also evident that many, if not all, remain committed to rectifying the meanings of the national from outside, or below the state. Their commitment to the "national" is perhaps best manifested in their drive to engage with the social and political dilemmas that beset their own societies, as well as to dismantle hegemonic definitions of national identities, which often take the forms of ethno-chauvinist identifications.

Given the postcolonial intellectual conditions within which the latter generations operate, they have tended to focus more than their predecessors on subaltern capacities and agency which, to an extent, escape the regimes of nationalist power in the informal, everyday, or peripheral spaces of human creativity. Predictably, this is also a universal trend in scholarship, to which younger scholars are especially attuned. This sometimes creates tensions between different generations manifested in contestations over experiences and meanings of the "national". This is pointed out by Abinales who uses emerging critiques against the nationalist imaginations of senior Filipino intellectuals such as Ileto by young upstarts in the Filipino academe as one such example. What such competing views about the "national" reveal is that senior scholars had the experience of having to deal with colonial and statist domination, making them focus on the power and consequences of these forces. Given the different social, historical, and changing intellectual conditions, younger scholars have distinct concerns. In some instances, as in this Filipino case, this has involved criticisms of the work of the older generations of local scholars. However, there is also a need to guard against establishing clear distinctions between the concerns of senior and younger scholars. Conditions change with time and scholarship will respond to the change. Ileto himself has declared that "Philippine history could fruitfully become less nation state focused and more decentred", although his passion for interrogating the ways nationalist histories are actually read and localized remains undiminished. We must also remember that scholarship on Southeast Asia is inevitably group- or school-oriented and not merely individualistic. Alongside intergenerational tensions and differences, there are always also more continuities across generations than meet the eye. How will all these intergenerational dynamics eventually be localized in Southeast Asia? What kinds of stories will local scholars tell forty or fifty years from now?[56] Only time will tell.

For now, the diverse thinking over the meaning of nation and national sensibilities reveals at least two significant trends: first, that the definitions of the nation are never reducible to the political pursuits of the state alone; and second, that the category of the nation, while disputed, deconstructed and problematized, remains meaningful to intellectuals in the region. In a region which has given rise to some of the major nationalist movements in the twentieth century, nationalism, while often hijacked by the various Southeast Asian states, remains a necessary means to express shared geo-historical and ethno-cultural sensibilities even at levels below the state. Hence while deplorable atrocities, marginalization, and manipulation have taken place in its name, the "national" also has its appeal and meaning in local/regional histories.

Therefore, it is important for us to grasp the complex meanings of the "national" beyond the simple dichotomy between state and non-state, or the ethical versus the immoral, if we want to go beyond the preconceptions inherent in western human scientific frameworks of the national. As has been pointed out by many Western scholars, the relationship between the state and nationalist discourses is only historical and never teleological (see Karl 2002, p. 24). Taking ethno-cultural or nationalist sensibilities seriously does not necessarily mean agreeing with the state. Contemporary Southeast Asian nationalism may, in fact, provide us with grounds to think about alternative conceptions of society and political agency in the contemporary world. Such a project speaks directly to the challenge to decentre and pluralize Western social scientific discourse.

Hence, rather than eschewing national frameworks, it seems the more important task is to decouple nation and state and to explore how people make their own histories and meanings of decent/rightful human existence within the constraints of political and economic realities, as well as cultural imaginations and social categories. Perhaps as a start we need to remember that the formation and transformation of social and political orders are necessarily informed from the start by people's shared histories, emotive allegiances, as well as their self-orienting recognition of what counts as justice, equality, rights, emancipation, and so on.

Conclusion

The rethinking of Southeast Asia from the perspective of the local/regional, as this book suggests, is a project which cannot be divorced from social and historical context, as well as personal political-theoretical commitments to study social and political dilemmas that beset us in Southeast Asia. A project entangled with, yet also distinct from, Western disciplinary and theoretical influence, regional conceptualizations are shaped by the attempts to use the humanities and the social sciences to respond to local needs. A vital reason to prioritize the "local" and to articulate the specificities of historical processes and subjectivities in the region is the disjuncture between theory and lived realities. As regional scholars interrogate the differences between the region and the Western world, as well as "local" imperatives behind the production of knowledge in both the West and the region, moments of the highly local in the constitution of Western humanities and the social sciences are better revealed, and notions about its universality questioned.

The narratives presented in this book offer us alternative perceptions of Southeast Asia from scholars coming from the region. This volume represents one response by regional scholars to the call to decentre and diversify knowledge production. The disciplinary configurations and epistemological considerations highlighted in this book suggest that we need a great deal more versatility than we can get from sticking rigidly to conventional disciplinary and theoretical categories, if we want to grasp the complex dimensions of human existence and meanings in Southeast Asia better.

It is clear that the project to build more coherent and integrated perspectives on the questions of Southeast Asian knowledge remains far from being complete. However, we can also conclude that the intergenerational experiences and concerns described here bring out important lessons on the production of (local/regional) knowledge in the human and social sciences. The project of theorizing the local/regional is never merely about differences between local/non-Western perspectives and contexts. It is also about intergenerational and intraregional tensions, differences and continuities in terms of shared conditions, commitment, and struggles.

In the changing stakes of area studies in the post–Cold War era, regional efforts to rethink the region may provide evidential and theoretical grounds on different modalities of political and ethical imaginings of human existence and emancipation. Unless alternative theoretical-political logics and rationalizations on social formations and human action which are different from, yet *not* unconnected to, Western ideas, modernity, and capitalism, are acknowledged and reconciled by a diverse/polycentric universal project of knowledge, the progressive call for the decentring of Eurocentric knowledge will remain locked in its own cultural and political relativism, inhibiting a true transformation of knowledge production.

Notes

1. It was Edward Said's critique of representations of the "non-West" in *Orientalism* (1978) that provided a watershed for an emergent critique of area studies. Vicente Rafael (1999) has identified several reports that documented the crisis faced by area studies in a post-Saidian and post–Cold War era such as *Items* (the

1994–1995 issues) by the Social Science Research Council in New York, and essays in *What's in a Rim: Critical Perspectives on the Pacific Region Idea*, edited by Arif Dirlik (1993), and *Southeast Asian Studies in the Balance*, edited by Charles Hirschman, Charles F. Keyes, and Karl Hutterer (1992).

2. A growing number of works seeking to go beyond area studies has served to cement the sense of a crisis in area studies. These works include: Neil L. Water's edited volume on *Beyond the Area Studies Wars: Toward a New International Studies* (2000); Martin Lewis' and Karen Wigen's essay on "A Maritime Response to the Crisis in Area Studies" in *Geographical Review* 89, no. 2 (1999): 161–68; Harry Harootunian's *History's Disquiet: Modernity, Cultural Practice and the Question of Everyday Life* (2000); Itty Abraham's report on *Weighing the Balance: Southeast Asian Studies Ten Years After* (1999); Masao Miyoshi and H.D. Harootunian's *Learning Places: The Afterlives of Area Studies* (2002); Peter J. Katzenstein's "Area and Regional Studies in the United States" in *PS: Political Science and Politics* 34, no. 4 (2001): 789–91; and Arif Dirlik's "Asia Pacific Studies in an Age of Global Modernity" in *Inter-Asia Cultural Studies* 6, no. 2 (2005): 158–70.

3. Anxieties over disciplinary and institutional issues have long run deep within the field of Asian Studies since the 1950s. Some works which provide an insight into these anxieties are Felix Keesing's "Problems of Integrating Humanities and Social Science Approaches in Far Eastern Studies" in *The Far Eastern Quarterly* 14, no. 2 (1955): 161–68; Milton Singer's "The Social Sciences in Non-Western Studies" in *Annals of the American Academy of the Political and Social Science* 356 (1964): 30–44; Wm. Theodore De Bary's "The Funding on Asian Studies" in *Journal of Asian Studies* 30, no. 2 (1971): 389–412; Robert Ward's "Presidential Address: A Case for Asian Studies" in *Journal of Asian Studies* 32, no. 3 (1973): 161–68; George McT. Kahin's "Presidential Address: The Polarization of Knowledge: Specialization on Contemporary Asia in the United States" in *Journal of Asian Studies* 33, no. 4 (1974): 515–22; Richard D. Lambert's "Presidential Address: An Action Agenda for Area Studies" in *The Journal of Asian Studies* 35, no. 1 (1975): 7–19; and David Buck's "Forum on Universalism and Relativism in Asian Studies" in *Journal of Asian Studies* 50, no. 1 (1991).

4. See, for example, David Szanton, ed., *The Politics of Knowledge: Area Studies and the Disciplines* (Berkeley and Los Angeles: University of California Press, 2004); Laurie J. Sears, ed., *Knowing Southeast Asian Subjects* (Seattle and Singapore: University of Washington Press and NUS Press, 2007); Cynthia Chou and Vincent Houben, eds., *Southeast Asian Studies: Debates and New Directions* (Singapore: International Institute for Asian Studies and the Institute of Southeast Asian Studies, 2006); Itty Abraham, "Southeast Asian Studies Whereto?" in *Weighing the Balance: Southeast Asian Studies Ten Years After*, edited by Itty Abraham (New York: Social Science Research Council, 1999), pp. 43–59; and Anthony Reid and Maria Serena I. Diokno, "Completing the Circle: Southeast Asian Studies in Southeast Asia", in *Southeast Asian Studies: Pacific Perspectives*, edited by Anthony Reid (Tempe, AZ: Program for Southeast Asian Studies, 2003), pp. 93–107.

5. For example, see Achille Mbembe, *On the Postcolony* (Berkeley: University of California Press, 2001); Ali Mazuri, "Forward to the Past: African Intellectuals in the 1990s", *African Commentary* (June 1990): 32–38; and Reynaldo C. Ileto, "On the Historiography of Southeast Asia and the Philippines: The 'Golden Age' of Southeast Asian Studies — Experiences and Reflections", proceedings of the Workshop on "Can We Write History? Between Postmodernism and Coarse Nationalism" (Institute for International Studies, Meiji Gakuin University, 9 March 2002).

6. For an excellent discussion of the influence of North American scholarship on the study of Southeast Asia, see Vicente L. Rafael, "Regionalism, Area Studies, and the Accidents of Agency", *The American Historical Review* 104 (1999): 1208–20.

7. The nature and consequences of the quarrel over disciplinary and theoretical differences in the North American academe have been extensively discussed in a volume by Loius Menand, ed., *The Future of Academic Freedom* (Chicago: The University of Chicago Press, 1996). A later volume edited by Amanda Anderson and Joseph Valente on *Disciplinarity at the Fin de Siecle* (2002) attempts to put an end to this fight by showing how disciplines are inevitably products of both disciplinary and anti-disciplinary practices.

8. This workshop was organized in 2002 in my capacity as consultant to the Southeast Asian Studies Programme, Social Science Research Council, New York, under the sponsorship of a Ford Foundation seed grant (No. 1005-0128). It was aimed at initiating an intergenerational and interdisciplinary dialogue amongst Southeast Asian scholars as a basis for planning an intellectual retooling project for young Southeast Asian researchers. This planning workshop eventually led to a workshop series from 2004–05 which brought twenty-five scholars comprising "junior" and "senior" Southeast Asian researchers into conversation. This workshop series was funded by a Toyota Foundation Initiative Fund (No. D03-P-003 28), and jointly organized with Reynaldo Ileto. The workshop series was titled "Local Scholarship and the Study of Southeast Asia: Bridging the Past and the Present".

9. Some examples of classical debates on Southeast Asian Studies are J.C. Van Leur, *Indonesia Trade and Society: Essays in Asian Social and Economic History* (The Hague: van Hoeve, 1967); John R.W. Smail, "On the Possibility of an Autonomous History of Modern Southeast Asia", *Journal of Southeast Asian History* 2, no. 2 (1961): 72–102 (reprinted in Laurie J. Sears, ed., *Autonomous Histories, Particular Truths: Essays in Honour of John Smail* [Madison Wisconsin Centre for Southeast Asian Studies, 1993]: 39–70); Craig Reynolds, "A New Look at Old Southeast Asia", *Journal of Asian Studies* 54, no. 2 (1995): 419–46; and Donald K. Emmerson, "Issues in Southeast Asian History: Room for Interpretation — Review Article", *Journal of Asian Studies* 40, no. 1 (November 1980): 43–68.

10. For some examples, see Syed Hussein Alatas, *The Democracy of Islam: A*

Concise Exposition with Comparative Reference to Western Political Thought (The Hague: W. van Hoeve, 1956); Syed Hussein Alatas, *Intellectuals in Developing Societies* (London: Cass, 1977); Syed Hussein Alatas, *The Myth of the Lazy Native* (London: Frank Class, 1977); Maung Htin Aung, *A History of Burma* (New York and London: Columbia University Press, 1967); Salazar Zeus A. *The Malayan Connection* (Lunsod Quezon: Palimbangan ng Lahi, 1998); Teodoro Agoncillio, *A Short History of the Filipino People* (University of the Philippines, 1960); and Reynaldo C. Ileto, "Orientalism and the Study of Philippine Politics", in *Knowing America's Colony: A Hundred Years from the Philippine War* (Hawaii: Centre for Philippines Study, University of Hawaii at Manoa, 1999), pp. 41–66.

11. Miyoshi (2002, p. 45) has pointed to the self-serving use of the history of victimization to demand payment in some cases.

12. For an overview of these debates, see Ignas Kleden, "Alternative Social Science as an Indonesian Problematique", *New Asian Visions* (1986), pp. 6–22; Laurie J. Sears, "The Contingency of Autonomous History", in *Autonomous Histories, Particular Truths: Essays in Honour of John Smail*, edited by Laurie Sears (Madison Wisconsin: University of Wisconsin Centre for Southeast Asian Studies, 1993), pp. 11–13; Itty Abraham, "Southeast Asian Studies Whereto?" pp. 43–59; Ananda Rajah, "Southeast Asia: Comparatist Errors and the Construction of a Region", *Southeast Asian Journal of Social Science, Special Focus: Reconceptualizing Southeast Asia* 27 (1999): 41–53; Vicente L. Rafael, "The Culture of Area Studies in the United States, *Social Text* 41 (Winter 1994): 106–07; Ariel Heryanto, "Can There Be Southeast Asians in Southeast Asian Studies?" *Moussons* 5 (2002): 3–30. [Reprinted in Sears, *Knowing Southeast Asian Subjects*, pp. 75–108]; Abu Talib and Tan Liok Ee, eds., *New Terrains in Southeast Asian History* (Athens and Singapore: Ohio and Singapore University Press, Southeast Asian Series No. 107, 2003): ix–xxv; Paul H. Krastoska, Remco Raben, and Henk Schulte Nordholt, "Locating Southeast Asia", in *Locating Southeast Asia: Geographies of Knowledge and Politics of Space,* edited by Paul H. Krastoska, Remco Raben, and Henk Schulte Nordholt (Singapore: Singapore University Press, 2005), pp. 11–20; Thongchai Winichakul, "Trying to Locate Southeast Asia from Its Navel: Where is Southeast Asian Studies in Thailand?" in *Locating Southeast Asia*, op. cit., pp. 113–32; Thongchai Winichakul, "Writing at the Interstices: Southeast Asian Historians and Postnational Histories in Southeast Asia", in *New Terrains in Southeast Asian History*, op. cit., pp. 3–29; Anthony Reid and Maria Serena I. Diokno, "Completing the Circle", op. cit., pp. 93–107; Victor T. King, "Southeast Asia: Personal Reflections on a Region", in *Southeast Asian Studies: Debates and New Directions*, edited by Cynthia Chou and Vincent Houben, pp. 23–45.

13. See, for example, Ignas Kleden, "Social Science in Indonesia: Action and Reflection on Southeast Asian Perspective", in *Social Science in Southeast Asia: From Particularism to Universalism*, edited by Nico Schulte Nordholt and Leontine

Visser, *Comparative Studies* 17 (Amsterdam: VU Press, 1995), pp. 9–34; Paul H. Krastoska, Remco Raben, and Henk Schulte Nordholt, "Locating Southeast Asia", pp. 11–20; Thongchai Winichakul, "Trying to Locate Southeast Asia from Its Navel", pp. 113–32; Thongchai Winichakul, "Writing at the Interstices", pp. 3–29; Victor King, "Southeast Asia: Personal Reflections on a Region", pp. 23–45; Robert Cribb, "Region, Academic Dynamics and Promise of Comparativism: Beyond Studying 'Southeast Asia'?" in *Southeast Asian Studies*, op. cit., p. 48.

14. Adrian Vickers has cautioned against taking the Saidian critique of Orientalist representations to an extreme in the study of Southeast Asia. He argues on the importance of textual reading as a form of knowledge contribution and a means for translating meanings across different societies within and beyond Southeast Asia (2009).

15. King has gone on to write two disciplinary-based books on Southeast Asia, i.e., *Anthropology and Development in Southeast Asia* (1999) and *The Sociology of Southeast Asia* (2008).

16. King has disputed Heryanto's opinion on the marginalization of Southeast Asian scholars in Southeast Asian Studies (see King, "Southeast Asia: Personal Reflections on a Region", pp. 23–44).

17. I owe this insight to Joel S. Kahn.

18. Zomia refers to the mainland massif of Southeast Asia which extends from the Central Highlands of Vietnam westward all the way to North-eastern India and the South-western provinces of China.

19. See note 7.

20. For an elaboration of the problems of the dependency and inequalities in knowledge production between the First and Third worlds, see Farid Alatas' article in *Current Sociology* 51, no. 6 (2003): 599–613, and his book on *Alternative Discourses in Asian Social Science* (2006).

21. Expatriate scholars form a big component of the academic community in the two main national universities in Singapore, i.e., the National University of Singapore and Nanyang Technological University. I want to thank Joel Kahn for highlighting this point to me.

22. Arif Dirlik had raised this point in an article on "Asia Pacific Studies in an Age of Global Modernity" in *Inter-Asia Cultural Studies* 6, no. 2 (2005): 158–70.

23. "Circles of esteem" is a concept introduced by Robert Cribb (2006). This concept defines Southeast Asian Studies as a field whereby knowledge production is constituted by complex and hierarchical scholarly networks which produce a system of professional evaluations driven primarily by esteem and derision.

24. Arif Dirlik (2005, p. 158) has also pointed to newer reconfigurations of Asia and the Pacific studies as scholars responded to the crisis of area studies. He identifies the study of "civilizations, oceans, diasporas, Asianization of Asian studies and indigenous studies" as newer paradigms replacing earlier area studies.

25. Workshop participants not represented in this volume are Diana Wong from Malaysia, Kasian Tejapira from Thailand, and Liu Hong from China.
26. In the face of such difficulties, some scholars have dismissed the recourse to ethics as a rhetorical practice that grew out of ideological splits and ambiguities of the modern condition since the sixteenth century (Simpson 2002). Others have instead pointed to the fact that antinomies over ethics have been experienced all across the history of knowledge production (see Jay 2002, pp. 32–33).
27. This book will cite scholars according to surnames in the usual academic practice. However, in cases following patronymic naming practices, where there are no family names but personal names followed by the father's name, references will only make use of personal names.
28. Wallerstein (2003) has defined contemporary disciplinary conventions as comprising three simultaneous things: (i) intellectual categories or modes of defining a field of study with some kind of boundaries; (ii) institutional structures in the form of departments, degree programmes, prizes, and so on; and (iii) shared cultures of scholarship styles, classical texts, and approaches. Wallerstein, "Anthropology, Sociology, and Other Dubious Disciplines", *Current Anthropology* 44, no. 4 (2003): 453.
29. For a recent volume discussing the impact of American social sciences on Indonesian social sciences since the Cold War, see Vedi R. Hadiz and Daniel Dhakidae, eds., *Social Science and Power in Indonesia* (Jakarta and Singapore: Institute of Southeast Asian Studies and Equinox Publishing, 2005).
30. ASEAN was formed in 1967 in Bangkok by five founding countries, that is, Thailand, Malaysia, Singapore, the Philippines, and Indonesia. Brunei joined in 1984, followed by Vietnam in 1995, Laos and Myanmar in 1997, and Cambodia in 1999.
31. See also Vedi R. Hadiz and Daniel Dhakidae, *Social Science and Power in Indonesia*, p. 4; and David Ransom, "The Berkeley Mafia and the Indonesian Massacre", *Ramparts* 9, no. 4 (1970): 27–49.
32. These comments were made by Kasian Tejapira during workshop discussions on 30 November 2002.
33. For a view on the origins and alternative practices of Southeast Asian Studies in China, see Hong Liu, "Sino-Southeast Asian Studies: Towards an Alternative Paradigm", *Asian Studies Review* 25, no. 3 (2001): 259–83.
34. For the origins of conceptions of Southeast Asia in Japan, which dates back to the post–World War I era, see Shimizu Hajime, "Southeast Asia as a Regional Concept in Modern Japan", in *Locating Southeast Asia*, edited by Paul H. Kratoska, Remco Raben, and Henk Schulte Nordholt, pp. 82–132. In my recent brief affiliation at the Centre for Southeast Asian Studies, Kyoto University, in 2008, I discovered that the centre practises a unique model of truly interdisciplinary area studies where natural and human scientists are engaged in collaborative studies of the region.

35. For accounts of these developments, see Anthony Reid and Maria Serena I. Diokno, "Completing the Circle", pp. 93–107; Charnvit Kasetsiri, "Southeast Asian Studies in Thailand", in *Southeast Asian Studies: Pacific Perspectives*, edited by Anthony Reid, pp. 109–17; UP Asian Centre, "Southeast Asian Studies in Asia: An Assessment" (Philippines: Asian Centre, University of the Philippines, 2003). Conference-Workshop Proceedings, 8–10 January 2002, Quezon City, Philippines; Shamsul Amri Baharuddin, "Malaysia: The Kratonization of Social Science", in *Social Science in Southeast Asia: From Particularism to Universalism*, edited by Nico Schulte Nordholt and Leontine Visser, *Comparative Studies* 17 (Amsterdam: VU Press, 1995): 87–110; Taufik Abdullah and Yekti Manauti, eds., *Toward the Promotion of Southeast Asian Studies in Southeast Asia* (Jakarta: Indonesian Institute of Sciences, 1994); See Shaharil Thalib, "The Department of Southeast Asian Studies, University of Malaya, 1976–1993", in *Toward the Promotion of Southeast Asian Studies in Southeast Asia*, edited by Taufik Abdullah and Yekti Manauti, pp. 39–86; and Heryanto. "Can there be Southeast Asians in Southeast Asian Studies", op. cit., pp. 3–30.

36. At the University of Malaya, Thai was introduced as an undergraduate subject in 1976, followed by Talagog in 1984, and Vietnamese in 1993. The Southeast Asian Studies Programme at the University of Malaya became a fully-fledged department in 1989 (see Shaharil Talib, "The Department of Southeast Asian Studies", pp. 39–86).

37. At the National University of Singapore, the Southeast Asian Studies Programme, established in 1991, introduced Bahasa Indonesia in 1992, followed by Vietnamese in 1995, and Thai in 1998. In 2007 Bahasa Malaysia became the fourth language offered to majoring students. Apart from the university, the Institute of Southeast Asian Studies (ISEAS), established in 1968, is a leading Southeast Asian Studies research and publication centre. ISEAS publishes two main journals dealing with Southeast Asia: *Sojourn* (since 1986) and *Contemporary Southeast Asia* (since 1979). Other major Southeast Asian journals in the region are based at the National University of Singapore. These are the *Journal of Tropical Geography* (from 1953) [prior to the separation from University of Malaya], *Journal of Southeast Asian History* (from 1960), which became the *Journal of Southeast Asian Studies* from 1970, and the *Southeast Asian Journal of Social Science* (1973).

38. The Centre for Southeast Asia Social Studies at Gadjah Mada University was the first department of Southeast Asian Studies in Indonesian universities. It was set up on 19 December 2000 (Personal communication with Aris Mundayat). A research centre for Southeast Asian Studies was established by LIPI, the Indonesian Institute of Sciences, under its Research Centre for Regional Resources on 5 July 2001 (Personal communication with Yekti Manauti).

39. In Thailand, a programme of Asian Studies was introduced at Chulalongkorn University as early as 1967. It became the Institute of Asian Studies in 1976. In 1971, a programme of Thai studies was established at Thammasat University which became the Thai Khadi Studies Institute in 1975. In 1974, a research

programme of Southeast Asian language and cultural studies was established at Mahidol University, but it became the Language and Cultural Research Institute for Rural Development in 1981. Silapakorn University started an MA programme in Southeast Asian history in 1974. A Southeast Asian Studies undergraduate degree programme was established at Thammasat University in 2001. See Charnvit Kasetseri, "Southeast Asian Studies in Thailand", pp. 112–17.

40. In Vietnam, a Department of Southeast Asian Studies was established in 1973 within a government research organization known as the Vietnam Social Sciences Committee. It later became the Institute of Southeast Asian Studies within the Vietnam Academy of Social Science. See Anthony Reid and Maria Serena I. Diokno, "Completing the Circle", p. 101.

41. The University of the Philippines introduced the teaching of Malay and Austronesian languages in the 1920s. See Anthony Reid and Maria Serena I. Diokno, "Completing the Circle", p. 96.

42. For an optimistic view on the distinctiveness of Southeast Asian studies in the United States, in particular, the interaction between the study of the region and disciplinary knowledge and its contribution to theory building, see John Bowen, "The Inseparability of Area and Discipline in Southeast Asian Studies: A View from the United States", *Moussons* 1 (2000): 3–19. For a contrasting view on the situation in the United Kingdom, where individual country studies matter more than the study of Southeast Asia as a region, see Victor King, "Southeast Asia: An Anthropological Field of Study?" *Moussons* 3 (2001): 3–31.

43. Takashi Shiraishi, a historian of Indonesia, who was once based at Cornell University, has earlier pointed out the institutional autonomy of Southeast Asian Studies programmes in Japan, which depart from the American model of area studies. See Takashi Shiraishi, "New Initiatives from Japan", in *Southeast Asian Studies*, edited by Anthony Reid, pp. 141–53.

44. The Southeast Asian Studies Programme, NUS, obtained approval from the University Senate to change its name from Programme into Department on 16 February 2011.

45. Talal Asad has noted that "It is not always clear what critics mean when they claim that there is no such thing as 'the West' because its modern culture has diverse genealogies taking it outside Europe. If Europe has a geographical 'outside' doesn't that itself presuppose the idea of a space — at once coherent and subvertible — for locating the West?" (2003, p. 14).

46. For the subject of Asian values, see Chua Beng-Huat, "'Asian Values' Discourse and the Resurrection of the Social", *Positions* 7, no. 2 (1999): 573–93; Khoo Boo Teik, "Nationalism, Capitalism and 'Asian Values'", in *Democracy in Malaysia: Discourses and Practices*, edited by Francis Loh Kok Wah and Khoo Boo Teik (Richmond, Surrey: Curzon Press, 1998), pp. 51–73. For studies on Islamic politics, nationalism, and democracy in Southeast Asia, see Syamsuddin, M. Din. "Responses of Muslim Social Scientists toward Indonesian Modernization", in *Social Science in Southeast Asia: From Particularism to Universalism*, edited

by Nico Schulte Nordholt and Leontine Visser, pp. 79–86; Farish A. Noor, "Blood, Sweat and Jihad: The Radicalization of the Political Discourse of the Pan-Malaysian Islamic Party (PAS) from 1982 Onwards", *Contemporary Southeast Asia*, 25, no. 2 (2003): 200–32; Robert Hefner, "Global Violence and Indonesian Muslim Politics", *American Anthropologist* 104, no. 3 (2002): 754–65; and Vidhu Verma, "Debating Rights in Malaysia: Contradictions and Challenges", *Journal of Contemporary Asia* 32, no. 1 (2002): 108–30.

47. Saba Mahmood has precisely made a plea on how subjugated subjects can still work out resistance within authoritative regimes in her work, *Politics of Piety: The Islamic Revival and the Feminist Subject* (Princeton, NJ: Princeton University Press, 2005).

48. For examples, see Taufik Abdullah and Maunati Taufik Abdullah, *Toward the Promotion of Southeast Asian Studies in Southeast Asia*; Ananda Rajah, "Southeast Asia: Comparatist Errors and the Construction of a Region, pp. 41–53; UP Asian Centre, *Southeast Asian Studies in Asia*; Heryanto, "Can There Be Southeast Asians in Southeast Asian Studies"; Abu Talib and Tan Liok Ee, *New Terrains in Southeast Asian History*.

49. In particular, see Paul H. Krastoska, Remco Raben, and Henk Schulte Nordholt, *Locating Southeast Asia*, pp. 1–19; and Heather Sutherland, "Contingent Devices", in *Locating Southeast Asia*, ibid., pp. 20–59.

50. A defence of the continued importance of regions to knowledge production vis-à-vis globalization has been made by two anthropologists studying the Caribbean: Karla Slocum and Deborah A. Thomas, "Rethinking Global and Areas Studies: Insights from Caribbeanist Anthropology", *American Anthropologist* 105, no. 3 (2003): 553–65.

51. The Toyota Foundation and Japan Foundation have co-sponsored the Southeast Asian Studies Regional Exchange Program (SEASREP). The Nippon Foundation funds the Public Intellectual Program for academics in their mid-careers.

52. In 2002, the Asian Centre in the University of the Philippines formed an Association of Southeast Asian Studies in Asia via a conference-workshop in Manila held in January 2002 with the theme "Southeast Asia in Asia: An assessment towards a Collaborative Action Agenda". Regional institutions and centres were invited to this conference. An existing institutional set-up for regional exchange is the ASEAN University Network which is based in Bangkok.

53. Comment by Melani Budianta (Workshop discussions, 30 November 2002).

54. The Southeast Asian Studies Programme at the National University of Singapore has established a two-way student exchange under a "Semester-in-Southeast Asia" programme since 2007. Its current partners to this exchange programme are Universitas Gadjah Mada, Thammasat University, Khon Kaen University, Vietnam National University, Hanoi, Vietnam National University, Ho Chi Minh City, and Ateneo de Manila University.

55. See James Scott in Itty Abraham, *Weighing the Balance*, p. 27.

56. Vickers has noted that recent PhDs graduates from Southeast Asian universities

have shifted research agendas on the region to study narrative and cross-cultural forms and, as a result, contributed to more equal interaction between local and Western scholarships (2009).

References

Abraham, Itty, ed. *Weighing the Balance: Southeast Asian Studies Ten Years After*. Proceedings of two meetings held in New York City on 15 November and 10 December 1999. New York: Social Science Research Council, 1999.

———. "Southeast Asian Studies Whereto?" In *Weighing the Balance: Southeast Asian Studies Ten Years After*, edited by Itty Abraham. New York: Social Science Research Council, 1999.

Abu Talib and Tan Liok Ee, eds. *New Terrains in Southeast Asian History*. Athens and Singapore: Ohio University Press, Southeast Asian Series No. 107 and Singapore University Press, 2003.

Agoncillio, Teodoro A. *A Short History of the Filipino People*. University of the Philippines, 1960.

Alatas, Syed Farid and Vineeta Sinha. "Teaching Classical Sociological Theory in Singapore: The Contest of Eurocentrism". *Teaching Sociology* 29 (2001): 316–31.

———. "Academic Dependency and the Global Division of Labour in the Social Science". *Current Sociology* 51, no. 6 (2003): 599–613.

———. *Alternative Discourses in Asian Social Science: Responses to Eurocentrism*. Thousand Oaks: Sage, 2006.

Agoncillio, Teodoro. *A Short History of the Filipino People*. University of the Philippines, 1960.

Alatas, Syed Hussein. *The Democracy of Islam: A Concise Exposition with Comparative Reference to Western Political Thought*. The Hague: W. van Hoeve, 1956.

———. *Intellectuals in Developing Societies*. London: Cass, 1977.

———. *The Myth of the Lazy Native*. London: Cass, 1977.

Ananda Rajah. "Southeast Asia: Comparatist Errors and the Construction of a Region". *Southeast Asian Journal of Social Science, Special Focus: Reconceptualizing Southeast Asia* 27 (1999): 41–53.

Anderson, Amanda and Joseph Valente. *Disciplinarity at the Fin De Siecle*. Princeton and Oxford: Princeton University Press.

Antlov, Hans. "Preface' in *Social Science and Power in Indonesia*, edited by Vedi Hadiz and Daniel Dhakidae, pp. xix–xxi. Jakarta and Singapore: Equinox Publishing and Institute of Southeast Asian Studies, 2005.

Asad, Talal. *Formations of the Secular. Christianity, Islam, Modernity*. Stanford, California: California Press, 2003.

Asian Centre, University of the Philippines. "Southeast Asian Studies in Asia: An Assessment". Conference-Workshop Proceedings, 8–10 January 2002, Quezon City, Philippines.

Berman, Marshall. *Adventures of Marxism*. New York: Verso, 1999.

Bowen, John. "The Inseparability of Area and Discipline in Southeast Asian Studies: A View from the United States". *Moussons* 1(2000): 3–19.

Buck, David. "Forum on Universalism and Relativism in Asian Studies". *Journal of Asian Studies* 50, no. 1 (1991): 29–34.

Chua Beng-Huat. "'Asian Values' Discourse and the Resurrection of the Social". *Positions* 7, no. 2 (1999): 573–93.

Chou, Cynthia and Vincent Houben, eds. *Southeast Asian Studies: Debates and New Directions*. Singapore: International Institute of Asian Studies and Institute of Southeast Asian Studies, 2006.

Chou, Rey. "Theory, Area Studies, Cultural Studies: Issues of Pedogogy in Multiculturalism". *In Learning Places: The Afterlives of Area Studies*. Durham, NC: Duke University Press.

Cribb, Robert. "Region, Academic Dynamics, and Promise of Comparitivism: Beyond Studying 'Southeast Asia'". In *Southeast Asian Studies: Debates and New Directions*, edited by Cynthia Chou and Vincent Houben. Singapore: International Institute of Asian Studies and Institute of Southeast Asian Studies, 2006.

De Bary, Wm. Theodore. "The Funding on Asian Studies". *Journal of Asian Studies* 30, no. 2 (1971): 389–412.

Dirlik, Arif, ed. *What's in a Rim: Critical Perspectives on the Pacific Region Idea*, 2nd ed. Lanham, MD: Rowman and Littlefield, 1998.

———. "Asia Pacific Studies in an Age of Global Modernity". *Inter-Asia Cultural Studies* 6, no. 2 (2005): 158–70.

Emmerson, Donald K. "Issues in Southeast Asian History: Room for Interpretation — A Review Article". *Journal of Asian Studies* 40, no. 1 (November 1980): 43–68.

Farish A. Noor. "Blood, Sweat and Jihad: The Radicalization of the Political Discourse of the Pan-Malaysian Islamic Party (PAS) from 1982 Onwards". *Contemporary Southeast Asia* 25, no. 2 (2003): 200–32.

Halib Mohammed and Tim Huxley, eds. *An Introduction to Southeast Asian Studies*. London: Tauris, 1996.

Harootunian, Harry. "Tracking the Dinosaur: Area Studies in a Time of 'Globalism'". In *History's Disquiet: Modernity, Cultural Practice and the Question of Everyday Life*. New York: Columbia University Press, 2000.

———. "Postcolonial's Unconscious/Area Studies' Desire". In *Learning Places: The Afterlives of Area Studies*, edited by Masao Miyoshi and H.D. Harootunian. Durham, NC: Duke University Press, 2002.

Hefner, Robert. "Global Violence and Indonesian Muslim Politics". *American Anthropologist* 104, no. 3 (2002): 754–65.

Heryanto, Ariel. "Ideological Baggage and Orientations of the Social Sciences in Indonesia". In *Social Science and Power in Indonesia*, edited by Vedi Hadiz and Daniel Dhakidae. Jakarta and Singapore: Equinox Publishing and Institute of Southeast Asian Studies, 2005.

————. "Can There be Southeast Asians in Southeast Asian Studies?" *Moussons* 5 (2002): 3–30. Reprinted in *Knowing Southeast Asian Subjects,* edited by Laurie Sears. Seattle and Singapore: University of Washington Press and NUS Press, 2007.

Hirschman, Charles, Charles F. Keyes, and Karl Hutterer, eds. *Southeast Asian Studies in the Balance: Reflections from America.* Ann Arbor, Michigan: Association for Asian Studies, 1992.

Hong Liu, "Sino-Southeast Asian Studies: Towards an Alternative Paradigm". *Asian Studies Review* 25, no. 3 (2001): 259–83.

Ileto, Reynaldo C. "Orientalism and the Study of Philippine Politics". In *Knowing America's Colony. A Hundred Years from the Philippine War.* Hawaii: Center for Philippines Study, University of Hawaii at Manoa, 1999.

————. "On the Historiography of Southeast Asia and the Philippines: The 'Golden Age' of Southeast Asian Studies — Experiences and Reflections". Proceedings of Workshop on "Can We Write History? Between Postmodernism and Coarse Nationalism". Institute for International Studies, Meiji Gakuin University, 9 March 2002.

Jay, Martin. "Speaking Azza". *London Review of Books* 24, no. 23, (2002): 32–33.

Kahin, George McT. "Presidential Address: The Polarization of Knowledge: Specialization on Contemporary Asia in the United States". *Journal of Asian Studies* 33, no. 4 (1974): 515–22.

Kahn, Joel. *Other Malays: Nationalism and Cosmopolitanism in the Modern Malay World.* Singapore: Singapore University Press and NIAS Press.

Karl, Rebecca E. *Staging the World: Chinese Nationalism at the Turn of the Twentieth Century.* Durham, NC: Duke University Press, 2002.

Kasetsiri, Charnvit. "Southeast Asian Studies in Thailand". In *Southeast Asian Studies: Pacific Perspectives*, edited by Anthony Reid. Tempe, AZ: Program for Southeast Asian Studies, 2003.

Katzenstein, Peter J. "Area and Regional Studies in the United States". *PS: Political Science and Politics* 34, no. 4 (2001): 789–91.

Keesing, Felix. "Problems of Integrating Humanities and Social Science Approaches in Far Eastern Studies". *Far Eastern Quarterly* 14, no. 2 (1955): 161–68.

Khoo Boo Teik, "Nationalism, Capitalism and 'Asian Values'". In *Democracy in Malaysia. Discourses and Practices*, edited by Francis Loh Kok Wah and Khoo Boo Teik. Richmond, Surrey: Curzon, 1998.

————. "Value(s) of a Miracle: Malaysian and Singaporean Elite Constructions of Asia". *Asian Studies Review* 23, no. 2 (1999):180–92.

King, Victor. *Anthropology and Development in Southeast Asia. Theory and Practice.* New York: Oxford University Press, 1999.

————. "Southeast Asia: An Anthropological Field of Study?" *Moussons* 3 (2001): 3–31.

————. "Southeast Asia: Personal Reflections on a Region". In *Southeast Asian Studies: Debates and New Directions*, edited by Cynthia Chou and Vincent Houben.

Singapore: International Institute for Asian Studies and Institute of Southeast Asian Studies, 2006.

———. *The Sociology of Southeast Asia: Transformations in a Developing Region.* Copenhagen: NIAS Press, 2008.

Kleden, Ignas. "Alternative Social Science as an Indonesian Problematique". *New Asian Visions* (1986): 6–22.

———. "Social Science in Indonesia: Action and Reflection on Southeast Asian Perspective". In *Social Science in Southeast Asia: From Particularism to Universalism*, edited by Nico Schulte Nordholt and Leontine Visser. Amsterdam: VU Press, 1995.

Krastoska, Paul H., Remco Raben, and Henk Schulte Nordholt. "Locating Southeast Asia". In *Locating Southeast Asia: Geographies of Knowledge and Politics of Space*, edited by Paul H. Krastoska, Remco Raben, and Henk Schulte Nordholt. Singapore: Singapore University Press, 2005.

Lal, Vinay. *Empire of Knowledge: Culture and Plurality in the Global Economy.* London, Sterling, Virginia: Pluto, 2002.

Lambert, Richard D. "Presidential Address: An Action Agenda for Area Studies". *Journal of Asian Studies* 35, no. 1 (1975): 7–19.

Lewis, Martin and Karen Wigen. "A Maritime Response to the Crisis in Area Studies". *Geographical Review* 89, no. 2 (1999): 161–68.

Maung Htin Aung. A *History of Burma.* New York and London: Columbia University Press, 1967.

Mazuri, Ali. "Forward to the Past: African Intellectuals in the 1990s". *African Commentary*, June (1990): 32–38.

Mbembe, Achille. *On the Postcolony.* Berkeley: University of California Press, 2001.

———. "African Modes of Self-Writing", translated by Steven Rendall. *Public Culture* 14, no. 1 (2002): 239–73.

Menand, Louis, ed. *The Future of Academic Freedom.* Chicago: University of Chicago Press, 1996.

Mignolo, Walter D. "Colonial and Postcolonial Discourse: Cultural Critique or Academic Colonialism?" *Latin American Research Review* 28, no. 3 (1993): 120–34.

———. "Afterword: Human Understanding and (Latin) American Interests — The Politics and Sensibilities of Geocultural Locations". *Poetics Today* 16, no. 1 (Spring 1995): 171–214.

———. *Local Histories/Global Designs: Coloniality, Subaltern Knowledges, and Border Thinking.* Princeton, New Jersey: Princeton University Press, 2000.

Mitchell, Timothy. "The Middle East in the Past and Future of Social Science". In *The Politics of Knowledge: Area Studies and the Disciplines*, edited by David Szanton. Berkeley and Los Angeles: University of California Press, 2004.

Miyoshi, Masao and H.D. Harootunian. *Learning Places: The Afterlives of Area Studies.* Durham and London: Duke University Press, 2002.

Nordholte, Nico Schulte and Leontine Visser, eds. *Social Science in Southeast Asia: From Particularism to Universalism*. Amsterdam: VU Press, 1995.

Rafael, Vicente L. "The Culture of Areas Studies in the United States". *Social Text*, no. 41 (Winter 1994): 106–107.

———. "Regionalism, Area Studies, and the Accidents of Agency". *American Historical Review* 104 (1999): 1208–20.

Ransom, David. "The Berkeley Mafia and the Indonesian Massacre". *Ramparts* 9, no. 4 (1970): 27–49.

Reid, Anthony. *Southeast Asian Studies: Pacific Perspectives*. Tempe, AZ: Program for Southeast Asian Studies, 2003.

Reid, Anthony and Maria Serena I. Diokno. "Completing the Circle: Southeast Asian Studies in Southeast Asia". In *Southeast Asian Studies: Pacific Perspectives*, edited by Anthony Reid. Tempe, AZ: Program for Southeast Asian Studies, 2003.

Reynolds, Craig, J. "A New Look at Old Southeast Asia". *Journal of Asian Studies* 54, no. 2 (1995): 419–46.

Saba Mahmood. *Politics of Piety: The Islamic Revival and the Feminist Subject*. Princeton, NJ: Princeton University Press, 2005.

Said, Edward. *Orientalism*. London: Routledge and K. Paul, 1978.

Salazar Zeus A. *The Malayan Connection*. Lunsod Quezon: Palimbangan ng Lahi, 1998.

Sears, Laurie J. "The Contingency of Autonomous History". In *Autonomous Histories, Particular Truths: Essays in Honour of John Smail*, edited by Laurie Sears. Madison, WI: University of Wisconsin Centre for Southeast Asian Studies, 1993.

——— (ed). *Knowing Southeast Asian Subjects*. Seattle and Singapore: University of Washington Press and NUS Press, 2007.

Shaharil Thalib. "The Department of Southeast Asian Studies, University of Malaya, 1976–1993". In *Toward the Promotion of Southeast Asian Studies in Southeast Asia*, edited by Taufik Abdullah and Yekti Manauti. Jakarta: Program of Southeast Asian Studies, Indonesian Institute of Sciences, 1994.

Shamsul Amri Baharuddin. "Malaysia: The Kratonization of Social Science". In *Social Science in Southeast Asia: From Particularism to Universalism*, edited by Nico Schulte Nordholt and Leontine Visser. Amsterdam: VU Press, 1995.

———. "Southeast Asia as a Form of Knowledge: Of Production/Reproduction, Analyses and Approaches". Keynote paper for the Singapore Graduate Forum on Southeast Asian Studies: ASEAN Graduate Workshop organized by Asia Research Institute, National University of Singapore, 28–29 July 2006.

Shimizu Hajime. "Southeast Asia as a Regional Concept in Modern Japan". In *Locating Southeast Asia: Geographies of Knowledge and Politics of Space*, edited by Paul H. Kratoska, Remco Raben, and Henk Schulte Nordholt. Amsterdam: VU Press, 1995.

Shiraishi, Takashi. "New Initiatives from Japan". In *Southeast Asian Studies: Pacific Perspectives*, edited by Anthony Reid. Tempe, AZ: Program for Southeast Asian Studies, 2003.

Singer, Milton. "The Social Sciences in Non-Western Studies". *Annals of the American Academy of the Political and Social Science* 356 (1964): 30–44.

Simpson, David. *Situatedness; Or Why We Keep Saying Where We're Coming From.* Durham: Duke University Press, 2002.

Slocum, Karla and Deborah A. Thomas, "Rethinking Global and Area Studies: Insights from Caribbeanist Anthropology". *American Anthropologist* 105, no. 3 (2003): 553–65.

Smail, John R.W. "On the Possibility of an Autonomous History of Modern Southeast Asia". *Journal of Southeast Asian History* 2 (1961): 72–102. Reprinted in *Autonomous Histories, Particular Truths: Essays in Honor of John Smail*, edited by Laurie Sears. Madison: Madison Wisconsin Centre for Southeast Asian Studies, 1993.

Spencer, Johnathan. "Writing Within: Anthropology, Nationalism, and Culture in Sri Lanka". *Current Anthropology* 31, no. 3 (1990): 283–300.

Suryadinata, Leo. "Southeast Asian Studies in Singapore: Past and Present". In *Toward the Promotion of Southeast Asian Studies in Southeast Asia*, edited by Taufik Abdullah and Yekti Manauti. Jakarta: Program of Southeast Asian Studies, Indonesian Institute of Sciences, 1994.

Sutherland, Heather. "Contingent Devices". In *Locating Southeast Asia: Geographies of Knowledge and Politics of Space*, edited by Paul H. Kratoska, Remco Raben, and Henk Schulte Nordholt. Singapore: Singapore University Press, 2005.

Syamsuddin, M. Din. "Responses of Muslim Social Scientists Toward Indonesian Modernization". In *Social Science in Southeast Asia: From Particularism to Universalism*, edited by Nico Schulte and Leontine Visser. Amsterdam: VU Press, 1995.

Szanton, David, ed. *The Politics of Knowledge: Area Studies and the Disciplines*. Berkeley and Los Angeles: University of California Press, 2004.

Taufik Abdullah. "Past Performance and Future Directions". In *Social Science in Southeast Asia: From Particularism to Universalism*, edited by Nico Schulte Nordholte and Leontine Visser. Amsterdam: VU Press, 1995.

Taufik Abdullah and Yekti Manauti, eds. *Toward the Promotion of Southeast Asian Studies in Southeast Asia*. Jakarta: Program of Southeast Asian Studies, Indonesian Institute of Sciences, 1994.

UP Asian Centre. *Southeast Asian Studies in Asia: An Assessment*. Philippines: Asian Centre, University of the Philippines, 2003. Conference-Workshop Proceedings, 8–10 January 2002, Quezon City, the Philippines.

Van Leur, J.C. *Indonesian Trade and Society: Essays in Asian Social and Economic History*. The Hague: W. van Hoeve, 1967.

Van Schendel, Willem. "Geographies of Knowing, Geographies of Ignorance: Jumping Scale in Southeast Asia". In *Locating Southeast Asia: Geographies of Knowledge and Politics of Space*, Paul H. Kratoska, Remco Raben, and Henk Schulte Nordholt. Singapore: Singapore University Press, 2005.

Vedi R. Hadiz and Daniel Dhakidae, eds. *Social Science and Power in Indonesia*. Jakarta and Singapore: Institute of Southeast Asian Studies and Equinox, 2005.

Verma, Vidhu. "Debating Rights in Malaysia: Contradictions and Challenges". *Journal of Contemporary Asia* 32 (2002): 108–31.

Vickers, Adrian. "Southeast Asian Studies After Said". Keynote Address at Third International Conference on Southeast Asia. Kuala Lumpur, 9 December 2009.

Wallerstein, Immanuel, "Anthropology, Sociology, and Other Dubious Disciplines. Sidney W. Mintz Annual Lecture for 2002". *Current Anthropology* 44, no. 4 (2003): 453–65.

Walters, Neil L., ed. *Beyond the Area Studies Wars: Towards a New International Studies*. Hanover and London: University Press of New England, 2000.

Ward, Robert. "Presidential Address: A Case for Asian Studies". *Journal of Asian Studies* 32, no. 3 (1973): 161–68.

Winichakul, Thongchai. "Writing at the Interstices: Southeast Asian Historians and Postnational Histories in Southeast Asia". In *New Terrains in Southeast Asian History*, edited by Abu Talib and Tan Liok Ee. Athen and Singapore: Ohio University Press, Southeast Asian Series No. 107 and Singapore University Press, 2003.

—————. "Trying to Locate Southeast Asia from Its Navel: Where is Southeast Asian Studies in Thailand?" In *Locating Southeast Asia: Geographies of Knowledge and Politics of Space*, edited by H. Kratoska, Remco Raben, and Henk Schulte Nordholt. Singapore: Singapore University Press, 2005.

Wolters, O.W. "Southeast Asia as a Southeast Asian Field of Study". *Indonesia* 58 (1994): 1–17.

2

POST-IMPERIAL KNOWLEDGE AND PRE-SOCIAL SCIENCE IN SOUTHEAST ASIA

Wang Gungwu

All literate knowledge stemmed from the transmissions of sacred texts before the scientific revolution of the seventeenth century in Europe. By the twentieth century, following the expansion of the West, most scholars in Asia accepted that science education had an equal place with their own classical humanities. It was not until the second half of that century that social science was taken seriously in Asian universities. The impact of that on the humanities has yet to be fully felt, but many universities already treat traditional learning as something akin to pre–social science. For those who believe that the humanities are vital to any civilized society, the challenge is not only to protect the humanities from further erosion, but also to use scientific methods and ideas to study the nature of Asian traditions in changing societies without these studies becoming simply pale imitations of imperial knowledge from the West.

This chapter does not examine directly the implications of taking up that challenge. It only describes my experiences with an early stage of transition, one moving from what could be described as imperial knowledge brought from the West, to new local and national efforts in Southeast Asia to respond to the introduction of social science. In that context, the chapter deals primarily with the decade in the 1940s and 1950s of my own apprenticeship as a student, during which I studied in three places: Nanjing in China, 1947–48;

Singapore as part of British Malaya, 1949–54; and London at the School of Oriental and African Studies, 1954–57.

I began my studies of history without thought of what social science was and what it was not. My history teachers certainly did not call themselves social scientists. However, from today's perspective, my educational background could be described as more than one-third social science and nearly two thirds humanities. So I may be said to represent something called pre–social science. I agreed to participate in this volume because I believe that the history and sociology of knowledge could be useful to those who wonder about current trends and potentials, and wish to see some of the problems today in a wider context. The fact is, I studied history in the imperial traditions of a humanities education and, while welcoming the stimulus of social science analysis, decided not to pursue any training in a specific social science discipline. This has determined the way I have worked for over five decades. Another reason I am writing here stems from my concern that some academic disciplines have become too narrowly focused on quantitative techniques and do not emphasize enough the many dimensions of time and place that all social problems possess. The sacred cow of a universalistic *science* is threatening to reduce the *social* to a set of ciphers that diminishes the relevance of empirical practice and the power of human judgment and action. Southeast Asian Studies needs to consider if this is the direction to go. I hope that my pre–social science experiences can show that there are alternative ways that are more inclusive and that openness to ideas and respect for actual experience should not give way to theory worship.

There are now thousands of Asians who have studied social science subjects as undergraduates and then gone on to pursue graduate studies in their respective fields within their countries or elsewhere in Europe, North America, and Australasia. Some, from countries such as India, Japan, and China, had begun their studies prior to World War II, and a few among them mastered their fields so well that, with new data and fresh observations, they offered insights that enriched both theory and method in their chosen disciplines. Southeast Asian students came to the social sciences later and new generations of them were exhorted to serve the new nation states of the region with their practical skills. Most of them tried hard to adapt what they learnt from Western theories and models to stimulate economic development, improve standards of governance, and meet urgent social needs in their respective countries. Since the 1960s, with the increase in the number of universities, new opportunities have been available to do independent research that has encouraged some to hope that new and more relevant theories and methods might emerge from their local research.

Is the pursuit of better theories to replace those discovered elsewhere the way to go? Or should social scientists in Asia concentrate on effective application of received knowledge to make their countries safer, stronger, more prosperous, and orderly? Or should they examine and re-evaluate the cultural roots of their societies in order to find the native genius that might transform the social sciences from their alien origins into new sources of inspiration for their leaders and peoples? These questions are now being asked in many parts of Asia, but they were already being asked, albeit in less focused ways, in the 1950s and 1960s, even in former colonies in Southeast Asia on the eve of independence and nation building. I recall some experiences related to the transition from received traditions to rejection and activism and to sceptical scientific inquiry in the humanities and the social sciences. I will offer here my reflections on those transition years, afterthoughts on my experiences, and ideas about what directions might be fruitful in the future. I suggest that what occurred in the long process of decolonization in British Malaya, and later, Malaysia and Singapore, may tell us something useful about social science education and its value to Asian states and communities.

EMPIRE KNOWLEDGE

I came to the study of history rather indirectly. I saw it as an interesting approach to self-knowledge at a time of political revolution and cultural turmoil, with no thought whatsoever whether the discipline belonged to the humanities or the social sciences. My high school in Ipoh in the Malay state of Perak was a colonial school where the medium of teaching was English and the curriculum followed was that used in most schools in the British Empire. I later learnt that, in almost all subjects, the same textbooks were used throughout the empire. In addition to English literature, I studied history and geography (our school did not offer economics), science, mathematics, and advanced mathematics. The science was mainly basic physics and chemistry. No one mentioned social science, but I was taught to think that the word "science" was the key to any kind of progress.

The most important part of my growing social awareness during my later high school years in 1945–46 was the sense that a new world was dawning in Asia. In Malaya, after the British defeat in 1941–42 and the three-and-a-half years of Japanese Occupation, there was growing resistance to colonial rule. There were the strikes organized by left-wing trade unions backed by the Malayan Communist Party; the racial clashes between Malays and Chinese;

the shortages of food and all imported goods; the angry accusations made against incompetent and corrupt officials; and the anti-colonial, anti-imperialist slogans everywhere. From the street activities all over Malaya, one could see that British power was being challenged and could hear the many voices exhorting people to prepare for a Malaya that local leaders would some day control. Obviously, these were problems that social science disciplines would have helped us understand. No one mentioned it, but I think I had begun to ask "social science" questions in my mind simply by living through those times. And that did affect my choice of reading matter in our library.

My own interest when I left school was to study literature, a subject my father and my teachers taught me to love. In any case, the two universities at which I studied in 1947–48 and 1949–54 had different policies on the question of the humanities and social science. My first campus was in Nanjing, the capital of the Republic of China, while my second was the new University of Malaya founded in Singapore in 1949 by the departing British colonial power. Neither were interested in drawing clear boundaries between the humanities and social science. The National Central University in Nanjing admitted freshmen directly to an academic department in which they would remain for four years of study, and it was the Department of Foreign Languages that accepted me. This placed me in the Faculty of Arts where the main departments were those of history, literature, and philosophy.[1] Subjects such as geography and psychology were located in the Faculty of Science. I do not recall if the university offered sociology and political science and believe that economics was a core subject in the Faculty of Commerce. At the time, there was another national university in Nanjing, the Zhengzhi (Politics) University (a cross between Sciences Po in Paris, and the London School of Economics in London, but guided by the belief that such an institution should be controlled by the party in power, in this case, the Kuomintang), and that university certainly offered political science (including international relations and public administration) and economics.

My education in Malaya did not prepare me to understand events in China during my time in Nanjing, from April 1947 to December 1948. There the students, all on full national scholarships, were deeply involved in post-war China's political debates. Our teachers were dutiful in class, but had to hold several jobs outside the campus in order to make a living. So we saw little of them and learnt much more from our peer groups. Hyperinflation dogged everyone's daily lives. There were frequent mass demonstrations in Nanjing at which opponents of the national government (including students) were arrested and beaten up, all of them described as communists or communist sympathizers. Outside the capital, the civil war in the north was going badly for the government. At the same time, my parents in Malaya kept me informed of the outlawing of the Malayan Communist Party, the armed rebellion that led the British to introduce Emergency Regulations for all of Malaya, and of the economic turmoil that resulted from that. They also told me of the political deal struck by the British with the Malay elites to establish a new Federation of Malaya in which very few non-Malays could qualify to be citizens. Thus, from the end of the war in 1945 till my return to Malaya in December 1948, not a day passed without something happening that could have been a core topic for social science study.

My second university, the University of Malaya, was much smaller and its offerings more basic. It had adopted the Scottish system of having Arts students do a three-year BA (General) degree after which a select number of students qualified to do a one-year specialization for an honours degree. For the general degree, there were no majors and we were each made to take three subjects. The university gave us little choice and offered only English literature, history, geography, economics, and mathematics in the Faculty of Arts. I took literature, history, and economics and only decided to specialize in history in my fourth year. I liked literature best, and inexplicably found economics uninteresting at the time. In the end, I chose history because the professor of history, C. Northcote Parkinson, encouraged us to look for local documents and probe the ideas behind them that could explain complex events relevant to the way Malaya was developing.[2] He challenged us to discover what facts accounted for historical changes, including lessons that would help us understand some of the dramatic developments in Asia, and especially in our neighbourhood. It did not occur to me or anyone else to ask whether history belonged to the humanities or the social sciences.

What was more important for me was the range of books available in our respective libraries, and the conditions in which I was free to read books beyond those that our teachers recommended. Even more influential for my attitudes towards knowledge was the temper of the times that enlivened campus lives.

When I joined the University of Malaya in October 1949, I was introduced to the discipline of economics and found some of the courses stimulating. It was taken for granted that the methods we used and the theories that were applied to our region were drawn from experiences in the developed economies of Western Europe and North America. We were also taught about the technical programmes and methodologies that were considered to have been efficacious in other tropical or subtropical areas such as southern India or Africa or the West Indies. It was axiomatic that economic principles were universal and as valid as the laws in the physical sciences. It was assumed that the political values and legal and administrative framework of the colonial state would remain and, therefore, what was good for the British Empire should be able to serve the future postcolonial nation equally well. The students were being prepared to inherit that state structure and its philosophical underpinnings. Our courses concentrated on technical knowledge and rarely touched on the conflicting social and cultural values and political and economic challenges that prevailed outside the campus. The Emergency conditions prevented open discussions about the debates that were dividing the world. We were left to discuss these issues among ourselves.

My understanding of the social sciences during the decades of decolonization was that the academic disciplines called the social sciences began to evolve in Europe in the nineteenth century and spread quickly to North America. In Europe, some social scientists benefited from opportunities to test their theories on the conquered peoples of Asia and Africa. For them, imperial tasks such as surveying and mapping the world, defining civilization and barbarism through the study of ethnography and ethnology, and extending the frontiers of geology and natural history were strongly supported by colonial governments. In economics, the writings of Adam Smith and Jeremy Bentham, among others, were brought in to assist the European expansion that followed the scientific revolution and the rise of industrial capitalism, notably in India and beyond the Strait of Malacca. In addition, scientific theory and method were extended to challenge the authority of theology and classical studies, and question prevailing social and political philosophy. This later gave rise to new fields such as sociology and political science. There grew other fields that were acknowledged during the twentieth century, but the boundaries drawn between the humanities and the natural sciences were not always clear. For empires, it was more important to use the knowledge to serve their interests than to explore lofty ideals of theoretical sophistication.

As has been much argued since the late 1970s, the study of classical and biblical studies, extended to West Asia, developed into Edward Said's "Orientalism", which showed that the way that knowledge was presented came to serve various kinds of empire building after 1800.[3] Such perspectives enabled the underlying premise of European power, whether it was more Greco-Roman or more Judaeo-Christian, to spill over to the rest of the Asian continent. For example, the ideas about civilization of the classical age enabled the British to mix practical and technical dedication with racial condescension in India, and for the Dutch to be singularly diligent in the study of the multiplicity of peoples and cultures in the Netherlands East Indies. The French in turn were deeply committed to bringing civilization to their oriental natives. Despite the Enlightenment ideals that shaped the rise of modern Europe, they too were deeply influenced by classical ideas of empire and racial superiority.

As for America, eschewing imperialism while guided by missionary zeal, their schools and colleges in East Asia (including its colony in the Philippines) were open and ready to introduce practical social science disciplines, often linked to their faculties of commerce or business. Not troubled by imperial burdens, their social scientists were eventually more drawn to the ideals of scientific perfection and the sacred mission of developing universal theories. Before the end of the age of European empires, however, European scholars took their superiority for granted and did not think it necessary to proclaim such a mission.

In the first two decades after the end of World War II, social science disciplines that looked to the United States were increasingly taught in universities in Japan, Korea, and the Philippines. This was free of explicit imperial baggage. In British Malaya, however, and throughout most universities in the Commonwealth tradition, classical education was still well regarded. Whatever the social sciences might have done for the empire, British officials did not consider it necessary for local universities to emphasize such academic disciplines. Even in the universities of Cambridge and Oxford, sociology and politics did not merit separate academic departments until recently. Only the field of economics was recognized early and the little awareness I had of social science came from attending classes in economics for my first three years at the University of Malaya. The excellent textbooks by John Hicks, notably *The Social Framework*, Paul Samuelson's *Economics: An Introductory Analysis*, and Kenneth Boulding's *Economic Analysis*, together answered many technical questions and introduced me to fine points of theory. But, in retrospect, what was more important was the way the courses opened me to macroeconomic issues relevant to the ideological debates of the time. For example, what John Maynard Keynes stood for, and how that was challenged by the writings of Frederick Hayek, illuminated clearly for me some major problems in politics.[4] It even stimulated my interest in history, including the modernization experience of Western Europe, the United States, and Japan.

I recall reading R.F. Harrod's biography of Keynes soon after it was published and was inspired by that to read the works by leading members of the Fabian Society, including Sidney Webb and Harold Laski, and other leading lights of the London School of Economics.[5] Their writings also led me to the work of sociologists such as Emile Durkheim, Max Weber, and the wayward thoughts of Pitrim Sorokin.[6] They represented what I understood to be social science and it did not surprise me that many of them, almost seamlessly, were linked to historians and literary writers such as George

Bernard Shaw, H.G. Wells, and Lytton Strachey.[7] In short, I found at the time no great divide between social scientists and various creative writers and philosophers, or with some of the historians who wrote on the period between the two world wars. These engaged intellectuals ranged from Arnold Toynbee and E.H. Carr to George Orwell, Arthur Koestler, and W.H. Auden,[8] and to philosophers such as Bertrand Russell, Friedrich Hayek, Karl Popper, and Jean-Paul Sartre.[9]

The ideas and methodologies of these authors had shaped some of my thinking before I decided to specialize in history. As I turned to the study of historical documents and interpretations, I found that their writings illuminated some critical developments in Asian history. The more I linked their theories to the research I was doing, the more they helped me to become a historian who was conscious that the social science disciplines have much to offer us. The correction was something I needed. My reading of history taught me that the colonial system depended on classically educated officials for whom social science education was minimal. The model of the Roman Empire, later influenced by the Chinese examination system, ensured that the social sciences were only marginal to imperial needs. And when some of the colonial administrators turned to scholarly pursuits, they almost invariably began with history, languages, philology, Oriental classical texts (if available), and natural history. Their best work led to the development of new fields such as tropical geography and anthropology, and even transformed Orientalist preoccupations into what became modern Area Studies. For me, perhaps the most important contributions came from the rise of social and cultural anthropology and the injection of their methods into some areas of sociology.[10]

The courses I took in literature had the least to do with social science but, in the context of the white man's burden, it was easy to see connections with colonization in the Americas, slavery and exploitation in Africa, the Orientalism of the Muslim and Hindu worlds, and even the contempt for the "heathen Chinese".[11] But for my generation, I believe it was the books read in the library and borrowed from friends that seemed to have better explained our turbulent times. We looked for policies and ideas that would answer the key questions on our minds: independence and freedom from the imperial powers, building new nations, the appeal of socialism, the revolutionary movements among the young all over Asia. Not finding much in the classroom, we looked elsewhere. Most books on anti-colonialism and revolutions were banned and we were challenged to find them to read. I did manage to read some proscribed works by Marx and Lenin and (in Chinese) some wartime writings of Mao Zedong and realized that they were more calls to action than systematic expositions.[12] There were similar writings on the anti-revolutionary side that condemned all communists as terrorists and exhorted us to reject their attacks on capitalism and imperialism. Clearly, these did not represent social science but, at a time when political life was simple, economic conditions desperate, and social tensions violently divisive, the colonial university offered too little to help explain the world and we had to look elsewhere to the active and the engaged for help.

I did not dwell long among the revolutionary writers because alternative explanations also caught my attention. Aside from the courses in history that were largely about Western expansion into Asia, I had read widely about the French and Russian revolutions and the Spanish Civil War. I was impressed by Orwell's *Animal Farm* and even took part in broadcast readings of the book on Radio Malaya.[13] Closer to home, I admired the work of Victor Purcell on the Chinese in Southeast Asia and took his side against the flattering essay on General Gerald Templer by my professor of history, C.N. Parkinson.[14] Nevertheless, I was stimulated by Parkinson's course on the evolution of political thought, where he challenged us with his conservative and anti-Fabian ideas.[15] But it was not until I began to do research on Southeast Asian and Chinese history myself that I began to appreciate the use of European social science concepts and methodologies in Asian research.

Three men opened my eyes to the use of social science methods to deal with Southeast Asian questions. One was J.S. Furnivall whose books on Burma and the Netherlands East Indies, especially his *Colonial Policy and Practice*, provided a rigorous examination of the colonial state from within. Another was Rupert Emerson. As an American political scientist, he wrote more from the outside and I found his pre-war study of *Malaysia: A Study in Direct and Indirect Rule*, more enlightening than anything written by historians. The third was the posthumous work of J.C. van Leur, introduced to me in 1954 by W.F. Wertheim.[16] I recall eagerly waiting to read his collection of essays, *Indonesian Trade and Society*, when it was translated and published in 1955. But, when I chose to do my doctoral research on tenth century Chinese history, I set aside my Southeast Asian interests and did not pursue the exciting lines of inquiry that these writers had opened up. There were two other reasons for this. My teachers in London were not advocates of the social sciences and my desire to re-discover Chinese sources and traditions of historiography sent me back to classical Sinology to learn a new trade.

All the same, the exposure I had to a few social scientists working in Southeast Asia continued to influence my thinking. Thus, even as I shifted my focus to China, I remained attracted to the work of scholars who were less conventionally Orientalist and more ready to apply the methods of sociology and politics to the study of pre-modern China. For example, I read Wolfram Eberhard, Hsiao Kung-chuan, and Owen Lattimore with great interest.[17] Eberhard used methods of historical sociology to dissect pre-modern Chinese history in refreshing ways. Hsiao, who was trained in political science, skilfully reinterpreted the history of Chinese political culture and the imperial dynasties. As for Lattimore, his application of the frontier theory to the borderlands between Chinese and the nomadic peoples of the steppe, was one of the most important works of historical geography that I have ever read.

I was similarly drawn to the work of Karl Wittfogel even before he published his book on *Oriental Despotism*. With the help of Feng Chia-sheng, he had reframed the history of the northern borderlands through the study of Khitan-Chinese society and power relationships.[18] Neither Lattimore nor Wittfogel were trained as social scientists, but their research methods were innovative and their early writings contributed richly to fields such as geography and historical sociology. And then there were the two books on the Chinese gentry by Chang Chung-li. His combination of historical and political data with careful sociological analysis showed me how a great number of questions could be answered through a mix of disciplines.[19] There were many others whose work I encountered rather erratically, but nevertheless influenced my thinking even as I tried to acquire some sinological skills. The methodologies employed by R.H. Tawney, E.H. Carr, Max Weber, and, not least, the work of Lewis Namier, especially his *The Structure of Politics at the Accession of George III*, influenced in one way or another the way I approached the study of the protagonists seeking to reunify China during the chaotic tenth century.[20]

But, as long as my research was about early Chinese history, social science was only marginally useful. It was only when I was asked to write on the Chinese overseas in transition to postcolonial nation building in Southeast Asia that my early readings of Furnivall, Emerson, and van Leur once again loomed large.[21] This was especially true of the work of social anthropologists. The doyen of historical anthropology was Maurice Freedman.[22] I had not paid attention to his early report, "Colonial Law and Chinese Society", and only vaguely heard, when I was in London, that he had completed an excellent doctorate at the London School of Economics. But when I was back in Singapore and came to read his new book, *Lineage Organisation in Southeastern China*, I was fascinated. Through him, I was led back to the work of Fei Hsiao-tung, Lin Yueh-hwa, Chen Han-sheng, Francis L.K. Hsu, and Chen Ta, that first generation of Chinese trained in sociology and anthropology, some in Britain and others in the United States.[23] It was Freedman's appreciation of the pioneering work of a handful of sociologists who worked in China, such as Daniel H. Kulp, Marcel Granet, and J. Lossing Buck, that made me realize how powerfully this branch of social science had influenced the Chinese themselves.[24] At that point, for the first time, I regretted that, as students at the University of Malaya in the early 1950s, we were not exposed to a wider range of social science disciplines.

I was drawn to the study of the Chinese overseas somewhat by accident. It began when I was invited to give a series of eight lectures on the history of the Nanyang Chinese by Radio Sarawak, the state of Sarawak at that time still a British colony.[25] After reading the available sources in Chinese, I returned to the work of Victor Purcell. This was the moment when Purcell reviewed the new book on the history of the Chinese in Thailand by the American anthropologist, G. William Skinner. In that review, Purcell revealed how strongly the classically trained scholar was sceptical of the social science methods adopted by Skinner. I was surprised by my reaction. Instead of agreeing with a fellow historian, my sympathies were entirely with the anthropologist who offered an "analytical" history.[26] The 1950s marked the gradual retreat of imperial classicism in the face of non-imperialist American social science. In Southeast Asia, the new names were George Kahin and Clifford Geertz on Indonesia, and Lucien Pye on Malaya and Burma.[27] For me, there was also the discovery that the Philippines was different. Because the Americans brought social science education to the country early, it already had its own social scientists. Several of them had already begun to explore their own brand of theory and method and I found it inspiring to read, among others, the work of O.D. Corpuz, Cesar Majul, and Horacio de la Costa.[28] They pointed to what can be done when local Southeast Asians are masters in their respective social science disciplines. By this time, it was clear to me that the multiple disciplined (even undisciplined) start in my university education had taken its toll on my history training, and my excursion into sinology (close to Chinese traditions where knowledge did not have borders) was the final straw. I could no longer claim ownership in any branch of knowledge that required the drawing of academic borders.

CONCLUSION

Let me end with some thoughts on how all this may be relevant to Southeast Asian Studies. From the start, the most successful social scientists were those who majored in economics. Their quantitative skills made their theories more credible and both national governments and large corporations appreciated the rigour of that kind of training. Others have done well who trained in disciplines such as sociology and psychology. Yet others found the study of politics or government satisfying and were able to transfer their knowledge to their jobs in a wide range of public service positions. Those who studied anthropology and linguistics were more likely to be drawn to teaching and research, but some governments have found them invaluable in dealing with community affairs as well. As for historians who thought that their subject belonged to the humanities, some are now content, even grateful, for their field to be included as a social science. This is still true in most modern universities of Asia, with economics at one end of the spectrum, and history at the other, with the others at different points in between. The precise point often depends on the stage of economic development of the country, the political and bureaucratic system in operation there, and the social-cultural mix of its population.

The criteria that determine where each discipline is placed is stricter today and often decided by how quantitative the methodologies used are, and how prepared the protagonists are to make theoretical contributions to knowledge. It is this concern with theory that is exercising young scholars in Asia. While most have mastered the quantitative skills and others have contributed fresh qualitative insights by using data collected in Asia, there are few breakthroughs in theory that have come from their research. Many now ask if they should continue to accept existing theories worked out by Western scholars as universal, or if they should make greater efforts to discover their own original theories.

I have no doubt that when more Asian scholars analyse their data and find that new theory is needed to explain unfamiliar or even unknown phenomena, changes will happen. They understand the history of how the social sciences evolved in the West, how the various disciplines grew out of classical and philosophical quests for truth and knowledge. Those quests had come from a tradition that was very different from the social and moral pursuits found in Asia. For me, this was especially so with reference to ancient East Asian thought. But how Western goals and methods of knowledge creation were introduced to Asia is also relevant when we try to understand the current efforts among Asian social scientists to find their own voices. In order to advance new theories and methodologies, many would need to master not only one or more existing social science disciplines, but also familiarize themselves fully with the underlying assumptions of traditional Asian values. In that way, they could discover distinctive ways to explain the new realities in a globalizing Asia.

As someone who came to appreciate the contributions of social scientists without being trained as one, I am not qualified to examine the processes involved in such a transformation. What is clear is that social science in the

West grew out of having empirical studies analysed within a philosophical tradition that refined logical and objective thinking and created modern science. In Southeast Asia, we need to learn all we can about that science and also learn all we can about the multiple conditions, both past and present, of each local society. By doing so we can see how much social science can explain what we see, and how we might derive new concepts and theories to illuminate what has not been successfully explained. If we can acquire deep knowledge of the origins of our societies and the ways they are changing, being pre–social scientists is not a barrier to such research and scholarship. The danger for Southeast Asian Studies would come from excessive emphasis on "disciplinary rigour" drawn from social science models developed elsewhere. Any turning inwards in search of new paradigms or universal theory is not the best that social science can do for the region. My experience suggests that much more can be gained from deep engagements with one's own society and through fostering intellectual curiosity and scepticism of academic boundaries. This can best be done by returning to the spirit of inquiry that only reading, thinking, and action can produce.

Notes

1. All these subjects have been officially considered branches of science since the Communist victory in 1949. Together with a group of subjects linked with economics, they were taken out of the Academy of Science in 1977 to form the Chinese Academy of Social Sciences. More recently, several Chinese universities have rebelled against this and established new institutes or centres to focus on the study of the humanities. Some have revived the old idea of *wenxueyuan* or Faculty of Arts to distance the humanities from any pretence to be scientific.

2. C.N. Parkinson's later work made it even less clear whether history belonged to the humanities or social sciences. From naval and maritime history, he turned to writing a history of political thought and then went on to discover Parkinson's Law; *Parkinson's Law* (Boston: Houghton Mifflin, 1957). The law, "work expands to fill the time available", has a status that may be compared to that of social science theory and has become a valuable concept in public and business administration.

3. My early encounters with the word "Orientalism" was innocent of political content, and merely described the work of humanities scholars who specialized in the study of ancient Asian languages, literature, history, and philosophy. After Edward Said published his book, *Orientalism* (New York: Pantheon Books) in 1978, the word has never been the same again.

4. My teachers conveyed to me some of the excitement of the debates over the ideas of John Maynard Keynes as I struggled to read his classic study, *The General*

Theory of Employment, Interest and Money (London: Macmillan, 1936), and then Friedrich A. Hayek's *The Road to Serfdom* (London: Routledge, 1944). My textbooks were John Hicks, *The Social Framework: An Introduction to Economics* (Oxford: Clarendon, 1946); Paul Samuelson, *Economics: An Introductory Analysis* (New York: McGraw-Hill, 1948); Kenneth Boulding, *Economic Analysis*, revised edition (New York: Harper, 1948).

5. Roy Harrod, *The Life of John Maynard Keynes* (London: Macmillan, 1951). I only read one book by Sidney Webb, *The History of Trade Unionism* (London: Longmans, Green, 1935). Like many students of my generation, we were more attracted to the books by Harold Laski. For example, I recall being impressed by *Liberty in the Modern State* (London: Faber & Faber, 1930); *A Grammar of Politics*, 5th ed. (London: Allen & Unwin, 1948); *The Rise of European Liberalism* (London: Allen & Unwin, 1936); and *The Foundations of Sovereignty and Other Essays* (London: Allen & Unwin, 1931). They could all be described as studies in the ambit of the social sciences.

6. I benefited much from reading at the time Emile Durkhem's *The Division of Labour in Society* (Glencoe: Free Press, 1949). Later, his *Moral Education: A Study in the Theory and Application of the Sociology of Education* (New York: Free Press of Glencoe, 1961), made me revise my views about education. As for Max Weber, he was a powerful influence on many of us, notably his *The Protestant Ethic and the Spirit of Capitalism* (New York: Scribner, 1948); but it was the collection of essays, *From Max Weber: Essays in Sociology* (London: K. Paul, Trench, Trubner, 1947), which I read again and again, and they took me further to another stimulating set of essays, *The Religion of China: Confucianism and Taoism* (Glencoe: Free Press, 1951). Pitrim Sorokin was, I remember, rather challenging to read, but I did learn from his *Society, Culture, and Personality: Their Structure and Dynamics, a System of General Sociology* (New York, Harper, 1947).

7. I mention these three to underline my own "lack of discipline": I read most of Shaw's plays and some of his Fabian tracts, several of Wells' socialist essays and early novels, as well as *The Outline of History: Being a Plain History of Life and Mankind* (New York: Garden City, 1931; revised edition, the first was published in 1920). As for Lytton Strachey, his brilliant biographies (*Eminent Victorians*, 1918; and *Queen Victoria*, 1921) and historical essays were writings that many social scientists admired.

8. A.J. Toynbee moved easily between classical history, contemporary politics and international relations, and he stunned the world with his massive *A Study of History*. (London: Oxford University Press, 12 volumes, 1934–45); E.H. Carr was similarly engaged before he completed his great *History of Soviet Russia* (London: Macmillan 1950–78). As for George Orwell, I was introduced to his *Burmese Days* (first published in 1934) to support my anti-colonial feelings, but when I read his *Animal Farm* soon after it was published in 1945 (London: Secker & Warburg), it led me to read everything he has ever published. I still

think that modern fable was one of the most powerful political documents of its time. Similarly, some of the early writings of Arthur Koestler: *Darkness at Noon* (English translation first published in 1941) and *Promise and Fulfillment: Palestine, 1917–1949* (London: Macmillan, 1949), read like politics, history, and literature all in one. In a less direct way, W.H. Auden worked his politics into his poetry and demonstrated how needless some academic divisions can be. His *Journey to a War* (first published in 1939, New York: Random House) led me to look out for his *Collected Poetry*, first published in 1945 (also by Random House in New York).

9. All four were great writers. When we compare a major book by each of them, it becomes clear how impoverishing it can be to be obsessive about academic boundaries; for example, Russell's *Roads to Freedom: Socialism, Anarchism, and Syndicalism* (first published in 1918), Popper's *The Open Society and its Enemies* (1945), Hayek's *The Road to Serfdom* (1944), and Sartre's *The Age of Reason* (translation published in 1947). It should also be noted that Russell, after a brief visit, published an analysis of what he called *The Problem of China* (New York: Century, 1922). Although his knowledge of Chinese politics was clearly inadequate and his views about the country's economy hardly any better, the book offered insights into the dangers of revolution that were debated and criticized within China for years. It is interesting that a full translation by Qin Yue into Chinese was published in Shanghai in 1996, long after Russell's comments on revolution could be of any help.

10. Maurice Freedman influenced me most to think in this way. I eventually came to read his "Colonial Law and Chinese Society" in *Journal of the Royal Anthropological Society* 80, 1950, and it was an eye-opener. When we met in London and he showed me his work on *Chinese Family and Marriage in Singapore* (published in 1957) and the draft of his brilliant study of *Lineage Organization in Southeastern China* (1958), he convinced me that historians of Asia do need to have a good understanding of anthropology.

11. It is ironic that this term came, not from European imperialists in China, but from an American poet Bret Harte writing about the Chinese in the United States (first published as *Plain Language from Truthful James*, in 1870).

12. Here I came up against a brand of social science that served also as messianic and political inspiration for revolutionary action. The writings of Lenin and Mao were proscribed in British Malaya and also in the Federation of Malaya (and Malaysia) and Singapore. But it was possible to find a few essays by Marx in the University of Malaya library and certainly books about the ideas of Marx and Lenin, for example, Sidney Hook's *From Hegel to Marx: Studies in the Intellectual Development of Karl Marx* (New York: Humanities Press, 1950); and Edmund Wilson's *To the Finland Station: A Study in the Writing and Acting of History* (New York: Doubleday, 1953, first published in 1940), both of which I read with immense interest. As for Mao Zedong, I read a few wartime essays by him when I was a student in Nanjing in 1947–48. In them, I saw him more as a

nationalist with Stalinist ideas, than someone dedicated to Soviet Communism. I did not read anything by him in English until I got to London in 1954, the year when his *Selected Essays* were first published by Lawrence and Wishart in four volumes.

13. Radio Malaya used a radio drama version in which we acted out the parts of Napoleon, Snowball, Boxer, and some of the others. The producer felt sorry for me and one of the parts that I read was that of Boxer, the workhorse who came to a sad end in Orwell's story.

14. Parkinson's book was *Templer in Malaya* (Singapore: Donald Moore, 1954). Purcell offered a very different image of Templer, one that is not so heroic, in his book, *Malaya: Communist or Free?* (London: Gollancz, 1954).

15. His book, *The Evolution of Political Thought* (London: University of London Press, 1958), was based on the course of lectures he gave to the History honours class at the University of Malaya between 1952 and 1956.

16. J.S. Furnivall, *Netherlands India: A Study of Plural Economy* (Cambridge: Cambridge University Press, 1939); and *Colonial Policy and Practice: A Comparative Study of Burma and Netherlands India* (Cambridge: Cambridge University Press, 1948). Rupert Emerson, *Malaysia: A Study of Direct and Indirect Rule* (New York: Macmillan, 1938). W.F. Wertheim recommended the work of J.C. van Leur that was eventually put together in *Indonesian Trade and Society: Essays in Asian Social and Economic History* (The Hague: van Hoeve, 1955).

17. These three books were particularly helpful: Wolfram Eberhard, *Conquerors and Rulers: Social Forces in Medieval China* (Leiden: Brill, 1952); Hsiao Kung-ch'uan [Xiao Gongquan], *Rural China: Imperial Control in the 19th Century* (Seattle: University of Washington Press, 1960); and Owen Lattimore, *Inner Asian Frontiers of China* (New York: Capitol and American Geographical Society, 2nd edition, 1951; first published by Oxford University Press in 1940).

18. Karl A. Wittfogel and Feng Chia-sheng [Feng Jiasheng], *History of Chinese Society: Liao, 907–1125* (Philadelphia: American Philosophical Society, and New York: Macmillan, 1949). It was not until I returned from my studies in London in 1957 that Wittfogel's *Oriental Despotism* was published (New Haven: Yale University Press, 1957). There the former revolutionary social scientist dissected the origins of totalitarianism in China (he called it "total power") by drawing from ancient Chinese classical texts. I was certainly bemused by his turnaround. Of course, his use of social science terms, and even methods, followed that of Marx's earlier analysis of Greek and Roman classical history. Most Chinese were not impressed and, as far as I know, no translation of Wittfogel was published. Interestingly, the only use of the term for China was polemical. This was by a scholar in Taiwan: C.L. Chiou, *Democratizing Oriental Despotism: China from 4 May 1919 to 4 June 1989 and Taiwan from 28 February to 28 June 1990* (New York: St Martin's, 1995).

19. Chang Chung-li [Zhang Zhongli], *The Chinese Gentry: Studies on their Role in 19th Century Chinese Society* (Seattle: University of Washington Press, 1955); and

the follow-up volume, *The Income of the Chinese Gentry* (Seattle: University of Washington Press, 1962).

20. R.H. Tawney, *Land and Labour in China* (London: Allen & Unwin, 1932; new edition of the report he presented to the Institute of Pacific Relations in 1931). For Carr and Weber, see notes 6 and 8 above. Lewis Namier's *The Structure of Politics* was published in London by Macmillan, 1957.

21. See note 16. All three scholars underlined aspects of the region's plural societies that helped me to see the *huaqiao* (overseas Chinese) in a new light.

22. See note 10. In Maurice Freedman's lecture to the China Society in June 1964, he surveys the early efforts to study the Chinese in Southeast Asia and sums up very well the way we were examining that phenomenon in the 1950s; *The Chinese in South-East Asia: A Longer View* (London: China Society, 1965).

23. Notably the following books: Fei Xiaotong [Fei Hsiao-t'ung], *Earthbound China: a Study of Rural Economy in Yunnan*, revised edition (Chicago: University of Chicago Press, 1945); and *China's Gentry: Essays in Rural-Urban Relations*, revised edition (Chicago: University of Chicago Press, 1953). The others are by Lin Yaohua [Lin Yueh-hwa], *The Golden Wing: A Sociological Study of Chinese Familism* (New York: Oxford University Press, 1948); Chen Hansheng [Chen Han-seng], *Landlord and Peasant in China: A Study of the Agrarian Crisis in South China* (New York: International Publishers, 1936); Francis L.K. Hsu, *Under the Ancestor's Shadow: Chinese Culture and Personality* (New York: Columbia University, 1948); Chen Da [Ch'en Ta], *Emigrant Communities in South China: A Study of Overseas Migration and its Influence on Standards of Living and Social Change* (New York: Institute of Pacific Relations, 1940).

24. Daniel H. Kulp, *Country Life in South China: The Sociology of Familism. Vol. one: Phoenix Village, Kwangtung, China* (New York: Columbia University Teachers College, 1925); Marcel Granet, *Chinese Civilization*, English translation first published in New York by Knopf, 1930; and J. Lossing Buck, *Land Utilization in China: A Study of 16,786 Farms in 168 Localities, and 38,256 Farm Families in 22 Provinces, 1929–1933* (Chicago: University of Chicago Press, 1937).

25. The lectures were published shortly afterwards as *A Short History of the Nanyang Chinese* (Singapore: Donald Moore for English University Press, 1959).

26. G. William Skinner, *Chinese Society in Thailand: An Analytical History*, and *Leadership and Power in the Chinese Community in Thailand*, both published by Cornell University Press, Ithaca, in 1957 and 1958 respectively. Victor Purcell's review was in *Journal of Asian Studies* 17, no. 2 (February 1958): 223–32. See reply by Ronald Dore in the same journal, vol. 17, no. 3 (May 1958): 513–14 in Skinner's defence.

27. All three authors have been prolific. The earliest to make an impact on social science research in Southeast Asia were George McT. Kahin, *Nationalism and Revolution in Indonesia* (Ithaca, NY: Cornell University, 1952); Clifford J. Geertz, *The Religion of Java* (Glencoe: Free Press, 1960); and Lucian W. Pye, *Guerilla Communism in Malaya, Its Social and Political Meaning* (Princeton: Princeton

University Press, 1956), and *Politics, Personality, and Nation-building: Burma's Search for Identity* (New Haven: Yale University Press, 1962). Lucian Pye's earliest work was actually on China: his PhD thesis at Yale University in 1951 was only made available in 1967 and a shortened version was published as *Warlord Politics: Conflict and Coalition in the Modernization of Republican China* (New York: Praeger, 1971).

28. Onofre D. Corpuz, *The Bureaucracy in the Philippine* (Quezon City: Institute of Public Administration, University of the Philippines, 1956); Cesar Adib Majul, *Mabini and the Philippine Revolution* (Quezon City: University of the Philippines, 1960); and Horacio de la Costa, *The Jesuits in the Philippines, 1581–1768* (Cambridge: Harvard University Press, 1961). More conventionally a historian was Teodoro A. Agoncillo, whose *The Revolt of the Masses: The Story of Bonifacio and the Katipunan* in 1956, and *Malolos: The Crisis of the Republic* in 1960 (both published by The University of the Philippines), were important landmarks in Filipino historiography.

References

Agoncillo, Teodoro A. *The Revolt of the Masses: The Story of Bonifacio and the Katipunan.* University of the Philippines, 1956.
———. *Malolos: The Crisis of the Republic.* University of the Philippines, 1960.
Auden, W.H. *Journey to a War.* New York: Random House, 1939.
———. *Collected Poetry.* New York: Random House, 1945.
Boulding, Kenneth. *Economic Analysis.* Rev. ed. New York: Harper, 1948.
Buck, J. Lossing. *Land Utilization in China: A Study of 16,786 Farms in 168 Localities, and 38,256 Farm Families in 22 Provinces, 1929–1933.* Chicago: University of Chicago Press, 1937.
Carr, E.H. *History of Soviet Russia.* London: Macmillan, 1950–78.
Chang Chung-li [Zhang Zhongli]. *The Chinese Gentry: Studies on Their Role in 19ᵗʰ Century Chinese Society.* Seattle: University of Washington Press, 1955.
———. *The Income of the Chinese Gentry.* Seattle: University of Washington Press, 1962.
Chen Da [Ch'en Ta]. *Emigrant Communities in South China: A Study of Overseas Migration and its Influence on Standards of Living and Social Change.* New York: Institute of Pacific Relations, 1940.
Chen Hansheng [Chen Han-seng]. *Landlord and Peasant in China: A Study of the Agrarian Crisis in South China.* New York: International Publishers, 1936.
Chiou, C.L. *Democratizing Oriental Despotism: China from 4 May 1919 to 4 June 1989 and Taiwan from 28 February to 28 June 1990.* New York: St Martin's, 1995.
Corpuz, Onofre D. *The Bureaucracy in the Philippines.* Quezon City: Institute of Public Administration, University of the Philippines, 1956.
de la Costa, Horacio. *The Jesuits in the Philippines, 1581–1768.* Cambridge: Harvard University Press, 1961.

Dore, Ronald. "Letter 2 — No title", *Journal of Asian Studies* 17, no. 3 (May 1958): 513–14.

Durkhem, Emile. *The Division of Labour in Society*. Glencoe: Free Press, 1949.

———. *Moral Education: A Study in the Theory and Application of the Sociology of Education*. New York: Free Press of Glencoe, 1961.

Eberhard, Wolfram. *Conquerors and Rulers: Social Forces in Medieval China*. Leiden: Brill, 1952.

Emerson, Rupert. *Malaysia: A Study of Direct and Indirect Rule*. New York: Macmillan, 1938.

Fei Xiaotong [Fei Hsiao-t'ung]. *Earthbound China: A Study of Rural Economy in Yunnan*. Rev. ed. Chicago: University of Chicago Press, 1945.

———. *China's Gentry: Essays in Rural-Urban Relations*. Rev. ed. Chicago: University of Chicago Press, 1953.

Freedman, Maurice. "Colonial Law and Chinese Society". *Journal of the Royal Anthropological Society* 80, (1950).

———. *Chinese Family and Marriage in Singapore*. London: HMSO, 1957.

———. *Lineage Organization in Southeastern China*. London: Athlone, 1958.

———. *The Chinese in South-East Asia: A Longer View*. London: China Society, 1965.

Furnivall, J.S. *Netherlands India: A Study of Plural Economy*. Cambridge: Cambridge University Press, 1939.

———. *Colonial Policy and Practice: A Comparative Study of Burma and Netherlands India*. Cambridge: Cambridge University Press, 1948.

Geertz, Clifford J. *The Religion of Java*. Glencoe: Free Press, 1960.

Granet, Marcel. *Chinese Civilization*. English translation first published by New York: Knopf, 1930.

Harrod, Roy. *The Life of John Maynard Keynes*. London: Macmillan, 1951.

Harte, Bret. "Plain Language from Truthful James". *Overland Monthly and Out West Magazine* no. 5, Issue 3 (September 1870): 287.

Hayek, Friedrich A. *The Road to Serfdom*. London: Routledge, 1944.

———. *The Road to Serfdom*. Chicago: University of Chicago Press, 1944.

Hicks, John. *The Social Framework: An Introduction to Economics*. Oxford: Clarendon, 1946.

Hook, Sidney. *From Hegel to Marx: Studies in the Intellectual Development of Karl Marx*. New York: Humanities Press, 1950.

Hsiao Kung-ch'uan [Xiao Gongquan]. *Rural China: Imperial Control in the 19th Century*. Seattle: University of Washington Press, 1960.

Hsu, Francis L.K. *Under the Ancestor's Shadow: Chinese Culture and Personality*. New York: Columbia University, 1948.

Kahin, George McT. *Nationalism and Revolution in Indonesia*. Ithaca, NY: Cornell University, 1952.

Keynes, John Maynard. *The General Theory of Employment, Interest and Money*. London: Macmillan, 1936.

Koestler, Arthur. *Darkness at Noon* (English translation first published in 1941).

————. *Promise and Fulfilment: Palestine, 1917–1949.* London: Macmillan, 1949.

Kulp, Daniel H. *Country Life in South China: the Sociology of Familism.* Vol. 1: *Phoenix Village, Kwangtung, China.* New York: Columbia University Teachers College, 1925.

Laski, Harold. *Liberty in the Modern State.* London: Faber & Faber, 1930.

————. *The Foundations of Sovereignty and Other Essays.* London: Allen & Unwin, 1931.

————. *The Rise of European Liberalism.* London: Allen & Unwin, 1936.

————. *A Grammar of Politics.* 5th ed. London: Allen & Unwin, 1948.

Lattimore, Owen. *Inner Asian Frontiers of China.* 2nd ed. New York: Capitol Publishers and American Geographical Society, 1951 (first published by Oxford University Press in 1940).

Lin Yaohua [Lin Yueh-hwa]. *The Golden Wing: A Sociological Study of Chinese Familism.* New York: Oxford University Press, 1948.

Majul, Cesar Adib. *Mabini and the Philippine Revolution.* Quezon City: University of the Philippines, 1960.

Mao Zedong. *Selected Essays.* Lawrence and Wishart, 1954.

Namier, Lewis. *The Structure of Politics.* London: Macmillan, 1957.

Orwell, George. *Burmese Days.* New York: Time Inc., first published in 1934.

————. *Animal Farm.* London: Secker & Warburg, 1945.

Parkinson, C.N. *Templer in Malaya.* Singapore: Donald Moore, 1954.

————. *Parkinson's Law.* Boston: Houghton Mifflin, 1957.

Popper, Karl. *The Open Society and its Enemies.* London: Routledge and Kegan Paul, 1945.

Purcell, Victor. *Malaya: Communist or Free?* London: Gollancz, 1954.

————. *The Evolution of Political Thought.* London: University of London Press, 1958.

————. "'Scientific Analysis' or 'Procrustean Bed'?" *Journal of Asian Studies* 17, no. 2 (February 1958): 223–32.

Pye, Lucian W. *Guerilla Communism in Malaya, its Social and Political Meaning.* Princeton: Princeton University Press, 1956.

————. *Politics, Personality, and Nation-building: Burma's Search for Identity.* New Haven: Yale University Press, 1962.

————. *Warlord Politics: Conflict and Coalition in the Modernization of Republican China.* New York: Praeger, 1971.

Russell, Bertrand. *Roads to Freedom: Socialism, Anarchism, and Syndicalism.* New York: Henry Holt, 1919 (first published in 1918).

————. *The Problem of China.* New York: Century, 1922.

Said, Edward. *Orientalism.* New York: Pantheon Books, 1978.

Samuelson, Paul. *Economics: An Introductory Analysis.* New York: McGraw-Hill, 1948.

Sartre, Jean-Paul. *The Age of Reason*. Gallimard, Knopf, Vintage Books, translation published in 1947.

Skinner, G. William. *Chinese Society in Thailand: An Analytical History*. Ithaca, NY: Cornell University Press, 1957.

———. *Leadership and Power in the Chinese Community in Thailand*. Ithaca, NY: Cornell University Press, 1958.

Sorokin, Pitrim. *Society, Culture, and Personality: Their Structure and Dynamics, A System of General Sociology*. New York: Harper, 1947.

Strachey, Lytton. *Eminent Victorians*. London: Chatto & Windus, 1918.

———. *Queen Victoria*. 1921.

Tawney, R.H. *Land and Labour in China*. London: Allen & Unwin, 1932 (new edition of the report he presented to the Institute of Pacific Relations in 1931).

Toynbee, A.J. *A Study of History*. London: Oxford University Press, 12 volumes, 1934–45.

van Leur, J.C. *Indonesian Trade and Society: Essays in Asian Social and Economic History*. The Hague: van Hoeve, 1955.

Wang, Gungwu. *A Short History of the Nanyang Chinese*. Singapore: Donald Moore for English University Press, 1959.

Webb, Sidney. *The History of Trade Unionism*. London: Longmans, Green, 1935.

Weber, Max. *Protestant Ethic and the Spirit of Capitalism*. New York: Scribner, 1948.

———. *From Max Weber: Essays in Sociology*. London: K. Paul, Trench, Trubner, 1947.

———. *The Religion of China: Confucianism and Taoism*. Glencoe: Free Press, 1951.

Wells, H.G. *The Outline of History: Being a Plain History of Life and Mankind*. Rev. ed. New York: Garden City, 1931 (first published in 1920).

Wilson, Edmund. *To the Finland Station: A Study in the Writing and Acting of History*. New York: Doubleday, 1953 (first published in 1940).

Wittofgel, Karl A. and Feng Chia-sheng [Feng Jiasheng]. *History of Chinese Society: Liao, 907–1125*. Philadelphia: American Philosophical Society and New York: Macmillan, 1949.

———. *Oriental Despotism*. New Haven: Yale University Press, 1957.

3

FROM THE EDUCATION OF A HISTORIAN TO THE STUDY OF MINANGKABAU LOCAL HISTORY

Taufik Abdullah

Unlike most present day history students, I enrolled in the Department of History by conscious personal choice. While most of my high school classmates preferred to enter the faculties of economics, law, or social and political sciences, I opted for the commonly assumed economically less promising subject of study. In a time when the youthful idealism of the newly sovereign nation state was still very much part of the game — after all my classmates and I were the living witnesses of the bloody national revolution — I thought some of us should study the history of our newly independent country, so I consciously made the sacrifice "for the sake of our future". Well, I must confess, liking the subject matter did not exactly make this a difficult sacrifice. I made the decision on the ship taking me and my friends to Java from Sumatra.

The Department of History of the Gadjah Mada University in Yogyakarta was then a part of the Faculty of Letters, Pedagogy, and Philosophy. In 1956, two years after I matriculated, the faculty was divided into two and the Department of History became a part of the Faculty of Letters and Culture. Looking back at the first two or three years of my study, I can now remember my bewilderment with the way the department was run. Not only because I had to follow the Continental system of free study, but there was also no clear-cut boundary between the subjects to be examined in the first year and those in the third year. Or, perhaps I was not properly aware of it. Since it was entirely dependent on my decision, I just attended the lectures on whatever subjects were offered. The lecturers and professors were apparently not too certain about the subjects of study to be offered to future historians. After all, the study of history was still something new in the tradition of higher learning in Indonesia. None of them had a formal degree in history. Now, several decades later, I can only express my gratification to the rather awkward programme of the department, as it exposed me to different kinds of disciplines and subjects of study.

Perhaps because the dean of the Faculty of Letters, Pedagogy and Philosophy was a psychologist, all first year students were required to attend his lectures on psychology and pedagogy. Even though the students of the Department of History were not obliged to take the exams, I still managed to enjoy these lectures very much. I stopped attending the class after the Faculty of Letters, Pedagogy and Philosophy was divided into two and we no longer shared the same campus halls. Whatever the case, by the time I received my bachelor degree, I had already taken courses in the history of art (from ancient Egyptian to the European Romantic period), the cultural history of ancient India, the history of ancient and modern Indonesia, Islamology (that is, Islamic doctrine), the cultural history of Islam, the history of Old China, introductory philosophy (plus logic and ethics), ethnology (studies on some isolated ethnic groups) and anthropology, history of modern Europe (from the Renaissance to the nineteenth century), Malay classical literature, Old and New Javanese, Indonesian modern literature, linguistics, and an introduction to comparative languages.

At the time I was about to receive my bachelor degree, the Department of History reorganized its system. The graduate study or what was then called *doktoral*, was to be divided into Western and Indonesian sections. Soon after I received my BA degree I decided to join the section of Western history. The reason for this decision was very simple and, perhaps, also a little naive. I hoped I could be sent abroad to study. I thought it was impossible to get that opportunity if I concentrated on studying Indonesian history. Not only this, but I had also been appointed as a teaching assistant in Western history.

MY LOVE AFFAIR WITH THE SPECULATIVE PHILOSOPHY OF HISTORY

Although the graduate or *doktoral* students would have to take an exam on the critical philosophy of history or, as was stated in the programme, "the theory of history", I was more interested in reading the speculative philosophy of history. Arnold Toynbee was then at the peak of his popularity. A weekly magazine (its name was *Star Weekly*, but it was an Indonesian language magazine) summarized his theory on universal history for several consecutive weeks. I still remember the time when the great historian gave a lecture at our university, but I could not really understand his lecture. Perhaps I was more accustomed to hearing a Hollywood accent, or his lecture was simply above my head, but more likely it was a combination of the two. Until today I still do not have the courage to read his eleven thick volumes of *A Study of History*. I was, however, less of a stranger with a few of his much shorter writings and, of course, the two-volume summaries of his theory on universal history. Motivated by a very inspiring course on the theory of history, given by a Dutch professor (who was a Christian theologian as well as an accomplished scholar on the history of Islamic philosophy, and historical philosophies of the old philosophers, ranging from Herodotus and Thucydides to Hegel and Karl Marx), I also tried to get acquainted with the ideas of Oswald Spengler, Karl Jaspers, and Pitirim Sorokin. One of Sorokin's books (*Social Philosophies of An Age of Crisis*, 1950) summarizes the ideas of a number of modern philosophers of history. I also enjoyed reading Pieter Geyl's criticisms (*Debates with Historians*, 1962) on Toynbee and other great historians.

These above mentioned books fuelled my interest in the historical grand narrative and speculative philosophy of history as did the courses I had taken. These courses covered various aspects of the cultural history of Europe, such as the foundation of Western civilization (Greek and Roman civilizations, and Judaism and early Christianity) and the modern cultural history of Europe, from the Renaissance to the 1848 Revolution, as well as the intellectual and socio-political predicament of Europe, which had been forced to accept the leadership of the United States. Edith Hamilton was my favourite author on the Greek and Roman civilizations (*The Greek Way to Western Civilization, The Roman Way to Western Civilization*, and *Mythology*). I liked her rather popular style of writing. Huyzinga's classic, *The Waning of the Middle Ages*, was, in my opinion, an example of serious scholarship that finds its affinity with literary beauty. Actually, the original Dutch title of the book was more poetic — *The Autumn of the Middle Ages*. The writings of two Dutch scholars, Jan Romein and Beerling, which had been translated into Indonesian, really opened the gates to understanding Europe for a young Indonesian like myself. Jan Romein said it was the deviation of Europe from what he called *algemeen menselijk patroon* (general pattern of mankind), that had made Europe so different from the rest of the world. Beerling's books, written in the mid-1950s, not only explored the intellectual history of Europe and described the recent philosophical trends, but also discussed the sense of intellectual crisis that was occurring in Europe following World War II. I also admired

Benedotte Groce's reflective history of Europe in the nineteenth century. One of the required readings for the theory of history was an excellent little book by W.H. Walsch, *"An Introduction to the Philosophy of History"*. The book not only touches on some important controversial subjects in history, such as "objectivity", "explanation in history", and the like, but it also gives succinct summaries on the ideas of several historical thinkers. It was through the guidance of this book that I dared to read R.G. Collingwood's difficult book, *The Idea of History*. Collingwood's approach with this book was particularly attractive. I read it at a time when people were trying to understand historical events from the perspective of the actors of history. This was a part of the liberation of history from colonial perspectives, which characterized the intellectual climate of Indonesia in the 1950s. I also enjoyed reading a rather entertaining book by Rowse on "the use and abuse of history".

The 1950s was the time when Mentor Books published many wonderful paperback books on European history, which cost no more than fifty U.S. cents each. In spite of the fact that there was a difference between the formal and "informal" exchange rate, the price of the books was still relatively low by Indonesian standards. Although I did not always have the time or, perhaps, the urge, to read all the books I bought, I still have some of the English translations of the Greek and Roman classics. That was also the time when many English translations of Russian classics, such as the writings of Tolstoy, Dostoevsky, Pushkin, and others, in addition to straightforward communist-oriented books, such as the collected writings of Lenin and some short accounts by Marx and Engels and others, could easily be purchased at very modest prices. There was no doubt in my mind that these books were subsidized, or perhaps imported, by the embassy of the Soviet Union. However, in spite of all these facilities offered by the market, by the time I received my *doctorandus* degree, my love affair with the speculative philosophy of history and the grand narrative of history had turned sour. The subjects of study were intellectually "too expensive" for me. I could no longer be a passive consumer of such branches of knowledge.

I have never regretted the fact that I dared to write a long *skripsi doktorandus* (a required thesis for PhD candidates in the old Continental system that was used in Indonesia until the early 1970s) on nationalism and nationalist movements in Europe after the French Revolution. In preparing the *skripsi* I learned not only the genesis of the divergent nationalist movements in Western Europe, their heroes, their actions, and the ideas of the nationalists, but also theories on nationalism and its related ideologies. It was while studying European modern history that I realized the importance of the knowledge of history, as a reconstruction of past events, in the process of nation formation.

Studying Europe made me more aware of how significant the debates on history, which had taken place since I enrolled in the history department, were. I felt I could better understand the nature of the intellectual climate that I had been through.

A PERIOD OF CULTURAL AND INTELLECTUAL ADVENTURE

When I received my *doktorandus* degree, the intellectual enthusiasm and, of course, the political instability of the 1950s, had become the past to contemplate. Sukarno's Guided Democracy and Soeharto's New Order regimes tended to look down at the 1950s — the period they saw as the time when the nation had almost forgotten its revolutionary zeal (as Sukarno never forgot to tell the nation), or as the period when ideological conflicts had taken the state away from the promises of the Proclamation of Independence (as Soeharto said when he took over the presidency). They might be right, but they only looked at one historical dimension of the era. The 1950s can also be seen as the time when the nation, and the newly sovereign nation state, dared to venture into uncharted intellectual territories. Several literary figures might claim themselves to be "the legitimate inheritors of world culture", but others tried to define what it meant to acquire a New World — the world of an independent nation — while some others strove to rediscover the genuine roots of the nation. It was indeed a period of cultural and intellectual adventure. I do not know how else one could explain the fact that a Muslim film producer, who was also a leader of an Islamic political party, collaborated with a Filipino film producer, to produce the first Indonesian movie in colour. They made a film called *Rodrigo de Villa*, a story of a gallant Spanish hero who fought against the crooked Moors! It was also during that period that many Indonesian intellectuals began to talk about the need for liberating "our" history from colonial domination. How could the so-called *Neerlando-centric* view of history be transformed into an *Indo-centric* one? Whose history really mattered — the Europeans who came and conquered "our country", or that of the struggling people and their efforts to liberate themselves from the fate that had been imposed on them? In spite of all types of political instability and conflict that to some extent characterized the 1950s, this historical episode can still be seen as a period of cultural innocence, just like the situation between the early 1920s and the early 1930s can be perceived as a decade of ideologies. If in the early and mid-1950s the concern for cultural orientation seemed to have separated itself from the conflicting political interests, in the 1920s–1930s the ideological debates among the nationalists were conducted without directly touching on the questions of the proper basic foundation of legitimate power. Indonesia was then, as the radical nationalists never forget to emphasize, ruled by the illegitimate colonial power, but in the 1950s the name of the game had changed. Indonesia had become a sovereign state. Within this newly emerging framework one can imagine that the moment cultural concern entangled itself with power politics was also the moment the era of cultural innocence began to fade away.[1]

A DISCOURSE TO REFLECT ON

In the period when the relatively free intellectual climate was about to be overturned by the rapid change of political events, the University of Indonesia and Gadjah Mada University co-sponsored the first National History Seminar in December 1957 on the campus of the Gadjah Mada University. Many big and less than big names in the contemporary historical discourses — thinkers, scholars, teachers, textbook writers, even leaders of political parties, and military officers — were among some 800 participants of the seminar. I will never forget this event. Not only because it was the first seminar I ever attended, although as no more than a curious observer, but also because the seminar was in many ways a historical event. That was the first time every possible understanding and view on the so-called national history was openly discussed and debated. Did we really need "a philosophy of national history" or could we simply talk about the effort to write the history of our nation? How should the series of events from prehistoric times to the present be organized? The periodization of history was indeed not only a matter of dividing history into several periods, but it also reflected the philosophical or, perhaps, even ideological, understanding of the course of history. What kind of "periodization" should be made, and used, as the tools in history teaching? How about textbook writing and the methods of history teaching? To a young and aspiring novice like myself it was a very lively seminar, and also a big eye-opener. History was not only something you might want to learn and comprehend, it was apparently also a discourse to reflect on.

The national seminar, however, was the last opportunity for the concerned intellectuals to independently explore the realm of historical ideas and orientations. By that time a move towards the establishment of Guided Democracy had already been under way. Although, according to the 1950 Provisional Constitution, the president "can do no wrong", because he was only the head of state, President Sukarno appointed himself the cabinet *formateur* and formed the National Council, which would help him as a kind of pseudo-cabinet. In short, as the opposition parties accused him, Sukarno had not only made himself the chief executive, but also the personification of the Constituent Assembly. "Was it not the exclusive right of the elected Constituent Assembly to set up such a high level state institution?" they argued. The unstable political process reached its climax with the issuance of the presidential decree of 5 July 1959. Indonesia "returned to the 1945 Constitution", the rather executive-heavy constitution, drafted shortly before the capitulation of Japan and the outbreak of the Indonesian revolution. With that decree, Guided Democracy had been officially established. Gradually the new regime began to make itself the holder of the hegemony of discourse and meaning. President Sukarno, who had become the chief executive, but preferred to be called the Great Leader of the Revolution, instructed the citizens of the nation state, most notably students and civil servants, to follow the indoctrination programmes. With the formation of Guided Democracy, Indonesia had officially entered the long period of the greedy state in its contemporary history. This was the state that could not satisfy itself with the monopoly of power and economic patronage, but also wanted to control the political consciousness of the people and the collective memory of the nation. It took several decades before the state would again treat its people as adult citizens, who could be expected to know their rights and their duties in the modern nation state.[2]

Meanwhile in our classroom Sartono Kartodirdjo, who was the first Indonesian to get a university degree in history, led us, the *doktoral* students, to take various historical problems, such as historical truth and national history, as topics of discussion. By that time we already had at our disposal the posthumously published books of C. van Leur (*Indonesian Trade and Society*, 1956) and B. Schrieke (*Indonesian Sociological Studies*, two volumes, 1955), along with W.F. Wertheim's sociological history of Indonesia (*Indonesian Society in Transition*, 1958). George Kahin's *Nationalism and Revolution in Indonesia* (1952) was also available in the bookstore. I really enjoyed reading this book for it described the revolutionary events that were very close to my heart. Although the book barely mentioned the region where I was born and spent my childhood, by reading the book my reminiscences on the glorious events became more alive and understandable. I liked to look at myself as "a son of the revolution" — too young to be part of the great event, but old enough to remember.

Van Leur's criticisms of colonial history and on what he regarded as the fragmentation of Indonesian history (ancient history was the territory of archaeologists, the Islamic period was the subject of study of philologists, while the coming of the Western powers was the specialty of archivists) might have opened the eyes of the historians on the need to review the existing historical body of knowledge, but how should they change the perspective? M. Yamin, the poet, lawyer, and politician, was perhaps most responsible for advocating the so-called *Indo-centric view* of history. He not only displayed this approach in his historical plays and poems, but also demonstratively showed how a nationalist oriented history should be written. It was, however, also during this period that G.J. Resink (whose articles were later translated and collected in his *Indonesia's History between the Myths*, 1962) the poet and the expert on international law, emphasized the need for detailed study, and showed the danger of the *regio-centric* view of history. No less important, Resink also debunked the myth of "350 years under Dutch colonialism". He did this when President Sukarno was still repeating the myth over and over in his speeches. But then, of course, to Sukarno, history was never meant to be an attempt to discover the truth of the past. History to him was a way to search for inspiration in the never ending struggle to reach the promising future. It was not the dynamics and the structure of the chain of events in the past that really mattered to him, but the "flame of history" that might enliven nationalist imagination. It was the inspiration that could be garnered from the remembered past that really mattered to him.

National history as a theoretical and methodological problem was certainly not Sukarno's intellectual interest. However, by that time it was exactly these kinds of problems that had become the major academic and intellectual concerns of historians. Sartono sought to find the solution by avoiding philosophy and taking sociology instead. History could only be properly explained if both the chain of events, as a process, and the many facets of the structural settings were taken into consideration. In the meantime John Smail had written his seminal short paper in the old *Journal of Southeast Asian History* (published by the then named University of Malaya, Singapore) on autonomous history. Smail made a clear differentiation between ethical judgment and historical perspective. The easy solution suggested by school teachers and history textbook writers, of simply changing the foundation of ethical judgment, as a matter of fact, changed nothing. With this kind of strategy it was then thought that "national history" would remain the captive of "colonial history". The latter continued to be the dominant factor in determining what events should be included in the reconstruction of the past. The problem was therefore how to formulate the right historical perspectives. Smail actually took up this problem first raised by van Leur. It was the understanding of the "autonomous history" that really mattered.[3]

Before he left for Yale University (1962) Sartono persuaded me to move to Jakarta, where he said I might get a better chance to continue my study. He was right. After working for one year at the bureau of what was then called the Indonesian Council of Sciences (MIPI) and about one-and-a-half years as a research assistant at the newly established National Institute for Economic and Social Research of MIPI (in 1967 it became the Indonesian Institute of Sciences, or LIPI) I was sent to study abroad. Out of the seven candidates, I was the only non-economist selected. Even though I could enrol as a student majoring in history I had to make a promise to the institute that I would take courses in economic history and development theory.

STUDYING LOCAL HISTORIES

When I arrived at Cornell University, Ithaca, in late summer 1964, I was still not sure about my study programme. But Cornell was, at least to my mind, the most hospitable university to foreign students who were not too certain about what they really wanted to study. I could only say to my academic adviser that I liked the works of Schrieke, van Leur, and Wertheim, who treat history from a sociological perspective. Professor Oliver Wolters, whose book on the early history of the Srivijaya Empire was then about to be published, thought for a while and finally advised me to see Professor Lauriston Sharp, the anthropologist, and a well-known expert on Thailand. Before I fully realized what had happened, my study programme was already in my hands. I would be majoring in Southeast Asian history with anthropology as my minor. I was expected to get my MA, and it was hoped, if my grades permitted, I could continue to the PhD programme.

If I now reflect on my student days at Cornell, I must say that I was fortunate to have had an expert on the ancient history of Southeast Asia as my academic adviser. Professor Oliver Wolters was not only a demanding teacher and a challenging adviser, his lectures and seminars were also very stimulating and enlightening. By carefully revealing the dynamic of history in ancient times, he indirectly persuaded his students to look much deeper into the roots of the modern course of history. At the same time, the dimensions of anthropology made me aware of the importance of divergent types of social networks and cultural traditions, which might influence the course of history at the local or even national level. At that time, however, I was more attracted by the questions of myth and system of belief.

In the meantime the political and economic situation in Indonesia had steadily deteriorated. Scattered local rebellions had indeed been subdued, but Indonesia was facing internal, horizontal agrarian conflicts, as well as international isolation. On university campuses in the United States, students were beginning to get restless because of the escalation of the Vietnam War. That was the time I really felt lonely and uncertain about my future as a

student. Would I be able to continue my study? What would happen to
Indonesia? Would Indonesia be able to maintain its integrity? What was the
future of national integration? The political and social calamities of 1965–66
really disturbed me, but by the beginning of 1967, a better political climate
had returned. I could again look at the future in a more optimistic mood.

By the end of my first semester, I had already decided that I would take
nationalist movements in Aceh and West Sumatra during the colonial period
as the topic of my master's thesis. This decision, I have to admit, was made
out of intellectual anger. In spite of the fact that we might have gradually
liberated our history from colonial perspectives, we were apparently trapped
in — what Resink had warned in the 1950s — the *regio-centred* view of
history. The so-called national history still concentrated too much on the
events that took place in Java, as if other islands and other regions had no
history. So I decided to study the nationalist movement in the two regions
in Sumatra. Not only did Aceh have the reputation of being one of the last
regions to be included in the fold of the *pax Neerlandica*, but it was also the
only Republican territory that remained free from Dutch occupation during
the revolution. West Sumatra, the region of the Minangkabau people, had
produced a great number of revolutionary leaders, both in the Republican
government and in the opposition faction. It was also one of the most
important centres of the nationalist movement during the colonial period.
However, hardly any history textbooks ever touched on the histories of the
two regions. I had by then decided to study local history. I thought the so-
called Indo-centric view of history would be more relevant if an Indonesian
historian took local histories before he embarked on national history. By
studying local history, I thought, one would not easily slip into the trap of
the so-called mainstream of national history. This was an intellectual trap
that would easily lure one to concentrate on the region "where the action
is" and to ignore the divergent types of local dynamics. Furthermore by
studying local history the historian would have a deeper understanding of
the actors' life situation and a better comprehension of their interpretation
of empirical realities. These types of knowledge were very important in the
effort to appreciate the courses of actions these actors might have taken in
certain historical situations. Perhaps my courses in anthropology and on the
history of the countries in Southeast Asia had some influence on my decision
to approach history from this perspective.[4]

Since I had made this decision, in my spare time I read books on Aceh.
I naturally took Snouck Hurgronje's classic study on the region (*The Acehnese*,
1911) as the first priority. Jim Siegel, who had just joined the Cornell
faculty, had also written a book on Aceh with a poetic title, which was, by

the way, taken from the Qur'an, "*The Rope of God*" (1965). I also began to collect materials from newspaper summaries prepared by the colonial intelligence service. I still had not touched Minangkabau when I finally decided to give up Aceh. After reading a thesis on the comparative study of the careers of Mongkut, the king of Thailand, and Mindon, the king of Burma, written by a Thai historian, I realized I might not be in a position to make a proper comparative study of the two regions. It would not be fair. Although I had not done any research on Minangkabau, I spoke the language and had lived through its tradition. But what did I know about Aceh? I had never been to Aceh and I did not know the meaning of even a simple Acehnese sentence. Of course my knowledge on Aceh was not wasted. My later writings on Islam in Indonesia and Southeast Asia clearly reflect my youthful acquaintance with Aceh.[5]

It was in the anthropology seminar that I tried to understand what Minangkabau was. For an academic exercise I picked the most crucial aspect in Minangkabau cultural and political tradition — the relation between Islam and *adat* (customs), as the ideal pattern of behaviour, as well as the customary law. I still remember the amazement of G.H. Bousquet (*Introduction à l'étude de l'Islam Indonésien*, 1938), a French scholar who wrote a book on Islam in the Netherlands Indies, when he came across this cultural and political tradition of the Minangkabau. How come the thoroughly Islamized ethnic community was also the one with a very strong attachment to its non-Islamic inheritance law and kinship system?

In my exercise paper I suggested that the relation between Islam and *adat* in Minangkabau should be seen from the multiplicity of conflicts in the Minangkabau conception of their own world. It had two rather distinct *adat* political traditions that not only recognized the legitimacy of each other, but also needed the presence of each other. In the course of time Islam, which was first seen as the perfection of *adat*, gradually — although precipitated by the outbreak of the Padri war in the early nineteenth century — came to be treated as the legitimate foundation of *adat*. "Religion designs, *adat* applies". Before I was really aware of what I had been saying, I had apparently been discussing the functions of conceptualized conflict situations in the course of social dynamics. The paper was later published in *Indonesia,* the biannual journal of the Modern Indonesian Project, Cornell University (1966).[6]

This academic exercise had, to some extent, helped me chart the kind of MA thesis I was about to write. I took up the subject of social change in Minangkabau in the early twentieth century as the topic of my thesis. There was only one book on the same period, but it specifically concentrated on the nationalist movement in the region. The book (*Enige Beschouwingen Over de Ontwikkeling van het Indonesisch Nationalisme op Sumatra's Westkust*, 1949) was a thesis by H. Bouman, a Dutch scholar, on the Indonesian nationalist movement in West Sumatra. However, not only were his sources rather limited, but somehow I also had the impression that he was more interested in proving his thesis on modern Minangkabau as a society that had been trapped in the triangular conflict of *adat*, Islam, and Western ideas. He might be right, but I was more interested in telling the stories of what happened in the past. My problem in preparing the thesis was the rather limited number of sources available. In spite of the fact that the Wason Collection of the university library was quite rich, the sources on my subject were rather scant. I could get access to the summaries of the press prepared by the Dutch intelligence service, some memoirs, and of course, the excellent collection of old colonial journals, but this was not adequate enough to tell a detailed story. How could I fill the gaps in the sources? My understanding of the society might help, I thought. I remembered the differences between "*verstehen*" (understand) and "*erklären*" (explain), but perhaps these should not be treated as two opposing approaches. After all historians should have to face two types of realities — one that is something he managed to reconstruct from existing sources, and the other, the kind of reality perceived by the actors of history. When dealing with the former, historians have to rely on their ability to read the divergent and sometimes conflicting sources critically, and to use whatever methodology he prefers, whereas when dealing with the latter type of reality, the historian has no other way except to see it through the eyes of the actors of history. Therefore a deeper understanding of the life situation and world view of the actors is very important. The writings and statements of the actors may help, but they do not always give reasons for their actions. And how can we be sure that all actions are the result of rational reactions to the situation? Irrationality in the process of selecting the kind of action to be taken can also be part of the game. Historians, therefore, have to find the foundations of whatever actions have been taken by the actors of history. On this particular point I found my academic exercise and understanding of Minangkabau society and tradition very useful.

I felt myself very fortunate because after successfully defending my MA thesis,[7] I passed my preliminary exam, which meant I could enrol as a PhD candidate. Soon I embarked on another subject matter. I thought it would be better if I could also get a better understanding of the Minangkabau conception of power and their image of the past. I wanted to find out if these two aspects played a role in the selection of actions when dealing with their understanding of the predicament at present. Again an anthropology seminar gave me the opportunity to work on these problems. I took as the subject of my seminar paper the *Kaba Tjindua Mato* (A Story of Tjindua Mato), a piece of traditional literature which I later labelled as the Minangkabau state myth. The *kaba* (story) had been widely seen as the most important piece of literature in the Minangkabau tradition. In the process of writing the paper on this piece of traditional literature, which was and still is seen as the description of the working system between the Minangkabau kingdom and its centre, Pagaruyung, I had to learn about the methods of text criticism and to see the possibility of using Levy-Strauss' concept of myth. The story describes the situation where the well-ordered world is threatened by unwanted elements. The whole range of the system of power had to be put into action because that was also the time when the inherited notions of justice and wisdom had to face the most serious test. The *kaba* treats the mother of the king (Rajo *Alam)*, Bundo Kanduang, as the symbol of wisdom and the source of legitimacy. By looking at the kinds of events described in the story, I thought the *kaba* must have been written in the late seventeenth or early eighteenth century — that was the time when the integrity of the Minangkabau kingdom had been threatened by outside powers.

I was already in the field conducting research for my PhD thesis, when I received a letter from Ruth McVey, urging me to revise the paper for publication. The revised paper was published a few months after I returned from the field (1970).[8]

As a grantee of the London-Cornell Project, I had to write a progress report every three months from the field. But what should I be writing about? I had only been three months in the field. Since I had written a thesis on Minangkabau in the early twentieth century, perhaps I could develop some ideas I happened to touch on briefly in the thesis. Since I had done some further research on the subject, I just focused my report on the behaviour of a certain *adat* leader, who promoted the idea of "progress" on the basis of his understanding of the Minangkabau view of history. How and in what way could the traditional view of history find affinity with the demand of the *dunia maju,* or "progressive world"? The first thing I did was look into the nature of the Minangkabau *tambo* (traditional historiography), which describes the genesis and the formation of the Minangkabau world. It depicts how the world slowly and gradually unfolded itself. After that I looked at the *adat* attitude towards unavoidable change and the need for maintaining continuity. How did these elements influence the course of action in a society that had been facing the incessant intrusion of outside elements? Of course I did not forget to list whatever effects the Dutch rule had brought to the society. The problems became more complicated when the Islamic reformers joined the search for the religiously proper *kemajuan* (progress), and the growing number of the so-called young Western educated intellectuals also became eager to participate in the discourse.

By chance, during my fieldwork Jim Siegel came to Jakarta and asked me about my report. Perhaps because he liked the field report, he told Ben Anderson and Claire Holt about it. They apparently asked Clifford Geertz's opinion about my report. On my return to Ithaca, after spending a year in Indonesia and five months in Holland, Claire Holt asked me to write an article on the basis of the rough draft of my field report. After working on it for almost two months I finally gave the article the rather fancy title of "Modernization in the Minangkabau World". That was my contribution to Claire Holt et al., eds., *Culture and Politics in Indonesia*.[9]

Although the article deals with the Minangkabau as a whole, it was in Padang, the capital of the residency, that most of the action took place. Despite the fact that its history can be traced back to the earlier centuries, even to the period before the Acehnese sultanate managed to establish its authority temporarily (early seventeenth century) in Padang, the important role of this coastal town to the highlands in the interior really began after the Dutch East India Company (VOC) had secured the existence of its fortified factory. The VOC managed to establish its factory on the seaport by allying itself with the local forces to kick out the Acehnese. However, the friendship did not last long. Soon after the VOC secured its position it became the target of almost incessant attacks from the surrounding villages. At one time, as the Dutch report stated, the attack was led by someone from Pagaruyung, the seat of the king of Minangkabau. Whatever the case, both Aceh and the VOC planted their deep impact on the social arrangement of Padang. Unlike in the highlands, the land of their origin, the people of the coastal town developed a certain kind of aristocratic class. It was this stratified society that had also undergone a process of maturity, which saw Padang gradually change into a colonial town. However, what type of colonial town was Padang? What kind of relationship did it ever have with the place of origin of most its population, the highlands in the interior? I had the occasion to look at Padang more closely nineteen years after the publication of the above article when the Center for Southeast Asian Studies of the University of Kyoto invited me to participate in its project on urban civilization in Southeast Asia (1991).[10]

I finally finished my PhD thesis in August 1970. The thesis was later published "as it is" by the Cornell Modern Indonesia Project in 1972. My PhD thesis deals with the nationalist movement in West Sumatra in the years 1927–33. Or, to set it against historical events, the thesis deals with the social and political situation from the outbreak of the so-called communist rebellion in the small village, Silungkang (January 1927), to the arrest of several Minangkabau radical nationalist leaders. The arrests, like the case in Java, sharply curtailed the activities of the *kaum pergerakan*, the nationalists. It just happened that most of the local nationalist leaders were the graduates of the Islamic "modernist" schools, or as the term I used at the time, the *kaum muda* schools. In the thesis I tried to answer the question of why the graduates of the religious schools should emerge as the local leaders of the nationalist movement. Opposition to the colonialism and imperialism of the *kafir* power might be one answer. But then what was the content of the religious teaching that drove people to behave the way they did? In some ways the thesis is a continuation of my MA thesis, but, of course, this time I was almost overwhelmed by the rich sources I managed to assemble from archives and contemporary publications and, of course, from personal interviews with a number of the former activists. In both works I tried to address the questions on the ways the local leaders perceived themselves, and the factors that led them to see and treat their local and ethnic community as being part of the struggling nation called Indonesia. It was after completing the study that I became more convinced that by taking up separate local situations as the initial focus, the attempt to construct national history could become more meaningful.[11]

FROM A RELIGIOUS ANGLE

However, since I had — perhaps by accident — touched on the question of how actions are influenced by the understanding of religion, I had the urge to follow it through. Was the case in West Sumatra just a sheer historical accident, or could it be explained from the perspective of the role of a system of belief in determining the choice of action? After I returned to Indonesia I began to familiarize myself with the literature on the sociology and anthropology of religion and wrote articles from these angles. Since I was also entrusted by the Minister of Religious Affairs to lead a research team on "religion and social change", the efforts to deepen my knowledge of the problems had become a professional necessity. In addition to supervising the research project, I also edited a book on Islam in Indonesia and later on Weber's theory of religion. I worked on the later book because I thought that one of the ways to promote social science was to introduce the classics to the would-be social scientists. I was at that time the director of the National Institute for Economic and Social Research of the Indonesian Institute of Sciences (Leknas-LIPI), the institute that sent me abroad, and the chairman of the Indonesian Association for the Promotion of Social Sciences (HIPIIS), as well as a member of the board of Social Science Foundation.

I had to admit that I was quite proud of my efforts to edit a collection of writings on Islam in Indonesia. In the book I included the translated writings of Jim Siegel, A. Johns, Clifford Geertz, Harry Benda, and W.F. Wertheim (in the second edition, I also included the translation of my article on *adat* and Islam). In the rather long introduction I specifically touched on the problems of the social dimensions of religion: how people interpreted the holy texts and translated them into the structure of their society and into a pattern of proper social conduct and actions.[12] A number of people, particularly those who had been teaching Islam as a religion, told me that they were quite surprised with the book. They told me it was the first time they had read about Islam from the perspective of its adherents, not from that of the doctrine of the religion.

I was glad to learn that the book I edited on Weber's theory of religion, which particularly concentrated on his "Protestant ethics" thesis, was used as required reading by some postgraduate study programmes.[13] In addition to the long introduction that I wrote, I included two pieces of Weber's work and several empirical studies that, to some extent, tested his thesis. After the publication of the book some political leaders began to talk about the need to enhance the "work ethos" of the people. Since the book was published during the "era of national development", as the New Order preferred to call the period, it was understandable that the probable relationship between religion and work ethos could catch public imagination.

During this period I contributed a chapter to a book on the sociology of religion, published by Sage Publications, London.[14] The editor of the book, who also happened to be the president of the Research Commission of the Sociology of Religion, officially launched the book in a session of the World Sociology Congress in Uppsala, Sweden, in 1978. I was invited to talk about the article I had contributed to the book. Perhaps because he knew that I had been sacked from my position as director of the Leknas-LIPI for criticizing the New Order Government's crackdowns on students' activities, he nominated me as the vice-president of the group. And I was elected vice-president of the study group of the Sociology of Religion. In the same year I also co-edited (with a Dutch anthropologist) a collection of the writings of Durkheim, specifically those that dealt with the question of social morality. Again I wrote a long introduction, but I had to pay a price.[15] A historian colleague, who was a close personal friend as well, accused me of being a "traitor".[16] He thought I had abandoned historical studies. I simply told him, "No, I just don't want to be a stupid historian." Whatever the case, I did not dare introduce the social theory of Karl Marx. Firstly, because I thought I was not academically qualified to do so, and secondly — well

I have to admit this — I was not stupid enough to introduce Marx in the strongly anti-communist New Order regime. And not least important, which publisher would be daring enough to publish it?

After I came to a conclusion that religion could be used as an ethical foundation in interpreting empirical realities, and, therefore, might also function as a basis for choosing a course of action, I realized that I had to be able to grasp the way people make sense of their religious doctrine. How would they translate their understanding of religious texts into a system of action? With this question in mind, I began to read theories of the sociology of literature and text criticisms. I never abandoned my vocation as a historian, but I hoped these branches of knowledge might provide me with the tools to understand the dynamics of history on a major scale, as well as the nature of events in little incidents. I had the opportunity to use this new awareness in my attempt to evaluate the significance of three important pre-war Indonesian novels as potential historical sources. Two of the novels (*Sitti Nurbaya* and *Salah Asuhan*) dealt with the cultural dilemma that had to be faced by the growing number of Minangkabau Western-educated groups, and another one (*Belenggu*), on the intellectual predicament of the indigenous educated class in colonial Batavia. Since it was my first attempt to approach literary work from a historical perspective, I simply started my paper by quoting the last sentences of each novel and treating them as if they were sources of history. By doing this I managed, at least to my understanding of history, to delineate the gradual change of urban mentality of colonial Indonesia from the maintenance of traditional notions of propriety, through the crisis of personal identity, to the sense of absurdity in the implanted modernity. Well, this may not be the real empirical situation, but that was the impression I could get from the novels that were published from the late 1920s to the early 1940s. I presented this paper at the Indonesia-Dutch History Conference held in Yogyakarta, 1982. Only after the participants gave their comments did I know that I had actually approached the problems by using the deconstruction method.[17]

DISCOVERING ANOTHER FACE OF THE MINANGKABAU

Until the end of the 1970s (except my articles on *adat* and Islam, and on the traditional literature), all my published writings on Minangkabau deal with the twentieth century events. This was except for one unpublished paper on the Padri movement and war (1803–37), which later illustrated to me the complexity of understanding the intellectual climate of the Minangkabau in the early twentieth century. The dramatic events of 1803–37, which began as a radical religious reform movement, ended up as a war of opposition to the intrusion of colonial power. The Padri war not only sealed the fate of the Minangkabau monarchy, with its centre in Pagaruyung, but also marked the beginning of the imposition of forced coffee cultivation. In other words, after the Padri war, Minangkabau was included within the expanding colonial *pax Neerlandica*. That was an empirical fact, but how did this proud ethnic group deal with the fact that they were actually no longer the master of their destiny? How could they maintain a relative peaceful situation? But then, as if out of nowhere, scattered rural rebellions broke out in many parts of the Minangkabau region. What happened? After learning about the continuing decline of coffee production in 1908, the colonial government finally decided to introduce a personal tax system. The relatively calm situation suddenly erupted into scattered rebellions in several places, and mass demonstrations in others. These scattered rural rebellions are still part of the local collective memory. The violent events were — and still are — remembered as "the Kamang war", because it broke out in Kamang in the district of Agam, or "the Mangopoh war", in the district of Padang-Pariaman, and others. After the tragic events that had caused so many people to lose their lives, either by fighting or simply facing their final days at the hands of the colonial hangmen after the "wars" had generally subsided, the region experienced a relatively rapid economic growth and became an important centre for the Islamic reform movement and nationalist propaganda. In other words the intellectual climate that I had described in my contribution to Claire Holt's volume was only one face of Minangkabau in the early century. The significance of the intellectual climate cannot be fully understood without taking these tragic events into consideration.

How should I explain this phenomenon? I had no choice but to look a little deeper into the situation after the Padri war. The opportunity to do this came when I participated in the first Dutch-Indonesia History Conference held in 1976. My question was "what happened after the Padri war"? Forced coffee cultivation, the spread of *tariqah* (mystic) schools, as well as the theological controversies among them, and the resumption of trade relations between the coastal towns, which had since the seventeenth century been under the domination of the Dutch and the highlands in the interior, the introduction of supra-*nagari* (village) administrative units, and, of course, the writing as well as the rewriting of *tambo* (cosmology, myth, social mores and values, and "history" rolled into one coherent historical discourse) and *kaba* ("stories" told in the traditional literary style) were some of the events that took place after more than three decades of social, cultural, and political calamities. The people apparently took everything in their stride as if nothing fundamental had taken place. Why? One of the explanations

I found out was because of the people's attitude to *plakat panjang* (long declaration), issued by the governor general of the Netherlands Indies in 1833, during the short lull in the Padri War. In the document the governor general stated that the *kompeni* (the Dutch) did not come to Minangkabau to govern, but only to trade. The Minangkabau would remain under the rule of their respective *penghulu*, or *adat*-chiefs. However, since the *kompeni* would also want to establish schools, safeguard the villages against the possibility of inter-*nagari* warfare, and to maintain roads, it required the people to cultivate and sell coffee to its *pakhuis* or warehouse. Later, after the fall of the fort of Bonjol, the most important bastion of the Padri, which practically meant the defeat of the Minangkabau, the people still thought they remained "independent", even though they were still required to cultivate coffee. By taking the declaration at its face value, the Minangkabau gradually created a make-believe political sphere in which they could continue with their life uninterrupted. This was the political and social sphere I called a *schakel* society, the intermediary society, which existed in the boundary between the real and imagined reality. Without this make-believe sphere, the psychological burden of being a subjugated people would be too heavy to bear. And a host of symbols and myths were created to emphasize the authenticity of this make-believe world. Naturally the Minangkabau were not alone in their efforts to create a cultural sphere of this kind of *schakel* society. Practically all regions that had been subjugated by force created and entertained this make-believe social and cultural sphere. The problems, however, emerged when the colonial government introduced a policy that blatantly stated it was the real ruler, not, as people wanted to believe, the allies who came from the country above the wind.[18]

One may say that the genesis of the *schakel* society was planted when the "mythologization" of a historical event was undertaken. That was the process when a simple event or statement, or perhaps even only a gesture of non-hostility, had been glorified in the local collective memory. The myth had gradually moulded the way people looked at their empirical reality, and then perhaps influenced the course of events, or history, if you like. It could also have induced the process of "historization of the myth", when myth and history merge into undifferentiated systems of knowledge. That was the cultural sphere where "fact" and "meaningful imagination" rolled into one seemingly coherent primal myth. A social or even political crisis would take place if the sanctity of this myth was debunked by the curse of event or by the brute use of power. This was what happened in the "anti-tax rebellions" of 1908, as I described in a paper I presented at the Human Sciences Congress in 1977.[19]

CONCLUSION

Now, if I look back at my writings on Minangkabau history, I realize that I was then very much the son of my time. That was the time when the call for the liberation of history from colonial domination was very strong, and that was also the period when the desire to look at history "from within" was beginning to be voiced. Of course, I must admit I was also very much concerned with the regional imbalance in the body of knowledge in the history of Indonesia. From the beginning I was very much intrigued by the idea of closing the gaps.

I started my attempt to understand Minangkabau from the way the people translated their adopted religion into their inherited social system and cultural values. This attempt was also my way of trying to get an account of the Minangkabau culture. "Why should they embrace the new religion?" "Why should such basic cultural transformation have to take place?" Only after getting some ideas on these questions did I begin to look at the series of events that took place in the period I had been studying. In the process, I had not only tried to reconstruct the course of events and tried to find the linkages of the events, but I had also tried to find answers to the questions of why the actors behaved the way they did in the past.[20]

If the colonial archives can be taken as a clue, then I can definitely say that the region of West Sumatra was as politicized as Batavia/Jakarta and Bandung (both still at that time parts of West Java province). While on most regions the colonial intelligence service gave its regular reports on political activities of the people only every three months, it was not the case with the *Residentie* of West Sumatra. The intelligence service always sent its report to The Hague every month. How should I explain these rather hectic political activities of Minangkabau? No less important was the question of how I should make sense of the popularity that the "all-Indonesia" political parties had among the Minangkabau people, despite their divergent ideologies. What was the basis of Indonesian nationalism? The moment this kind of question came to my mind I realized how important it was to study local history.

I still believe in the importance of the proper study of local history. It is vital for the sake of knowledge and, indeed more importantly, for a better understanding of the challenges that face this multi-ethnic and multi-historic nation, Indonesia.

Notes

1. See Taufik Abdullah, "Inherited Identity and the New Nation: The Politics of Cultural Discourse in Indonesia", *Identity, Locality and Globalization: Experiences*

of India and Indonesia (New Delhi: Indian Council of Social Science Research, 2001).

2. Taufik Abdullah, *Indonesia: Towards Democracy* (Singapore: Institute of Southeast Asian Studies, 2009), pp. 290–306, 381–97.

3. Taufik Abdullah, "The Study of History". In *Sciences in Indonesia*, vol. 1, edited by Koentjaraningrat (Jakarta: Indonesia Institute of Sciences, 1972), pp. 79–120. See also Taufik Abdullah, "On the Questions of History Seen from Within: The Case of Southeast Asia" in *Arung Samudra: Persembahan Memperingati Sembilan Windu A.B. Lapian*, edited by Edi Sedyawati and Susanto Zuhdi (Depok: Pusat Penelitian Kemasyarakatan dan Budaya. Lembaga Penelitian, Universitas Indonesia, 2001), pp. 645–60.

4. For example, Taufik Abdullah, *Islam dan Masyarakat: Pantulan Sejarah Indonesia* (Jakarta: LP3ES, 1987). See also Taufik Abdullah, "Islam and the Formation of Political Tradition in Indonesia", *Itinerario*, no. 13 (Special Issue, 1989).

5. Taufik Abadullah, "The Making of Malay Political Tradition" in *The Making of Islamic Discourse in Southeast Asia*, edited by A.J. Reid (Clayton, Victoria: Monash University, 1993).

6. Taufik Abdullah, "Adat and Islam: An Examination of Conflict in Minangkabau", *Indonesia* 2 (1966): 1–24.

7. Taufik Abdullah, "Minangkabau 1900–1927: Preliminary Studies in Social Development", unpublished MA thesis, Cornell University (Ithaca, NY, 1967).

8. Taufik Abdullah, "Some Notes on the *Kaba Tjindua Mato*: An Example of Minangkabau Traditional Literature", *Indonesia* 9 (April 1970): 1–22. See also Taufik Abdullah, "*Tambo, Kaba*, and History: Tradition and the Historical Consciousness of the Minangkabau" in *Walk in Splendor: Ceremonial Dress and the Minangkabau*, edited by Anne Summerfield and John Summerfield (Los Angeles: The Fowler Museum and Cultural History, UCLA, 1999).

9. Taufik Abdullah, "Modernization in the Minangkabau World: West Sumatra in the Early Decades of the Twentieth Century" in *Culture and Politics in Indonesia*, edited by Claire Holt (with the assistance of R.O'G. Anderson and James T. Siegel) (Ithaca, NY and London: Cornell University Press, 1972), pp. 179–245.

10. Taufik Abdullah, "Padang in the Minangkabau World: The Return of the Lost Child", in *The Formation of Urban Civilization in Southeast Asia II*, edited by Yoshihiro Tsubaochi (Kyoto: Center for Southeast Asian Studies, Kyoto University, 1991), pp. 1–51.

11. Taufik Abdullah, Schools *and Politics: The Kaum Muda Movement in West Sumatra, 1927–1933* (Ithaca, NY: Cornell Modern Indonesia Project, 1972).

12. Taufik Abadullah, ed., *Islam di Indonesia* (Jakarta: Tinta Mas, 1974).

13. Taufik Abdullah, ed., *Agama, Etos Kerja dan Perkembangan Ekonomi* (Jakarta: LP3ES, 1979).

14. Taufik Abdullah, "Identity Maintenance and Identity Crisis in Minangkabau"

in *Identity and Religion: International Cross Cultural Approaches*, edited by Hans Mol (London: Sage Studies in International Sociology, 1978), pp. 151–68.

15. Taufik Abdullah and A.C. van der Leeden, eds., *Durkheim dan Pengantar Sosiologi Moralitas* (Jakarta: Yayasan Obor, 1987).

16. Of course I could not be accused of being a "traitor" because around the same time I edited and wrote several introductory notes, as well as a lengthy epilogue, to a book on local history. It was a collection of several colonial archives, reports, articles on various historical events in divergent localities in the Indonesian archipelago. All articles and reports were originally written in Dutch. I used my introduction to explain the nature and scope of local history. It is a history that is an inseparable part of the history of a larger geographical entity; call it national history or whatever you like. In a way, the book can also be seen as a vista of local histories because I (with the help of some senior colleagues) not only selected the cases from many regions, but also selected divergent types of writings on local history. For the epilogue I touched on the problems of writing social history in a local perspective. The book has since been published five times. Taufik Abdullah, ed., *Sejarah Lokal di Indonesia* (Yogyakarta: Gadjah Mada University Press, 1978).

17. Taufik Abdullah, ed., *Literature and History* (Papers of the Fourth Indonesian-Dutch Historical Conference, Yogyakarta, 24–29 July 1983) (Yogyakarta: Gadjah Mada University Press, 1986).

18. Taufik Abdullah, "The Making of a *Schakel* Society: The Minangkabau Region in the Late Nineteenth Century" in *Papers of the Dutch-Indonesian Historical Conference* (Leiden and Jakarta (Reprinted in *Majalah Ilmu-Ilmu Sosial* 11, no. 3, 1976).

19. Taufik Abdullah, "The Anti-tax Rebellions In West Sumatra of 1908: The *Schakel* Society in Crisis" in *Southeast Asia I, The 30ᵗʰ International Congress of Human Sciences in Asia and North Africa, 1976*, edited by Gracia de Lama (Mexico: El Colegio de Mexico, 1982), pp. 135–53.

20. Taufik Abdullah, "Islam, History, and Social Change in Minangkabau", in *Change and Continuity in Minangkabau*, edited by Lynn L. Thomas and Franz von Benda-Beckmann (Athens: Ohio University, Center for International Studies, 1985), pp. 141–56.

References

Abdullah, Taufik. "Adat and Islam: An Examination of Conflict in Minangkabau". *Indonesia* 2 (1966): 1–24.

———. "Minangkabau 1900–1927: Preliminary Studies in Social Development". Unpublished MA Thesis. Ithaca, NY: Cornell University, 1967.

———. "Some Notes on the *Kaba Tjindua Mato*: An Example of Minangkabau Traditional Literature". *Indonesia* 9 (April 1970): 1–22.

———. "Modernization in the Minangkabau World: West Sumatra in the Early

Decades of the Twentieth Century". In *Culture and Politics in Indonesia*, edited by Claire Holt (with the assistance of R.O'G. Anderson and James T. Siegel). Ithaca, NY and London: Cornell University Press, 1972.

———. *Schools and Politics: The Kaum Muda Movement in West Sumatra, 1927–1933*. Ithaca, NY: Cornell Modern Indonesia Project, 1972.

——— ed. "The Study of History in Koentjaraningrat". *The Social Sciences in Indonesia*, vol. 1. Jakarta: Indonesia Institute of Sciences (1972): 79–120.

——— ed. *Islam di Indonesia*. Jakarta: Tinta Mas, 1974 (second edition, 1990).

———. "The Making of a *Schakel* Society: The Minangkabau Region in the Late Nineteenth Century". In *Papers of the Dutch-Indonesian Historical Conference*. Leiden and Jakarta. Reprinted in *Majalah Ilmu-Ilmu Sosial* 11, no. 3, 1976.

———. "Identity Maintenance and Identity Crisis in Minangkabau". In *Identity and Religion: International Cross Cultural Approaches*, edited by Hans Mol. London: Sage Studies in International Sociology, 1978.

——— ed. *Sejarah Lokal di Indonesia*. Yogyakarta: Gadjah Mada University Press, 1978 (fifth printing, 2005, with minor revisions).

——— ed. *Agama, Etos Kerja dan Perkembangan Ekonomi*. Jakarta: LP3ES, 1979 (second printing 1982).

———. "The Anti- tax Rebellions in West Sumatra of 1908: The *Schakel* Society in Crisis". In *Southeast Asia I, The 30ᵗʰ International Congress of Human Sciences in Asia and North Africa, 1976*, edited by Gracia de Lama. Mexico: El Colegio de Mexico, 1982.

———. "Islam, History, and Social Change in Minangkabau". In *Change and Continuity in Minangkabau*, edited by Lynn L. Thomas and Franz von Benda-Beckmann. Athens, OH: Ohio University, Center for International Studies, 1985.

———. "Historical Reflection on Three Novels of Pre-war Indonesia". In *Literature and History (Papers of the Fourth Indonesian-Dutch Historical Conference, Yogyakarta, 24–29 July 1983)*, edited by Taufik Abdullah. Yogyakarta: Gadjah Mada University Press, 1986.

———. *Islam dan Masyarakat: Pantulan Sejarah Indonesia*. Jakarta: LP3ES, 1987.

———. "Islam and the Formation of Political Tradition in Indonesia". *Itinerario*, no. 13, Special Issue, 1989.

———. "Padang in the Minangkabau World: the Return of the Lost Child". In *The Formation of Urban Civilization in Southeast Asia II*, edited by Yoshihiro Tsubaochi. Kyoto: The Center for Southeast Asian Studies, Kyoto University, 1991.

———. "The Making of Malay Political Tradition". In *The Making of Islamic Discourse in Southeast Asia*, edited by A.J. Reid. Clayton, Victoria: Monash University, 1993.

———. "*Tambo, Kaba*, and History: Tradition and the Historical Consciousness of the Minangkabau". In *Walk in Splendor: Ceremonial Dress and the Minangkabau*, edited by Anne Summerfield and John Summerfield. Los Angeles: The Fowler Museum and Cultural History, UCLA, 1999.

————. "On the Questions of History Seen from Within: The Case of Southeast Asia". In *Arung Samudra: Persembahan Memperingati Sembilan Windu A.B. Lapian*, edited by Edi Sedyawati and Susanto Zuhdi. Depok: Pusat Penelitian Kemasyarakatan dan Budaya. Lembaga Penelitian, Universitas Indonesia, 2001.

————. "Inherited Identity and the New Nation: The Politics of Cultural Discourse in Indonesia". In *Identity, Locality and Globalization: Experiences of India and Indonesia*. New Delhi: Indian Council of Social Science Research, 2001.

————. *Indonesia. Towards Democracy*. Singapore: Institute of Southeast Asian Studies, 2009.

Abdullah, Taufik and A.C. van der Leeden, eds. *Durkheim dan Pengantar Sosiologi Moralitas*. Jakarta: Yayasan Obor, 1987.

Collingwood, R.G. *The Idea of History*. London: Chatto & Windus, 1949 (first published in 1932).

Geyl, Pieter. *Debates with Historians*. Cleveland, OH: Meridian, 1958.

Hamilton, Edith. *Mythology*. New York: New American Library, 1953 (first published in 1942).

————. *The Greek Way to Western Civilization*. New York: Mentor Books, 1953.

————. *The Roman Way to Western Civilization*. New York: Mentor Books, 1963.

Hurgronje, Snouck. *The Acehnese*. Leiden: Brill, 1906.

Huyzinga, J. *The Waning of the Middle Ages: A Study of the Forms of Life, Thought and Art in France and the Netherlands in Fourteenth and Fifteenth Centuries*. Middlesex: Penguin, 1955.

Kahin, George F. McT. *Nationalism and Revolution in Indonesia*. Ithaca, NY: Cornell University Press, 1952.

Schrieke, B. *Indonesian Sociological Studies*. The Hague: W. van Hoeve, 1955.

Siegel, Jim. *The Rope of God*. Berkeley and Los Angeles: University of California Press, 1969.

Sorokin, Pitirim. *Social Philosophies of An Age of Crisis*. Boston: Beacon, 1950.

van Leur, C. *Indonesian Trade and Society*. The Hague: W. van Hoeve, 1956.

Wertheim, W.F. *Indonesian Society in Transition: A Study of Social Change*, 2nd ed. The Hague: W. van Hoeve, 1959.

Walsch, W.H. *An Introduction to the Philosophy of History*. London: Hutchinson's University Library 1956 (fourth printing).

4

SCHOLARSHIP, SOCIETY, AND POLITICS IN THREE WORLDS
Reflections of a Filipino Sojourner, 1965–95

Reynaldo C. Ileto

Interacting in this forum with colleagues from around the region, I am struck by how our scholarship, though addressing similar concerns and sharing common discourses, is shaped by our location in nation states with very different pasts. Filipino scholars have a domestic intellectual tradition shaped by the experience of successive colonial regimes, coming to terms with them while struggling for reforms, and, ultimately, independence. At the turn of the eighteenth century, for example, Filipino seminarians and priests were already grappling with issues of race and nationality in their struggle for equal treatment with the Spanish friars within the Catholic Church. By the 1880s, intellectuals shaped by the Enlightenment (and thus called *ilustrados*), such as Jose Rizal and Isabelo de Los Reyes, both based in Spain, were engaging with mainstream debates at that time in history and ethnography, including how the "indigenous" might be retrieved in the creation of a national identity. These late-nineteenth century scholars were also propagandists who campaigned for the establishment of racial equality and liberal governance in the colony and, later, took up varying positions in relation to the revolution against Spain and the intervention of the United States. This pattern — a parallel trajectory of scholarship and politics — would be repeated in the following century.

The process of simultaneously being formed by and contesting the political, social, and cultural hegemony of Spain and the United States, and to a lesser extent Japan, has made most Filipino intellectuals keenly aware of the dilemmas in positing pure forms of the "Western" or the "indigenous", or the local versus the global. Filipinos, moreover, are not physically "fixed" themselves; their "nation" also travels to the nooks and crannies of the wider world they inhabit. The shifting locations — such as Spain, America, Japan, and Australia — from which they have voiced their political concerns, further complicates the identification of a domestic intellectual tradition. To some extent this pattern applies to my own career. Inspired by this forum's call to meditate on our personal intellectual trajectories as Southeast Asian scholars, I sketch in the pages that follow a narrative of my sojourns in the academic worlds of the Philippines, the United States, and Australia from roughly 1965 to 1995. This narrative is bound to be partial and fragmented; no doubt other events will come to light on further reflection on my past. My aim here is to sketch the outlines of those initial thirty years of my career and to reflect on the patterns that emerge with the hope that this essay can contribute to the ongoing debates about local knowledge production and "the West".

GROWING UP IN THE PHILIPPINES

I was born in Manila in October 1946 just three months after the Philippines gained its nominal independence from the United States. The previous year, Japan had surrendered to the Allied forces, ending its three-and-a-half years of occupation of the islands. My Ileto grandfather, who passed away in 1945 at the age of ninety-five, was a product of Spanish colonial rule, having been educated as a seminarian in the Colegio de San Jose and then working as a bookkeeper for a landlord in central Luzon. He was implicated as a "revolutionary spy" in the resistance against U.S. occupation in 1899, but nevertheless joined (or "collaborated with") the new colonial system as a mathematics teacher in 1904.

My father, Rafael, grew up under the American and Commonwealth regimes, oblivious of the fact that his father had participated in the Filipino-American war. He was sent to the United States Military Academy at West Point for officer training in 1939, and there he developed a strong debt of gratitude (*utang na loób*) to America for this perceived gift. In 1944, now a lieutenant in the U.S. Army, he returned to his homeland to "liberate" it from the Japanese occupiers. Shortly after I was born he turned down an offer of American citizenship and decided instead to commit himself to building the army of the newly independent Philippines, rising to become one of its top commanders. His military and diplomatic career, however, was fraught with questions of where his ultimate loyalty lay: to the Philippines or the United States? Although he was brought up in solidly Tagalog towns in Bulacan and Nueva Ecija, and spoke English only when he commenced his higher education, my father's American sojourn transformed him into somewhat of a Filipino-American binational. My own identity, personal and intellectual, could not but be formed also in relation to his dominating personality.

For better or worse, my mother, named after Russian ballerina Olga Preobrajenska, had a decidedly stronger influence on the shaping of my identity. Her father was a Tagalog from Polo, Bulacan, who entered Manila politics armed with a law degree from the University of the Philippines (UP). Her mother traced her origins to immigrants from Amoy, or Xiamen, in the late eighteenth century. Technically, then, Olga was a "Chinese mestiza", whose mother's generation had come to embrace Spanish rather than Hokkien and identified with the Filipino nationalist cause. Her uncle Isidoro de Santos, of the same part-Chinese ancestry, is mentioned in our history books as the chairman of the Filipino revolutionary committee in Singapore that hosted Emilio Aguinaldo's visit in 1898. Another uncle pursued his medical training at the Tokyo Imperial University.

My mother was sent to the United States for her college education in 1939 but, to my knowledge, this sojourn did not create identity issues for her as it did my father. In her spare moments while raising her seven children, she involved herself in drawing, painting, and art history. Fluent in English, Tagalog, and Spanish, she was too reticent to flaunt her talents while playing — rather badly by comparison with her peers — the role of general's or ambassador's wife. Her triumph would rest on her ensuring by her speech and presence that her children would internalize her feminine and ironic sensibilities. Although I did not become aware of much of this family background until I was a graduate student in my twenties, it has helped me to identify and position myself as a "typical" middle-class Filipino intellectual whose writing bears a peculiar heritage bestowed by the ghosts of empires in the Philippines and the odd couple that my parents were.

History was not a field that interested me as a liberal arts student in the Ateneo de Manila. I was drawn more to the sciences and engineering and was gearing up for a career in the rapidly expanding field of electronics. In June 1965, however, my Chinese-mestiza grandmother, to whose generosity I owe my university education, took me and my sister on a vacation to Japan and Hong Kong — my first overseas trip. She herself had spent part of her childhood in the safety of Hong Kong and Singapore (where she learned English) during the tumultuous years of the revolution against Spain and the American invasion. I am certain that this background, with the lessons it held, was part of the reason she gifted each of her grandchildren with a trip to nearby countries. Our tour of Tokyo, Nikko, Hakone, and Hong Kong was nothing out of the ordinary, but what I saw and experienced of other cultures during those ten days powerfully affected my self-perception as "Asian". Whatever prejudices I may have picked up in childhood against the *Hapón* (Japanese) turned into respect and even admiration of another culture worthy of emulation.

My Ateneo education, too, was displaced by travel. Although I enjoyed physics, chemistry, and practical subjects such as technical drafting, I found it increasingly difficult to hold on to the idea, endorsed by my school guidance counsellors as well as my military father, that my "natural" career was in engineering. I made the momentous decision in October 1965 to shift my focus entirely to the arts and social sciences. I transferred to a truly "liberal arts" degree programme called "Humanities", which allowed me to choose practically any subject I wished to take. For three semesters and a summer, I did intensive coursework in history, philosophy, politics, English literature, art, music, and Asian Studies in the form of Indian philosophy, Chinese and Southeast Asian history, and a newly introduced Japanese language course.

Ever since my momentous shift to the humanities, the notion of academic "discipline" has meant little to me. A discipline could bestow intellectual rigour, occupational identity, and even a source of authority if needed, but it could also lead to a sort of mental closure. Although I developed a preference for what was labelled "philosophy", I also liked communication arts, literature, Chinese history, and physics. What mattered more, it seemed, than the particular discipline in which a course or subject was located, was the kind of person a lecturer was and whether the readings were interesting and meaningful. Because of my "humanities" background, recent debates on "discipline" versus "area study" have generally failed to excite me.

Educated for fourteen years in a Jesuit school, I was taught to belong to both the Filipino nation state and to the wider world of Roman Catholicism. So the kind of Philippine history I learned was nationalist. I don't think there could have been any other kind of history taught in the schools, but this one was unique because it firmly established the contribution of the Catholic Church to the making of the nation. At that time I was almost totally oblivious to the other, more anticolonial and socialist, variety of nationalist history being propagated by the UP historian, Teodoro Agoncillo. Instead it was Jesuit Father Horacio de la Costa's documentary history of the Philippines that I was taught. I really didn't see anything unusual about this liberal, Catholic, nationalist variety of history because in fact the issues of revisiting and rewriting the colonial past or challenging Western hegemonic scholarship were not introduced to me in the Ateneo during the mid-1960s.

At the same time, I picked up some ways of thinking that would become useful later in developing my critical approaches to history. Precisely because the Ateneo was a Jesuit university, my more memorable teachers had studied at universities in predominantly Catholic countries such as France, Germany, and Italy. At this early stage I became familiar with the thinking of (in addition to St Thomas Aquinas) Sartre, Buber, Husserl, Merleau-Ponty, Heidegger, and Weber. Most of my American trained lecturers, on the other hand, were into behavioural and structural-functional social science. My favourite Harvard-trained lecturer in history, while being extremely knowledgeable in his field of Chinese history, taught it in terms of an uncritical modernization paradigm, which is how any student of John K. Fairbank would have proceeded. What I was learning at the Ateneo about continental European philosophy offset what I was being taught by my politics and history teachers, although at that time the theoretical fault lines were not clear to me.

STUDYING HISTORY IN AMERICA

Although I had been recruited as an instructor in philosophy at the Ateneo, an offer of a Cornell University scholarship to study Southeast Asian history made me decide to major in history instead, and to focus my sights on the region in which the Philippines was located. History was clearly not among my favourite subjects at the Ateneo. It was only at Cornell, under the guidance of British historian Oliver Wolters that I began to appreciate the exciting possibilities of historical writing. If, like Wolters, one can write books and articles on Southeast Asia in the seventh to thirteenth centuries, based on precious few stone inscriptions and Chinese accounts, imagine what one could accomplish with a handful of Tagalog and Spanish texts! Wolters showed me how to squeeze the most out of what was available. He stressed the need not only for historical detective work, but also for complex and nuanced readings of texts, to which end he directed me to anthropologists, literary critics, or anyone else who could enrich my understanding of the past. He himself deployed social science concepts such as "localization" and "man of prowess" in organizing his narratives. Through him I learned to appreciate history, but not as a shackled "discipline". This was my first direct academic encounter with "the West".

After a year of graduate coursework, I decided to develop an expertise in Indonesian history, innocently anticipating later warnings against doing Southeast Asian studies only to study one's own country. I took Bahasa

Indonesia for two semesters, followed by Dutch reading lessons. In the summer of 1969, however, I was told that, being a foreign student, I had to produce a Master's thesis first, even though I was on a four-year PhD scholarship. That meant having to write two theses in four years! It seemed unfair that, unlike my American classmates, I had to prove my capabilities first before proceeding to a doctorate, as if something was terribly lacking in my Ateneo honours degree. Perhaps this was my first experience as a postcolonial native. Nevertheless, I welcomed the chance to actually write history for the first time.

Unfortunately, a year of learning both Indonesian and Dutch (on top of French the previous year) was insufficient to mount a major thesis exercise using sources in these languages. But I was also reluctant to fall back on Philippine history proper and so, after much discussion, D.G.E. Hall, the temporary chair of my committee, proposed a compromise: Look "in between" Indonesia and the Philippines. Surely, he pointed out, Muslim Mindanao belongs historically to the Indonesian archipelago more than to the Philippines. Hall had read and admired De la Costa's book, *The Jesuits in the Philippines*, which contains extensive accounts of early Jesuit relations with the sultans and *datuk* of Moro Mindanao. He had found the skills of this Harvard-trained Jesuit historian to be exemplary and surely worthy of my emulation. And so the die was cast: I would study Magindanao history in lieu of an Indonesian topic, and I would pursue De la Costa's initial explorations of the subject.

Returning from his sabbatical in the fall of 1968, Wolters echoed Hall's advice. Having recently published a book on early commerce in the Indonesian archipelago and the rise of Srivijaya, Wolters was interested in the place of Mindanao and Sulu in those trading networks and encouraged me to explore this topic. Moreover, like Hall, he admired the work of the Jesuit De la Costa, almost as much as he disdained the work of the UP scholar, Teodoro Agoncillo. My two British advisers actually knew De la Costa and Agoncillo much more than I, the "native" scholar, did, and they seemed to be nudging me in a certain direction. "Do not write like Agoncillo!" Wolters warned me at our first meeting. "Take Father de la Costa as your model", suggested Hall. The political and ideological implications of such injunctions did not register with me at that time. During my Ateneo days, I hardly saw De la Costa, who was stationed in Rome most of the time, while I had never even heard of Agoncillo. Being a neophyte in historical studies, I accepted the advice of my British teachers without hesitation.

My MA thesis, *Magindanao, 1860–1888: The Career of Datu Uto of Buayan*, was a graduate student's application of socio-economic and cultural history methods to a specific time and place. The scholarly literature on factionalism, patron-client ties, trading networks, indigenous social structures, and so forth, was part of our required reading. By merging these perspectives with the skills in historical detective work that I picked up from Wolters, I was able to churn out a thesis using a few late nineteenth century sources. Although one can discern echoes of Wolters' "man of prowess" in my portrayal of Datu Utto, a "Moro" who led a movement to resist Spanish subjugation, my choice of this topic to pursue was determined not by my teachers, but by the political climate of the times. Hall, a servant of Queen Victoria's empire in Burma, defended the British conquest of that land. Wolters had landed in academia after a decade as district officer in British Malaya, neutralizing Communist terrorists, as he was wont to call them. These were no historians writing against the empire. I took a sharply divergent path when I joined the anti-war (and implicitly anti-imperial, anti-colonial) movement in the United States from 1968 onward. It was via my exposure to the Vietnam War that I began to revisit the multitude of "revolts" that seem to dot Philippine history. The "Moro wars" were part of this. Could we begin to understand the "Moro" in his own terms, just like the Vietnamese "enemy" was beginning to be understood as a figure arising from his or her own social, political, and cultural milieu?

I wrote about Datu Utto with the knowledge that a year earlier (1968) Datu Udtog Matalam, former governor of Cotabato, had founded the Muslim (later, Mindanao) Independence Movement in the historic site of Pagalungan. My MA thesis was published in the Cornell Southeast Asia Data Paper series in 1971, and reprinted cheaply in 1984 by the Mindanao State University in order to give Filipinos access to the work. An annoying requirement of the graduate school turned out in the end to be a politically useful work, in addition to initiating me into the proper discipline of history. The past of Datu Utto has continued to hover over the tense political situation in Mindanao from the 1970s to the present. The Moro Islamic Liberation Front (MILF) is a direct descendant of Utto's movement. The recent massacre of members of the Mangudadatu family by a scion of the government-allied Ampatuans contains echoes of the past: Is it a mere coincidence that a Datu Manguda belonged to Datu Utto's alliance of upriver *datuk* that warred against the downriver *datuk* who were allied with the Spanish?

I was a neophyte with respect to the Magindanao, ignorant of their language and culture, and whatever I knew about Islamic notions of community and struggle came only from books. Given the time constraints of my scholarship, there was no time to immerse myself in that world. That is why, for my PhD research, I turned to the Tagalog region, whose language and literature I could master in a relatively short time, and to the Christian religion, whose workings in the popular mind I could freely explore, given my exposure since childhood to its teachings and practices. I also turned to another body of historical writings that I had the skills to interrogate: Tagalog religious texts and patriotic literature.

Two Indonesianists at Cornell were particularly helpful in honing the approach I would take in my doctoral thesis. One of them was the anthropologist, James Siegel, whose 1969 book, *The Rope of God*, together with his reading of the Acehnese epic, *Hikayat Potjoet Mohammad*, provided models I could emulate. Another Cornell lecturer who inspired me was Benedict Anderson, whose essay "The Idea of Power in Javanese Culture", though much maligned nowadays by critics reading it out of context, was to me a brilliant example of an interdisciplinary approach combining phenomenology, political sociology, history, and literature. It was also Anderson who in conversation initially encouraged me to think of Jesus Christ as a religio-political figure, a notion he would have picked up from his part–Irish Catholic background. I could detect in both Siegel and Anderson echoes of what I had been taught by the practitioners of philosophy and literature at the Ateneo de Manila. Only at this point did I cease to feel alienated from the "American social science" atmosphere that pervaded Cornell.

My doctoral work saw an even closer alignment than my MA thesis between scholarship and political context. The late 1960s witnessed the American military "surge" in Vietnam and a corresponding intensification of the anti-war movement. This was also the time of the Great Proletarian Cultural Revolution in China, the French student revolt, the founding of a new Communist Party in the Philippines, and the rapid growth of the radical student movement in that country. While the American "silent majority" continued to support U.S. militarism, the academe generally opposed it. George Kahin, a specialist in Indonesian politics and one of the founders in 1951 of the Cornell Southeast Asia Program, led the way by organizing in May 1965 a fifteen-hour national teach-in opposing U.S. military involvement in Indochina. The political environment in the United States, being closely intertwined with Southeast Asian realities, made intellectual life at Cornell meaningful for me. Seriously protesting against the saturation bombings, the massacre of civilians, the propping up of a puppet regime in Saigon, I was led by all this back to the history of American intervention in the Philippines, the so-called "first Vietnam". It was only sometime in 1968 that I realized that there had been a full-blown war of resistance from 1899 to 1902 that led to the loss of nearly half a million Filipino lives. This was my first serious questioning of my father's legacy. The simple addition of the Filipino-American war — not the Spanish-American War, nor the Philippine Insurrection — to my knowledge of Philippine history, made me re-examine everything I had learned previously in school.

Wolters' stern advice in August 1967 that I should not write in the manner of the nationalist historian Agoncillo came, in fact, not long before UP-educated fellow students I had befriended at Cornell began to herald me with stories about this fabled "Agoncillo" and other radical professors at the State University. This made me all the keener to read Agoncillo and to write like him, building on the foundations laid down in his 1956 book, *The Revolt of the Masses: The Story of Bonifacio and the Katipunan*. Reading about the "real" Indochina and the "real" Philippine Revolution drew my attention to what my Jesuit education had omitted. For a while, I was bitterly angry at the Ateneo for having taught me only one side of the story, so to speak. In the context of the Cold War and the Catholic Church's alignment with the Right, it is understandable how certain radical or militant dimensions of the Filipino experience could be suppressed by the educational system in the 1950s and 60s. By 1970, however, many students and teachers from the Ateneo itself had joined the movement for radical change; the UP-Ateneo divide was starting to crumble.

"Radical change" could mean a variety of things depending on the movements concerned and their ideological orientations. A common denominator, however, was the view that the 1896 "revolt of the masses" had not run its course; it had not turned into a social revolution. The wealthy and educated class in the cities had abandoned the cause as pressure from the Americans mounted towards the end of 1898. The eventual U.S. conquest then turned the Philippines into its political, economic, and ideological satellite — the reality behind the rhetoric of democratic tutelage — making independence since 1946 a bit of a sham. From the mid-1960s up to the early 70s, anticolonial nationalism expressed itself in criticisms of, and even calls to expatriate, American academics in the UP, and even American Jesuits in the Ateneo, for perpetuating neocolonial scholarship. Frank Golay, a Cornell economist who spent some years in the Philippines, had been a casualty of this pressure. I was totally innocent of this background when I first encountered him as director of the Cornell Southeast Asia Program in the late 1960s.

My studies at Cornell did not lead to a gap between what I was learning from "the West" and from the homeland. There was always a critical interrogation of knowledge from both ends. As I learned about the history and anthropology of China and Southeast Asia from my Cornell teachers, I also learned about the radical nationalist and socialist traditions developed in the Philippines since the 1950s from reading the works of Agoncillo, Cesar Majul, Renato Constantino, and others. Furthermore, while I was in the United States, I increasingly became involved in Filipino student organizing, which included a substantial conference held in Ithaca of Filipino students on the East Coast of the United States, followed by the setting up of a national student association to help promote the aims of the student movement in the Philippines overseas.

What made radical ferment among diasporic Filipino intellectuals possible, in my view, was a strong sense of history, marked by a common awareness that, a hundred years back, Filipino propagandists called *ilustrados* were involved in the same kind of activity in Europe. The ability to view our activities as part of a deeper historical flow was facilitated by the fact that all of us, whether educated in Catholic or government schools, knew the basic facts about the nineteenth century and the Philippine revolution through our nationalist textbooks. We could discern parallels between the student uprising of 1970, and the 1896 "revolt of the masses", and identify a role for ourselves in an ongoing historical event.

This is not to downplay the value of graduate training in the West and the positive effects of being distanced from the homeland. Ironically, being in the heart of the English-speaking world made me more aware than ever of an "other language" that had always served as a supplement to my basically English linguistic universe. As I alluded to above, one of the valuable things I learned at Cornell was how to read texts methodically and critically. I took a particular interest in traditional Tagalog metrical romances called *awit*, a literary genre foreign to me as I was growing up. I belong to the generation of Ateneo schoolboys who were fined fifty centavos if caught speaking in the vernacular languages rather than English. But this never happened to me because English was the language of my childhood despite my Bulacan-Tagalog family background. Having met during the war as students in the United States, my parents decided that their children's future would be best ensured if they spoke English well. This was at the expense of Tagalog, as a result of which I nearly failed my third year in high school owing to my extremely poor grades in Pilipino, and my spending too much time with a rock band.

Since the Tagalog language figured heavily in my thesis project, I began to acquire the skills to handle "deep Tagalog", initially by plodding through old texts with the help of a dictionary. But the crucial part of internalizing the language came when, as part of my graduate fieldwork in 1971–72,

I stayed at my wife Loolee's ancestral home in Tanauan, Batangas, the basement of which had been converted into St John's Clinic. Conversing with people from all walks of life who came to be treated by my father-in-law made me sensitive to the nuances of everyday Tagalog speech. Moreover, Loolee's grandmother, Maria Gonzales Carandang, a remarkable woman who had lived (and suffered) through the wars with Spain, America, and Japan, lived in that house and spoke to me solely in Tagalog. Our conversations started me thinking about historical memory, particularly relating to past wars. In sum, my Tanauan experience helped me to understand, through their manifestations in the present, the "categories of meaning" I was discovering in old Tagalog literature.

My focus on religion and popular movements in Luzon was initially a displacement of my limited efforts to understand Muslim Magindanao. It became an obsession, however, following the student uprising in Manila in January 1970 — dubbed the "First Quarter Storm" — and calls for a new revolt of the masses. How was this actually to happen in a culture shaped by centuries of Spanish, Catholic influence? As part of my thesis research, I returned to the Philippines in mid-1971 to ground my ideas and book knowledge in fieldwork. I mentioned above my experience in Tanauan, which, together with explorations of the surrounding areas, took up roughly a third of my fieldwork year. Another third was devoted to the usual research in archives and libraries. The final third was spent engaging in the political activities and debates of this period.

There was a lot of talk about revolution in Manila universities at that time, made possible to some extent by the historical studies carried out by Agoncillo, Majul, Constantino, and other pioneering nationalist scholars that I alluded to earlier. More than just academic texts, these served as an inspiration to young radicals pursuing the "unfinished revolution" in the early 1970s. New readings of the Philippine revolution inspired by Mao Zedong's writings had by then proliferated as well. During this time I met regularly with a study group comprising a number of my former Ateneo classmates, to discuss works which would have been totally proscribed by our Jesuit teachers in the mid-sixties. Of particular salience to us was the example of China, whose modern history from the Christian-influenced Taiping rebellion to the rise of Mao, I had studied under the guidance of Knight Biggerstaff, a Cornell professor sympathetic to the Chinese Revolution (and hounded for it by Senator McCarthy's red baiters). In the process I began to think of similarities and differences between China and the Philippines. All three components of my "fieldwork" mutually interacted in the end to make me question the uncritical universalism and the developmentalist assumptions underlying the revolutionary slogans of the time emanating from Manila and other urban centres — a mirror image, ironically, of the "modernization theory" then still in vogue in American area studies.

I returned to the United States in mid-1972 to do further research in the archives in Washington and thereafter to write my thesis. My take on Agoncillo's "revolt of the masses" theme would be to explore the mentality that informed popular movements in the nineteenth century. My critical lenses were focused on American liberal-democratic and Filipino nationalist-democratic discourses that obscured, if not suppressed, the perceptions and visions of the so-called inarticulate masses. My enthusiasm for thesis work withered, however, in September of that year after President Marcos, with the encouragement of the United States, declared martial law, jailed all the activists he could get hold of, and clamped down on criticism. I was, again, drawn to the protest movement, this time against Marcos' martial law, and by early 1973 was inclined to abandon my PhD studies in order to engage in full-time activism. But there was a problem: Could the diaspora really be a place for effecting political change in the homeland? What was the point of talking about a "revolt of the masses" if one could not even see and hear them? The *ilustrados* engaged in the Propaganda in Spain had faced the same question a century earlier.

My decision to physically withdraw from the anti–martial law movement and concentrate on writing my thesis was only partly due to gentle reminders from Wolters. In early 1973 another mentor figured in my intellectual trajectory — the Filipino Muslim Cesar Majul, a Cornell PhD graduate of the late 1950s who had returned to his alma mater on a visiting professorship. It was Majul who prevailed on me to finish my thesis and to publish it as a contribution, precisely, to the movement for political and social change back home. I suppose Majul's air of certainty about what I must do stemmed from his long experience as a professor of history, politics, and Asian Studies at the UP. In the late 1950s and early 1960s he published seminal works on the revolutionary tradition of 1898 (based on his Cornell thesis) as his contribution to the "political awakening" of university students. In the 1960s, he devoted his energies to writing a monumental history of Muslim Mindanao and Sulu, which would inform Muslim separatist movements in later years. Having written about intellectuals who shaped the 1898 revolution, as well as being a scholar-activist for the Muslim Filipino cause himself, Majul offered me irresistible advice.

Despite my renewed commitment to the academe, returning to the homeland would not be a simple task. I had already been identified as an anti-Marcos figure and was advised by my father not to return to Manila since I was on a government blacklist and would be arrested on arrival. Fortunately, a timely offer of a postdoctoral fellowship came from Anthony Reid at the Australian National University (ANU). Thus, in February 1974, having successfully defended my thesis draft, I set off for Canberra with my wife and our baby daughter, Malaya Amihan, to commence a new phase in my career. From Australia, I reckoned, I would be able to figure out my return to the Philippines.

RETURNING TO MANILA VIA AUSTRALIA

Until political necessity provoked it, I had never thought of Australia as a meaningful site for Southeast Asian Studies. But, glancing at the map of the region, I asked why not? In the early 1970s, Australia under the Whitlam government was seriously coming to terms with its British colonial and "White Australia" past in its efforts to tie itself more closely to Asia. Australia offered, to me at least, a different experience of what we commonly generalize as "the West".

A desire to position itself within the Asia-Pacific in more than geographical terms enhanced Australia's commitment to Asia-Pacific studies in key universities such as the ANU. Seeking to develop its own trajectory and momentum, Southeast Asian Studies in Australia was particularly open to change. I enjoyed the ANU's full support in expanding my thesis into a book, despite the reigning positivist and empiricist environment. At least the latter would spur me to undertake more archival research. Pretty thin, indeed, were the documentary fruits of my 1972 fieldwork because I was mostly in southern Luzon, immersed in the Tagalog language and cultural practices, or discussing Marx's *Manifesto* and Mao's "On Contradiction" with my discussion group. Taking the cue from Tony Reid, who felt that my work on Magindanao was still more "solid" historically, I started a long-term project on the social history of the revolution and resistance to U.S. occupation in Southern Luzon — research which up to now has provided substantial empirical backing for my "theoretical" explorations.

I made my peace with the Marcos government prior to a brief visit to the Philippines in December 1975, while still a postdoctoral fellow at the ANU. The worrisome threat of being arrested was thus reduced to a benign "interview" by the Constabulary Intelligence Service on my arrival at the airport. I finally settled down in Manila in late 1976, and in June the following year, took up an assistant professorship in the UP history department. This was rather unusual for a graduate, like me, of the Ateneo de Manila, since at that time there continued to be a lingering distrust in the UP of anyone educated by the Jesuits. But my involvement in the Filipino student movement in the United States, where I worked closely with a number of UP graduates, facilitated my entry. No less a personage than Professor Agoncillo himself seconded the departmental chairman's motion to hire me.

It was not as if all was well after I landed the UP job, though. At the first university commencement after my arrival, the graduating students turned their backs on the guest speaker, Madame Imelda Marcos, who understandably was miffed and would take her revenge. Thus, throughout my UP days we had one budget crisis after another, making my teaching career there more of a social and political commitment than an "academic career", as we conventionally put it.

As a lecturer in the University of the Philippines, I could never see history just as an academic exercise. For one thing, I was — or had to be — a nationalist scholar. Far from the pejorative connotation it has come to bear since the ending of the Cold War, "nationalist" at that time meant being committed to constructing a broad collectivity transcending family, religious, or ethnic lines. It meant being conscious of an "unfinished revolution", suppressed by imperial conquest and colonial knowledge, but having the potential of being resurrected and fulfilled if we applied ourselves to it. I had to engage with Maoist intellectuals as well as historians writing under the Marcos signature, all of whom laid claims to the nationalist mantle. My students, who invariably waved the flag of nationalism, from time to time respectfully disputed my historical interpretations with quotations from Constantino's *A Past Revisited* or even Amado Guerrero's *Philippine Society and Revolution*, the guide book of the Communist-led National Democratic Front. Some of them even took to the hills (*namundok*), never to be seen again.

Teaching at the UP also brought me into close relationship with scholars who were attempting to indigenize Philippine history and anthropology, employing the use of the Filipino language in academic writing as the first stage in the process. Again, as in 1971 when I was doing fieldwork for my Cornell thesis, at the UP in 1978–81, questions of local knowledge and domestic rhythms of change versus universalist categories of meaning and change, were being debated, although sometimes polemics got tied up with rather irreducible differences or rivalries among competing groups or powerful professors. Nevertheless, the work was exciting because we were extending the frontiers of Philippine history by doing more local/regional studies, tracing the linkages between the local and the national, applying different models from Spengler to Mao, writing in the vernacular to reach the masses, decolonizing history, and so forth.

In 1978 I even experienced, as close as I could get, how the state, or Marcos, or more specifically the group of scholars writing under Marcos' signature, sought to harness history to promote nation state projects. For six months I was involved with the *Tadhana* history project and produced a chapter on cultural changes in the late eighteenth century. To my mind it was an open question as to who was using whom: Marcos or the nationalist historians writing in his name? Six months in the fringes of the "inner circle", though not to the point of meeting with the president himself, were enough to teach me the folly of gross generalizations about "dictatorship", "collaboration", "nationalist", "democracy", etc., in any sensitive account of local scholarship in Southeast Asia. The *Tadhana* project was but one instance of a general pattern, since the late nineteenth century, of Filipino intellectuals attaching themselves to institutions of learning as well as the state, constructing and reproducing history for revolutionary or nation building purposes.

The Marcos/*Tadhana* attempt to decolonize history was particularly effective in challenging the Catholic Church's emplotment of Philippine history. It was really the Agoncillo challenge to De la Costa all over again, but in the hands of much more skilful and "disciplined" historians. Nevertheless, it seemed to me that the basic scaffolding of Philippine national history was not being questioned. Marcos' New Society simply installed itself as the end-point of a Hegelian historical trajectory — history recolonized by the state. A critical point in my Philippine sojourn arrived after I turned down the invitation to become a full member of the Tadhana project and subsequently withdrew entirely from it. My energies henceforth would be focused on the publication of *Pasyon and Revolution: Popular Movements in the Philippines, 1840–1910*.

Although it started out as a Cornell thesis and an ANU book manuscript, *Pasyon* was overhauled and expanded during my interactions with a number of UP graduate students in 1978 and after a few more trips to the north and south of Manila to observe popular religious rituals. I began to care less about the latest global trends in scholarship and felt compelled instead to write about what I saw and felt on the ground in the context of a repressive political environment. Could this be why the final manuscript was rejected by some prominent U.S. academic presses? I realized then that I was misguided in initially thinking that the book should be published in "the West" in order to get ahead in the field.

The intended audience of the book would be Filipino, first and foremost — such had been my intention in writing the thesis in the first place. The nationalist ethos of the UP history department in which I worked could only strengthen this sentiment. In October 1979, a trip to the People's Republic of China with a group of historians confirmed my decision. Totally mesmerized by this brief visit, which included meetings with Chinese academics and an exiled leader of the Filipino student movement, I was driven more than ever to write for the sake of empowering the "masses", however naive or quixotic this may seem in retrospect. Instead of rewriting my manuscript to suit the expectations of U.S. publishers, I would keep it the way it had evolved during my UP teaching days and have it disseminated by the Ateneo University Press. It was launched in December 1979.

Aside from its scholarly virtues as a university press publication, *Pasyon and Revolution* is a veiled critique of the "empty exteriorities" of the Marcos dictatorship, as well as the Communist Party's mass line policies, although there is no direct reference to the present, or to the actual targets of my criticism. I am told that the book, which enjoyed an extensive Filipino readership soon after it saw print, actually contributed to Marcos' downfall in February 1986 through the so-called People Power revolution in which religious icons were manipulated with the backing of the Catholic Church. The dramatic assassination by Marcos agents of the opposition leader Benigno Aquino provided the ingredients for a martyr figure that could hold a mass movement together. The book, among others, provided historical and cultural foundations for such a reading. The prescient Majul was right after all. This did not mean, however, that the rest of the academe would share his view.

In the West, *Pasyon and Revolution* was well received, thanks in no small measure to its origins as a Cornell thesis and its affinity with the works of Siegel, Anderson, and James Scott. In Manila, the book was welcomed by the likes of Bien Lumbera and Prospero Covar, advocates of indigenous literature and culture, but swiftly encountered difficulties with the historians. As early as the book's launch, the venerable Agoncillo, whom I had personally invited, became visibly disturbed as he paged through the copy I had presented to him. What had I done wrong now? The resistance to my book was due, I think, not to any real disagreement with its more obvious conclusions, or even to its veiled critique of the regime in power. In the wake of debates I was engaged in during my teaching career in the UP and my involvement with Tadhana, I began to wonder if my work was really up against a hegemonic linear and developmentalist form of historical emplotment that would not easily go away.

In the process of replying to critics of my book, which was not initially accepted as a proper work of history, I began to openly deploy "theory", citing Barthes, Foucault, Marx, Maurice and Marc Bloch, Nietzsche, and so forth. Much of this was polemical, however. In the end what mattered was not so much becoming an "expert" in these modes of understanding, treating them as ends in themselves, but rather in being on the lookout for gems of thought that could help me make sense of local conditions. The tendency for scholars who have gone to the West for their higher degrees is, unfortunately, to wave the banner of new methodologies in order to trounce perceived old ways of thinking back home. I came dangerously close to that.

Towards the end of my UP sojourn, I wrote a critique of nationalist historiography that highlighted its progressivist, Enlightenment lineage, its linear construction, and the exclusions that invariably accompanied such an emplotment. Mimicking Foucault, I called for the resurrection of suppressed knowledges and the writing of history that resists incorporation into the nation state's metanarrative. I was obviously attuned to "global trends" in historiography that identified and denounced the violence nation state histories have inflicted on local and regional narratives and concerns. In critiquing nationalist historiography — and in celebrating the contingent, the local, and the nonlinear — I was trying to write against the ideological underpinnings of the Marcos state, whose history textbooks bore the same structural features as Agoncillo's.

My essay was eventually published in Singapore in 1988 as "Towards a Nonlinear Emplotment of Philippine History". For many years it was never, to my knowledge, reviewed or cited. However, with academic criticism of nationalist historiography rising to mantra-like proportions in the 1990s, the piece was reprinted in a collection put out by Duke University Press in 1997. Since then I have wondered why this essay was so warmly received in the West in the late 1990s, while in the Philippines it was not. I stand by my contention that Philippine history could fruitfully become less nation state focused and more decentred. But could it be, as well, that changing intellectual fashions in the wake of the Cold War had actually predetermined my conclusions about the kind of history labelled "nationalist" that I was lambasting? My critique of Agoncillo/Marcos history was framed by the politics of the late 1970s and early 1980s, but would it apply to all kinds of nationalist history at all times? What was lacking in my essay was a closer interrogation of the ways in which national(ist) histories were actually read and understood in schools and social movements, their localization (to echo Wolters) in a Filipino environment.

THE PHILIPPINES VIEWED FROM AUSTRALIA

My stint at the UP, combined with another full-time job at De La Salle University from early 1984 (to make ends meet), was physically exhausting.

After a period of illness in 1985, I decided to "take a break" by accepting a temporary lectureship in history at James Cook University (JCU) in the north-eastern city of Townsville. In keeping with the Australia-in-Asia mood of the times, and acting on the advice of Wang Gungwu (who was then Professor of Far Eastern History at the ANU), JCU had decided some years back to develop a niche programme in Philippine Studies. I arrived in Townsville in early February 1986, just before a military rebellion and the People Power demonstrations were to profoundly alter the political scene in the Philippines. The downfall of Marcos coincidentally marks the end of my formal Philippine career because the "break" in Australia eventually turned into a long-term stay for family and career reasons. My father, as it happens, also took up prominent, and sometimes controversial, positions in Corazon Aquino's cabinet from 1986 to 1992. That tricky familial connection might have adversely affected my career had I stayed around.

Being based in regional Australia brought about a shift in my intellectual concerns. Part of the background to this was being racially vilified by drunken white Australians or being told to go back where I came from after I had written critical letters to the editor of the *Townsville Bulletin*. All too real was my fear that rocks would be hurled at my house because I wrote against common media misrepresentations of Filipinos or crudely justified attempts to limit Asian immigration. This was the context in which colonial discourse and race relations became vital concerns for me and ushered in a period of consuming interest in Edward Said's book, *Orientalism*. I had bought a copy of, but never read, it in 1978 since it did not seem to be particularly useful for the arsenal of ideas I needed in order to engage in debates in Manila. In Townsville, however, Said became meaningful and relevant, opening up to me the extensive literature on postcoloniality.

North Queensland was the perfect place for me to observe the workings of colonialism and racism in "the West" itself. There I encountered a significant population of Torres Strait Islanders and even discovered that Filipino pearl fishers and traders dominated the economy of Thursday Island (in the Torres Straits) at the end of the nineteenth century. Heriberto Zarcal, the 1898 Philippine Republic's representative (or "ambassador", according to some textbooks) to Australia, was actually a Filipino merchant based on Thursday Island, who owned a fleet of pearling vessels christened the *Aguinaldo*, the *Llanera*, and the *Natividad* after three Filipino generals who won victories against Spanish forces in 1897. Zarcal was actually part of a network of revolutionary supporters that included my grand uncle in Singapore. To my surprise and delight, I discovered that even the far north of Australia is inscribed in the Filipino national narrative. Zarcal's fortunes declined, however, shortly after the White Australia policy was introduced with Federation in 1901. I experienced the vestiges of that policy from 1986 and could imagine how life must have been for Zarcal and other Filipinos in northern Australia at the turn of the century.

In Townsville, Aborigines were present in far greater numbers than I had ever encountered in my previous sojourns in the southeast corner of Australia. This demographic situation, and the history it begged, encouraged a kind of scholarship at JCU that harks back to the role Agoncillo played at UP, and Kahin at Cornell. Their counterpart at JCU was the historian Henry Reynolds, a prolific Reader proudly lacking the title Doctor, who championed the cause of the Aborigines as victims in the past and present. That White settlement amounted to an invasion was a controversial idea he and other progressive Queensland historians tried to insert into public discourse as well as the state history textbooks. Such creative melding of scholarship and activism was all too familiar (and inspiring) to me — in fact I was reminded a bit of the UP historians trying to "use" Marcos for injecting a more radically anticolonial perspective into the Filipino national narrative. Australian colleagues such as Reynolds above and Noel Loos, who wrote on the Torres Strait Islanders, shared my commitment to "history from below" — one reason I stayed on despite the positivism and empiricism that continued to dominate Australian historical studies in the late 1980s.

In teaching Southeast Asian and Philippine history to Australian students, it became increasingly clear to me that Australian self-perception, or the national imaginary, hinged a lot on a view of the "other", both within and without, as inferior, exotic, aboriginal, black, or oriental. I found it pointless to teach Philippine history in the conventional manner because the Philippines would then become just another exotic place they could *know* about and incorporate into their conceptual universe of "us" versus "them". And so my teaching, at least at the advanced levels, gravitated towards making students examine what Europeans, Americans, and educated Filipinos have said about the "natives", or about themselves in relation to the natives, and how these representations follow from certain "Great Ideas" emanating from Europe. Philippine history became a study of how texts are produced about the "Oriental other" of a Euro-American civilization surging forward to incorporate the rest of humanity into its universe.

Surprising though it may be to those who think in terms of global "branding", the history department at JCU in the late 1980s was a most conducive place to develop my thinking about "postcolonial theory". The Australian far north was historically at the edge of White settlement, where the clash of cultures and the "tyranny of distance" from Europe were most keenly felt. Townsville up to the 1930s had been the start off point for Aboriginal headhunting expeditions, yet it also became a stronghold of labour unionism and nationalist agitation — topics of consuming interest for JCU historians. I discovered how anticolonial nationalism in predominantly white Australia could be intellectually productive when it led people to understand how many of the ills of society could be traced to the nation's past as a backwater of the British Empire and its failure to cut the umbilical cord, so to speak, with Mother England and, now, America. So how different was this place from the Philippines, really? It didn't take much effort to develop in my department a group of colleagues and students, spearheaded by Rodney Sullivan and Elizabeth Holt, devoted to the study of the American empire and colonial discourse in the Philippines. Feminist theory was eventually introduced in conjunction with postcolonial criticism — a really productive combination evidenced in Holt's PhD thesis on American representations of Filipino women during the Filipino-American war and after.

My initial foray into the critique of colonial discourse came in the form of a review of Stanley Karnow's popular book, *In Our Image: America's Empire in the Philippines*, published in 1989. I acknowledged that, as an expert on the Vietnam War, Karnow had taken great pains to establish the Philippine-American war as one of the major wars America has had to fight, one that needed 30,000 U.S. troops to win and which took the lives of close to half a million Filipinos. But, taking the cue from historian Glenn May, he attributes the Filipino revolutionaries' defeat (in contrast to the Vietminh) to their failure to overturn the social order dominated by the "oligarchs". A victorious America then tried to refashion the Philippines according to its image, but failed, owing to the strength of a so-called "Filipino tradition" and value system. The Filipino characters in Karnow's book are ruled by passions, kinship ties, debts of gratitude, personal loyalties, and so forth. In effect they are portrayed as a variant of America's classic image of their little, brown brothers whose persistent cultural lack demanded an almost indefinite deferral of their independence. Images of the Filipino constructed by Worcester and Foreman a century or so before Karnow to justify the American military conquest, reappear in modern social science garb in this Pulitzer Prize-winning book.

The real problem, it seemed to me, was not the journalist Karnow himself, but the array of esteemed academics whose works undergird the book and are generously cited in the footnotes. The intertextual signs were there of a discourse in operation, and so in the years that followed I began a systematic deconstruction of these writings: from Glenn May's work on the Philippine-American war, to Carl Lande's classic work on patrons, clients, and factions in party politics, to Al McCoy's various writings on factions and families in history, and so forth. When I first presented it at an Australian conference in 1994, I felt all too keenly the resistance of particularly the American academic establishment to this new interest of mine. An anonymous reviewer for a prominent journal in my field even described my revisiting of the literature on patron-client ties, with a critical focus on Lande's book, as a typical Third World nationalist tirade cloaked in postmodernist garb. After languishing in the back-burner for five years, this was reworked into a Burns Chair lecture titled "Orientalism and the study of Philippine politics", delivered at the University of Hawaii in 1997 and published two years later *as a lecture* by the Center for Philippine Studies at Hawaii.

The fact is, the work being done by my white Australian comrades in the Australian "backwater" of Townsville was met with the same kind of resistance from the historical establishment there. At the end of the day, what some of my colleagues deemed of utmost importance was systematically filling in the gaps in a comprehensive history of Australia — or, more specifically, of north Queensland — that they dreamt of constructing. They claimed that the newfangled theories the handful of us were introducing to the students were just pulling them away from the serious task of historical documentation and reconstruction. The reaction reached the point of obstacles being placed on the successful completion of student theses informed by postcolonial and feminist theory. The publication by the JCU history department in 1993 of a collection of essays titled, *Discovering Australasia: Essays on Philippine-Australian Interactions*, was the Philippine Studies group's first and last statement of note.

By 1994, I felt it was time to leave Townsville and, just like in the past, I was fortunate in having an "escape route" to facilitate my retreat. Help came from my academic allies at the ANU through whose advice and assistance I won an appointment as Reader in the Faculty of Asian Studies in early 1995. How timely, for at about this time a new liberal-conservative regime under John Howard was elected to power. I could feel strange echoes of Marcos and martial law. Relations with Asia would be downgraded; the prime minister would begin to strut about as America's deputy sheriff in the southern Pacific. Worst of all, residues of a "White Australia" mentality that feared contamination by blacks and Asians, would be increasingly exploited by Howard for political gain in the guise of immigration debates.

While Southeast Asian studies in the ANU, located in the nation's capital, would survive the regime change, JCU in the north would not so. Shortly after my departure, funding was cut for Asian studies. Indonesian and Thai would no longer be taught. The group of scholars that was beginning to produce exciting new readings of Philippine history from the periphery, so to speak, would quietly fade away. Even the great Henry Reynolds would be pilloried by conservative historians from the south who, with the visible support of the prime minister, called for a return to a "factual" and "sensible" narrative of the Australian nation.

In August 1995, on the fiftieth anniversary of the end of World War II in the Pacific, I experienced the uncanny return of "Japan" in my academic sojourn in far north Australia. Townsville had been an important R&R destination during World War II and the city invested heavily to commemorate the half-centennial of V-J Day. A massive street parade was held, and I was there to observe discreetly what people were celebrating. For one thing, Japanese people were not invited to the Townsville event. Also, those Japanese visitors who tried to attend the parade, such as our students at JCU, were harassed, and one or two even physically abused. Racial hatred towards the (Asian) enemy could be felt even as late as 1995, whereas such sentiments had largely disappeared from the Philippines, despite its having borne the full brunt of the Japanese army's advance into Southeast Asia. Appropriately timed with the election of the Howard government, a pristine Australian national identity was being mobilized against a Japanese "other".

CONCLUSION

Let me return to the beginning of my narrative: In the 1940s my father's Filipino-American binational identity depended much on a shared opposition to a despised Japanese enemy. But the "shock" of my first visit to Japan, the old "enemy", in 1965 opened up possibilities of other models to emulate aside from the America I had inherited. It pointed me, as well, towards another career path in history and Asian studies. My trajectory as an intellectual and academic would commence from that point. Further encounters with other cultures and academic environments in Ithaca, Tanauan, Manila, Canberra, and Townsville, and my admiration for the Chinese path to development, did not lead to anxiety about what was authentic and original versus what was foreign and threatening. I somewhat sensed from the very beginning that the "outside" was always already inscribed in my being, from the day I was born in Manila of disparate parents who had met and married in the United States, to my Roman Catholic education, and even to my marriage to a Tagala from Batangas province. I identified with a national narrative anchored in a revolution that featured characters "from below" as well as from beyond — that is, in the diaspora. My academic trajectory has seen me weaving in and out of the homeland, with lengthy sojourns in the United States, Australia,

Japan, and Singapore. Navigating through these diverse paths I have sought to explore the possibilities they opened up for a deeper understanding of the Philippines, my primary focus of research. My intellectual trajectory, if one can speak of such, has to take into account the shocks, turnings, and improvizations that have come with linking my experiences in varied places to my ongoing love for the Filipino nation.

References

Agoncillo, Teodoro A. *The Revolt of the Masses: The Story of Bonifacio and the Katipunan.* Quezon City: University of the Philippines, 1956.

Anderson, Benedict R.O'G. "The Idea of Power in Javanese Culture". In *Culture and Politics in Indonesia*, edited by Claire Holt et al. Ithaca, NY: Cornell University, 1971.

Constantino, Renato. *The Philippines: A Past Revisited.* Quezon City: Tala, 1975.

Costa, Horacio de la. *The Jesuits in the Philippines, 1581–1768.* Cambridge: Harvard University, 1961.

Guerrero, Amado. *Philippine Society and Revolution.* Philippines: Revolutionary School of Mao Tsetung Thought, 1970.

Holt, Elizabeth M. *Colonizing Filipinas: Nineteenth-Century Representations of the Philippines in Western Historiography.* Quezon City: Ateneo de Manila University, 2002.

Ileto, Reynaldo C. *Magindanao, 1860–1888: The Career of Datu Uto of Buayan.* Data Paper no. 82. Ithaca, NY: Cornell Southeast Asia Program, 1971; revised edition by Anvil Publishing, 2007.

———. *Pasyon and Revolution: Popular Movements in the Philippines, 1840–1910.* Quezon City: Ateneo de Manila University, 1979; 7th printing, 2009.

———. "Towards a Non-linear Emplotment of Philippine History". In *Reflections on Development in Southeast Asia*, edited by Lim Thek Gee. Singapore: Institute of Southeast Asian Studies, 1988; reprinted as "Outlines of a Nonlinear Emplotment of Philippine History" in *The Politics of Culture in the Shadow of Capital*, edited by Lisa Lowe and David Lloyd. Durham and London: Duke University, 1997.

———. "Orientalism and the Study of Philippine Politics". In *Knowing America's Colony: A Hundred Years from the Philippine War* (The Burns Chair Lectures, 1997). Occasional Papers Series. Center for Philippine Studies, University of Hawaii, 1999; reprinted in *Philippine Political Science Journal* 22, no. 45: 1–32.

Ileto, Reynaldo C. and Rodney Sullivan, eds., *Discovering Australasia: Essays on Philippine-Australian Interactions.* Townsville: James Cook University, 1993.

Karnow, Stanley. *In our Image: America's Empire in the Philippines.* New York: Random House, 1989.

Majul, Cesar A. *The Political and Constitutional Ideas of the Philippine Revolution.* Quezon City: University of the Philippines, 1957.

————. *Muslims in the Philippines*. Quezon City: University of the Philippines, 1973.

Marcos, Ferdinand E. *Tadhana: The History of the Filipino People*. Manila: 1976.

Said, Edward W. *Orientalism*. New York: Pantheon Books, 1978.

Siegel, James T. *The Rope of God*. Berkeley: University of California, 1969.

————. *Shadow and Sound: The Historical Thought of a Sumatran People*. Chicago and London: University of Chicago, 1979.

5

FROM CONTEMPLATING WORDSWORTH'S *DAFFODILS* TO LISTENING TO THE VOICES OF THE "NATION"

Wong Soak Koon

To look back on one's intellectual journey and development is one of the hardest tasks. Perhaps one should not even attempt it. Now in my sixtieth year, I hope I may be able to do so with some equanimity and honesty. I shall also try to link this trajectory with some of the key concerns of this volume. As I look back, it seems to me that the main difference between the earlier and later phases of my literary criticism has to do with the shift from an F.R. Leavisian unitary sense of "The Great Tradition" and a New Criticism approach, to my later concern with literature as a part of cultural politics. The later phase thus propelled me into examining issues such as the narratives of nation formation and how these are inflected by gender, class, and ethnicity; the hybridity of identity which is constantly in flux in a global-local interface. These issues have also directed me to look more closely at Malaysian writers, both those who write in English and those who use the Malay language. This does not, however, mean that I have abandoned my old loves (Virginia Woolf, Jane Austen, Shakespeare, E.M. Forster, Dostoyevsky, Tolstoy, and Turgenev in translation, etc.).[1]

THE EARLY DAYS

Enrolled as a primary pupil in St Mary's School, then run by Anglican missionaries, in 1955, just before Malaysia (then known as Malaya) achieved its independence in 1957, I was very much schooled in the colonial mould. Yet there was no critique on my part of this colonizing of the mind. In fact, to my young mind, the world of school was sane and orderly, a sanctuary for identity building, away from the tensions of a dysfunctional fourth-generation migrant Chinese family (my great-grandfather joined the hordes who sailed to the Nanyang regions and chose Malaya to seek his fortune, but by the time I was born, the family wealth from tin mining enterprises had been lost). The English language itself was, for me at the time, a vehicle for imagining landscapes and lifestyles which allowed for "escape". The lilt and rhythms of the poems in Palgrave's *The Golden Treasury*, for example, invigorated me and the foreignness of snowy climes, of vales and dales with grazing sheep, did not estrange. I remember the little cupboard where I kept my small collection of English books, its doors pasted over with just such pastoral scenes which I had studiously cut out from various magazines. Even today, I cannot go wholeheartedly into a postcolonial daffodil bashing of Wordsworth's much maligned flower. A poem such as Wordsworth's was, and still is, able to give me recollections "too deep for tears". It did not matter that I had not then seen a daffodil; I shared the poet's sentiments, "And then my heart with pleasure fills/And dances with the daffodils".

When I later studied the works of other heirs to migrant families, for example, *The Return* by K.S. Maniam and the short stories and autobiography, *Among The White Moon Faces: Memoirs of A Nonya Feminist* by Shirley Lim, I saw that this love of the English language was not unusual with migrants in colonial settings. And yet, it was always accompanied by ambivalence because of the unmooring from communal Chinese or Indian values this attachment to the colonialist's language inevitably engenders. Ravi, K.S. Maniam's protagonist in *The Return*, a third-generation migrant Indian, may have escaped the "madness" which his father's recalcitrant clinging to Indian cultural mores breeds, but Ravi's own identity at the end of the novel is an uncertain one. Straddling migrant Indian and colonial legacies as well as an embryonic Malaysian national identity, Ravi discovers that "words will not serve". Instead, words "will be vague knots/of feelings, lustreless, cultureless" (Maniam 1993, p. 173).

In my first year at the University of Malaya, I was still very much moved by the aesthetics of English literary studies. Wavering between majoring in history or in English, I finally chose English because it fed my joy in solitary reading. The English Department gave us an excellent foundation in the close reading of texts for which I am very grateful. We acquired a confident grasp of nuanced, careful reading as we studied diction, imagery, tone, and other essential details of a text. This New Criticism kind of approach, often dismissed in the contemporary race for theory, is not to be thrown out with the bathwater.[2] Poststructuralist, postcolonial, and feminist theories which are applied without clear relevance to detailed analyses of texts can take away our pleasure in the literary works themselves, and obfuscate, rather than enlighten. One can well understand Carolyn Heilbrun when she says, "Since my retirement, I have lost my taste for literary criticism, not only because of its turgid vocabulary but because it seems, now, so distant from the works it pretends to illuminate." She is quick to add that she feels ashamed "in sounding petulant about the young and those who ask unfamiliar questions" (Heilbrun 1997, p. 183).

THE DEVELOPMENT OF UNFAMILIAR QUESTIONS

In retrospect, it seems to me that I began tentatively to ask unfamiliar questions, questions beyond literary analysis, when I looked at catchphrases such as "nation building", "national unity", and "a Malaysian identity" after the traumatic racial riots of 13 May 1969 which shook the complacency of the Malaysian citizenry. My almost exclusively aesthetic concern with literary analysis was shaken by a need to be more engaged with the socio-political realities of Malaysian society. I was in my second year of varsity studies and had just chosen to major in English when a curfew was imposed because of the riots. The colonial legacy of a multiracial country made up of migrants, mainly from China and India, and the "indigenous" majority Malays had fissures which greatly taxed the political ingenuity of the early architects of the Malaysian nation state as well as their ability to compromise. As a leading Malaysian historian puts it:

> In order to end colonial rule and achieve national independence for Malaya, the UMNO [United Malays National Organisation] nationalists were compelled by the British officials to work out a formula of inter-racial co-operation, unity and harmony among the various races in the country. In 1955 and again in 1956 they negotiated and achieved a "Social Contract" with the two major non-Malay parties, the Malayan Chinese Association (MCA) and the Malayan Indian Congress (MIC), on the basic principles for co-operation, partnership and administration of the future nation-state. (Cheah 2002, p. 2)

The "Social Contract", worked out by the Alliance Coalition was strained by contradictions and was sorely tested by post-independence socio-economic developments. The Alliance's defeat at the hands of opposition parties in the

1969 Elections brought the underlying conflicts to the surface. A Malaysian sociologist sums up the causes of the 13 May riots in this manner:

> There was certainly widespread discontent among the workers, farmers, middle classes as well as urban settlers. The state's racially discriminating policies only served to create further divisions among the people and the 1969 election results clearly reflected this growing polarisation. (Kua 2007, p. 39)

As I had chosen to major in English Literature in the Department of English, the events of 13 May motivated me to study texts outside the Anglo-American and European canons. It seemed to me that to understand the Malaysian situation better, one could do worse than to examine the works of writers from other countries who explore the legacies of colonialism, such as the dislocation due to migrancy, the tensions of multiracial societies, and the Herculean task of shaping a national identity. Fortunately, the Department of English was then helmed by Professor Lloyd Fernando who steered the curriculum expertly into what were then new waterways in the department's flow of ideas. Thus, a course such as "Commonwealth Literature" offered undergraduates an opportunity to examine the works of writers from the Caribbean, Africa, and Australia, to mention some locales. As Fernando sees it:

> The Department of English in the University of Malaya teaches *English Literature*. Emphasis on the words together, separately, and alternately. Not just British Literature which would keep us tied to a specific culture when the basis for such an exclusive tie is now gone, but also literature by writers in the English language from the most diverse backgrounds imaginable — Patrick White in Australia, R.K. Narayan and Raja Rao in India, N.V.M. Gonzales in the Philippines, Chinua Achebe in West Africa, V.S. Naipaul in the West Indies. (Fernando 1986, p. 84)

Enrolling eagerly in the "Commonwealth Literature" course, I was excited by the Guyanese writer, Wilson Harris, who writes in his own unique, visionary style about the fragmented history of British Guiana. In retrospect, it seems to me that Harris was ahead of the now fashionable postcolonial and subaltern theorists in looking at the postcolonial condition. Be that as it may, his Guyanese novels exhibit an original creative impulse and an inimitable style. Both in content and technique, Harris' novels question the unitary vision of the individual and of society enshrined in Western Enlightenment epistemology, which privileges linear chronology. In the "Author's Note" to *The Whole Armour*, Harris describes his work as set in "a landscape saturated with the traumas of conquest" (Harris 1973, p. 8). The brooding Guyanese jungle, the great rivers and magnificent waterfalls watch over the violent encounters of men. Like the Nigerian writer, Chinua Achebe, Harris does not want to suggest that violence began with the arrival of the European conquerors. Guyana's past exhibits a historical palimpsest of traumatic events, first, among the indigenous Arawak Indians, then, between them and the Spaniards, and between the conquistadores and other Europeans. The quest for El Dorado which beckons to all men is a universal slogan for Man's perennial search for power and wealth. The decimation of the indigenes, such as the Amerindians; the toll on the colonialists themselves; the transplantation of people from one locale to another as colonial labour thematized in Harris' oeuvre are commonly explored in postcolonial literature.

When I first read Harris' fascinating yet disturbing novels, I had not even heard of theorists such as Homi Bhabha, or of poststructuralism and postcoloniality. Looking back, I can see that Harris was already challenging the tyranny of a unitary self that is unquestioningly lodged in a society that has a unitary scale for evaluating values. Thus, Harris eschews the constraining boundaries of what he terms "the novel of persuasion". He elaborates on the restrictions of this kind of novel:

> The novel of persuasion rests on grounds of apparent common sense: a certain "selection" is made by the writer, the selection of items, manners, uniform conversation, historical situations, etc., all lending themselves to build and present an individual span of life which yields fashionable judgements, self-conscious and fashionable moralities. The tension which emerges is the tension of individuals — great or small — on an accepted plane of society we are persuaded has an inevitable existence. (Harris cited in the Preface to *Palace of the Peacock* 1960, pp. 3–4)

In contrast to "the novel of persuasion", in Harris' novels, for example, *Palace of the Peacock*, social particulars and detailed delineation of the Guyanese landscape are evoked only to be reworked in order to suggest the fluidity of past and present, and the limitations of linear time. Characters who are residing in the present almost magically merge with characters from the past, bearing the same names in a simultaneity which loosens the dominant grip of linear chronology. Harris thus offers the patient reader fresh, new insights into Guyana's historical inheritance.

In *Palace of the Peacock*, the narrative centres around a crew's boat journey upriver through the Guyanese jungle. Their goal is an Amerindian settlement named "Mariella", but the indigenes have fled leaving behind an old Amerindian woman to guide them as they continue to pursue the folk. The leader of the crew, Donne, is "a type of Elizabethan conqueror and conquistador". The crew are the heirs of various races, "Europeans, Africans, Portuguese, Indians — belonging historically to different centuries and to successive waves of migrants to the Caribbean" (Ramchand 1960, p. 9). By eroding the normalized boundaries between past and present, Harris encourages a continual revisiting of history. By establishing a strange, yet convincing, psychic identification between "conqueror" and "conquered", he intimates that guilt and culpability are diffuse and complicated. Thus, it is not easy for any party to evade responsibility for historical instances of human violence. Perhaps this aspect of Harris' novels was of particular appeal to me after the brutalizing turmoil of the 13 May racial riots in Malaysia. Harris prompts us to be self-reflexive and self-critical so that we can reassess our egoistic upholding of "self-conscious and fashionable moralities" (Harris 1960, p. 3) in a climate of finger pointing and recrimination.

In *Palace of the Peacock*, the characters break out of the finite confines of society in dream states that are heightened states of consciousness. In these visionary moments, which seem to transcend, almost mystically, linear history, Harris' protagonists sense the subtle links and incestuous bonds between men in locales where identities and histories are fragmented. Thus, the dreaming narrator in *Palace of the Peacock* identifies with Donne, the representative of imperial desire: "I felt my heart come into my mouth with a sense of recognition and fear ... he was myself standing outside of me while I stood inside of him" (Harris 1973, p. 23). Both conqueror and conquered, colonialist and colonized, are culpable in the complex interactions engendered by imperial-colonial power relations as men colluded with one another, opposed one another or imitated one another. Greed and idealism, losses and gains, love and animosity, are inextricably knitted into subtle links that tie together men (both masters and slaves) of different racial origins, in a colonial legacy that intimates incestuous connections. Harris' vision of a transcendence of hate and revenge appealed to me then as it does now in spite of his obscure prose. Harris' prose moves the reader rapidly from one abstract thought to its opposite: from conflict to reconciliation, from destruction to creation, from estrangement to identification, from animosity to compassion, all the while suggesting their symbiotic ties. Such a renegotiation of binary opposites breaks the Manichaean mindset which makes the "alien", the "Other". It destabilizes the power of the hegemonic "I" to assign negative values to the people who are not like us. I remember, as an undergraduate, being alternately bewildered and excited by Harris' convoluted prose. Today, I still enjoy Harris' works, but a better knowledge of postcolonial theories has helped me to see that some readers may take Harris to task for an allegorizing of power relations which leaves almost no room for the quotidian particularities of political agency. For some, Harris' oeuvre does not contribute to a sense of political constituency; even his evocation of a kind of "hybridity" may be subject to critique.[3]

At the time, however, I was drawn to Harris' tone of reconciliatory calm and to his exploring of a state that is akin to what Conrad once described as "floating supine above the chaos". It is thus not surprising that I chose to work on Patrick White for my MA thesis.[4] Like Harris, White is another writer who moves us into a visionary grasp of an expanded consciousness. In such a state of awareness, one can accommodate opposites as well as sense the luminescent thread tying together different cultures. Like Harris, who depicts the traumas of Guyana's fragmented history, White is drawn to the painful memories of the Australian past. Basing his novel, *Voss*, on the mysterious disappearance of the enigmatic explorer, Leichardt (1813–48), while on an expedition into the Great Australian Outback, White employs the journey motif too and, like Harris, endows this universal literary convention with localized meanings. Just as Harris' depiction of the Guyanese jungle and rivers resonates with history and local legends, so too White's vision of the Australian outback becomes a luminous montage of the Australian landscape and historical experiences. Thus, in *Voss*, the members of the expedition setting out into the Great Australian Outback are carefully chosen so as to represent a cross-section of early settler society. At one end, there is Judd, the emancipated convict with a past, and at the other, are the colonial gentry who try to dissociate themselves from the emancipists. Other members of the group journeying inland represent the free settler, the working class, the enquiring spirit of European science, and the tradition of Christian faith. The artist in the group, Le Mersurier, reveals the artistic temperament which struggles to portray the experiences which the outback bestows on each member of the expedition. White's inclusion of Jackie and Dugald, two aboriginal figures, completes the representative character of the exploring party.

For my MA thesis, I focused on White's characters whom he himself calls "illuminates", who are capable of an expanded consciousness that can accommodate irreconcilable opposites. Like Harris' protagonists, they challenge a finite grasp of time and space. These "illuminates" comprehend, in very brief instances, the unity within themselves, and between themselves and others from diverse cultural backgrounds. And yet, White does not simply portray these moments of illumination as sudden mystical insights which are unrelated to the protagonists' everyday experiences. In contrast to this expanded awareness of some characters in *Voss*, White gives us a picture of the narrow-mindedness of the "huddlers", that is, those who cluster into cities and towns, mainly on the coastal fringes. They "huddle" as if in instinctive fear of the Australian continent's ancient presence, which is most strongly felt in the outback. At the end of the novel, Voss' legacy remains, especially for Laura Trevelyan, whose extraordinary connection to Voss is powerfully evoked by White so that the explorer's experiences as he journeys inland are depicted as available to Laura as she waits in the Bonners' home, described as a typical refuge for the gentry in New South Wales. It is as if some human beings "have a power to project towards others by some means which is beyond the normal faculties of reason and emotion, although less than the conventionally understood faculty developed by mystics" (Fernando 1986, p. 243). Both Harris and White unseat the tyranny of linear time and, to use verbs common in the vocabulary of postcolonial and poststructuralist theories, *interrogate* the finite confines of characterization, *renegotiate* binary categories, *destabilize* a unitary self, splitting the self into different subject positions and showing it to inhabit liminal spaces.[5] White and Harris give us new insights into the historical and psychological legacies of colonialism and of a coming together of different cultures. Nonetheless, some may prefer a more politically grounded narrative approach, one which focuses more on the delineation of socio-economic and political minutiae. One may also ask how Malaysian writers deal with the themes of colonialism, deracination, migration, and nation building after independence. My study of Malaysian writings, in some depth, only began after my return to Malaysia after doctoral studies in the University of California, Berkeley,[6] where I registered in the PhD programme in English in 1975.

GROWING TOWARDS THE DIFFICULT QUESTIONS

Berkeley was my first and only experience of studying abroad; all my subsequent trips overseas were for research or short teaching stints. In fact going to the United States in 1978 was the first time I had travelled so far from Malaysia. It was with some trepidation that I embarked on the PhD programme in Berkeley although I was already over thirty years old (older than most of the other graduate students) and had had some teaching experience. Initially, my younger, but much more articulate course mates intimidated me.

I was fortunate to be supervised by Professors Masao Miyoshi and Alex Zwerdling from the Department of English, and Professor Todd Willy from the Department of Rhetoric as I worked on Joseph Conrad's novels with an Eastern setting. And yet, in retrospect, I now see that, though my choice of supervisors was excellent, my choice of author to study was much less so. Did I really feel passionate about Conrad's oeuvre? Did I not, even then, have some misgivings about Conrad's portrayal of women, for example, his depiction of Lord Jim's fiancée whom he called "The Intended" instead of naming her? Was not Conrad's portrayal of non-Europeans a problem? With hindsight, it is clear that I hurriedly chose a topic because my employer back home in Malaysia, the University of Science in Penang, had granted me leave for only three years to complete the PhD. In Berkeley at that time, it was almost unthinkable to attempt the completion of a PhD degree in anything less than six to seven years. The foreign language requirements as well as coursework usually took some time to fulfil. After five years spent in the Bay Area, arguably one of the most fascinating locales in America, I was obliged to return in 1983 to resume my teaching duties without completing my dissertation. Fortunately, I had done my comprehensives and had drafts of the first few chapters when I returned. After teaching for a year back home, I completed the dissertation, returned to submit it, and the PhD was conferred in 1986.

The Bay Area and the University of California, Berkeley did much to help me grow both academically and personally. Berkeley's vibrant campus life was fed by a student body made up of different races, cultures, and classes. Sproul Square at lunch hour was frequently alive with speeches given by the scholarly and the eccentric. Although Berkeley in the late seventies and early eighties was not quite the Berkeley of the Vietnam War protests, lecturers and other Bay Area residents continued to take up causes such as the anti-apartheid demonstrations. I was also able to take in the diverse cultural activities of the Chicano, African-American, and Asian-American students. A world of discourses with multiple perspectives opened up even though graduate studies was, in the final analysis, a gruelling and often lonely affair. Towards the end of my stay in Berkeley, Professors David Lloyd and Abdul Jan Mohamed joined the Department of English and I benefited from their talks on postcoloniality and cultural politics.

Yet it was really important socio-economic and political changes in Malaysia, which I observed after I returned from Berkeley in 1985, that motivated me to look at key issues in postcolonial writing, in particular, the ways writers explore the problematics of nation building in a multiracial country such as Malaysia. The state's narrative of "nation" elides contradictions and solders over potential fissures in its effort to downplay ethnic and class differences, as well as draw attention away from the dominance of UMNO within the ruling coalition. I decided that literary analysis would profit from a cross-disciplinary approach. One may need to traverse the boundaries of academic disciplines to bring out the socio-political saliency of a literary text, while not neglecting the text's literary-aesthetic dimension. On my return to the University of Science in Penang, I was fortunate to enjoy academic dialogues with some colleagues from the School of Social Sciences. These friends helped me understand the Malaysian polity better.[7] The prevalent atmosphere of self-censorship among Malaysian academics at the time, engendered by an increasingly authoritarian state, did not deter some of them from asking so-called sensitive questions on the effects of rapid economic development in Malaysia.[8] Then a major event in post-independence Malaysia erupted, namely "Operation Lalang". It was the mass arrests under "Operation Lalang" beginning from 27 October 1987 that propelled me into asking difficult questions, such as: What is a Malaysian identity? What is equity in a multi-racial nation where communal feelings envelop nation building efforts in a miasma of mutual distrust? How are these concerns reflected in contemporary Malaysian literature, even if I can only access works written in English and Malay since I cannot read works written in the vernaculars?

"Operation Lalang" is arguably as deeply etched in the memory of Malaysians as the racial riots of 13 May 1969. According to a book put out by the "Committee Against Repression in the Pacific and Asia" (CARPA), just prior to the massive arrests, communal animosity and intra-ethnic UMNO conflicts added to the tensions of the following conditions:

> Popular disaffection with the Mahathir administration had been growing with the protracted economic crisis of the eighties. Together with rising unemployment and declining public expenditure, especially for the social services and subsidies, there is now more public awareness of "money politics" (reflecting increasing political access to wealth acquisition) and of various major scandals and corporate failures that have been taking place, as well as of growing curbs on civil liberties and democratic rights. (CARPA 1986, p. 3)

A total of a hundred and nineteen people were arrested and Mahathir accused the detainees of racial and religious extremism when, in fact, most of those taken in were not associated with political parties. A number of those arrested were social activists who "had been trying (admittedly with limited success) to develop non-communal alternatives for Malaysian society" (CARPA 1986, p. 6). I had myself joined a social reform movement, Aliran, just before the "Operation Lalang" arrests.[9] My Berkeley sojourn and the socio-political developments in Malaysia on my return had shaken me out of a hitherto rather uninvolved stand in spite of the fact that, during my undergrad years, the 13 May riots did affect me. I remember that when I started my MA thesis in 1971, Professor Lloyd Fernando, my supervisor, was taken aback by my residual nonchalance. He told me, "How can anyone live in Malaysia and not be concerned?" "Operation Lalang" certainly made it hard to remain an observer. The then president of Aliran, Dr Chandra Muzzafar, was one of those arrested. I recall waiting for a ride from another Aliran member to go to the Aliran office to strategize and write letters of appeal to local and international bodies, asking them to pressure the government to release those arrested or to give them their day in court. Waiting in the gathering gloom of the brief Malaysian dusk, I felt a sense of foreboding. A thick silence fell as night came. Even the neighbourhood dogs did not bark.

"Operation Lalang" is one of the most brutalizing moments in Malaysian history. After such an event, the citizen-subject had to question her identity as formed within communal and national boundaries. Identity may have to be constantly renegotiated. It seemed to me then that contemporary Malaysian writing may yield some insights into this difficult process. Malaysia in the eighties and nineties, with its accelerated modernizing project creating a diversity of responses, is rich ground for the creative writer to mine for raw materials which the imagination may work on. Perhaps I was looking for writers courageous enough to recognize the fissures which had been covered up by the optimistic rhetoric of nation building. Is it unpatriotic to examine the inconsistencies of the nation state? Or, is it love for a country that makes one unwilling to absorb uncritically official rhetoric on integration and unity because this rhetoric elides problems? I knew that I would not choose migration (the diasporic route) as I had decided that Malaysia would be the place to plant stakes; it is, after all, the country where I was born, a fourth-generation migrant Chinese whose great grandfather migrated to Malaysia, then known as "Malaya", in the nineteenth century to work out his destiny. As the national anthem goes, Malaysia is "tanah tumpahnya darahku".[10] With a renewed interest in the challenges of nationhood, I began to analyse the works of contemporary Malaysian writers who write in English and Malay (the languages I am fluent in). In examining such contemporary works, some of the issues which continue to draw me in are: the legacies of migrant and colonial histories; the interrogation of the state-proffered narrative of "nation" as writers decouple the quotidian lived experiences of the people from the state rhetoric of nation building so as to expose the complexities of identities-in-flux; the examination of the effects of modernization; a relook at those interstices of history which are ignored by official state history. Contemporary Malaysian writers, Malay and non-Malay alike, take up such issues, but because of space constraints, and for my purpose here, I shall only refer to Malay writers as they help me to traverse my own ethnic boundaries in order to understand another community better.

MALAY WRITERS COMPLICATING THE NATION STATE AND "MALAYNESS"

The group of writers I shall now discuss are Malay writers who use either Malay or English. They belong to a younger generation in comparison to veterans such as Usman Awang, Shahnon Ahmad, or Mohamad Haji Salleh. Their thematization of identity, community, and affiliations destabilize a slogan, regularly used by diehard ethno-nationalists, that is, "Ketuanan Melayu" ("Malay Dominance" or, as some would like to translate it, "Malay Sovereignty"). These contemporary Malay writers inflect the resonances of Malay identity, seeing it through a prism of challenging perspectives. In so doing, they remind me of Wilson Harris and Patrick White, mentioned earlier in this chapter. Like Harris and White, these contemporary Malay writers boldly complicate historical legacies and communal stereotypes, thus highlighting intra-ethnic differences (a refreshing departure from the usual tendency to focus on inter-ethnic divergences). They destabilize the idea of original purity, showing that the question "Who is a Malay?" may not be an easy one to answer. In evoking the ambivalence of human choices, they expose how unhelpful it is to divide the world into Manichaean and binary pairs. Heroes and villains thus become, as in Harris' and White's fiction, fascinatingly and disturbingly hard to differentiate. Perhaps we are all culpable in some way as we reflect on the less-than-positive legacies and present tensions of the Malaysian nation state.

The contemporary Malay woman writer, Che Husna Azhari, gives us a regional perspective on Malay identity. Hailing from the Opposition-led state, Kelantan, she produces short stories and a brief survey of Kelantanese history which decentre the primacy of the Malacca Sultanate in Malay cultural-historical identity. In her excavation of the Kelantanese past, she thus questions "the constant principles of national culture" (Bhabha 1994, p. 303). Che Husna says that the Kelantanese, "despair that the historians of Malay history collectively group our history with the Malacca-centric one of Malay culture. We feel that the flowering of our culture did not issue from the keris-kissing Malacca Sultanate" (Che Husna Azhari 1993, p. 61). In my analysis of her work (Wong 2003, p. 50), I note that she posits an alternative cultural-political identification for the Kelantan Malays whom she claims "have their own rich, established history, identifying with the civilization of the Malay Patani kingdom of southern Thailand and of the Chempas" (Che Husna Azhari 1994, p. 62).

In a similar vein, a Malay political scientist and human rights activist, Farish Noor, deconstructs the monolithic claim to *the* Malay identity often used emotionally by certain quarters. In so doing, he extends further a sense of hybridity. Perhaps a palimpsest of many layers accrue to all cultural identities; Malay identity is no exception. Farish Noor writes that,

> Malay culture and history is so deep, so rich and so vast only because the Malays of the past were themselves the inheritors of the traditions from all of Asia… Malay civilization, like all civilizations, is a hybrid amalgam of many civilizations. We were Hindus and Buddhists before, and before that we were pagan animists who lived at peace with nature. The coming of the great religions — Hinduism, Buddhism and Islam — and the arrival of new modernist schools of thought should not be seen as distinct episodes that keep our histories apart. (Farish Noor 2002, pp. 229–30)

My analysis of the Malay novel, *Empangan,* by Zakaria Ali, highlights a similar interrogation of an unproblematic, monolithic "Malayness". In fact, Zakaria suggests that such a unitary sense of identity may be due to the colonial administration's penchant for classifying the heterogeneous colonial subject, the Malay, under one category.

In *Empangan,* the protagonist, simply known as "J", pits himself against both colonial legacies and the authorities of the independent nation state who mobilize laws inherited from the colonialists to acquire land for development projects. Zakaria provides a regional perspective on nation building by focusing on the cultural specificities of Negri Sembilan (a state on the south-west coast of Peninsular Malaysia), just as Che Husna Azhari did with the state of Kelantan. In teasing out Zakaria Ali's interrogation of the hegemony of the nation state (Wong 2004), I highlight his thematization of the conflict between the traditional land inheritance practices upheld for generations by the people of the village of Kampong Paya, and federal laws. Thus, the postcolonial nation state is challenged by regional customary practices.

Zakaria also exposes the machinations of the powerful who accuse "J" of being a *pengkhianat* (a traitor) to national development goals when "J" sides with those who oppose development that would benefit only a few, mostly the elites. These goals are also seen as destructive to the natural environment. Though the villagers are Muslims, they are depicted as holding many natural phenomena in awe because animistic beliefs have not been entirely wiped out. The theme of being a "traitor" is enriched by Zakaria's foregrounding of the importance of oral history, or more specifically, oral heritage tales (*cerita-cerita warisan*) in a contemporary scenario. To the villagers this oral heritage remains important. It is suggested that official history, which is usually written history, can be inflected by local historical variants on the past. This aspect of the novel draws me especially since Zakaria presents "J" as enacting in a contemporary moment, the rebellious role of his forebear, Tukang Daud, a skilled maker of the *keris* (dagger). Tukang Daud had simply been seen by the powerful as a violent murderer who killed a rival *keris* maker. In the oral heritage tales, however, Tukang Daud is a man of honour who rebelled because of the gross injustice of being judged a loser in competitions to make the hilt of the *keris*. The award was twice unfairly given to another craftsman simply because this personage was the son-in-law of the powerful Datuk Endut Bondorong (the highest local figure of authority in the district). Like his ancestor, Tukang Daud, "J" too must take up a position against the powerful and the corrupt. The Harvard-educated "J" is a returning prodigal son who will not simply slip back quietly into village life. Instead, he opposes the elites and their supporters who would develop the village mainly for personal gain. The rhetoric used by these planners is that development will meet national and global economic imperatives.

As I examine contemporary works by Malay writers using either Malay or English, I find common themes such as the paradoxes of personhood thrown up by the nation state's modernizing efforts, and the psychological challenge of identity-in-flux clearly evident. In an essay in the collection, *Ceritalah: Malaysia in Transition*, Karim Raslan captures the dialectical pulls and instabilities underlying Malay-Muslim identity, in the midst of rapid development, in this manner:

> On the one hand a Malay was expected to conform to certain set norms — many of which were quasi-feudal in their emphasis on loyalty, obedience and blind devotion to authority. Despite this, on the other hand, he was also expected to be a dynamic, cosmopolitan businessman hunting down business opportunities in Yangon, Tashkent, Jo-burg and Santiago... Could I be a modern Malay and still be Malay? (Karim Raslan 1996, p. 13)

Karim Raslan's short stories also critique the extravagant lifestyles of the new Malay middle class. This theme of class differences cuts across the rhetoric of communal tensions which is commonly mobilized by sundry racialized politicians to garner vote, especially on the eve of elections. Other writers have also examined the theme of class differences, highlighting the lavish lifestyles of the rich, and the struggles to survive of those inhabiting pockets of urban and rural poverty. In *Green is the Colour*, for example, Lloyd Fernando depicts the spurious conviviality of the noveau riche from all ethnic groups, contrasting this with the pragmatic and arguably more genuine community feeling in locales not yet under rapid development. In their everyday encounters, people of various races, who are living almost below the poverty line, may share certain commonalities and show an innate decency, the kind of "decency" that George Orwell says is seldom brought into the corridors of power. In the final analysis therefore, class issues inflect and complicate "nation-ness". The possibility that identity by class may one day transcend ethnic divides must cause some politicians to have sleepless nights.

Gender is yet another inflection to the challenges of nationhood. In my analysis of a short story, "Ustazah Inayah", by Che Husna Azhari, I show how the female protagonist, Inayah, straddles unsteadily the demands of home and hearth and political responsibilities as a Member of Parliament under the ruling party (Wong 2001, pp. 149–53). Inayah feels culpable and responsible for the extravagant spending of the various state-affiliated women's groups whose indulgences she does not succeed in curbing. Her guilt is compounded when she observes the hardship endured by the poor women in her constituency who eke out a living working in tobacco barns. She feels as if she has not been able to make the voices of such women heard in the cacophony of voices asking for a piece of the national pie. Inayah's disillusionment forces her to take a sabbatical from party politics. Her putting on a veil (*tudung*), which is a personal choice having little to do with political strategy, is read as part of public political discourse. Her veiling causes the Opposition Islamic party to send an emissary to persuade her to party-hop. In such stories, I see how concerned writers evoke the tough struggle Malay-Muslim women take up in order to maintain agency amidst the Islamization strategies of the government and Opposition Islamic parties, each trying to up the ante on its rival. An interesting book, which I see as a breakthrough in terms of the exploration of Malay-Muslim women characters, is Fatimah Busu's *Salam Maria* (2004), which I analysed at a panel discussion when the book was launched.

In *Salam Maria*, Fatimah Busu boldly creates a near-utopian community within the nation state that challenges various assumptions about Malay-Muslim women's autonomy and agency. The protagonist of the novel, Maria, is viciously slandered (termed *fitnah* in Malay) because her singlehood makes her an easy target for lewd speculations and rumours. Even the mosque authorities, who should rightly exercise discernment and compassion, evict her from the place of worship. Leaving the society that has rejected her, Maria forms her own community deep in the jungle in a locale not yet exploited by logging companies. Her "constituency" (if we may call her group this) is made up of marginal women — the blind, the poor, and as the story develops, the abused who are the victims of incest and rape. In this "fantastical" community, Maria is the spiritual leader who is shown as very knowledgeable about the Qur'an and other key Islamic texts. In depicting Maria in this way, Fatimah Busu bravely interrogates the almost exclusively male right to Qur'anic interpretation long held by the official custodians of Islam in Malaysia. Indeed, Maria recalls Muslim women saints such as Rabeah al-Adawiyah and Sayyiddah Nafisah. An incident of incest in a prominent family resulting in the pregnancy of a *datuk*'s (a titled person's) daughter, who has to be kept out of public view, forces the *datuk* to bring the girl to Maria's jungle community. This episode offers Fatimah Busu ample opportunity to satirize the nation state's rhetoric on happy families ("keluarga bahagia" in Malay). Fatimah Busu criticizes the mother, the *datin*, for her indifference with regard to the incest. The indulgent pursuit of middle-class consumerism has eroded the *datin*'s parental responsibility and her moral sense. She is shown as following, without question, the *datuk*'s plan to hide their daughter away from public scrutiny. The *datuk* is exposed as a man who, instead of protecting his daughter as befits the head of the family under Islam, abuses her and then proceeds to hide his sin. The jungle locale, where Maria's community thrives while respecting nature, also provides Fatimah Busu with the opportunity to speak out against the destruction of nature because of ill-planned and rapacious development.

After studying a number of works by contemporary Malay writers, it seems to me that class, gender, and human rights, which had already been touched on by an earlier generation of writers, acquire fresh connotations and resonances today. Hopefully these fresh perspectives will inflect and complicate the usual communal-based themes and auger a courageous foraying into multicultural perspectives that have more depth than the surface stereotypes. Such a shift, when it comes, will be in keeping with the remarkable change shown by the people of Malaysia in the recent general elections on 8 March 2008. The Opposition parties attempted a multiracial approach and, after the elections, the Opposition Coalition took five states from the ruling alliance, the Barisan Nasional. The Malaysian electorate appears to have moved away from allegiance to narrow communal-based parties. Not since 1969 have the citizens denied the ruling government a two-thirds majority in Parliament. For me, it is heartening to see that the old fears of racial clashes, the memory of 13 May, so often used by certain incumbent politicians for political mileage, no longer haunt citizens the way they once may have. In fact many young voters, those below forty years of age, did not live through 13 May, that brutalizing moment in Malaysian history; they were not even born. The concerns of the younger generation of Malaysians centre on transparency, good governance, accountability, and the creation of genuinely democratic spaces. Some of the younger subjects of the nation state may even want to revisit the histories of the struggle for independence. The roles of socialist leaning figures in the anti-colonial phase such as Ibrahim Yaakob, Ishak Hj Muhammad, Lim Chin Siong, and others attract both scholarly and popular attention.

CONCLUSION

In my retirement, without the pressure of the regular assessment forms which Malaysian academics have to fill, I can choose to write and read whatever pleases me. I find myself drawn to autobiographies which seem to me to straddle the divide between facticity (or, referentiality) and the autobiographer's sense-making and language use. I like to read about the lives of those who have been rendered invisible by official discourses or relegated to a "villainous" role. This is not an attempt to valorize such figures. It is motivated by a simple curiosity about other lives which have had an impact on Malaysia's past and present, both for better and for worse. One example of such a figure would be Khatijah Sidek, the first leader of the women's wing of UMNO who was later asked to leave the party.[11] Women such as Khatijah Sidek reveal how diverse political choices can be. It seems to me that my earlier, youthful fascination with Wilson Harris and Patrick White, which I have discussed above, returns in my retirement to enrich my present engagement with Malaysian historical legacies as these are explored in fiction and autobiographies. Harris' and White's refusal to see life in Manichaean terms, their willingness to blur the demarcations between "self" and "other", engender the kind of compassion and tolerance I value. They reveal a brand of confidence which celebrates, rather than negates, differences. Their artistic vision of reconciliation and of a rising above narrow affiliations, speaks to the challenges facing the Malaysian citizenry and leaders at this juncture where a new political will should be forged. If we eschew communal sentiments it can be argued that "we must have a more holistic accounting of social solidarity that allows us to reduce inequalities by building capacities, enhancing capabilities, and making allowances for differences in abilities and cultures" (Khoo 2008, p. 20). Together with social scientists and those in other related fields, literary scholars and creative writers can play a vital role in times of political change. They do so by stretching the borders of the imagination and by providing fresh insights into the pragmatic, the quotidian, and the concrete.

Notes

1. I empathize with Mohan Ramanan who writes from India: "I want my Shakespeare and my dear Dickens. This does not mean that I am unpatriotic and that I do not want my Valmiki, Vyasa, Kalidasa and Sankara" (*New Straits Times*, 6 July 1994, p. 34).

2. In over three decades of teaching literature at a tertiary level, I have attempted to uphold close textual reading so that the theories, however fashionable, do not stamp out the texts. I remember a student telling me how hard it was to enjoy a literary work if one is constantly trying to see if one can apply a theory to fit it.

3. In an illuminating article, R. Radhakrishnan critiques metropolitan high theories which can have a universalizing drive thus eliding the specificities of local working out of terms such as "hybridity". He writes that while "metropolitan hybridity is ensconced comfortably in the heartland of both national and transnational citizenship, postcolonial hybridity is in a frustrating search for constituency and a legitimate political identity" (Radhakrishnan 1993, p. 753). He also observes that "postcoloniality" itself is an academic formation which "goes hand in hand with the development of cultural theory and studies" (p. 750). See R. Radhakrishnan, "Postcoloniality and the borders of Identity", *Callaloo* 16, no. 4 (Autumn 1993): 750–71. It seems to me that this metropolitan academic thrust can have its own hegemonic hold over the publication prospects of non-metropolitan academics who may employ its terminology to get published and so neglect local specificities.

4. I would like to record my heartfelt gratitude to Professor Lloyd Fernando who supervised my MA work for his unfailing encouragement, patience, kindness, and his discerning criticism which did much to allay the "fear and trembling" of a young, inexperienced researcher. Professor Fernando passed away in late February 2008 as I was preparing this essay. His passing is a great loss to literary scholarship and I agree with Kee Thuan Chye who writes, "Lloyd Fernando was truly a scholar and a gentleman. He was a man of grace and polish who invariably spoke well of others. He loved literature and imparted his knowledge of it to his students with such passion that it made an indelible impact on their lives" (*New Straits Times*, 2 March, p. 21).

5. See, for example, Bhabha, *The Location of Culture* (London: Routledge, 1994), pp. 1–65.

6. I am grateful to the Harvard-Yenching Institute for the award of a Doctoral Fellowship which made it possible for me to study abroad at the University of California, Berkeley.

7. Among those who made tea and coffee breaks at the canteen welcome hours of sharing are Dr Maznah Mohamad (now a fellow at the Asian Research Institute, National University of Singapore), Dr Johan Saravanamuttu Abdullah (presently senior fellow at ISEAS), Dr Goh Beng-Lan (then newly returned

from Japan after her MA), and Dr Mustafa Kamal Anuar of the School of Mass Communications.

8. The University and University College Act amended in 1975 constrained the freedom of academics and restricted the autonomy of universities.

9. Aliran (full name "Aliran Kesedaran Negara", or "National Consciousness Movement") is Malaysia's first multi-ethnic reform movement dedicated to justice, freedom, and solidarity. Listed on the Roster of the Economic and Social Council of the United Nations since 1987, Aliran has a consistent record of championing democratic rights. Guided by universal spiritual values, Aliran's struggle focuses on building unity by upholding human dignity and promoting social justice for all Malaysians. To conscientize the public, Aliran publishes *Aliran Monthly*, Malaysia's leading independent English news magazine. I have written pieces on various topics for this publication.

10. In the national anthem this Malay phrase refers to the foetal blood of birth in order to signify one's deep loyalty to the land.

11. See her memoir which is titled *Memoir Khatijah Sidek: Puteri Kesatria Bangsa.*

References

Abdul R. Jan Mohamed. *Manichean Aesthetics: The Politics of Literature in Colonial Africa*. Amherst: University of Massachusetts Press, 1983.

Bhabha, Homi, ed. *Nation and Narration*. London: Routledge, 1990.

———. *The Location of Culture*. London: Routledge, 1994.

CARPA (Committee Against Repression in the Pacific and Asia). *Tangled Web: Dissent, Deterrence and the 27 October 1987 Crackdown in Malaysia*. Kuala Lumpur: CARPA, 1988.

Che Husna Azhari. *Melor in Perspective*. Bangi: Furada, 1993.

Cheah Boon Kheng. *Malaysia: The Making of A Nation*. Singapore: Institute of Southeast Asian Studies, 2002.

Farish Noor. *The Other Malaysia: Writings on Malaysia's Subaltern History*. Kuala Lumpur, 2002.

Fatimah Busu. *Salam Maria*. Rawang: Absolute, 2004.

Fernando, Lloyd. *Cultures in Conflict: Essays on Literature and the English Language in South East Asia*. Singapore: Graham Brash, 1986.

———. *Green is the Colour*. Kula Lumpur: Silverfish, 2004.

Harris, Wilson. *Palace of the Peacock*. London: Faber and Faber, 1960.

———. *Tradition, the Writer and Society*. London: New Beacon, 1967.

———. *The Whole Armour and The Secret Ladder*. London: Faber and Faber, 1973.

Heilbrun, Carolyn G. *The Last Gift of Time: Life Beyond Sixty*. New York: Dial, 1997.

Karim Raslan. *Ceritalah: Malaysia in Transition*. Singapore: Times Books International, 1996.

Kee Thuan Chye. "A Scholar and a Gentleman". *New Straits Times*, 2 March 2008, p. 21.

Khatijah Sidek. *Memoir Khatijah Sidek: Puteri Kesateria Bangsa*. Bangi: Penerbit Universiti Kebangsaan Malaysia, 1995.

Khoo, Philip. "A New Dawn? Not Quite, but a Liberation all the Same". *Aliran Monthly* 2, no. 3 (2008): 2, 4–7, 19–20.

Kua Kia Soong. *May 13: Declassified Documents on the Malaysian Riots of 1969*. Kuala Lumpur, 2007.

Lim, Shirley Geok-Lin. *Life's Mysteries: The Best of Shirley Lim*. Singapore: Times Books International, 1995.

———. *Among the White Moon Faces: Memoir of a Nonya Feminist*. Singapore: Times Books International, 1996.

Lowe, Lisa and David Lloyd, eds. *The Politics of Culture in the Shadow of Capital*. Durham: Duke University Press, 1997.

Maniam, K.S. *The Return*. London: Skoob, 1993.

Maznah Mohamad and Wong Soak Koon, eds. *Risking Malaysia: Culture, Politics and Identity*. Bangi: Penerbit Universiti Kebangsaan Malaysia, 2001.

Palgrave, F.T. *The Golden Treasury of the Best Songs and Lyrical Poems in the English Language*. London: Thomas Nelson, n.d.

Ramanan, Mohan. "There's No Separating Language and Literature". *New Straits Times*, 6 July 1994, p. 34.

Ramchand, Kenneth. Preface to Wilson Harris' *Palace of the Peacock*. London: Faber and Faber, 1960.

White, Patrick. *Voss: A Novel*. New York: Viking, 1957.

Wong Soak Koon. "A Critical Study of Patrick White's Novels with Special Reference to his 'illuminates'". MA dissertation, Department of English, University of Malaya, 1975.

———. "Conrad's Eastern Novels: Cases of Intercultural Encounters". PhD dissertation, Department of English, University of California (Berkeley), 1985.

———. "Intervening into the Narrative of 'Nation': Che Husna Azhari's Kelantan Tale". *Sun Yat-Sen Journal of Humanities*, no. 16 (Summer 2003): 47–62.

———. "Identity, Community and Nation in Zakaria Ali's *Empangan*". Paper presented at Sephis Workshop on "Contested Nationalisms and the New Statism", Penang (Malaysia), 2–4 September 2004.

———. "Exploring the Framing and Unframing of Malay-Muslim Identity in Select Contemporary Fiction". In *Writing a Nation: Essays on Malaysian Literature*, edited by Mohammad A. Quayum and Nur Faridah Abdul Manaf. Kuala Lumpur: International Islamic University, 2009.

Wordsworth, William. *Poetical Works*, edited by Thomas Hutchinson. Revised by Ernest de Selincourt. London: Oxford University Press, 1969.

Zakaria Ali. *Empangan*. Kuala Lumpur, Dewan Bahasa dan Pustaka, 1990.

6

CRAFTING ANTHROPOLOGY IN MANY SITES OF FIELDWORK

Paritta Chalermpow Koanantakool

My anthropological training is the source and site of my knowledge making. I would like to describe two major "field sites" so to speak in the development of my career. One is the formative phase of my intellectual journey and the other is the concluding one. To write about these two phases poses two different problems. The formative phase took place some decades ago, and when I look back at it now, things seem like faded photographs. Dates, places, people, events, thoughts, and feelings seem like shadows lurking in a dim light and it makes me wonder whether I am picking up these pieces to construct a coherent image of a person who no longer exists, or never existed in the first place. On the other hand, my concluding phase is still ongoing, and to write when the dust is not yet settled, and without a vantage point of a view from afar, my eyesight must be clouded by the drudgeries of everyday life. I also suspect that my self-portrayal of an early period serves as a counterpoint of the agony of my present circumstances. Nevertheless this is my story.

ENCOUNTER WITH ANTHROPOLOGY

I grew up in a sheltered environment in the capital city of Thailand. My parents came from an urban background; both were descendants of well-to-do officials, but by the time I was born the family fortunes were already exhausted. Even so my parents sacrificed their moderate salaries to send my brother and I to a very good and progressive school. So in my childhood I was part of the majority, the mainstream Thai. Thailand was the country of the Thai. It never crossed my mind that there were other ethnic or language groups; diversity was never an issue. My maternal great grandfather was ethnically Chinese, but my mother always insisted that he had served the King and become a high-ranking official. Because of that his Chinese ancestry was of no consequence and he had become completely Thai. If there was any mention of non-Thai people, it was usually done in a tone that relegated them to an inferior position with ethnic stereotypes — our maid was a Lao (slow-witted, unhygienic) and vendors were Jek (unrefined, avaricious, but brainy). Thais were kind-hearted, good-mannered, but could not run businesses, so on and so forth. Such was the ethnic environment of my childhood.

Family peace and security came to an abrupt end at the time when I was finishing secondary education and preparing to take the university entrance exam along with various other scholarship exams — my father died of a sudden illness. So when I learned that I won a government scholarship to study Law in England, I decided to take it even if I had no inclination to become a lawyer. I had no idea what kind of career or options in life were open to a girl in those days, it was simply the family expectation of me to pursue my study as far as I could because of the commonly held view that education was the gateway to a secure future and success in life. So in 1969 I travelled to England, anxious to learn and absorb British education and culture, which at that time, was considered one of the best. In the first few years I suppose I was blind to most things that were going on in the world — the Vietnam War, student protests, etc. — as my energies were concentrated on improving my language skills and struggling with exam after exam. The switch from law to anthropology during my second year as an undergraduate at the University of Kent in Canterbury took place almost by chance. During my first year, law was taught with other social science subjects and I went to anthropology classes that talked about cross-cousin marriage and showed Levi-Strauss' diagrams with rows and columns of circles and triangles, and I was totally fascinated even though I could not make the slightest sense out of it. So I turned to anthropology and buried myself in classic ethnographies of the British school, from Frazer, Malinowski, Evans-Pritchard, Lienhardt, to works of the Année Sociologique school — Durkeim, Mauss, Hertz, Levi-Strauss and so on. Looking back, I enjoyed reading ethnographies perhaps because they represented non-western societies that I could respond and relate to because of my own non-western identity.

While I was an undergraduate student, I was working for Samakhii Samakhom, an association of Thai students in the United Kingdom. It was through their meetings, debates, talks, and journals that I began to learn more about the political situation in Thailand, about military dictators, corruption, student movements, and various social and economic problems. And it was through activities within the little overseas community of Thai students, coupled with the moral obligation that government scholarship students should give back to their country, that a sense of social responsibility was being formulated among Thai students of my generation in England. In 1973 I remember watching the TV news coverage of the 14 October student uprising that ousted the military regime with friends in the old lobby of the Thai government students office at 14 Princes Gate, London, that served as the association's office and library. A few days later we held a meeting in the same room. Dr Puey Ungphakorn, former governor of the Central Bank and later rector of Thammasat University who was on leave in England at that time, made a speech honouring students who had lost their lives in the uprising. He said he was ashamed that people as young as his children had to fight and sacrifice their lives so that people like him could enjoy democracy. I remember that despite the musty odour of that lobby furnished with tatty armchairs and couches, the atmosphere was charged with emotion and ideals that students such as us could do so much for our country. In retrospect, I suspect that I was attracted to anthropology because I thought it might provide a framework and methodology for me to understand my own society, to analyse how it has evolved, how it functioned or failed to do so, and somehow to contribute to its growth and development.

My interest in expressive aspects of culture led me to Cambridge where I met Barbara Ward, my first supervisor, who worked on Chinese opera in Hong Kong. Cambridge was not a great place for working on Southeast Asia, but they were generous enough to fund my research on the shadow play of southern Thailand. Why Thailand and not "other cultures" as anthropologists are supposed to do? Barbara told me "If you work on Thailand you will be ten years ahead of everyone else." So Thailand it was. The thought of spending ten more years as a postgraduate in England, on top of God knows how many already, did not appeal to me.

I returned to Thailand in 1976, and I could not have chosen a more fateful year to do fieldwork. A few days after arriving there, an old friend took me to a student meeting in Sanam Luang. It was a scene I had never experienced in my life. Half of the seventy-four *rai* (about thirty-five acres) of the spacious field was packed with students sitting on the ground listening to speeches. I was filled with excitement, but also apprehension. The atmosphere was tense. We had to sneak through rows of guards to get out. Shortly afterwards, I went down south, travelling in Nakhon Si Thammarat, Songkhla, Phatthalung, Pattani, to look for an appropriate fieldwork site. It was then that the events of 6 October took place. The violence in Bangkok did not affect me physically, but it was the first time I experienced life under a military regime. I remember going through all the books I brought with me and taking great care in covering every single one that had the word "Marx" on its cover. I made sure these would be at the bottom of my bags when I travelled in interprovincial taxis — typically old Mercedes in which eight to ten people were packed inside — in case we got stopped at checkpoints. In my head I had prepared answers in case men in uniform asked what a student like me was doing in isolated places in the south, and so on and so forth.

So I was doing fieldwork on shadow plays in the midst of those tumultuous years of 1976–77. I got to know a number of puppet masters, especially those who performed plays with political content concealed in jokes. Humour was the most difficult part of the performance, particularly for a Bangkok-born person like me to understand. I had to go through every line, every word, with anyone patient enough to explain these to me, before I could grasp the political commentaries puppet masters made about policemen, governors, district officers, and other government officials. It was fascinating to see puppets carved out to look exactly like some army generals who were ousted by students, or other characters that represented the president of a superpower country. When I decided to study folk performance in the mid-70s, the theoretical frameworks were the symbolism of puppetry and the social function of the performance-cum-ritual, but the political situation in Thailand at the time drew my attention to the power of artistes to make statements about the powers that be. Political engagement also shaped the identity of puppet masters who labelled themselves in those years as either "political" or "traditional" puppet masters. The identity of artistes and artiste imagined worlds became issues that I worked on later.

While I found myself in a precarious situation as a student in my own country, back in England where I went to complete my doctoral study, things seemed to have become even worse. I was living the wretched life of a student "writing up", struggling to make ends meet when all grants had run out. As if that were not bad enough, my husband and I were living in a run-down apartment in London where racial tension was beginning to erupt. Our place was in Wembley where the majority of the population was Indian. Streets were lined with Indian stores selling everything from spices to Indian silk. One day I went into a haberdashery on a high street to buy some sewing materials. This was an English shop, as one could tell from the look of middle-aged male assistants in tweed jackets and moustaches on their stern faces. I bought some small items which were put in a small brown paper bag, then carried that bag to a small cabinet with little drawers where they kept thread of different colours. While I was pulling out the drawers to find the thread I wanted, a voice behind me said "What are you up to now?" I turned and found a shop assistant staring at me suspiciously. I told him I wanted to get some thread and handed him the ones I wanted. He took them, but he also said "Let me see..." and snatched the brown bag from my hand and proceeded to empty all the contents out on a table and inspect them carefully to see if there were any stolen goods among them. Satisfied that I did not steal anything, he put everything back in the brown bag and handed it back to me as if nothing had happened. I could not describe how I felt — perplexed, dumbfounded, angry, sick. I was furious and yet I did not know what to say or what to do. I just walked out of the shop. It took me days to try to figure out why he behaved the way he did. Was it because I was an Asian, a foreigner? Because of my sloppy clothes? Because I fitted a shoplifter profile? I was angry with him, and I was angry with myself that I did not react to his rudeness. It was strange that I had been living in England for about twelve years and felt that those in English society I had come to know — a farming family in Somerset, my friends and teachers in college and university — might have found me different, but did not make me feel I was a complete "other". I even told myself that England was a second home to me. Even the notoriously nasty landlord of our apartment made us feel welcome as long as we paid the rent on time. But this little incident in a small shop was a fissure that opened up a new vista and allowed me to see a crack in what hitherto appeared seamless. It was ironic that I read about "other cultures", thought about southern Thai puppet masters as belonging to another culture, but the shop attendant in Wembley gave me a lived experience of being an "other". Not long after that I left Wembley, left England, and never went back.

It is often said that experiences of cultural clashes are major ingredients for the making of anthropologists. Malinowski and Boas, the great founding fathers of anthropology, were a Pole and a German who had spent their careers in an Anglo-Saxon environment. In my case, the alienation did not strike me in the face until near the end of my stay, but looking back, I suppose a person in my circumstance is always in-between. As a Thai student in a foreign country I was most of the time comfortable with English society and culture, but always felt the tug of obligation to be of service to my own country. Yet back in my own country during my fieldwork, where I observed, rather than lived, and in the years of political turmoil, I constantly felt the watchful eye of the state on my back. As an anthropologist, I always have a distance, a strange distance.

OUT OF UNIVERSITY: ANOTHER FIELD

My life as an academic was comparatively uneventful and I did not come up with any major work that would make my name worthy of being inscribed in the hall of fame of Thai anthropology. So instead of reflecting on why I have been so unproductive, I would rather talk about a recent chapter in my career that turned me from a university instructor into an administrator of a new kind of government agency, and how I struggle between looking back at the academic world with an outsider's perspective, looking forward at public service with reflexivity and often irrelevant critical comments, and trying to stay focused on the present in search of a tolerable identity.

The decisive moment happened six years ago. I will never know what came over me when I said yes to the invitation to become the director of a new organization called the Princess Maha Chakri Sirindhorn Anthropology Centre. The decision surprised all my friends and colleagues because in my twenty years of teaching anthropology at Thammasat University, I deliberately avoided all the usual administrative responsibilities that most professors have to undertake at some time or other. Instead, I confined myself to the limited pursuit of whatever issue interested me at the time, mainly, the identity of folk performers, and the development of Thai anthropology.

The idea to establish the centre was conceived in 1991 by Silpakorn University to honour Her Royal Highness, who was an alumnus with strong interests in epigraphy, archaeology, anthropology, history, and language. The centre was officially opened in 1999. The following year, its status was changed to a public organization, which is a new form of government agency that is designed to be more flexible, small, task-specific, and efficient than regular government departments. The Anthropology Centre was among a new batch of public organizations, together with other institutions such as schools, hospitals, educational accreditation institutes, and so on. When I was elected as director, the centre had been in operation as a public organization for only a year and was at the stage of searching for and defining its identity.

Moving out of the university and entering a public organization under the Ministry of Culture is like doing fieldwork in another tribe. I might have been in the civil service for two decades, but unlike civil servants in other government departments, university professors in those days were left to themselves. We spoke our mind, but nobody listened to us, and we listened only to ourselves and occasionally our colleagues. What a different world I have recently entered, brushing shoulders with high-ranking department heads, ministers, politicians, observing and absorbing a new culture.

Let me begin with a scene from my fieldnotes:

I stepped out of the van just before 9 a.m. The front entrance was already packed with men and women standing, talking, laughing, waiting. The men were in dark suits, women in smart silk outfits. Some men donned colourful silk jackets that made them look like minor stars in traditional dance drama. I was ushered into the front row together with department heads and other top management heads. People in the second row were deputy heads, third row sub-deputy heads, the row behind, the lesser rank. Civil servants know where to stand according to their rank. On one side of the parking space in front of the building stood two shrines ready to welcome the new boss.

9 a.m. The new boss arrived in a motorcade. I could hardly see him because as soon as he got out of his car he was swarmed by men and women who rushed to greet him and stay close to him as if he was a magnet. They all slided together like a wave of dark suits dotted with pretty silk jackets to the Brahman shrine where a woman deferentially presented him with some flower offerings. Then they moved to the land spirit shrine and presumably performed the same offering. Then they all slithered across the parking space to the other end to make an offering to the Chinese shrine. Then the whole crowd swooped past me into the building. I followed but could not squeeze myself into the inner circle. There was some commotion in the hallway. Some people presented the boss with some gifts or some petitions. The new boss was ushered into the lift with his aides and all the mandarins of the ministry. More people went up. I decided to wait. I had been up with the crowd on previous occasions and could visualize the scene. The new boss would go into his office at the auspicious moment set by some astrologer. He would joke a little bit with the press who would have their cameras ready, have photos taken, and greet mandarins who would present him with more flowers, enough flowers to turn his office into a greenhouse. Tables would be covered with paintings, Buddha images, books, and other gifts etc. I wonder if he would remember any face he saw that morning. Then he would take a lift to the meeting room for his first official meeting with the ministry's top people. He would smile, listen to the presentation of the ministry's outputs and plans, then he would begin his speech saying he thinks highly of the ministry even if it is considered a fourth rate ministry in terms of budget allocation. He would then give some broad and vague policies, and assure us he would like to treat us like friends and family members rather than subordinates etc., the usual stuff that makes me think they must have been coached by the same guru. Only there and then would I get to see the face and hear the voice of the new Minister of Culture.

This is of course not a daily experience, but in the past six years I have witnessed the ritual of welcoming a new minister to this ministry no fewer than four times. In fact there have been eight appointments to this office in six years. The year 2008 alone saw four ministers. As a result I have now become rather fluent in the script of the welcome ritual which is an inherent part of Thai bureaucratic culture. Having spent two decades leading an uneventful life of an anthropology instructor, I certainly found my new colleagues to be a new tribe. Though we speak the same language, look very similar, and eat the same kind of food, we belong to different tribes.

CULTURE, ANTHROPOLOGY, OR ANTHROPOLOGIES

If I have to choose an expression for what I am doing right now, as a former university professor among administrators of the culture ministry, and as a former academic in a public institution, that expression would be "building bridges" of many, many kinds.

One primary mandate is to create a space for public anthropology in a society where culture has largely been established as a conservative, nationalistic discourse. Put simply, "culture" is a coinage that developed in the 1940s in the period when nationalist sentiment was strong and state measures were taken in order to achieve "cultural reform"[1] that would make Thailand a civilized country. As a result, the legacy of that period is that culture remains the handmaiden of national values — nation, religion, and monarchy. The role of the recently created Ministry of Culture is described by one writer as a hegemonic identity production. It serves as a site of contestation between conservatively royalist-nationalist perspectives on Thai identity and progressive localists, and international understandings of Thai national identity.[2] The mainstream is the former. In bureaucratic practice, culture is pigeonholed into the tangible — archaeological sites, heritage sites, museum collections, traditional and contemporary fine arts, and the intangible — customs, ceremonies, and religions. Some departments define culture as a way of life and place emphasis on local wisdom and traditional values that should be upheld and instilled in the new generation; others define culture as something that must be guarded from corruption of moral values.

While the bureaucratic paradigm that is predisposed to essentializing culture is one thing, government policy and trends since 2002 have set another paradigm that has recently become a magic word for all policymaking: cultural capital. This term, as used among policymakers, has absolutely no relation with Bourdieu's notion, and simply means commodifying practices of turning culture into cash. Culture is increasingly seen as a ready-made product that serves as a new commodity for a new class of consumers. I went to interview the president of a major commercial bank to ask if anthropology could be of any relevance to the business class. The answer was a definite no: "You have to package anthropology as culture in the manner that the public can digest, you should invoke national pride. No use talking about tribal groups." Claiming that culture is the study of man, his everyday life, and world view, maybe with a leaning towards interpretation rather than hard science, and is critical and reflexive rather than celebratory, may make sense to anthropologists, but not to bankers.

Another aspect of the bridge-building is between academic and public anthropology. The mission of the Anthropology Centre is multifaceted. The royal decree establishing the centre spells out so many objectives that I wonder if anyone will ever be able to accomplish all of them. Basically it is set up to be a documentation centre for anthropological research materials, a research centre to promote research and foster a new generation of researchers, and to bring anthropology to the public to promote cultural diversity and peaceful coexistence. Anthropology for the academic community is something with which I am very familiar, but what anthropology for the public is, or should be, is another matter. The question has led me to "public anthropology".

Borofsky coined the term "public anthropology" in 2000 and defined its objective as "to promote the integration of anthropological perspectives and methods in solving human problems throughout the world; to advocate for fair and just public policy based upon sound research".[3] The idea proposed by the author is to advocate engaging with issues and audiences beyond disciplinary boundaries. Public anthropology may not resolve current dilemmas, but it can offer to reframe or ease them, and by doing so, it hopes to invigorate public conversations with anthropological insights, and reinvigorate the discipline.

Engagement with the public sounds most befitting to an agency that is known as a public organization. But the rationale of setting up public anthropology in the United States is premised on an American context, which is not necessarily the same in Thailand. Borofsky and other advocates of public anthropology argue that academic anthropology is becoming increasingly insular. The rapid expansion of the discipline in the 1960s meant that there is a big enough market for publications written especially for professors and college students. There exists a branch of anthropology called "applied anthropology" and, in fact, applied anthropologists argue that they have been doing what public anthropology claims as their terrain for a long time. But public anthropologists counter argue that they want to push the boundary further by not accepting "problem" issues that have already been framed and handed to anthropologists to engage with, but by reframing the frame itself.

While the debate between public and applied anthropology is ongoing, the divide between academic and applied/public anthropology in the Thai case is not so clear-cut. Anthropology here is a recent discipline, the tiniest and one of the most obscure disciplines of the social sciences. Thai anthropology came to be recognized as a discipline around the 1970s and, even so, at an early stage it was grouped under broader and better known disciplines such as sociology, social welfare, the humanities, or liberal arts. It was not until the 1980s that it began to have a separate identity. Even today it tends to be identified under the umbrella of "culture". So the critical mass of anthropologists in the academic community never happened in Thailand.

But the issue of size of audience aside, the divide between academic and popular outputs, or technical and non-technical writings, is less sharp than in a country such as the United States. Social scientists here practise as public intellectuals and write columns in newspapers, weekly magazines, popular magazines such as *Art and Culture* that reach a wide and lay audience. In addition to communicating with the wider public, the tradition of engaged scholars among Thai anthropologists has been strong on issues of slum dwellers, natural resources, community rights, politics of space and ethnicity, as well as migration, to mention a few.[4] So, contrary to the American case, Thai anthropology has been much involved in current issues and engaged in development work. So the question may not be engagement or non-engagement, but the direction and modalities of engagement.

Public anthropology is a challenge for someone like me who has had little experience with action research or advocacy. This led me to explore some past efforts of implementing public anthropology. Engaging with current issues has a range of practices in Thailand. Creating awareness among the public, or certain sectors of the public, can take the form of training courses or outreach programmes for bureaucrats, the business community, or members of the general public, on peace studies, conflict resolution, or multiculturalism. Some institutions collaborate with the media to produce television documentaries on cultural diversity or cultures of marginal groups. Some collaborate with non-governmental development organizations in dealing with government officials to find solutions for disadvantaged or ethnic groups facing problems of land rights or rights to natural resources.

Some of these experiments reveal that while anthropologists may advocate engaging more with public issues, some members of the public find our contribution too challenging and unsettling to their fundamental social values. One such case was an experiment in the United States in the 1970s. An attempt was made to introduce a year-long course entitled "Man, a Course of Study" for fifth grade students.[5] Books, course materials, and films were prepared by experts to be used in classes. The content of the course focused on the traditional annual migration cycle of the Netsilik (Inuit) with a twenty-one-hour long film produced under the direction of Asen Balikci, an anthropologist and filmmaker. The main purpose of the film was to give students a sense of what it is like to observe another culture. After a year or so, the project was discontinued due to protests by congressmen who had strong objections. While the course was premised on the view that the purpose of education is to equip students to think, question, and conclude based on their own ability to be critical, conservatives viewed education as the process by which students were inculcated with traditional values of society. Such exposure to an alien way of life was regarded as dangerous, unpatriotic, and heretical.

In an attempt to explore some routes to bridge anthropology and the public, I have dabbled in many things, but would like to single out two projects. The first one is engaged local community-based museums and the second is cultural fluency.

LOCAL MUSEUMS AND THE NEW MUSEOLOGY

For most Thais, mentioning the term "museum", which in the Thai coinage means a collection of many things, conjures images of a room cluttered with old, lifeless, and dusty objects. My exposure to museums is somewhat different. By the mid-1990s I was attending a number of seminars, workshops, and study tours that gave me a new understanding of museums and museology.

Museums have a long history in Thailand, but modern museums — particularly national museums supported by the state — began to be established in the early part of the nineteenth century. A new trend began in the mid-1980s when the economy was expanding and Asian countries were being dubbed as newly industrialized countries or NICs. Buddhist monasteries, schools, and government departments were encouraged to establish museums as sites of learning as well as sites of civilization. Private collections began and flourished and some began to be opened to the public. In addition to state encouragement, museums were seen by some intellectuals and development workers as forums for social and cultural development at the grass roots level. This has led to the local museum movement advocating local communities to perceive museums as a means towards discovering their own roots and fostering awareness of local history and pride in tradition. In the past decade, local authorities were allocated more resources and power to oversee a range of public services, including the promotion of art and culture. Because of this, local authorities have become important actors in establishing museums or creating projects to support local museums. So in the past two decades Thailand has experienced a museum explosion, resulting in the existence of more than 1,000 museums all over Thailand, out of which 300–400 are operated by some form of community organization.

This trend and movement led me to initiate collaborative on-site action research and development projects with three local museums located in Buddhist monasteries: Lai Hin Luang Museum in Lampang Province, Baan Don Museum of Nang Yai Shadow Puppetry in Rayong Province, and Tha Phut Museum in Nakhon Pathom Province. These collaborative projects involved a range of research, capacity building, and knowledge sharing activities. Capacity building activities covered topics such as conservation methods, classifying museum objects, and researching and interpreting the history of objects. In order to share experiences and lessons learned from the first three pilot projects in local museum management, workshops were organized for each of the regional museum networks. In addition, the Local Museums Research and Development project publishes a quarterly newsletter titled, *Moving Forward Together* (*Kao Pai Duaikan*), in order to provide yet another forum for sharing knowledge among members of the local museum community network.

In the process of carrying out the research I was led to literature on museum studies and discovered that it was a growing part of cultural studies. When the project started, I was somewhat apprehensive because I had no background in museology or museum studies, which forms a vast body of knowledge of its own. I was already familiar with anthropological views and critiques of museum representation.[6] The concept of "new museology" caught my attention because it aims to create a new space for seeing the museum in a wider context than the technical side of conservation, exhibition, and museum management.[7] But to approach museums from a vantage point of analyst and observer is quite different from engaging with museums and building the capacity for various actors involved. Then I discovered that there were works on the anthropology of museums that develop the concepts of "community-based museums" and "indigenous museology".[8] Our works with the three museums are guided by both these concepts and, at the same time, have dialogues with them.

The idea of the "community-based" museum, which focuses on the participation of the community in all major decisions concerning museum establishment and operation, raises questions about what a community is. What is "community" when one talks about a community-based museum? Who are the museum keepers? Contrary to images of modern museums run by curators and professionals, the groups of people who are involved in the setting up, running, and decision making in monastery museums are monks, schoolteachers, and members of the monastery committee who are connected by a complex web of traditional social relations — kinship, neighbourhood, religious organization, and festival networks — which serve as frameworks for mobilizing community support for, and participation in, museums. However, those who are key persons among museum keepers often have work and education backgrounds that facilitate linkages with outside networks and local administrative bodies that have recently become increasingly critical in securing resources.

"Indigenous museology" is a critique of Western-style museology as implemented by experts and government officials who perceive local and ethnic populations as lacking knowledge and expertise in museums. Christina Kreps argues that standard museology often overlooks the fact that local populations are the owners of their material culture and have, in fact, accumulated substantial knowledge about objects, albeit in a different mode from modern knowledge construction. I was curious to find out what local museum keepers and community members think of museums, what they know, and do not know. What I discovered was that the dividing line between Western and indigenous knowledge, if there is one, is far from clear-cut. It is true that some museum keepers and a number of community members have a lot of tips about object conservation that employ local herbal plants and substances, but their knowledge and practice are not confined within their home locality and they are exposed to new ideas and images that are transported across the globe. Many of the museum keepers have studied, or worked in Bangkok, and are fascinated by the wonders of technology and modern design. Community members, too, have travelled to work in cities or abroad. In Lai Hin village, the economy of the village since the 1980s has been sustained by export labour. As far as the images of museum and exhibition are concerned, indigenous museology may be more of a hybrid.

In addition to knowledge and perceptions of museums, museum practices are also embedded in the context of daily life and activities of monasteries, schools, or private owners. So, for example, it would be hard to find local museums that are open on a nine-to-five basis, or staffed with full-time employees. A lot of them are open during festival and monastery celebrations only, and it is not unusual for museums to be manned by elders or senior citizens. Museum keepers are often members of the monastery committee who perform other services for the monastery and double as museum keepers. In this sense local museums have their own personality, schedule, and community embeddedness that render them distinct from museums run by government departments or large establishments.

Our work with community museums has made me think hard about what kinds of tools or knowledge should be conveyed to, and exchanged with, community members, children, and museum keepers, and what use they will be for capacity building. We have realized that lifting contents and methodology from textbooks to use with the community will not work. Workshops become sites of hilarious scenes. When some researchers who are well trained in conservation techniques put on gloves before moving objects to show that they have to be handled with care, the museum keepers get impatient and unceremoniously scoop them up with their bare hands. Trying to talk about ethnographic methods in collecting life histories of objects, or showing children how to ask their grandmothers questions, becomes quite an art.

While I am not sure how to assess success or failure, or what benchmarks show our achievements, and there are many setbacks and ironies, I had a pleasant surprise recently. In one museum we have been working with for three years, the project culminated in staging a display of the history of the community and monastery. In the process of discussion and making decisions about what to include in the exhibition, I was rather frustrated that the narration and construction of the local history was framed by a standard version of national history. While I would like to see stories of local personalities and local daily life, museum keepers see it as too commonplace to draw the attention of local visitors. They want to portray local personalities as part of national history and emphasize scenes of visits by nationally known figures, such as kings and well-known figures at the national level. Local history is never on equal par with history in standard school textbooks. However, in a recent meeting of museum keepers in the north-eastern region of Thailand, one museum keeper was invited to talk about his work and projects. To our surprise, he said that his next exhibition will be on "the reform of local administration", focusing on the first municipal election since his village had been upgraded to a higher local administrative status. He planned to collect campaign posters, handbills, tapes, etc. to put on display. Though the new choice may not resist national narrative entirely, the museum's focus has shifted from the typical repository of art, antiquities, royal personalities, and national heroes, to a more mundane, local level political event. In this sense this local museum has given its space to representing the daily life experiences, concerns, and initiatives of the local community members.

CULTURAL FLUENCY

Trouble flared up in the deep south of Thailand in early 2004, followed by a chain of hideous violent incidents, some committed by the state, some by unidentified groups. The southernmost provinces on the Thai-Malaysian border are home to the Malay-speaking Muslim population and have a long history of unrest. Violence in this region, dubbed the "southern inferno" by the press, has generated discourses on ethnocultural conflicts, multiculturalism, peace, and conflict resolution. Some of the discourses have penetrated more quickly than actual practice and the conflicts are far from being resolved.

Bringing peace to the south is beyond the capacity of anthropology, but from the beginning it was noticeable that the coverage of southern violence in the Thai press painted negative, stereotypical images of southern Muslims as terrorists, separatists, and religious fanatics, and showed ignorance of their religion and culture. So we initiated a project to improve the cultural fluency of the Thai public, particularly state agents who are posted to the south in different capacities, to be well informed about the multi-ethnic and multi-religious relations of local groups. The output of the cultural fluency project would be a manual to be distributed in workshops and public spaces such as schools and public libraries. Prior to 2004, a few manuals had been produced by government agencies in the deep south, but our idea was to employ some ethnographic methods and materials in the manuals, and focus on inter-ethnic and inter-religious aspects, rather than centring on Muslim culture alone. The project started by enlisting the assistance of the academics of Prince of Songkhla University in Pattani to find graduate students, community leaders, and Muslim scholars to be our informants on various aspects of everyday life. We collected a lot of stories on how different religious groups lived side by side, sharing resources and devising customs that accommodated each other. Then these ethnographic accounts had to be written in a certain format. This was where the problems started and raised many interesting issues about simplifying or translating research materials for the public.

The research team made it clear from the beginning that this was not a manual written by religious experts, and it was not about religious principles, but religions as they were lived and practised. I felt that in the process of listening to story upon story, I learned so much about the dialectics of religious practice. But the interpretation of Islam is a sensitive issue. While we appreciated touching stories of how some local Muslims resented Islamization which may give anthropologists and scholars a humanistic view of the inconsistencies found in popular religious practice, we also knew that to record and publish these stories in the manual would at best be seen as a misunderstanding by the local communities and clerics, and at worst, an attempt to sabotage religion. How far should we go? How much should we compromise?

Another issue was the format of the manual. We realized that academics and the public are different readerships who have different tastes and manners of consumption. What kind of writing could convey facts and ideas collected and analysed by researchers, but still appeal and be digestible for the public? At first we thought of an FAQ format, breaking contents into bite-size sections. Then the writer had the idea of a children's fiction format, which sounded fine except that none of us is a Nobel laureate in literature. Fiction provides a nice framework for describing how Muslim, Chinese, and Buddhist children grow up in nearby villages. Scenes of rites of passage, language, everyday practices, and religious ceremonies can be woven in with ease. But when it comes to contradictory versions of the history about conflicts, it becomes awkward and we are still experimenting with it.

THE AUDIT CULTURE

I began by touching on the "agony" of the present, which I would like to elaborate in place of a conclusion. Experiments of building bridges certainly involve negotiating with the bureaucrat, the state discourse, the academic community, the public. It is a challenging learning process. But my job as director involves not only devising initiatives to meet these challenges, but also running a state organization. When I took the job I imagined that I would be doing similar things to what I always did, with less teaching and more research. How wrong and now naive I was. I am no longer teaching; I am doing a little bit of research; I spend a lot of time and energy struggling to cope with the Thai-style audit culture.

Since the economic crash of 1997, government organizations have undergone a series of restructuring and are increasingly imposed with more regulations to achieve accountability, efficiency, transparency, and many other magic words that define the goals of an ideal organization. I suppose I do not mind the idea of being audited if it challenges an organization to think of its intrinsic worthiness. Even though I find terms lifted from the world of marketing such as "vision", "strategy", "output", and "branding" fit badly with anthropology, I am prepared to negotiate and rethink to make them palatable, meaningful, and relevant to everyday practices. But the process of auditing allows no room for reflection, it is a coercive practice. Government auditing is framed and operated by a class of management experts who are from another tribe yet again and speak another language. They believe in the universality of their tools that can measure the success of anything from hospitals, schools, to research organizations. The emphasis on the power of numbers is so intense that the director of the Office of Public Sector Development Commission once told me in a discussion on the merit of indicators that he believed all qualities can be and must be quantified, end of discussion. These indicators are imposed from the top-down. The civil service commission dictates one set of indicators, the budget bureau another set, their internal auditor another set, another department yet another set. I am not quite sure how many sets of figures we have to deal with, but have to keep watch so that the figure in each box looks reasonable. At the beginning there was resistance from public organizations, albeit feeble, but as time went on, the audit culture established itself down to the local level. Even unconvinced by what it is leading to, the number games continue.

It was in the midst of frustration that I discovered "audit cultures" by Marilyn Strathern,[9] which gave me great relief to learn that the academic and education institutions in other parts of the world view the audit culture with similar ambivalence. It is refreshing to see that the audit culture can be addressed by the familiar discourse of social process, ritual, discipline, panopticon, technology of the self, and so on. But I like the idea that we are witnessing a new culture in the making, and I have first-hand experience observing and taking part in it fully. Whether this new culture will make an organization more competitive and transparent, organizational members more competent, or whether they will be more stressed and distrustful, may be a new problematic for me to reflect on. My fieldnotes keep growing; perhaps I shall have ample field data with me in whichever field site I find myself in next. In this sense the phase when the Anthropology Centre crosses my path can be seen as an extended ethnographic fieldwork of organization in the age of audit culture in which I have the curious role of observer, participant, and scriptwriter.

Notes

1. See discussion in Jiraporn Witayasakpan, "Nationalism and the Transformation of Aesthetic Concepts: Theatre in Thailand during the Phibun Period" (PhD dissertation, Cornell University, 1992); Scot Barme, *Luang Wichit Wathakan and the Creation of a Thai Identity* (Singapore: Institute of Southeast Asian Studies, 1993); Yukti Mukdawichit (in Thai) *Reading Community Culture: Poetics and Politics of Community Culture Ethnography* (Matichon, 2005).
2. Michael Kelly Connors, "Ministering Culture: Hegemony and the Politics of Culture and Identity in Thailand", *Critical Asian Studies* 37, no. 4 (2005): 523–51.
3. Robert Borofsky, "Public Anthropology: Where To? What Next?" *Anthropology News* 41, no. 5 (2000): 9–10.
4. For studies of communities of slum dwellers, see several works by Akin Rabibhadhana, for example, (in Thai) *Rise and Fall of a Bangkok Slum*, rev. ed.

(Phumpanya Foundation and Qualitative Research Association, 1993.) For natural resources and community management of natural resources, politics of space and ethnicity, see works by Anan Ganjanapan, Yos Santasombat, and Pinkaew Luangaramsri, for example, Anan Ganjanapan, ed. (in Thai) *Dynamics of Community Resource Management: Thailand Situation* 2 vols. (Thailand Reseach Fund, 2000); Yos Santasombat (in Thai) *Power, Place, and Ethnic Identity* (Princess Maha Chakri Sirindhorn Anthropology Centre, 2007).

5.   Jay Ruby, "Anthropology as a Subversive Art: A Review of *Through These Eyes*", *American Anthropologist* 107, no. 4 (2005): 684–93.
6.   See Richard Handler and Eric Gable, *The New History in an Old Museum: Creating the Past at Colonial Williamsburg* (Durham and London: Duke University Press, 1997).
7.   Peter Vergo, *The New Museology* (London: Reaktion Books, 1989).
8.   Christina F. Kreps, *Liberating Culture: Cross-cultural Perspectves on Museums, Curation and Heritage Preservation* (Routledge, 2003).
9.   Marilyn Strathern, ed., *Audit Cultures: Anthropological Studies in Accountability, Ethics and the Academy* (Routledge, 2000).

References

Barme, Scot. *Luang Wichit Wathakan and the Creation of a Thai Identity*. Singapore: Institute of Southeast Asian Studies, 1993.

Borofsky, Robert. "Public Anthropology: Where To? What Next?" *Anthropology News* 41, no. 5 (2000): 9–10.

Connors, Michael Kelly. "Ministering Culture: Hegemony and the Politics of Culture and Identity in Thailand". *Critical Asian Studies* 37, no. 4 (2005): 523–51.

Ganjanapan, Anan, ed. *Dynamics of Community Resource Management: Thailand Situation* (in Thai). 2 vols. Bangkok: Thailand Reseach Fund, 2000.

Handler, Richard and Eric Gable. *The New History in an Old Museum: Creating the Past at Colonial Williamsburg*. Durham and London: Duke University Press, 1997.

Kreps, Christina F. *Liberating Culture: Cross-cultural Perspectives on Museums, Curation and Heritage Preservation*. London and New York: Routledge, 2003.

Mukdawichit, Yukti. *Reading Community Culture: Poetics and Politics of Community Culture Ethnography* (in Thai). Bangkok: Matichon, 2005.

Rabibhadhana, Akin. *Rise and Fall of a Bangkok Slum* (in Thai). rev. ed. Phumpanya Foundation and Qualitative Research Association, 1993.

Ruby, Jay. "Anthropology as a Subversive Art: A Review of *Through These Eyes*". *American Anthropologist* 107, no. 4 (2005): 684–93.

Santasombat, Yos. *Power, Place, and Ethnic Identity* (in Thai). Princess Maha Chakri Sirindhorn Anthropology Centre, 2007.

Strathern, Marilyn, ed. *Audit Cultures: Anthropological Studies in Accountability, Ethics and the Academy*. London and New York: Routledge, 2000.

Vergo, Peter. *The New Museology*. London: Reaktion Books, 1989.

Witayasakpan, Jiraporn. "Nationalism and the Transformation of Aesthetic Concepts: Theatre in Thailand during the Phibun Period". PhD dissertation, Cornell University, 1992.

7

A NON-LINEAR INTELLECTUAL TRAJECTORY
My Diverse Engagements of the "Self" and "Others" in Knowledge Production

Yunita T. Winarto

I was bent on becoming an anthropologist when I decided to pursue my university education. My keenness to study anthropology was in part due to my interests in the subject of *Ilmu Bangsa-bangsa* (Science of Nations) at high school, during the Sukarno era. Enrolled in the cultural stream, I remember how the textbook used in this subject made me curious as to why there were no Indonesian anthropologists cited in this book on Indonesian society. As only Western anthropologists were cited in the textbook, I wondered why no Indonesians were studying Indonesia? Inevitably, my question was not due to the ideas of "Orientalism", which was unheard of then. Rather my concerns were influenced by my strong nationalist sentiment, which was a result of being raised to see myself as a part of a heterogeneous Indonesia. An ethnic Chinese and a Catholic, my father was a fervent nationalist, strongly involved in the political and social integration of ethnic and religious minorities into the Indonesian nation state during the Sukarno era. Influenced by my father's political inclinations, I was myself an active participant in various social and youth organizations at this time. The turmoil created by the Gestapu (Gerakan Tiga Puluh September) *coup d'état* of 1966 and the ideological pogroms which took on ethnic overtones, strongly motivated me to believe in the need for Indonesians to think about their own society. Although qualified to enter the more prestigious science stream during my senior high school, I chose instead to study the cultural stream. This was precisely because of my sentiment, youthful idealism, and my interest in dance and art performances. This decision marked the beginning of an intellectual journey that would lead me to study anthropology when I entered university.

Forty-four years have since passed. I can no longer easily presume that being an anthropologist is merely about studying my own society, or about relating my own self with the heterogeneity of Indonesian society. Instead I have gradually come to understand that "self" and "Other", "ethnicity", or any identity category are not to be understood merely within the confines of nation state boundaries. Over the years I have gained richer experiences, which have shown me that learning about one's "anthropological self" or even about "anthropologized Others" is not an easy and straightforward matter. It is not simply about applying theories and concepts learnt. Rather, I have learnt that knowledge is the result of a constant struggle to bring together theory/methodology and empiricism. This has been a journey through different habitats, disciplinary boundaries, and academic settings, wrought by personal and wider social circumstances, both intentional and unintentional. My intellectual journey is hence the result of a dialogical and dialectical interaction between my changing self and "Others" whom I have encountered — both subjects of my study, as well as people whom I have interacted with in my academic life and personal life — as I moved across different social, disciplinary, institutional, and spatial frontiers.

What follows is a narration of my intellectual journey as I tried to live up to my roles: first, as an anthropologist; then as a more interdisciplinary based human ecologist; and finally, as an academic professor with a mandate to merge the social sciences and humanities. It was through this latter role that I learnt about, and helped advocate, interdisciplinary and alternative "collaborative ethnographic studies" in the study of Southeast Asian and Indonesian peoples and their agricultural environments.

FROM "MONO-" TO "INTERDISCIPLINARY" PERSPECTIVES: BEING A HUMAN ECOLOGIST

As Wallerstein (2004) has pointed out, history plays a role in shaping the development of social science. Indeed not only history, but I would also add geography, had a lot to do with the kind of anthropological training I received for my bachelor's and magister's (equivalent to a master's) degrees in Indonesia. Indonesia's history as an ex-colony has had a significant impact on its education system and inevitably the development of its social sciences. It first adopted the Dutch university system, but switched to the American system in 1975 as part of its attempt to shake off the yoke of colonialism. Caught between this transition, my initial anthropological training was not only influenced by both the Dutch and American systems, but it also landed me with two equivalent bachelor degrees in anthropology.

I first enrolled in the Department of Anthropology at the Padjadjaran University in Bandung in 1969. This was at a time when the Indonesian university system was still modelled after the Dutch system. The first degree took five years; students were awarded a bachelor after three years of study, and a doctorandus (equivalent to a master's) upon completion of the five years. However, less than four years into my studies, after getting my bachelor's degree in anthropology, I got married and followed my husband to Jakarta in 1972. There I enrolled at the Universitas Indonesia (UI) in order to continue with my undergraduate studies. My study was, however, altered a year later when my husband had the opportunity to pursue his master's degree (MBM) in Manila.[1] Joining him,[2] I was able to take non-degree programmes with the Department of Sociology and Anthropology, at Ateneo de Manila University, and to resume my studies at UI in 1975 on our return to Indonesia. When I returned, the university system had changed to the American system. The first degree had been shortened to four years and a bachelor degree was awarded on completion of this. Being caught in this transition explained why I had two equivalent bachelor degrees when I completed my studies at UI in 1980.

Inevitably my anthropological training was influenced by the schools of thought found at both the universities I attended. At Padjadjaran University I was grounded in ethnographic methods as great emphasis was placed on actual fieldwork experience. This training emphasized the understanding of "Others" through fieldwork. It was a training which made me realize that I was also part of the Others whom I studied. I would say that it ingrained in me a strong awareness about reconciling formal anthropological knowledge with everyday realities as an ordinary Indonesian. My experience at UI taught me about classical anthropological theories. It also exposed me to wide knowledge on different regions of the world beyond Indonesia, such as the rest of Southeast Asia, Polynesia, Melanesia, and Africa.[3] Eventually, as I went on to my magister's studies at UI, and later for my master's and PhD studies abroad, my journey would take me from monodisciplinary to interdisciplinary awareness. This occurred as I became interested in human ecology and environmental science, which enriched my perspectives as an anthropologist. Let me begin with my initial training at Padjadjaran University.

KNOWING "OTHER" CULTURES: DOING ETHNOGRAPHY

The Department of Anthropology at Padjadjaran University, Bandung, where I was enrolled, was known for its ethnographic tradition. The anthropological curricula at this university placed much emphasis on ethnographic methodologies. My training there grounded me in the participant-observation method as actual fieldwork experience formed an important component of my studies. Students were required to conduct fieldwork each semester where we lived with the Others whom we were supposed to study in order to understand their cultures.[4] Yet, studying Others who were fellow Indonesians was not easy for me due to my own position as an ethnic Other in Indonesia. As I conducted my fieldwork exercises each year, I became increasingly perplexed by the gap between anthropological notions of the Other and my own complex position as a fieldworker studying the Others — who were fellow Indonesian citizens just like me — not to mention my own dislocated position as an Other within Indonesian society. My sensitivity to the problematic of the Other was due to circumstances of my personal life and my father's political activism.

I grew up in a family where my father was actively involved in social-political movements under the Sukarno era. When I was a senior high school student in the mid-1960s in Malang (my home town in East Java), Sukarno's national assimilation policy was at its peak. My father was appointed as a member of the state's initiative organization specially targeted to assimilate citizens of Chinese descent into the Indonesian "nation". I understood the state's policy then as one which viewed mixed marriages between those of Chinese origin and Indonesian people as an ideal means to produce what the state called "assimilation". As I learnt about anthropological concepts of "assimilation" and "acculturation" during my undergraduate studies, I began to question whether the state's notion of mixed marriages between different ethnic-cultural-religious persons could really be an effective way for "assimilation" to occur. Would a new kind of cultural entity be formed from mixed marriages? As I attempted to link conceptual knowledge and empirical reality, I ended up researching for my undergraduate thesis, the sociocultural life of a community of Chinese farmers who had married local natives in Tangerang — an area west of Jakarta. In this study I found that state assumptions about mixed marriages were wrong. If the local natives were women married to Chinese Confucian men, they and their descendants would become part of Chinese kin groups and communities, practising Chinese traditions. Religion became the point of reference in either sustaining or abandoning Chinese traditions, and not the mixed marriage per se (Pranaja 1972).

When I wrote my second thesis after moving to UI, I again sought to make links between the empirical realities I witnessed and formal theories which I had learnt. This time, however, I chose to work on the topic of capital formation. My choice of research topic was influenced by the strong push for development during the Soeharto regime at this time. There was then a state policy to improve small-scale enterprises. I became interested in this policy and wanted to find out the extent to which entrepreneurial culture could be developed amongst local small-scale entrepreneurs. My husband's profession in management probably had also some influence on my topic. I ended up researching small scale Betawi furniture shop owners, focusing on their processes of capital formation (Winarto 1980). At UI, there was an anthropological tradition to emphasize a holistic perspective when examining cultural aspects; hence my study of capital formation amongst small scale furniture shop owners had placed my analyses within the larger context of the sociocultural lives of these people.

The change in the Indonesian university system in the mid-1970s meant that my anthropological curricula changed towards American anthropology as various sub-disciplines within anthropology were introduced at UI.[5] Courses such as the anthropology of religion, political anthropology, medical anthropology, economic anthropology, psychological anthropology, and ecological anthropology soon dominated the UI curricula. Such an institutional shift would eventually influence my intellectual trajectory as the fields of human ecology and medical anthropology became available for the masters programme during the early 1980s — a programme which I would eventually enter.[6]

BECOMING INTERDISCIPLINARY: LEARNING TO BE A HUMAN ECOLOGIST AND ENVIRONMENTAL SCIENTIST

Having obtained my undergraduate degrees and following my husband's move to Medan, the capital of North Sumatera province, I was appointed a faculty staff at the newly formed department of anthropology at the University of North Sumatra in Medan in 1980. Coincidentally at this time the Soeharto government established a Ministry on Environment and Population. The minister of this new ministry issued a decree that all national universities would establish a centre for Environmental Studies in order to assist his ministry with research on environmental and population matters. In line with this push, a special training programme on human ecology titled "Man and Biosphere" was held in Bogor in 1981. This was jointly sponsored by the United Nations and the Indonesian Institute of Science in Bogor. I participated in this training programme on the basis of my ongoing research on the communities surrounding a plywood company in Besitang, North Sumatra. For the first time I not only learnt about human ecology but also about other disciplinary perspectives on the interaction between people and the environment. Lecturers and facilitators at this training programme came from various disciplinary backgrounds, and both Indonesians and foreigners from Southeast Asia participated in this programme. One of the main speakers at this programme was Andrew P. Vayda, a professor in human ecology from Rutgers University, United States. Vayda emphasized the importance of understanding and explaining human action, which affected the environment and vice versa, without the need to dwell on each disciplinary vantage point. On the contrary, by explaining the puzzling questions of the interaction between people and environment as the focus of study, any relevant conceptual and methodological tools originating from various disciplines could be drawn upon. Participating in that programme and responding to Vayda's invitation to pursue my studies in human ecology was a turning point in my scholarly life.

My decision to pursue further studies in human ecology[7] was, however, not as straightforward as I had thought. Although Vayda invited me to pursue my graduate studies in human ecology at his university and even helped me to get a Ford Foundation scholarship, I had to forgo this opportunity as I had to accommodate my husband's plan in furthering his studies in the United Kingdom. With two young children, it was hard to think about living separately on two continents. Since it was not possible for my husband to change his plan, I decided to withdraw my application to Rutgers University. However, as I did not want to give up my plans totally, I came up with a solution that enabled me to continue with my study plan while accommodating my husband's plans.[8] I decided to remain in Indonesia for two years before joining my husband in the United Kingdom. During this time (1982–84), I enrolled in the human ecology course in the magister's programme at UI while looking for an opportunity to further my studies in the United Kingdom. My search landed me in a Masters of Science in Environmental Technology course at the Imperial College of Science, Technology, and Medicine in London where I studied from 1984–85.[9]

My enrolment in the magister's programme at UI marked my serious engagement with the field of human ecology. This programme helped me move away from the functional-structural-systemic perspectives procured during my undergraduate studies to an actor-based approach focusing on human practices and/or its consequences on the environment (see Vayda 1983; 1996; Borofsky 1984). Vayda's ideas played a significant role in enabling me to move across disciplinary boundaries to explain the interaction between people and environment. His studies on the interaction between people and the forest in East Kalimantan influenced my perspective in approaching social-cultural-environmental phenomena as part of an "unbounded" entity, always in flux, full of diversity, the products and consequences of people's varied and dynamic actions (see Orlove 1980; Vayda 1983; 1996). My exposure to this new perspective made me realize that a phenomenon under study need not be bound merely to time or spatial dimensions, which further enriched the holistic perspective that I had picked up in my anthropological training at UI (Vayda 1983; 1996). Overall, my initiation into human ecology opened my eyes to interdisciplinary perspectives and the need for understanding the characteristics of ecosystems and problems under study. It helped me see that any emerging phenomenon is complex and not as simple as studying Others on the basis of their cultural universals.

Even though I had become more interdisciplinary in my intellectual disposition after my magister's programme, when I began my master's studies in environmental science — a programme with an interdisciplinary curriculum — in the United Kingdom in 1984, I felt like I was losing my grip as a social science scholar on the one hand, yet not firmly rooted enough in the more positivist/scientific approach of environmental science, on the other. This course was delivered over two terms: In the first term I studied various subjects encompassing social scientific perspectives and natural and life sciences' approaches to the environment; in the second term, I learnt about ecological management instead of studying about pollution, water management, and energy. My earlier studies of ecosystems helped tremendously in enabling me to follow some of the concepts introduced during my master's programme. The central difference between my master's and magister's studies, I would say, was that the latter made it clear from the start that it was a component of the anthropological sciences. My master's programme, however, offered a wide span of perspectives, including environmental law, environmental policy, geography, energy, biology, health, agronomy, and many others. To have a background in anthropology, with its constructivism/ideographic perspective, and yet pursue my studies in a positivistic/nomothetic perspective, led me to feel as if I was constantly jumping between two different paradigms.

Because I felt increasingly confused, by the second half of my master's programme I decided that I would keep my identity as an anthropologist — which, by the way, is reflected in my master's thesis — even as I had to prioritize agro-ecological frameworks throughout my studies (Winarto 1985).[10] For my master's thesis, I decided to bring in the narratives of the farmers whom I had observed and interviewed for my previous magister's thesis so as to enrich the human dimensions in my agro-ecological analyses. My supervisor's remark that, "Your thesis is very lively", was something I would never forget as I had previously been unsure if I was on the right track. His positive response strengthened my conviction about sustaining my identity as an anthropologist even as I continued to incorporate analyses from the natural sciences into my work. It became a way through which I could take on other scientific domains without losing my scholarly identity. This experience taught me that to be a human ecologist, an anthropological background can be a significant help. Yet, as I worked with, and learnt from, the world of "Other" scholars from other disciplinary backgrounds and encountered interdisciplinary ways of looking at the world, my anthropological "self" was also slowly changing as I shifted away from earlier assumptions. Such cross-disciplinary enrichment would continue to shape my PhD experience as I went back to the field of anthropology.

FROM "LOCAL" TO "REGIONAL" SETTINGS: BEING AN INDONESIAN SCHOLAR IN SOUTHEAST ASIAN STUDIES

I pursued my PhD studies at the Department of Anthropology, Research School of Pacific and Asian Studies (RSPAS), at the Australian National University (ANU) under the supervision of Professor James J. Fox. It was at ANU that I became aware of the study of regions beyond the world of anthropology. At ANU, professors and students are known not only for their research subjects, but also for the regions they study. Whilst the majority of foreign and Australian students were studying countries other than their own — a popular area being Indonesia — most Indonesian students, including me, were studying "ourselves". I was at first not bothered by this fact until one day when a fellow student asked my colleague, a Balinese anthropologist, "Why is a Balinese studying the Balinese?" I was surprised by this question as I had never thought that this was problematic. Although I was aware of the problem of value bias when one studies one's own society, I did not think that "Others" referred only to people outside one's own nation. Farmers, craftsmen, villagers in my studies were also part of the Others since I was different from them. I remembered then, that my interest to study my own people — on the basis of nation state boundaries — first began when I learnt about *ilmu bangsa-bangsa* (science of nations) during senior high school. But more than twenty years later, located at a university with an emphasis on studying regions and being questioned by fellow graduate students on why we — the Indonesian students — were studying our own societies within a nation state boundary, I began slowly to question my own restrictions in only studying Indonesia. It would be ten years after my PhD before I would venture out to study societies beyond Indonesia.

My PhD studies led me to carry out lengthy and detailed ethnographic fieldwork. I spent at least twelve months doing fieldwork — a trademark of PhD research requirements at ANU. I had a lot to thank my supervisor James Fox for for his reminder that I should not be bothered with applying the theories of others in my work. He insisted that a PhD student should be able to formulate her/his own theory and concepts from the ethnographic data collected. His remark haunted me throughout my work. I was unsure if I would be able to achieve this, as up until then I had always applied someone else's theory in my work.

My PhD research was on farmers' knowledge and practices under Green Revolution technologies as two planting seasons a year became feasible. Meticulously following each of the four planting seasons in 1990–92, my research investigated farmers' responses to pest outbreaks in rice farming, as well as their understanding of agro-ecology and ecosystems as they combined their existing knowledge, Green Revolution technologies, and the newly introduced Integrated Pest Management knowledge and strategies (see Winarto 1996). My previous training in human ecology and environmental technology proved helpful for writing a thesis on the formation of farmers' knowledge, which challenged the dichotomy between "scientific" and "local" knowledge. I showed how in situ knowledge on farming gradually became a true mixture of both "local" knowledge and "scientific" ideas. This thesis was later published as *Seeds of Knowledge* (Winarto 2004).

On the completion of my PhD degree, I returned to teach at UI, and at the end of 1998, was appointed the editor-in-chief of the journal *Antropologi Indonesia*. This was at a time when the Indonesian nation state experienced a drammatic change. It changed from the New Order regime towards the "reformation period" following the "May 1998 riot" and the toppling of Soeharto who had been president for more than three decades. Soon afterwards, a series of conflicts between different ethnic and religious groups in various parts of Indonesia erupted. At the same time, the new scheme of regional autonomy was also being set up. As the editor-in-chief of the journal, I was motivated to do something in that crucial period. Within a corridor as a scientific journal on Indonesia, I thought that examining the current turmoils of the Indonesian people was what the editors could and should do. I decided to organize a series of national and international symposia in collaboration with my colleagues from Indonesia, as well as the "Indonesianists" from abroad, to discuss and analyse the disturbing sociocultural phenomena occurring in Indonesia. As a result, we were able to publish a number of volumes of the journal *Antropologi Indonesia* and proceedings of the symposia, which examined a wide range of sociocultural problems that had emerged in Indonesia over the last two decades (the end of the twentieth century and beginning of the twenty-first century; see Winarto and Pirous 2008).[11] I perceived these works as something worthy I could produce for my own nation and people as an Indonesian anthropologist.

In the final year of my term as the editor-in-chief of the journal, I eventually had the chance to expand my research on farming beyond Indonesia, to the rest of the Southeast Asian region. This decision was in part motivated by the fact that the Farmer Field School model I was examining in the period of 1990–2000, which originated from the Indonesian National Integrated Pest Management Programme in Indonesia, had become widely adopted in other parts of Asia, Africa, and Latin America.[12] I wanted to understand and compare similarities and differences in the transmission of knowledge amongst farmers in the different countries and within the region. My endeavour to learn about farming in other Southeast Asian countries was facilitated by funding provided by the Toyota Foundation's SEASREP.[13] From this funding, I was able to carry out comparative studies in countries such as Vietnam, Cambodia, and Thailand. In addition, opportunities for visiting fellowships to the Centre for Southeast Asian Studies at Kyoto University and the Asia Research Institute at the National University of Singapore helped initiate me into networks of Southeast Asian scholars. In venturing to study countries beyond the nation state boundary of Indonesia, I was able to widen and enhance my understanding of farming and the dialectics between local and scientific knowledge in the Southeast Asian region. In turning to countries in Southeast Asia, I also developed an identity as a Southeast Asian scholar, rather than solely an Indonesianist.

Certainly, knowing other countries, apart from my own, was advantageous to my career. In 2004 I was invited to be a visiting professor of Southeast Asia by the Division of International Area Studies at Pukyong National University, in Busan, South Korea. On my return from Korea, I began coordinating a course on Southeast Asian ethnography at UI. However, an appointment as Academy Professor in Social Sciences and Humanities under the auspices of the Royal Netherlands Academy of Arts and Sciences

(KNAW) and the Indonesian Academy of Sciences (AIPI) in 2006 saw me moving to the Gadjah Mada University (UGM), Yogyakarta (2006–09), before returning to the University of Indonesia (2009–11) where I am currently working. This career move provided me with an opportunity to bring together academic knowledge and actual agricultural development programmes in Indonesia.

FROM AN ANTHROPOLOGIST TO AN ACADEMIC PROFESSOR: DEVELOPING A "NEW SCHOOL OF THOUGHT"

My appointment at UGM warranted me to improve the academic culture and scientific curiosity amongst social scientists and humanities scholars, as well as to strengthen the role of the social sciences and humanities in Indonesia. Hence, from being an anthropologist-cum-human ecologist, I had to take on the role as a professor of the broader disciplines of social sciences and humanities. Concomitantly, the UGM Graduate School invited me to develop a new school of "interdisciplinary thought" via synergizing the natural-environmental sciences and the social-humanities sciences through an interdisciplinary course for graduate students — a job that was right up my alley.

In order to achieve the goals with which I had been entrusted, I adopted three strategies: introducing interdisciplinary perspectives to graduate students; bringing newer visions of the human sciences to a nationwide audience; and finding alternative research methods whereby researchers and farmers could mutually learn from each other and shape knowledge.

My first step towards meeting my job's mission to develop a "new school of thought on the basis of an interdisciplinary study" was to introduce a new graduate course promoting such outlooks at the UGM Graduate Programmes. I learned from the Environmental Science Masters programme at UGM, which is strongly based on the study of ecosystems, of the division of their programmes into three different parts: the biotic system, the a-biotic system, and the sociocultural system. My aim on the other hand was to help foster awareness amongst students that human beings should not merely be seen as a component of the ecosystem, but as core agents utilizing and affecting natural resources. All aspects of the ecosystem are intermingling and affecting one another, criss-crossing parts of the ecosystem and their wider environment. For this purpose, I formulated a course titled, "Agency, Knowledge, and Nature" as an elective subject for students coming from diverse disciplinary backgrounds at Gadjah Mada University.

the final report was collaboratively written, farmers and ethnographers sat together, discussed the substance of the report, and wrote report items according to each other's interests. Although I finally edited and translated the report (Winarto 2007*b*), to my knowledge this was the first ethnographic report in Indonesia ever to be co-written by ethnographers and their study subjects.

Two collaborative films came out from these two research projects: the first is titled, "*Bisa Dèwèk*" (We Can Do it Ourselves, 2007) based on my collaborative work with Indramayu farmers, where this title was chosen by the Indramayu farmers themselves; and the second, *Lelakoné Menur* (The Story of Menur, 2007) which focuses on a group of female farmers from the research in Gunungkidul. Today, the farmers have used these two films as part of their campaigns to get state attention on their farming preferences and needs.[14] This strategy proved successful as the farmers managed to get official attention. The Indramayu farmers even received financial support from the Regency Agricultural Office to run the Participatory-Plant-Breeding Farmer Field School themselves. Both groups of farmers are indeed very proud of the films we produced together. This happy ending greatly improved my confidence that Indonesian social and human scientists could move forward to work with, and help address problems faced by, marginalized populations in the country (see Brookfield and Gyasi 2008, pp. 224–25).[15]

CONCLUSION

My simple interest to study the people of my society whom I saw as part of my self during my youth has undergone complex twists and turns over the last forty-odd years. From concerns with my own position as Other while studying my anthropological Indonesian Others during my fieldwork experiences in my undergraduate days, I eventually went on to discover broader interdisciplinary ways of thinking as I took up the study of human ecology and environmental science. As I learnt about insights from the natural sciences and tried to incorporate them into anthropological approaches, my original anthropological assumptions shifted as I tried to bring together the actions of human subjects and the forces of ecosystems. This shift marked an important turning point in my intellectual trajectory, and I gradually carved a new position for myself as an anthropologist-cum-human ecologist. My encounters with the study of regions during my PhD studies sparked my interests in studying other societies beyond my own several years after completing my PhD programme.

Yet, in 1998 my academic life brought me again to my own society as the editor-in-chief of *Antropologi Indonesia*. It was during this tumultuous time in history that I felt I had to do something worthy for my nation and people. Again, my latest appointment in the 2000s stimulated me to keep pursuing my work in pushing for better integration between the human and non-social sciences in natural resource management for the needs of my own country and society. Moving across the boundaries of the social sciences and humanities, my research interest on the interaction between people and environment led me to this latest opportunity to help foster interdisciplinary dialogues amongst the Indonesian academe. It also led me to meaningful relationships with the farming communities whom I studied and out of which an innovative model of "collaborative ethnography" through film production was born. The film and reports co-produced by farmers and researchers became an effective means to disseminate the world views, wisdom, and needs of the local farming communities. As the farmers experience ongoing problems in their lives, including, recently, climate change, my work in developing "collaborative ethnography" has also moved on to address these contemporary problems.

As I look back, the subjects of my research have revolved around my own society and/or Southeast Asia. Yet, the sources of ideas and theories which I have drawn upon, or become inspired by, have come from all parts of the world, both from Western and non-Western locales. I have found it hard to talk about anthropological knowledge in terms of "self" and "Other". However, it is equally hard to talk about knowledge in dichotomous terms of the "West" and the "non-West". Rather, looking at my own experiences, I see how my intellectual journey has been shaped by an intermingling of perspectives, theories, concepts, and empirical realities.

Notes

1. MBM stands for Master in Business Management, a degree at the Asian Institute of Management (AIM).
2. I took non-degree courses at the Ateneo de Manila University and the University of the Philippines while in the Philippines from 1973–74.
3. Two founding fathers of the Department of Anthropology, Faculty of Letters, Universitas Indonesia, were a Dutch anthropologist (J.B. Ave) and the first Indonesian anthropologist (Koentjaraningrat), who got his master's degree from Yale University, the United States and doctoral degree from the University of Indonesia. At the time of Koentjaraningrat's study at Yale University, the Human Relation Area Files was being expanded. Koentjaraningrat contributed the Javanese ethnographic materials to the Files.
4. At the time I was an undergraduate student (1969–72), each student had to pass a bachelor examination in the form of two kinds of exams. The first, an oral

exam, was based on theoretical and conceptual matters, and the second was a minor thesis each student had to write. After completing the bachelor degree, the student could move up the ladder to the graduate courses.

5. In the mid-1970s up to the early 1980s, a number of the first-generation anthropologists of the Universitas Indonesia took their master's and doctoral degrees in the United States. Each of them took elective courses in the subdiscipline they chose, e.g., in Religious and Urban Anthropology, Medical Anthropology, Folklore, and Biological Anthropology. Several second-generation anthropologists also pursued their studies in the United States with different specializations, e.g., Human Ecology and Social Organization. Outside the United States, England, Australia, the Netherlands, and Japan became the places for further training in anthropology for the other second- and third-generation anthropologists. The rest pursued their studies at the Universitas Indonesia.

6. The second major shift was the state's decision, through the hands of the Ministry of National Education and Culture in early 1980, to move each department of anthropology from the Faculty of Letters (it is now called the Faculty of Humanities, or Fakultas Ilmu Pengetahuan Budaya in Indonesian) to the Faculty of Social and Political Sciences in all universities in Indonesia. However, not all departments of anthropology obeyed the ministry's decree (e.g. Gadjah Mada University in Yogyakarta and Udayana University in Denpasar, Bali).

7. The late Professor Koentjaraningrat also played an important role in persuading me to pursue my study in human ecology. At that time (in early 1982), my husband was about to return from Medan, North Sumatra, to his institute in Jakarta, and had a plan to take his PhD degree in the United Kingdom. Knowing of my possibility of accompanying my husband abroad, Professor Koentjaraningrat and Professor Andrew P. Vayda wanted me to get my PhD degree in human ecology under Professor Vayda's supervision at his university (Rutgers University, the United States).

8. At the same time, the Graduate Programme in Anthropology at the Universitas Indonesia decided to run a graduate course specializing in human ecology with Professor Andrew P. Vayda as one of the lecturers. I decided to apply to that course while my husband was spending his one year in the United Kingdom for his literature studies (1982–83) and before returning to Indonesia for his research (1983–84).

9. Understanding my application withdrawal, but still concerned with helping me, Professor Andrew P. Vayda approached Professor Gordon R. Conway from the Centre for Environmental Studies, Imperial College of Science, Technology, and Medicine in London. Professor Conway was carrying out his agro-ecological research in Indonesia in collaboration with Indonesian scholars under the auspices of the Ford Foundation Regional Office in Jakarta. The underlying reason argued by Professor Vayda was the need to enlarge my knowledge of the ecological perspective from the standpoint of the ecosystem approach. At

last the Ford Foundation approved their support for my MSc programme in London.

10. For my MA thesis at the Imperial College of Science, Technology, and Medicine, I had used part of my research data from my magister's programme, together with other data on large dam development projects in the world, as I used agro-ecological analysis to analyse "drawdown" impacts on agriculture. Drawdown zones are open areas at the edge of a reservoir during the dry season when the reservoir water recedes for a period of about half a year. My magister's thesis was on state responses to, and planning over, secondary consequences of large-scale development projects, using the case of the drawdown area in the dam development in Wonogiri, Central Java, which was utilized by local people for crop farming. The large dam was built by evacuating a large number of people from the fertile areas of Bengawan Solo valley (see Winarto 1984).

11. See the volumes of *Antropologi Indonesia* of 1999–2004 and the proceedings of the 2000, 2001, 2002, and 2005 international symposia of the journal *Antropologi Indonesia*, published by the Department of Anthropology, Faculty of Social and Political Sciences, Universitas Indonesia.

12. The Farmer Field School or "a school without walls" is a training programme for farmers that lasts for an entire planting season (about four months). Each week, about twenty-five farmers get together to carry out observation, data collection, and analysis of their field conditions, and make decisions on what to do next in their planting strategy. The aim is to grow a healthy crop and to move away from any recommended strategy that is not based on field conditions and agro-ecosystem analysis. In relation to the National Integrated Pest Management Programme in Indonesia, the "school" aims to change farmers' practices in the injudicious use of pesticides that kill pests' predators. The Farmer Field School has now become a model of training and empowers farmers in various aspects of crop farming (see Fox 1991; Dilts and Hate 1996; Pontius et al. 2002; Winarto 2004).

13. SEASREP stands for Southeast Asian Studies Regional Exchange Program, funded by the Toyota Foundation.

14. The farmers in Indramayu regency organized film screenings in thirteen local districts spread all over the regency in 2007 to disseminate their capabilities and to gain the government's official support and recognition. The farmers themselves named their strategy "*Ngerogrog wité, murag uwohé*" (Shaking the bottom of the trees, the fruit is falling down).

15. My confidence was strengthened when — towards the final year of my position as the Academy Professorship Indonesia in Gadjah Mada University — I received a call from a farmer-fisherman in South Sulawesi with whom I did my first collaborative interdisciplinary work in rehabilitating and conserving mangroves at the end of 1990s. He expressed his happiness and gratitude that he would soon receive the Indonesian state's prestigious award in preserving the environment (*kalpataru*). He gained the award as someone successful in restoring

the mangrove forests in his area in South Sulawesi, a successful story of my first initiative in a kind of "collaborative-interdisciplinary" work with the local people and experts from other disciplines. These experiences made me feel confident to move forward in another "collaborative-interdisciplinary" work by facilitating farmers in their responses to the current global climate change. I know that I still have to travel a long journey to move along this path for the betterment of our planet and people now and in the future.

References

Borofsky, R. "The Cultural in Motion". In *Assessing Cultural Anthropology*, edited by R. Borofsky. New York: McGraw Hill, 1994.

Brookfield, Harold and Edwin A. Gyasi. "Academics among Farmers: Linking Intervention to Research". *Geoforum* 60 (2009): 217–27.

Dilts, R. and S. Hate. "IPM Farmers' Field Schools: Changing Paradigms and Scaling-up". *Agricultural Research and Extension Network* 59*b* (1996): 1–4.

Fox, James J. "Managing the Ecology of Rice Production in Indonesia". In *Indonesia: Resources, Ecology, and Environment*, edited by J. Hardjono. Singapore: Oxford University Press, 1991.

Lassiter, L.E. "Collaborative Ethnography". *Anthronotes* 25, no. 1 (2004): 1–14.

———. *The Chicago Guide to Collaborative Ethnography*. Chicago and London: University of Chicago Press, 2005.

Orlove, B.S. "Ecological Anthropology". *Annual Review of Anthropology* 9 (1980): 35–273.

Pontius, J., R. Dilts, and A. Bartlet. *From Farmer Field School to Community IPM: Ten Years of IPM Training in Asia*. Bangkok: FAO Community IPM Programme. Food and Agricultural Organization of the United Nations Regional Office for Asia and the Pacific, 2002.

Pranaja, J.T. "Akibat-akibat Sosial Budaya dari Perkawinan Tjampuran antara Masyarakat Indonesia Keturunan Tjina dengan Penduduk Asli di Desa Neglasari, Tangerang". BA (*Sarjana Muda*) dissertation. Bandung: Padjadjaran University, 1972.

Sen, A. *Development as Freedom*. Oxford: Oxford University Press, 1993.

Shiva, V. *Monocultures of the Mind: Perspectives on Biodiversity and Biotechnology*. London: Zed Books and Penang: Third World Network, 1993.

———. *Biopiracy: The Plunder of Nature and Knowledge*. Boston, MA: South End Press, 1997.

Vayda, A.P. "Progressive Contextualization: Methods for Research in Human Ecology". *Human Ecology* 11, no. 3 (1983): 265–81.

———. *Methods and Explanation in the Study of Human Actions and their Environmental Effects*. Bogor: Centre for International Forestry Research and World Wide Life for Nature, 1996.

Wallerstein, I. *The Uncertainties of Knowledge*. Philadelphia: Temple University Press, 2004.

Winarto, Y.T. "Pembentukan Modal dalam Usaha Kerajinan Kayu di Pondok Pinang: Suatu Analisa Antropologis". *Sarjana Sastra* dissertation. Jakarta: Universitas Indonesia, 1980.

————. "Perencanaan dan Konsekuensinya dalam Proyek Pembangunan: Kasus Proyek Bendungan dan Kawasan Surutan pada Bendungan Wonogiri". Magister's dissertation. Jakarta: Universitas Indonesia, 1984.

————. "An Ecological Analysis on the Consequences of Development Projects: A Case of the Drawdown Area in Dam Development Projects in Third World Countries". MSc dissertation. London: Imperial College of Science, Technology, and Medicine, 1985.

————. "Seeds of Knowledge: The Consequences of Integrated Pest Management Schooling on a Rice Farming Community in West Java". PhD dissertation. Canberra: Australian National University, 1996.

————. *Seeds of Knowledge: The Beginning of Integrated Pest Management in Java*. Monograph No. 53. New Haven: Yale Southeast Asia Council, 2004.

————."Menuju Paradigma Baru Pembangunan di Indonesia? Peranan Ilmuwan Sosial dan Humaniora". Professorship inauguration speech presented at the launching of the Academy Professorship Indonesia (API). Yogyakarta: Gadjah Mada University, 21 February, 2007*a*.

————. *Bisa Dèwèk*: Farmers' Empowerment through Film Production and Dissemination. [Masroni, Warsiyah, Nurkilah, Taningsih, I. Sumitro, Wartono, Muadib, Y.T. Winarto, R. Ariefiansyah, H. Adityasari, H. Prahara, S. Ma'arif, and Z. Rosidi]. Manuscript: Report to the Embassy of Finland. Depok: Undergraduate Program, Department of Anthropology, Faculty of Social and Political Sciences, Universitas Indonesia and IPPHTI-Indramayu, 2007*b*.

Winarto, Y.T. and I.M. Pirous. "Linking Indonesian Anthropology in Asia". Paper presented to the panel on Asian Anthropologists at the conference of The Asia Pacific and the Emerging World System. Ritsumaikan Asia Pacific University, Beppu, 13–14 December 2008.

Ethnographic Films

The Undergraduate Program, Department of Anthropology, Faculty of Social and Political Sciences, Universitas Indonesia and the Indonesian Integrated Pest Management Farmers Alliance, the Regency of Indramayu. *Bisa Dèwèk* (We Can Do it Ourselves). Supported by the Embassy of Finland in Jakarta and the Academy Professorship Indonesia in Social Sciences and Humanities. Depok, 2007.

The Academy Professorship Indonesia in Social Sciences and Humanities, the Graduate School, Gadjah Mada University and *Menur* Women Farmers Group in Wareng, Gunungkidul. *Lelakoné Menur* (The Story of Menur). Yogyakarta, 2007.

8

NEGOTIATING BOUNDARIES AND ALTERITY
The Making of a Humanities Scholar in Indonesia, a Personal Reflection

Melani Budianta

As an academician who teaches American literature and researches Indonesian literature and cultural studies, I have been accustomed to switching fields and exploring new territories. Yet, to write a chapter in a book on Southeast Asian Studies scholarship is like trespassing into somebody else's terrain — an awkward condition, which is not unfamiliar in my personal as well as professional history. I have internalized this disciplinary interpellation of asking myself "what right have you to be here". I remember my days as a graduate student at Cornell in the early 1990s, sneaking into James Siegel's and Benedict Anderson's famous Southeast Asian studies seminars, while writing my dissertation on the Representation of Otherness in Stephen Crane and the American 1890s. "You really don't need this course", said Professor Siegel, who was keen in keeping his class list rather short. Nevertheless, I stayed.

Years after returning home, I found my credentials once again questioned. It was during a recess in one of the meetings of the Majlis Bahasa Indonesia/ Melayu and Majelis Sastra Asia Tenggara — a three country (Malaysia-Brunei-Indonesia) intergovernmental body founded to promote Malay language and literature in the region. A Brunei representative looked at me rather closely, politely asking whether I am of Chinese descent. When I answered that I am a Peranakan, he went on to say, "But you must surely be a Moslem, right?" He was quite incredulous, when I answered negatively, confusing his understanding of what it required to be a national representative of a Malay body.

The list of similar experiences is uncannily long. Imagine strolling into a solo painting exhibition in Balai Budaya, one of the most prestigious art galleries in Jakarta in the 1970s, to see a pictorial expression of anger against "the way the Chinese-Indonesian abuses Indonesian language". (With no other guest around, the artist, from Surabaya, offered generously to lecture me on the subject, seeming quite aware of my physical ethnic affinity with the group he was attacking.) Once, in the mid-1960s, I went to a traditional arts performance with my sisters, where we found ourselves among crowds who, every half-hour, stood up and shouted unfamiliar patriotic yells, looking suspiciously at three timid girls who were awkwardly glued to their seats.

Wrong discipline, wrong place, wrong company, wrong ideology, wrong identity, wrong language, but, most blessedly, right timing. Had I lived much earlier, I might have gone berserk. Nowadays we witness the flourishing of scholarly terms such as "hybridity", "blurred genres", "transborder identity", "transnational/translational" condition, and "the postmodern diaspora", which, not only make sense of, but also valorize, the ambivalent, contradictory, and mismatched positions as "alternative" spaces for artistic creativity as well as political or ideological resistance.

However, romanticizing this position theoretically does not make daily life easier. In a time of conflict between Dayak and Madura in the late 1990s, families of mixed marriages suffered prosecution and separation. Before the peace deal of 2005, Acehnese women who initiated All Acehnese Women's meetings were intimidated by both warring sides, accused of betrayal and treason. In a safer academic zone, a colleague of mine, who is doing interdisciplinary gender studies of indigenous law, had her professorship deferred, because she was considered neither firmly entrenched in the discipline of law, nor sociology. While humanities scholars eagerly embrace deconstructive critical strategy, campus politics as well as cultural politics in Indonesia at the dawn of the twenty-first century keep on drawing rigid boundaries.

At the heart of the matter is this constant reworking of relations between theory and praxis, between ways of knowing and the condition of living —which are, at certain moments, complementary, at other moments, contradictory, coloured by gaps and ambiguities. How do the politics of daily life shape knowledge and cultural formation, and vice versa? And how does academic scholarship construct reality at a certain time and place in history?

Such complicated questions cannot be thoroughly answered by a microscopic personal account as narrated in this chapter. Moreover, as the accumulated scholarship on "border studies" has indicated, and the accounts of Dr Wong Soak Koon in Chapter Five of this book show, my hybrid personal experience and scholarly position is not at all unique. Besides, one might ask, what relevance does literary and cultural studies work, done by an Indonesian scholar trained in American studies and English literature, have for Southeast Asian Studies scholarship? From the perspective of area studies specialization, the answer might be *nil*. Yet, as Goh Beng-Lan explains in the introduction, by examining the ways knowledge is constructed in the lives of a number of Southeast Asian intellectuals, this book aims at mapping certain cultural and intellectual dynamics in the region at a certain historical juncture. Filling in a tiny slot in that broader perspective, I will narrate my engagement with the changing intellectual discourse and political climates of the day in my work as a (mismatched) humanities scholar, in thematic stages.[1]

Concurrent themes emerge here as in other chapters, that is, the use of Euro-American knowledge in making sense of local difference, the issue of gender, ethnic identity and identity politics, the complicated negotiation with the state and civil society forces, and the continuous quest to find alternative space for critical and interdisciplinary dialogue — among other things through the construction of an inter-Asian forum. This chapter elucidates how the process of knowledge and cultural formation — of knowing oneself in the context of others (the West, the Southeast Asian, the national self) — in Indonesia in the last two decades is heavily invested with boundaries making and crossing, of Othering and mirroring, which is facilitated or complicated by scholarship.

STAGES OF KNOWLEDGE MAKING: A RECOLLECTION

To talk about the way knowledge was formed in one's personal history, is to look back with the frames of the present, as it is not possible to recuperate the blank slate — if such condition ever existed. From the unfinished and unchartered process of knowledge making, I select three moments which were crucial to the development of my present projects. My engagements with American Studies, the Absurdist theatre, and Multiculturalism were three stages of my knowledge formation in graduate studies and teaching from 1980 to the late 1990s. These stages served not merely as the disciplinary baskets for the assortment of knowledge I amassed as a scholar in the humanities. They are also used here as metaphorical frames to describe how disciplinary subjects connect with daily experiences, and form the very lenses through which I construct meaning out of life around me.

THE INDONESIAN-AMERICAN STUDIES EXPERIENCE

If a number of American-scholars-turned-Asian-specialists received their cross-cultural initiation from peace corps or other intercontinental exchange programmes, I owe my training in area studies to a Fulbright scholarship, which introduced me to a master's programme in American Studies in the 1980s. Having finished an undergraduate thesis on the absurdist style of British playwright Harold Pinter at the then Fakultas Sastra, Universitas Indonesia (UI) in 1980 (supervised by the late theatre actress–scholar Toeti Indra Malaon), I plunged to the depths of the myth and symbol school of American studies at the University of Southern California (USC), Los Angeles. A half-hearted marriage (which ended in divorce not long after I graduated in 1981), between the English and History Department, the American Studies programme I undertook comprised half of courses in history, half in literature, as well as a summer school programme of interdisciplinary American Studies seminars on certain topics such as the 1920s or 1930s. I learned all I should know about U.S. literature and history from the courses of Dr Luther Luedtke, Dr Jay Martin, and the late Dr Richard M. Rollins, but got my actual "ethnographic" experience from the streets of downtown Los Angeles.

Staying in a slum area between Adams Street and 24th Street in Los Angeles, my husband, my two-and-a-half-year-old daughter, and I spent our first Christmas Eve in the United States, listening to what we thought were firecrackers, but turned out to be gunfights between the neighbouring black and Hispanic gangs. Living as a family on the scholarship budget for a single student, we experienced the pressure of holding on below the poverty line, in a super rich country. While discussing Richard Slotkin's *Regeneration Through Violence* in the classroom, we were mugged, watched people being mugged, and experienced racial harassment by L.A. police who suspected us to be Vietnamese shoplifters. Befriended by followers of Rev. Moon, we visited their brothers-and-sisters dormitory, sat through their promotion rituals and dinners, and discovered their recruitment strategy among immigrants and troubled teenagers. It was there that I learned the contradiction between secularism and religious fanaticism, and felt the irony of capitalism masked as spiritualism.

On the other side of the coin, our family also experienced how it was to live below the poverty line amongst the richer Indonesian community in Los Angeles. With few Indonesian families of graduate scholarship recipients in this community, we were a minority among rich Indonesian undergraduates, who were sent by their parents to this expensive American private university nicknamed the "University of Spoiled Children". Working then as a correspondent of the Indonesian *Tempo* news magazine, my husband was appointed to do a report on the way Indonesian students abroad celebrate their national holiday on 17 August 1980. As we were living in a temporary condition of being diaspora, we all shared this sense of heightened nationalism, as well as nostalgic feelings for the language, food and sights of home, which bonded us Indonesians together. However, it was soon apparent that our different lifestyle served as the gulf that separated the rich from the poor: the condominium lifestyle on the outskirts of the city — fancy cars, television in each room, a ten-times-higher monthly allowance — contrasted greatly to how my family and I were living. Weaved into my husband's report on the patriotic speeches and nationalist celebration of the 17 August activities of Indonesian students in Los Angeles, were offhand descriptions of this opulent lifestyle. As the *Tempo* editors in Jakarta put their scissors and glue to work, what came out in the next editorial was not the enthusiasm of the national holiday celebration, but the fancy lifestyle of Indonesian yuppies abroad.[2] For the rest of our stay in L.A., from October 1980 to January 1981, our daily life was full of terror, not from our American slum dweller neighbours, but from the rich Indonesian brotherhood. Midnight silent calls, stones thrown at the window, threats to revoke our Indonesian passports, and finally the "kidnap" and trial of my husband by about forty Indonesian students in a remote condo. Fortunately, a notable diplomat from the Indonesian Embassy, Pruistin Atmadjasaputra and her husband, poet Ramadhan K.H., knew us well. She intervened, refusing to bow to the demand not to renew our passports, and stayed throughout the "trial" to prevent physical abuse against my husband.

Our stay in Los Angeles in 1980–81 provided me with the experience of being the external Other, as well as the internal Other. It was eye-opening for me as an Indonesian, who was socialized since childhood to put the "belief in God" as the number one principle to adhere to, to see how the freedom of belief is practised in the United States at the cost of being a social hazard. America in the 1980s also alerted me to the gaps and contradictions, as well as the gender, race, colour, and class blindness of the discipline. There was a discrepancy between the myth and symbol paradigm hegemonic in 1980 within the discipline of American Studies — "the American Adam", "the Machine in the Garden", "the Virgin Land", and the sordid lived experiences of ordinary Americans, especially the urban poor. On the issue of democracy, it was quite disheartening to witness how media power captured voters during

the presidential election of 1980. Apart from learning new things about
America, I discovered that being Indonesian in Los Angeles was nothing
exquisite ("Indonesia? It must be near Indiana?"), but the brand of your car
("Indonesian? Oh, they drive fancy cars!") was a more telling marker in a
city at the end of the American-dream rainbow.

THE ABSURDIST THEATRE: COLD WAR AND THE
NEW ORDER INITIATION

Returning home from the United States in 1981 to teach Toeti Indra
Malaon's "Theatre of the Absurd" undergraduate seminar, I encountered
a peculiar experience. The second week after I introduced the history of
absurdist theatre, a student from another department requested to audit
that day's lecture. He began by reciting some lines from the Qur'an and the
first principle of Pancasila (Belief in God), and told me he suspected that
my lecture "contained elements of atheism, which is against Pancasila and
Islamic teaching". After convincing the intruder that I was disseminating
knowledge and teaching critical analysis, not preaching atheism, I was left
alone to resume my teaching.

What I experienced in the classroom that day was a reflection of the
academic environment during the New Order government in the 1980s
(Budianta 1997). I discovered that the student visiting my class was an
activist from the student senate, who had just completed his P-4 training, a
package of anti-communist ideological indoctrination initiated by the New
Order government.[3] It was quite shocking to see a student defending the state
ideology so strongly. A decade before, when I was still in the freshmen year,
I witnessed the anxiety of senior students in the same faculty preparing for a
street rally to protest against the New Order management of economic and
political affairs during Japanese Prime Minister Tanaka's visit.[4] By the late
1970s, however, campuses were "normalized" — the term for encouraging
students to refrain from political activism and turning their attention
instead to "professionalism". Earlier in the mid-1970s, a term called SARA,
an acronym for *Suku, Agama, Ras* and *Antar Golongan*, was introduced by
Admiral Soedomo, then the head of Operational Command of Security and
Order or Pangkopkamtib, to keep "sensitive issues" of ethnic, religious, racial
and class (or societal relations) out of public debate.

Apart from this small incident, however, the rest of my teaching career
was unhampered by any other intervention. Another person did raise questions
about my teaching Absurdist theatre, but it was in a different context.
Released from Buru Prison in 1979 after fourteen years of detention for his

alleged affiliation with the communist wing of a literary organization, the writer Pramoedya Ananta Toer lived in relative isolation in his Utan Kayu residence, not far from our rented house. My poet husband befriended him in spite of stern warnings from other literary friends, and from the head of the neighbourhood administrative unit (called RT or Rukun Tetangga) — who said that intelligence officers noted down the regular visits he made to Pram's residence. One afternoon I was quite surprised to see the face of this famous author peering into the big glass windows of our rented house. He said he was wondering why my husband missed his regular visit. My husband not being home, I let the renowned guest in for a short chat. Being a lecturer himself once,[5] he asked the subject of my teaching. He frowned at my answer, asking why I should teach such a nihilist literature. My explanation could not have satisfied him, for he kept insisting that a good work of literature must have a clear mission.

It was not a coincidence that Indonesian theatre in the 1970s (up to the early 1980s) was coloured by the absurdist style. Sapardi Djoko Damono (2007) noted that realism, which dominated the Indonesian literary scene in the 1950s–60s towards the end of the Sukarno era, was replaced by avant-garde experimentalism. The Cold War era in the Indonesian literary scene was won by those favouring freedom of expression; "l'art pour l'art, not aesthetics governed by politics". The New Order gave ample space and support for the "ideologically correct art" to grow, but in time the red scare and communist bashing atmosphere was getting to the point that it was unbearable. Bakdi Soemanto (in Sapardi 2007) indicated that Putu Wijaya's ground breaking absurdist play, Aduh, evoked the haunting atmosphere of the red scare. Sunu Wasono (in Sapardi 2007) recounted his experience watching the adaptation of Waiting for Godot in the campus theatre, which reminded him of the tediousness and absurdity of going through the P-4 anti communist indoctrination.

During this time, I was also involved in promoting the American Studies master's programme at my university. Indonesia in the 1980s was led by President Soeharto to enter into fast paced developmentalism, each phase consisting of a five-year progress plan, transforming urban landscapes with high-rises, toll roads, modern department stores, and real estate. The modern lifestyle looked towards America as a model. Indonesian universities took up the American-style credit system; chief economists of the New Order were American-trained, thus leading to the coinage of the term "Berkeley-mafia". To compete as a sustainable academic programme in this era of professionalism and developmentalism, the American Studies MA programme at UI was widening itself to a greater pool of adult students, from a limited pool of literary and history lecturers to diplomats in training, entrepreneurs, politicians. Eager to have a degree for promotion prospects and workable knowledge of "what makes America tick", the mixed audience was not quite ready for the critical, analytical approach of the humanities I was trained in. Academic disciplines in Indonesia were compartmentalized from the third grade of senior high school into sciences and social-humanities disciplines, the first acquiring the status of being superior and more important than the latter. I spent seven years doing the Sisyphean task of teaching Benjamin Franklin, Emerson, and Thoreau to professionals who considered American literature irrelevant to understanding things American. In 1988, with the help of another Fulbright scholarship, and the endorsement of Professor Sandra Siegel from the Department of English, Cornell University, who was a Fulbright visiting scholar at UI in the mid-1980s, I managed to take a break to do doctoral work in English literature for four years.

MULTICULTURAL LESSONS

While preparing for my trip, I met an American visiting scholar at UI who gave me personal advice to study in any university in the United States, except Cornell. Then he recounted the 1969 black students' takeover of one administrative building in Cornell to create Afro-American Studies.

In 1988 when I went to Cornell, no guns or takeovers were necessary to let graduate students study what they regarded as important for their education. True, the English department was still Europe-oriented, with heavy doses of the British classics, but the curriculum was balanced with a small, but good, selection of American literature courses. There was Henry Louis Gates' slave narrative classes, Chandra Mohanty's postcolonial theory, and Hortense J. Spiller's contemporary American literature. In the four years I was there, there was once a graffiti protest against the WASP (White Anglo-Saxon Protestant) orientation of the curriculum, but the department gave students a chance to propose topics for graduate reading classes. Students did write a petition to add "cultural studies" in the list of fields for concentration, and met outside classes to read Third World texts. I took Jonathan Cullers' famous literary theory class, which gave a foundation for deconstruction and postmodern theories. Literary studies were transformed by critical reading, which unravelled how relations of power and ideology informed literary texts.

In the late 1980s, multicultural sensitivity was being advocated in U.S. campuses as well as in the communities, especially in student family housing, where I stayed with my kindergarten-age son and middle-school-age daughter. I once attended a meeting organized by a students' multiracial association to prepare a "cross-cultural sensitivity workshop". Much to my embarrassment one evening the campus family housing superintendent called a special parents' meeting because she overheard my son making a racist remark towards a neighbour's son in the playground. It turned out that he had called out to his friend, who came from mainland China, "You, Chinese!" I apologized for my son's behaviour, but refrained from telling her the complicated story of our own Peranakan background. The boys were quite oblivious to any insults. Having a Javanese father, my son was always trying to figure out which part of his body was Chinese. He must have considered his friend Chinese from head to toe (Budianta 2003a). In the 1990s, the term "political correctness" (PC) was in the mass media — used derogatively by the conservative right — to refer to the atmosphere of social coercion to repress offensive behaviour and language, especially pertaining to one's (racial, ethnic, gender) identity. While multiculturalism as a paradigm opens up a wealth of cross-cultural issues unseen before by objective-structuralist approaches, my experience in the United States showed me that multiculturalism as a liberal discourse was not without its problems and contradictions.

While PC and multiculturalism produced public discussion in the United States and attempted to change certain language and behaviour, the SARA policy in Indonesia had created an effect of silencing any discussion of "sensitive issues". When I used multiculturalism as an entry point to talk about the diverse voices of American women writers in my literature classes after my return from the United States in 1992, my students alerted me to what was missing in Indonesian texts. After reading Maxine Hong Kingston, *The Woman Warrior*, they asked why the condition of Indonesian Chinese was never taken up by Indonesian writers of Chinese descent. When reading Leslie Silko's *Ceremony*, they thought of the marginalized Dayak, Irianese, and the unheard voices of the marginalized communities. Reflecting on self-hatred and the phenomenon of blacks "passing" for whites in Toni Morrison's *Beloved*, I shared my own personal struggle to accept "Chineseness" as a part of my identity. For my students and I, reading American literature in the framework of multiculturalism in Jakarta in the 1990s was a way to reflect critically on our own cultural problems, a precious opportunity in the political context of the time (Budianta 2000a).

This is not to say that critical voices from the arts, humanities, and social sciences were not available at that time. Since the mid-1980s, a number of Satya Wacana Christian University lecturers had been known among their students as "crazy lecturers" who stimulated students with critical thinking, and among them were Ariel Heryanto, Arief Budiman, and George Aditjondro.[6] From the mid-1980s Ariel Heryanto had written critically about Indonesian middle classes, the ideology of developmentalism, totalitarianism, and language, power and social change, and the students' movement, thereby opening the ground for cultural studies scholarship in the next decade. As it was random and unsystematic, state censorship did leave loopholes and cleavages for critical intellectual space — as long as one did not use it to attract public attention. The thirty-two year rule of the New Order government was also marked by the tightening or loosening of state control of freedom of expression, depending on the given socio-political conditions. In theatre, playwright W.S. Rendra performed his highly popular 1970s plays, which satirized corrupt government and the abuse of power, leading to his eleven-month imprisonment in 1978, and almost a decade of repression (Cohen 2008). With a number of exceptions, however, mainstream literary works in the New Order era were characterized by muteness on the issue of ideological and cultural differences.

THE MOMENT OF CRISIS: KNOWLEDGE FORMATION IN POST-REFORMASI INDONESIA

The explosive event of the Reformasi (1998) and its aftermath was a transformative moment for many Indonesian scholars. Although resentment towards the New Order government had escalated slowly but steadily through the years since General Soeharto obtained political control in 1966, no political and social scientist was quite prepared for the way things developed in the events of the late 1990s. Drastic changes occurred in the span of one year, from the extended economic crisis of 1997, followed by multidimensional crises and socio-political turbulence, to the dramatic end of the thirty-two-year rule of President Soeharto in May 1998. This volatile period challenged scholarly thinking in many ways. Indonesian academia, long established through the disciplinary separation of the sciences from the social-humanities since the secondary school level, were ill-equipped to handle complex multidimensional problems. The regional monetary crisis of 1997 was very much entangled with local socio-political repercussions, which overwhelmed finance and economics consultants. The social sciences, which for three decades had served the dictates of developmentalism, were similarly unprepared to deal with the chaotic backlashes of "progress", especially the animosity of intergroup conflict following the economic crisis, flared by the rhetoric of racial and religious differences which had, for three decades, been suppressed by military vigilance.[7] Artists and scholars in the arts and humanities were shocked into silence to witness the cruelty of the May looting of Chinese-owned shops, the victimization of urban poor children burnt in the department stores, and to hear the news of the brutal mass rapes of Indonesian Chinese women in the chaos of mid-May 1998 (Budianta 2003*b*).

GENDER AND POLITICAL ACTIVISM

The news of the mass rapes was especially troubling, causing conflict and division among scholars. The horrific acts of sexual brutality were mystified by denial and silence. Like a surrealistic event in a Gabriel Marquez novel, after the chaotic days from 12 May to 15 May of looting, rioting, and racial violence in Jakarta, which sent terror and an atmosphere of civilian war throughout Jakarta, not even a single trace of talk about the more than one hundred alleged cases of mass rape of Chinese women and children, could be found. Women and human rights activists, who directly dealt with the victims and witnesses refused to reveal any identification to protect them from further victimization.[8] At the same time news of the rapes had caused waves of pan-Chinese solidarity abroad. The government and the House of Representatives issued a denial, accusing activists of fabrication. Intellectuals and scholars used to positivistic methods of scientific investigation sided with the government in their scepticism and were complicit in pressuring for legalistic and scientific evidence.

The tragic events of May 1998, however, marked a new beginning in the history of Indonesian women's movements (Budianta 2003*c*). The violence against women and children, as well as racism and violence against the urban poor, resulted in the politicization of women from heterogeneous backgrounds. The seed of the movement was sown by an initiative called the Voice of Concerned Mothers, a strategy designed by a number of feminist scholars to launch street demonstrations to protest against the mismanagement of the government economic policy in February 1998. This campaign, using motherhood as a platform, and focusing on the rising price of powdered milk, managed to draw the sympathy of thousands of mothers from lower middle class communities across the metropolis who joined the cause. The interaction between these women and the feminist activists — although not without tension and conflict — formed the basis of solidarity for the May victims. Women of diverse background — class, religion, ethnicity — were more ready to forgo the need for evidence, for they knew what was at stake.

In this tumultuous period, many armchair women scholars felt a strong sense of emergency, and left the safety of their campuses to join street demonstrations, volunteer on forums, network for campaigns against violence, launch disaster relief initiatives, do research, investigate violence, and counsel victims and witnesses. As with many fellow women scholars, my own life as a scholar was transformed by the call of this emergency activism. The Reformasi years of 1998–99 gave me the chance to put theory into action, to suffer from frustration, disillusionment, and to renew my faith in engaged scholarship.

The May rapes forced me to face the issue of identity, and jeopardized my stance of academic neutrality. "As a woman and a Chinese Indonesian, why don't you speak up?" Somebody urged me. This kind of remark, uttered in a gesture of sympathy, was disturbing in conflicting ways. On the one hand, it was based on an essentialist notion of racial (and sexual) identity and the assumption of partisan identification on that basis — which I found unacceptable. On the other hand, I could not deny the fact that the brutal acts of the rapes were based on the double processes of Othering and "scapegoating" (of Indonesian Chinese, and women), something which cannot be condoned.

External circumstances dictated my way out of this double bind. The May rapes had drawn women from different religious, ethnic, class, and political backgrounds to work together through an interfaith, peace and non-violence movement. The rapes illuminated structured gender violence used in conflict areas and military zones from Aceh to Timor Leste. At the same time, however, the overseas Chinese heated reaction against the May rapes pushed the racial issue to the foreground so much that it complicated the interracial relations on the ground. In this kind of circumstance I opted, in agreement with many women activists, to use women as a political space for protesting against the crime, at the cost of downplaying — though not necessarily negating — the racial issue.[9]

The whole process of responding to the violence served as a political education for many women. A number of women's organizations emerged in these Reformasi years, and one important organization that emerged as a civilian response to the May rapes was the National Commission on Violence against Women. My involvement in women's activism in the Reformasi years was significant in moulding my scholarship. Working for the Division on Violence against Women of the Tim Relawan untuk Kemanusiaan (Voluntary Team for Humanity), I was often sent as a facilitator to discuss issues of racial and gender violence for high school children, religious communities, and neighbourhood gatherings. The processes of learning politics in everyday life confirmed for me the important position of engaged scholarship, and broke the walls between theory and praxis, scholarship and activism.

REGIONAL AWAKENING: INTER-ASIA NETWORK

It was in June 1998 — amidst the heated tension of women's activism — that I got an invitation to present a paper on the discourse of cultural identity and globalization in Indonesia during the 1997 economic crisis at a conference organized by the Asian Regional Network for New Alternatives (ARENA) in Taipei, Taiwan.[10] Formed in the mid-1980s by a number of scholar-activists in the region (among others, Arief Budiman from Indonesia), this organization "is a regional network of concerned Asian scholars — academics, intellectuals, activists, researchers, writers, and artists — which aims to contribute to a process of awakening towards meaningful and people-oriented social change".[11] This first encounter of a regional forum marked the beginning of my entrance into the inter-Asia network, opening my eyes to the wider issues of the region. Two years later at the ARENA congress of 2000, I was invited to join the organization formally as a fellow, and to serve both on the editorial board of ARENA and a new regional cultural studies journal (*Inter-Asia Cultural Studies*). A collaborative research project on responses towards authoritarianism in Indonesia and Malaysia initiated by Ariel Heryanto in 1998–99 helped me to connect with women activists in Malaysia and develop a comparative perspective.[12]

These regional interactions widened my horizons towards Asia and Southeast Asia. Interacting with diverse Asian scholar-activists with different strategies to pursue various agendas — from gender and economic justice, to the environment — was an important stage in advancing my interest in an interdisciplinary approach. The atmosphere of collegiality as well as the internal difficulties in managing diversity in a regional body such as ARENA served as a source of inspiration and lesson learnt for local activism.

On a personal level, my ARENA activity brought me to Beijing in 2001, and that first trip to mainland China helped me to come to terms with the issue of my "Chineseness". Being in the "homeland" to which I do not feel any cultural attachment, yet as Ien Ang (2001) argues, always made out by the state and others to beckon to you, helped me to internalize psychologically what I understood in theory, that race is a social construction (Hall 1993).[13] In the myriad of diversity among the Chinese population, my Indonesian tongue could be heard as one of hundreds of Chinese dialects. There I was as alien or as local as I might have been elsewhere. Among activists from Hong Kong, Taiwan, the Philippines, and Thailand, many of whom were in some way or another connected to the diasporic history of regional migration, I arrived home in homelessness.[14] In other words, I came to reconcile with my hybrid cultural position, taken not as given, but — without a sense of curse or of guilt — as an engaged point for action.

TRANSBORDER POSITION AND INTERDISCIPLINARY WORK

In a time when identity politics was on the rise and borders were more rigidly drawn globally as well as locally — I found it important to underline transborder positionality. When the thirty-two years of centralistic and authoritarian government were ended by the Reformasi movement, Indonesia entered a phase of rapid decentralization. The adoption of the Regional Autonomy Act in 2001 sped up the process, and was not without conflict and contradiction. On the one hand the policy of regional autonomy answered the demand for the distribution of political and economic power to the district level. On the other hand, the implementation of the policy often benefited the powerful local elites. The spirit of regional autonomy was also accompanied by the rise of *putra-daerahism*, an ideology of nativism which excluded the non-native population from local political power. In the euphoria of regionalism, the search for authentic local identity often overlooked hybridity and the cross-cultural processes which had occurred in history. Women activists were also concerned that the return to tradition often meant the return to patriarchy (Budianta 2006).

At the global level, the attack on the World Trade Center on 11 September 2001, followed by President G.W. Bush's war on terror campaign and the ensuing U.S. assault on Iraq, opened up a new page in world history after the end of the Cold War. These global issues had strong repercussions on intergroup dynamics in Indonesia, as they fuelled anti-U.S. or anti-West sentiments from right-wing Islamic groups. Usually made by citing Samuel P. Huntington's thesis on the clash of civilization, this anti-West discourse was often translated into condemnation of progressive Islamic groups, which were depicted as pro-West or Western-influenced, such as the Jaringan Islam Liberal (Network of Liberal Islam), and other moderate groups which make up the majority of the Indonesian population. In this time of tension, being Western-trained can be risky, as one's critical voice in representing the West can be hijacked by the extremist within. Similarly, voicing criticism about one's own country can be interpreted as an act of betrayal (Budianta 2007*d*).

The clamour of conflicting voices, using religion, race, or ideology as a political platform was not new in Indonesian history. Indonesia in the 1950s was seen by many scholars to be the heyday for the democratization process, which was unfortunately cut short by the "guided democracy" policy of the late President Sukarno, who used it to mask his strategy of totalitarian control. Sukarno's effort in orchestrating political harmony between nationalism, religion, and communism (Nasakom) suffered a heavy setback in the Cold

War–effect of the bloody communist cleansing in 1965. In 1998, after Soeharto stepped down from power, the Reformasi movement reset the democratization cycle in a different time and context. With such a past to remember, NGO activists, scholars, feminists, and cultural workers were eager to find alternative ways to manage conflicting differences with lower costs.

Islamic thinkers such as the late Nurcholis Madjid introduced the term *masyarakat madani*, a synonym for civil society, contextualized within an Islamic paradigm, modelling the peaceful and democratic society in the city of Madanniah during the Prophet Muhammad's time. The extreme right took issue with the term "liberalism" and "secularism/secularization". Among humanities scholars and cultural activists, the term "democratization" and "multiculturalism" became catchphrases. Although no single concept offered a panacea for fledgling democratization processes, I often used discussion forums on these concepts as entry points to speak of a critical stand which continuously transgresses essentializing cultural borders circulating in the current dominant discourses, in order to find humanitarian linkages and spaces for empowerment (Budianta 2004).

With the absence of liberal arts in tertiary education and weak humanities education in primary and secondary education, ground work still needs to be done to develop critical thinking among the general population in Indonesia. Recent studies show that radical religious groups recruit middle-class young people, insecure about their identity, especially from the faculty of sciences, ruled by a positivistic paradigm (Budianta 2007*d*). For me now, and in the years to come, literary and cultural studies serve as a strategic and critical space for building bridges between cultural borders and disciplinary entrenchments in post Reformasi Indonesia.

CONCLUSION

Teasing in and out between the self and cultural politics, this chapter cannot but avoid the fact that this tricky act of narrating the self is an act of representation, of self-fashioning. Behind this act of positioning is the question of audience. Am I talking to the academic community of Southeast Asianists whose field I am trespassing? But who is this scholar I am imagining? The stereotype of a Southeast Asianist in my imagination has an opposite route of scholarship from the one I have undergone. Unlike anthropologists, philologists, and historians, and area studies scholars, who spent a long time learning Southeast Asian languages and doing ethnography in one or more Southeast Asian countries, many Indonesian humanities scholars doing research on Indonesian culture started their training in Western literature. Sapardi Djoko Damono,

Bakdi Soemanto, Budi Darma, and the younger generation of literary and cultural studies scholars such as Manneke Budiman, and Intan Paramadhita, are British or American literature scholars by training, and Indonesian studies scholars by practice. In some way, they act as cultural translators[15] both ways, as they teach Western literary and cultural theory to Indonesian audiences, and present papers on Indonesian culture for international audiences, or do comparative studies.

Looking back at my own learning processes, I find that both what I learned formally from the Anglo-Saxon cultural studies and what I acquired locally by practice could not be untangled from each other. The way I internalized Western theories could not but be influenced by the cultural perspectives from which I came. The way I looked at the texts and reality around me cannot help but be framed by the theoretical lenses I acquired in my Western schooling. Yet to define the "cultural location from where I came from" is to already find mixed genres, heteroglossic voices of creative mixing, and playful translation and mistranslation of the West and the East — like the texts which make up diverse Indonesian literature.[16]

It is in this strategic appropriation of what is available to meet the local needs of the day, after the transfer of knowledge from European master teachers, that the discourse and scholarship in the humanities evolved in Indonesia, from new criticism to deconstruction, from philology to cultural studies. In some moments different genres and thoughts from different historical locations in Western history arrived, accidentally, thanks to various traffics of influences, at the same juncture (such as romanticism, realism, and absurdism,[17] or the euphoria of postmodernism, which came when the project of modernity was still being internalized). I realized that the moments when I received the best education was when I came across this kind of complexity and unsolved contradiction, including contradictions between what one learned and what one found on the ground, between scholarship and activism, and, especially, between what one saw in other places and in one's own. This position of alterity, of being an Other within and without, has moulded my intellectual journey.

My knowledge was constructed within the bounds of the vocabulary of the literary and cultural studies scholarship of the time — in the United States as well as in Indonesia. In the process of learning and the dissemination of knowledge, as a scholar I cannot but engage and negotiate the forces of the nation state — especially in the way it inscribed my race and gender — the forces of developmentalism and "glocal" capitalism, which fed educational institutions in Indonesia in the 1980s–90s, and the forces of the community with its demands and censorship during the New Order and Post Reformasi movement. My scholarship was significantly shaped by the political crisis in Indonesia in 1998, when race and gender violence broke for me the walls of scholarship and activism. Similarly the world crisis after the 11 September attacks activated in me critical responses against constructed ideological divides globally and locally. My regional perspective was widened by the transnational and regional networking which created and resulted from the changing global configuration of the twenty-first century. Moulded by time and history, I worked within the available space to expand the limits of disciplinary knowledge and to cross cultural boundaries. The story of my making as a hybrid humanitarian scholar in this historical juncture is not unique. It remains to be seen whether from this kind of biographical reflection a pattern of knowledge making in Indonesia or in the region can emerge. Experienced by a humanities scholar in Indonesia, this account — which might not fit the common understanding of Southeast Asian scholarship — speaks of a construction of certain forms of knowledge, among a limited circle of intellectuals and activists, in specific urban, cosmopolitan settings in Southeast Asia, in a certain, transient, historical moment.

Notes

1. For this kind of self narration, I will take the liberty to do self referencing. The references to my own work in this chapter serve as footnotes to my intellectual journey.
2. The report was published as a headline story in the monthly news magazine, *Tempo*, 4 September 1980.
3. First intended for civil servants, this training was later modified in different packages for students from elementary school to higher education. In the 1990s, there were initiatives to introduce this training also to workers and employees of the private sector.
4. Among others, Sylvia Tiwon, who is now faculty staff at the Asian Studies Centre, the University of Berkeley; Fauzi Abdullah, who now works as a legal aide for the marginalized.
5. In *Res Publica*, now renamed Trisakti University, in 1962–65.
6. The term quoted from Andreas Harsono's blog <http://www.andreasharsono. blogspot.com/2006/02/smak-sint-albertus.html> (accessed 21 March 1997). Andreas Harsono, now a media watch activist, was inspired by the Satya Wacana Christian University lecturers in his political activism as a student in Salatiga.
7. The crisis in the Indonesian social sciences — as it was uncritically co-opted by the New Order's developmentalism — was discussed in the 1970s and the topic re-emerged in the late 1990s when social sciences were considered unable to deal with social-political crises.
8. When one victim was about to leave Indonesia to testify in the United States, she was killed in an act of robbery one night before departure, and under

pressure, a psychologist collaborated with the police to put shame on the family by testifying that there was a record of a long history of incestuous sexual abuse on the body of the victim.

9. When Ariel Heryanto wrote his widely read newspaper column in the *Kompas* daily newspaper one month after the May rapes, titled "Saya Kapok Jadi Nonpri" (*Kompas*, 12 June 1998), I was inspired to write an open letter to the Minister of Women's Affair (who denied the existence of the May Rapes), mimicking Ariel's title, "Saya Kapok Jadi Wanita" (*Media Indonesia*, 1 July 1998).

10. Thanks to Ariel Heryanto, who introduced me to Cheng Kuan-Hsing, the convenor of the 1998 Inter-Asia Cultural Studies — Problematizing "Asia" Conference, Taipei. The output of the conference was the first edition of the *Inter-Asia Cultural Studies* journal, which included my article (Budianta 2000*b*).

11. From the ARENA homepage <http://www.arenaonline.org/content/view/17/54> (accessed 11 April 2008). For an overview of the rise of regional networks of social movements in Southeast Asia, see Teresa S. Encarnacion Tadem, "Globalization of Resistance 2002 — South-East Asia", 19 September 2003 <http://www.social-movements.org/en/node/view/319> (accessed 11 April 2008).

12. The output of the project is Ariel Heryanto and Sumit Mandal, *Challenging Authoritarianism, Comparing Malaysia and Indonesia* (London: Rutledge Curzon, 2003).

13. I am indebted to cultural studies concepts of constructed identity, such as Stuart Hall's definition of identity as cultural positioning (Stuart Hall, "Cultural Identity and Diaspora", in Williams, Patrick and Laura Chrisman, eds. *Colonial Discourse and Postcolonial Theory: A Reader* (Harvester Wheatsheaf 1993), pp. 393–402). The processes of coming to terms with my own Chineseness have helped me to observe the discourse of Chineseness in Indonesia in the aftermath of the Reformasi movement (Budianta 2007*b*).

14. One evening during a reflective sharing session in the little Buddhist temple on the outskirts of Beijing, Dessa Rosanna Quesada, ARENA fellow, senior artist-trainer from the Philippine Theatre Association and the Gender Wave against Violence and Exploitation, sang the lyrics she had created, which encapsulate the shared feelings of home in transborder homelessness among fellow activists:

Across the vast seas and the ragged peaks,
I fly alone through so many fields unknown.
I laugh with the rain, dance to the rhythm of the earth,
Follow the gaze of my sister sun.

I have been one with the wounded souls,
Who have yearned for the healing oil
I have tales from the battlefield
Yet, through it all, at night I ask myself:
Ref. Where is my home? Where is my home?
    Hmm... and I say,

> Home is where my heart will never have to fear
> Home is where my heart will find a place of peace
> Hmm...
> And my heart has found a place in you,
> My rainbow warrior.
>
> I have seen the fire from the breath of raging eyes,
> It feeds and I let it stay in my soul that never sleeps,
> My life has been blessed by the fire turned to spring,
> And I sing you songs that reach our common sky.
>
> I joined the circle of the earthly dreamers
> Placed a brick on a common house,
> Believing that our hopes mustn't die
> Yet, through it all, at night, I ask myself ...
> Ref. Where is my home? Where is my home?
>   Hmm... and I say,
>   Home is where my heart will never have to fear
>   Home is where my heart will find a place of peace
>   Hmm...
>   And my heart has found a place in you,
>   My rainbow warrior.
> (Copyright Dessa Rosanna Quesada, reproduced with permission).

15. Sapardi Djoko Damono and Bakdi Soemanto have translated a number of Western literary works from English to Bahasa Indonesia.
16. To get a picture of the diversity of cultural influences and intertextual variety of early Indonesian literature, see the anthology of Indonesian Literature before the 1920s, *Nona Koelit Koetjing, Antologi Cerita Pendek Sebelum 1920*, edited by Sapardi Djoko Damono et al. (Jakarta: Pusat Bahasa, 2006), and my discussion of that diversity in the introduction of the anthology, and another article I wrote on such diversity (Budianta 2007c).
17. To get a picture of the (mis)appropriation of western genres and literary movements, see Sapardi Djoko Damono (2007) and my introduction in the other literary movement series published by the Pusat Bahasa, 2004–07.

References

Ang, Ien. "Can One Say No to Chineseness? Pushing the Limits of the Diasporic Paradigm". In *On Not Speaking Chinese: Living Between Asia and the West*. London and New York: Routledge, 2001, pp. 37–51.

Budianta, Melani. "Lesson in Scholarship". *Menagerie 3*. Jakarta: Lontar, 1997.

———. "Saya Kapok Jadi Wanita". *Media Indonesia*, 1 July 1998.

———. "Double Texts: Representing America and Discussing Women's Issues in Indonesia". *American Studies International* 37, no. 3 (October 2000a).

————. "Globalization and the Discourse of Cultural Identity: The Case of Indonesia during the Monetary Crisis 1997–1998". *Inter-Asia Cultural Studies* 1, no. 1 (April 2000*b*): 109–28.

————. "Identitas Budaya dalam Masyarakat Multikultural" [Cultural identity in a multicultural society]. In *Budi dan Nalar: Harry Tjan Silalahi*. Jakarta: CSIS, 2003*a*: 601–612.

————. "Beyond Tears and Anger: Representations of Violence against Women". *Nivedini, Journal of Gender Studies* 1 (May/June 2003*b*): 1–23.

————. "The Blessed Tragedy: The Making of Indonesian Women's Activism in the Reformasi Years of 1998–1999". In *Challenging Authoritarianism in Southeast Asia, Comparing Malayisa and Indonesia*, edited by Ariel Heryanto and Sumit Mandal. New York: RoutledgeCurzon, 2003*c*.

————. "Multiculturalism: In Search of a Framework for Managing Diversity in Indonesia, Multicultural Education in Indonesia and Southeast Asia, Stepping into the Unfamiliar, Jakarta". *Jurnal Antropologi Indonesia*, 2004.

————. "Decentralizing Engagements: Women and the Democratization Processes in Indonesia". *Signs* 31 (Summer 2007*a*): 915–22.

————. "The Dragon Dance: Shifting Meaning of Chineseness in Indonesia". In *Asian and Pacific Cosmopolitans: Self and Subject in Motion*, edited by Katherine Robinson. Hampshire, UI: Palgrave, 2007*b*.

————. "Diverse Voices: Indonesian Literature and Nation-Building", in *Language, Nation and Development in Southeast Asia*, edited by Lee Hock Guan and Leo Suryadinata. Singapore: Institute of Southeast Asian Studies, 2007*c*.

————. "Beyond the Stained Glass Window: Indonesian Perceptions of the United States War on Terror". In *The International Perceptions on The U.S. War on Terror*, edited by David Farber. Princeton University Press, 2007*d*.

Cohen, Mathew Isaac. "Interview with W.S. Rendra". In *IIAS Newsletter Online*, no. 19 <http:www. aloa.nu/interviewmedRendra.html> (accessed 20 March 2008).

Damono, Sapardi Djoko et al. *Absurdisme dalam Sastra Indonesia*. Jakarta: Pusat Bahasa, Departemen Pendidikan Nasional, 2007.

————. *Nona Koelit Koetjing, Antologi Cerita Pendek Sebelum 1920*. Jakarta: Pusat Bahasa, 2006.

Hall, Stuart. "Cultural Identity and Diaspora". In *Colonial Discourse and Postcolonial Theory: A Reader*, edited by Patrick Williams and Laura Chrisman. Hemel Hempstead: Harvester Wheatsheaf, 1993.

Heryanto, Ariel. "Saya Kapok Jadi Nonpri". *Kompas*, 12 June 1998.

Heryanto, Ariel and Sumit Mandal, eds., *Challenging Authoritarianism in Southeast Asia, Comparing Malaysia and Indonesia*. New York: RoutledgeCurzon, 2003.

Tadem, Teresa S. Encarnacion. "Globalization of Resistance 2002 — South-East Asia", 19 September 2003 <www.social-movements.org/en/node/view/319> (accessed 11 April 2008).

9

BETWEEN STATE AND REVOLUTION
Autobiographical Notes on Radical Scholarship during the Marcos Dictatorship

Patricio N. Abinales

At middle age, Filipino intellectuals who matured politically as part of the student protests of the 1960s and the remarkable revival of communism, have elided from a posture of unswerving militancy to more deliberative, less passionate, and self-critical encounters with power in society. Growing old, combined with the safety of some tenured post (a member of the professoriate, a pundit's niche in media, the NGO "sector", or a corporate boardroom) are frequently the most immediate reasons for this political "moderation". In certain cases, it is the fact that one is simply getting old, and this, combined with the debilitating allures of petit bourgeois comforts, have a way of tempering one's militancy. Yet, there are also the profound changes in the political scene, especially after the Communist Party of the Philippines (CPP) lost its morally hegemonic position in 1986 and soon afterwards, despite its "reaffirmation" of Maoist principles, started acquiring the same vices that its class enemies have been notoriously known for. Lastly, on the broader social canvas, the diminution of one's political passion can likewise be the result of one's disappointment with "the masses" as they refuse to rally to the red flag, but instead gave their whole to conservative religiosity, and who, instead of acting as the makers of history, have decided to work abroad. Writing about one's present without taking these multiple contexts into consideration can thus be difficult and disheartening. The likely tendency for a lot of ageing former activists and progressive intellectuals is to minimize their radical past or not talk about it so as to avoid justifying contemporary compromises. A few even go to the deep end, disavowing any connections with that past and going to the extreme of becoming rabid defenders of reaction and conservatism. Then there are those who embellish the radical past as if to say that having "done my fair share" in the struggle, they now deserve to "slow down" or even "retire" from active politics.[1] This is what has made this autobiographical essay profoundly difficult to write. Will one simply list his/her contributions to the revolution and then accept the risk that, at middle age, he/she could be labelled a compromiser or, worse, an opportunist? Or can one detach the political experiences that made possible the development of one's ideas and evaluate the latter on their own terms?

This predicament becomes more evident once we factor in the Marcos dictatorship. For under authoritarian rule, the political choices were said to be starkly simple: you were either for the state or for the revolution, for the "fascistic few" or the "nation/people". While the fall of Marcos and the near-breakdown of the CPP after 1986 had complicated this dichotomy, a lot of intellectuals of that period continue to cling to this binary as the measure of political commitment. And today, there appears no way that one can avoid this "either/or" choice that the Marcos era bequeathed on those who lived under it. But perhaps a way out of this dilemma is to view the authoritarian period as a spectrum where between state and revolution are found different shades of political choices. These hues were constantly pressured by these extremes, but managed to keep their distinctiveness. By recognizing this nuanced spectrum it is possible to explore a terrain that is fraught with complexities of exegeses, choices, and praxis, far different from the polarized portrait of state and revolution that has become the standard feature of the martial law era.

This chapter explores this "third way" by looking at progressive/radical writings which were critical of both state and revolution. While these writings never precipitated a "revolution within the revolution", they revealed important major flaws in the CPP's perspectives and strategy that prompted senior Party leaders to recognize them as a threat to Maoist ideological purity. The "debates" that ensued, however, never bore fruit, and some of the issues raised continue to haunt the Left to this very day. This chapter is also autobiographical in form in part to conform to the overall theme of this edited volume, and in part because I want to situate my personal, political, and intellectual journey in this intra–left wing struggle of ideas. I begin with an overview of the contexts in which my pilgrimage began, and then move to a brief discussion of my works in relation to these settings. I close by suggesting that intellectual (and political) exile does not only always produce what Ben Anderson calls "long-distance" nationalism; on the contrary, the appearance or *non-appearance* of this nationalism from afar depends on where one began one's intellectual and political pilgrimage.[2] In my case, "exile" ended up increasingly denying the legitimacy of the nation state in favour of subaltern sentiments that are the product of my encounters with the local histories of my home island.[3]

BEGINNINGS: ACADEMIA AND THE REVOLUTION

It took almost four months before the Marcos dictatorship allowed schools to open after martial law was declared on 21 September 1972.[4] No sooner were classes allowed when the University of the Philippines (UP) was hit by "silent marches" and intermittent "pillbox" attacks on the police led by CPP cadres and "national democratic" activists who escaped detention or had decided not to join their comrades in the armed struggle in the countryside.[5] While giving a psychological boost to a radical student movement in disarray, these counter-attacks were politically ill advised: the more activists staged them, the more they got arrested and jailed. Those who thought that these protests would inspire students to join them were disappointed; the majority had accepted the new order or were too scared to defy it. These "ultra-leftist tendencies" were eventually reined in and a reconstituted urban party leadership began the tedious process of rebuilding the underground network in the schools. At UP, and in certain schools on Mindanao island, the southern Philippines, communist cadres initiated the re-establishment of legally allowed (i.e. apolitical) organizations, which became the sources of new recruits for the underground, the urban slums, factories, and the New People's Army (NPA).[6] Recruits were told to prepare themselves for "higher forms of struggle", go to where the "masses" live, and thus complete the process of casting off their petit bourgeois imperfections in preparation for full "proletarianization". But as long as they were still in the universities, these activists were to spearhead a "propaganda and education campaign" against the dictatorship and on behalf of the revolution.[7]

The CPP had both ideological and practical reasons for continuing with this pre-martial law programme for student recruits. First, the protests of the late 1960s and early 1970s showed that students — when properly motivated — could become a powerful propaganda and organizing force for the revolution. Articulate and educated, they could provide the intellectual education that the relatively "backward" masses lacked. And indeed, in the early 1970s, there were signs that the first student-led NPA guerrilla units were doing well in the areas where they set up base.[8] Secondly, as the younger of two communist parties, the CPP also had to play catch up with its older rival, the Partido Komunista ng Pilipinas, in terms of organizing "the basic masses", and thus had to rely on its strongest and biggest constituents — the students. In fact, the first generation of CPP cadres came mainly from the student front, and when martial law crippled the Party, its leaders had no choice but to continue recruiting in the schools even if they suspected the students of being infected by the virus of petit bourgeois individualism and opportunism. Thus, every new legal organization and Party cell formed inside these associations was oriented towards producing cadres for the urban underground and the guerrilla war.[9]

The romance of the pre-martial law street battles against government troops during the so-called "First Quarter Storm" (FQS) of the 1970s fired up the imagination of the first recruits under martial law. But as the years advanced and new generations of students entered the university, the appeal of the pre-martial law protests began to fade. Vaguely familiar with or completely ignorant of the radical past, their political education was further stymied by martial law. Unlike their elders who were honed in political debates and exposed to various kinds of radical literature, they were ignorant of the battles of correct political lines, the nuances of Marxist and Maoist thought, and of activism as a mark of distinction. The recruits from these generations overcame the stultifying impact of martial law, but even inside the "movement", they were not as exposed to a life of constant debate and study. It was sufficient that they be introduced to the Party's *Basic Mass Course*, some readings on nationalism, Mao Tse Tung's *Red Book* of quotations, and stories of the revolution by the Party newspapers. There was no need to delve further into Marx before and after the *Manifesto*, nor Lenin and the stories behind *What Is To Be Done?* The priority was to bring in more recruits, not dabble in deeper theorizing. For hasn't the CPP chairman, Jose Ma. Sison, already defined the "line of march" for revolutionaries?

Recruitment into the underground began to slow down as it became more difficult to convince the increasingly apolitical "martial law babies" of the imperatives of revolution. The few times when these "martial law babies" joined activist-organized mobilizations, were when they felt threatened economically. Protests over school fee hikes brought thousands of students out of the classrooms, but once activists "raised" the issue to "a higher level", by linking fee increases to the Marcos dictatorship, participation dwindled significantly.[10]

The CPP's response to this growing apathy was not to tackle it head on, but to ratchet up the rhetoric to open criticism of the "U.S.-Marcos dictatorship" and tales of mass poverty and oppression to play on the guilt, compassion, and anger of the petite bourgeoisie. This tactic failed and the numbers of student participants in mass actions continued to drop. As this organizational crisis became evident, academics sympathetic to the movement began to propose an alternative strategy to reverse the decline: make the schools themselves a major ideological battleground against the dictatorship.

Inspired by the writings of the French philosopher Louis Althusser on ideological state apparatuses, these academics argued that the role of universities in a "development-authoritarian" society such as the Philippines was to infuse students with a pro–status quo outlook. Accordingly, the task of the activist as student was to break this ideological straitjacket through a rigorous criticism of the state of university and national affairs to their constituents. And while those who decide that their fortunes lay in the factories and the guerrilla zones should not be discouraged, activists must also provide an alternative for those who prefer to remain in the cities and on the legal front, or even just remain sympathetic to the revolution. To accomplish these goals, communists must do the opposite of what the Party policy was towards student politics. Instead of preparing students to become guerrillas or underground cadres, thereby treating their school terms as merely a minor transition, activists must take their being students seriously, excelling in class as they would in politics, and thereby gain the admiration of their cohort. They had to show that their politics stood on a rich lode of elaborate Marxist theorizing and not simply on a series of incantations from the *Red Book*. This was the only way to attract students whose lack of political experience had reinforced their petit bourgeois desire to excel in schools and enter the capitalist world with better chances of rising through the ranks.[11]

The CPP condemned this proposal as reactionary and branded those pushing for a rethinking of political work on the student front as "renegades" and "opportunists" out to undermine the revolution. Yet, at the middle level, there were cadres who expressed openness to dialogue with these heretics and even accepted the validity of their criticisms. These cadres began to explore new options for students, including the possibility of developing a "radical middle class", i.e., students or professionals who would not become guerrilla or trade union activists, but who would occupy critical ramparts in the private sector, government offices, and universities.[12] The discussions did not resolve the major areas of difference, but a middle ground was struck when both sides tried to help each other in preserving a strong Left presence inside the UP campus. In 1980, despite the disapproval of the CPP Manila leadership, local cadres pursued this "tactical collaboration" to the fullest, bringing about left wing victories in student council elections in many units of the university. This was only the second time the Party became a hegemonic force in university student politics.[13]

A HERETIC'S HUB[14]

This left wing challenge to the CPP's ideological orthodoxy at UP began to cluster with other similar views around the Third World Studies Program, a research unit created in 1976 by the university's College of Arts and Sciences.[15] To avoid being tagged a subversive organization by the regime, it did not use terms such as "Marxism" or "revolution", using concepts such as dependency and world systems theories instead to push for alternative explanations. Despite limited funding, the programme immediately made its presence felt in the academic community. Starting with reprints of the top scholars from these perspectives (notably Andre Gunder Frank, Immanuel Wallerstein, and Henrique Fernando Cardoso), the programme soon began publishing original research done by its growing network of "fellows" (many of whom were former CPP members).

Whether it was because Marxist books were banned and thus inaccessible, or because they were convinced by the main arguments of dependency and world systems theorists, the programme's fellows began to actively promote these frameworks as a means of understanding the Philippine political economy under Marcos. The results were a flurry of studies on the growth of dependent/peripheral capitalism as evidenced by the expansion of joint ventures between Japanese and American capitalists with cronies of the Marcos regime, and the growth of export crop agriculture.[16] These studies' adoption of the dependency argument that capitalism was the dominant "mode of production" in the Philippines put them on a collision course with the CPP's position that, like China, the country's social formation was "semi-feudal and semi-colonial". The implications of the dependency argument cut deep into the heart of the Party's strategy: since capitalism now reigned in the Philippine countryside, why must the CPP continue to insist on organizing poor peasants around the issue of land reform and protractedly build a rural army among them?[17] Should not the Party instead invest all its resources into forming trade unions and poor peasant associations on issues such as wages as part of a larger worker-centred revolutionary strategy?[18]

Party ideologues wasted no time in attacking these heresies, with responses ranging from the most theoretical to the most bizarre (e.g., the argument that there is no "real" capitalist society to speak of today because even countries such as the United States or Japan were captive to "rent-seeking activities", i.e., "semi-feudal" practices).[19] Others, however, took the criticism more positively, seeing in the criticisms of the dependency theorists a chance to strengthen the CPP's fundamentals. Two CPP-influenced institutions — the Church-based Luzon Secretariat for Social Action (LUSSA) and the Alternate Resource Centre (ARC, based in Davao city) — published a series of studies on the agriculture and fishing sectors.[20] ARC itself devoted a special issue on the dependency debates for the political education of communist activists and cadres on the southern island of Mindanao.[21] ARC went the furthest in agreeing to work with the *dependistas* to conduct parallel studies on Mindanao agriculture. The first ever Marxist-influenced studies on the changing political economy of Mindanao were the results of these discussions.[22] The Party's Mindanao Commission also became interested in the strategic implications of the dependency school's arguments, noting that the success of the *welgang bayan* (popular uprisings) in the 1980s was partly the result of the Party taking to heart *dependista* suggestions that the loci of capitalist development and exploitation on the island — the factories, slum communities, and plantations — were as vital as the rural areas.[23]

From political economy the inquiries expanded to examinations of the theoretical underpinnings of authoritarian rule, with some Third World fellows positing the idea that the Marcos regime was a "Bonapartist" state, while others, inspired by New Left theoreticians Ernesto Laclau and Nicos Poulantzas, drew attention to the dictatorship's relatively autonomous position vis-à-vis civil society.[24] By the 1980s, with the CPP now a national presence, the programme sought to understand the dynamism of the revolution itself, resulting in the publication of two successful edited volumes. The essays in its *Marxism in the Philippines* series explored the tensions between the CPP's Maoism and Christianity, the mode of production question, and the problems of revolutionary strategy in the late Marcos period.[25] Putting the first of these two volumes out while still under martial law was already a daring act. But its audacity also had to do with the programme — now renamed a centre — deciding to bring out the problems facing the communist movement at a time when it appeared to be the most formidable opponent of the dictatorship. Again CPP defenders hit hard on this project, particularly after it became a regular feature of the centre's activities, but interest in the lectures and the positive reception to the series mitigated such attacks.[26]

If there was this considerable radical theorizing outside of the CPP and between the CPP and a small group of left wing critics, why then did Kathleen Weekly correctly observe that, despite the CPP's practical experiences and intellectual/ideological debates within itself and with other forces, these issues were "never theorized substantially, nor was the coherence of the basic [Maoist] framework onto which they were being hung ever assessed thoroughly"?[27] What were the limits to the contributions of a radical hub such as the Third World Studies Center to the revolution? Let me offer three possible explanations behind this failure to debate. The first has to do with the interaction of authoritarian rule's impact and the nature of Filipino Maoism. One cannot deny the toll on human and intellectual capital that the dictatorship had wrought on Filipino leftists. The number of cadres known for their organizational expertise and theoretical competence, who were either killed or imprisoned for long periods of time, deprived the CPP of a stable personnel core that could have continued the major theoretical project began by Jose Ma. Sison.[28]

Two examples are worth citing here. The once leader of the largest moderate student organization, Edgar Jopson, joined the CPP after martial law was declared. He worked in the trade union movement in Manila, was promoted to the Manila regional organization, and then assigned to Mindanao where he pushed for additional research on the island's political economy. Jopson was killed while overseeing the creation of an island-wide coordinating body, the Mindanao Commission.[29] The former priest, and one of the leaders of the Party's National Democratic Front (NDF), Edicio de la Torre, spent most of his time in jail, with very little chance to ruminate on an issue that got him fascinated in the revolution and ultimately convinced him to join the Party: the dialectics between the theology of liberation and Filipino Maoism.[30] On his first release from prison, De La Torre returned to united front work and initiated secret meetings with other anti-Marcos forces to sell the idea of forming a broad tactical alliance against the dictatorship. He was rearrested and exiled to Rome. After the downfall of Marcos, he returned to these issues, but by then had become so much of a renegade in the Party's eyes that he was eventually forced to resign.[31]

By closing all venues for open political articulation, martial law also validated Sison's prediction that the state would eventually turn "fascistic" as it tried to stem the crisis of the political economy and slow down the inevitability of revolutionary triumph. The appropriate response to this authoritarian turn, therefore, was to speed up the accumulation of arms and the development of a peasant guerrilla army. The CPP must also quickly educate "the masses" on the political line, and given their low "educational levels", a simplified form of Marxism and Mao Tse Tung's hortatory moralizing were enough. All that was necessary was the Party *Basic Mass Course* (which were simplified summations of the arguments of the CPP's main bible, *Philippine Society and Revolution*, or *PSR*) and then impart this to the masses. There was neither the time nor need for complicated, nuanced radical inquiry. Those insisting that the CPP take a pause and "ideologically consolidate" were simply slowing down the revolution. Moreover, what use would probing deeper into Marx's theory of surplus value or Lenin's theory of imperialism serve, when these have no direct impact on mobilizing the masses whose main concern was state repression?

This line of argument served the CPP well in its early years, but Maoism's powerful anti-intellectual strain was not enough to sustain a movement that, by the early 1980s, was already shaping up to be a complex national organization that was spread over a society altered significantly by the dictatorship. The dependency debates and the discussions of the role of universities and academics in the revolution were intimations that radical intellectuals and some cadres (notably the Mindanao Commission) were aware of the limits of Filipino Maoism. The former, however, continued to be treated with disdain by Party intellectuals who saw them as engaging in "ivory tower" theorizing — a worthless exercise unvalidated by the crucible of political "practice".[32] Moreover, once the Mindanao Commission decided to go full speed with its urban uprisings, no other CPP unit took up the debates. When the assassination of Marcos' rival Benigno Aquino sparked thousands of protests nationwide, everyone saw very little value in pushing for a debate on the spread of capitalism or the Marcosian state. At this point, what became imperative were the conjunctural explanations that offered practical approaches to fighting a weakened dictatorship.[33]

A minor theoretical revival took place after 1986 when the Party broke into factions, but after 1992, with Sison regaining the leadership and the centre's fellows drifting away to seek other pursuits (see below), Third World Studies shifted its priorities away from just enriching radical theory to "broader" issues such as development and neo-liberalism, civil society politics, peace studies, and more polymorphous multi-issue "social movements".[34] The thrust now was on how to expand the "democratic spaces" opened up by the post-authoritarian order, through expanding the dialogue and discussions (and fewer debates) with various social forces and with a government that appeared more receptive to "popular pressures". The centre's publications now began to veer away from straightforward critical evaluations of the strengths and weaknesses of the post-authoritarian state, towards positing concrete policy recommendations on how to expand "popular democracy" under President Corazon Aquino.[35]

Once it became institutionalized as a major unit of the university, its aura as an out-of-place hub that attracted wayward radical intellectuals began to fade. The first casualties of its normalization were the left wing discussions by the centre's fellows who were concerned less with academic requirements and more involved in issues which university authorities saw largely as outside their academic priorities. The centre quietly dissolved its network of fellows, and those once active eventually drifted away from the hub to immerse themselves in "civil society" work, take their academic careers more seriously, or embrace mainstream traditional patronage politics, thereby breaking completely from their radical pasts.[36] A parallel problem plagued pro-CPP intellectuals as the mass struggles that animated and gave substance to their defence of the orthodoxy receded with the decline of student activism and the loss of Party exclusive rights on urban protest. The new next generation of Party defenders in UP was more detached from the realities of everyday resistance and compensated for this delinking by further romanticizing and reifying the revolution, albeit this time finding theoretical sustenance from the self-conscious incoherence of postmodernism.[37]

PERIPHERIES AS CENTRES (MARGINAL NOTES ON THE PERSONAL)

The Third World Studies Center was not simply known for its critical commentaries on the Left; it also became famous for being one of the few Manila institutions interested in the political economy of the southern Philippines. The immediate attraction was Marcos' development vision for the country's largest and poorest land frontier and the rebellions that this interventionist programme spawned.[38] Shortly after martial law was declared, the Moro National Liberation Front (MNLF) launched its "war of liberation" to separate Mindanao, the smaller Sulu Archipelago, and the island of Palawan from the Republic. For the next two years, the Muslim zones of Mindanao became major battlegrounds as the MNLF and the Armed Forces of the Philippines (AFP) fought each other for control over these territories.[39] The war stalemated in the late 1970s, but the ensuing peace negotiations never restored stability to the Muslim areas.[40] By the 1980s, the "Christian" provinces also became battle zones, with the AFP fighting to contain successful communist expansion. These rebellions took a heavy toll on the people of Mindanao, but also chipped away at ramparts of the dictatorship, forcing it to expend valuable resources and manpower.[41] And, as happens with unwinnable wars, the failure of the AFP to score decisive victories against the MNLF and the CPP, plus widespread corruption inside the dictatorship, increased the alienation of young military officers towards Marcos, to the point where some of them eventually tried to overthrow him in 1986.[42] All this was happening against the backdrop of a profound transformation of Mindanao's local economy. Mindanao was no longer the "empty and dark", underpopulated, and undeveloped region of the country; it had become central to every national economic development plan conceived by Manila. When the Third World Studies Center sent a research team to south-eastern Mindanao, it was to attempt to understand "the economic origins of social unrest".[43]

I grew up in Ozamiz City in northern Mindanao, but — like many provincial kids of my time — was sent by my mother to UP, where I majored in history and politics. Already at this early point in life, my feeling as an outsider was evident. Coming from Mindanao, I was immediately associated with its political and social instabilities, criminals and exiles, its informal economies, complemented by Manila's fear of "Muslims" and its bigotry against non-Filipino speakers.[44] These prejudices were, however, mitigated by the attractiveness of the revolution and the idea that despite our diverse origins we were one with the "Filipino people". We joined the "movement", but my participation did not last long. I began to drift slowly away from it, having difficulty in reconciling the Party's Stalinist excuses with its radical democratic rhetoric.[45] I ended up working at the Third World Studies Center in 1979, just when it was making its mark as a haven for radical heretics, and I was sent to south-eastern Mindanao as part of a team that was involved in a long-term study on the fast growing export banana industry.[46]

On the side I was also starting to contribute essays on different issues — from right wing vigilantes in northern Mindanao and the social bandits of Metropolitan Manila — to a news magazine owned by a Marcos crony that was, ironically, trying to test the limits of the regime's censorship laws.[47] I thus found myself in several sites — in a left wing academic research centre, working on the southern "periphery", while being continuously exposed to growing opposition inside the media, and a fellow traveller to a revolution that was going awry. These locations defined the succeeding years of my academic and political life and were instrumental in making me gradually understand my own peculiar multiple marginality: provincial kid in the national university, worker at an institute which operated at the fringes of the university, and fellow traveller of a growing national revolutionary movement which challenged issues of domination and tried to centralize a southern periphery. The grids of my young mental map were at variance with many of my intellectual, academic, and political peers.

The ouster of Marcos in 1986 was profoundly unsettling for many who described themselves as leftists. The much-anticipated final battle between state and revolution never took place. Instead it was displaced by a non-violent, religious, and comical forced removal of an ailing dictator by the most bewildering coalition of forces — bourgeois politicians rebounding from weakness, social democratic splinters, bungling military coup plotters, and a broad cross-section of Manila society.[48] The new regime promised the full restoration of "democracy", but after repeated attempted coups by and against her, and her refusal to implement a comprehensive land reform programme, President Corazon Aquino steadily abandoned her left flank, leaving social democrats, liberals, and leftists who supported her disconsolate and weakened.[49] But no one could take advantage of this turn of events. The CPP's decision to boycott the 1986 elections brought out festering divides inside the organization that turned into violent factional debates over outdated strategies and viewpoints and a Stalinist authoritarian culture.[50] Even those of us on the edges looking into the Party were as befuddled as those on the inside. To my political confusion were added anger and uncertainty when two close friends and comrades were assassinated by elements identified with the military. I had thought these sordid acts would not happen under a restored democracy; but they did.

It was to get some breathing space and take stock of my life that I applied for a one-year fellowship for Southeast Asian Studies at Cornell University in 1988, which, after I was accepted, was upgraded to a full PhD programme in Government. This gave me the opportunity to work with Benedict Anderson whose own life history was also marked by constant dislocation until he settled at Cornell.[51] Upstate New York was a nice respite from the political battles back home and an opportunity to brood over the political issues of my immediate past. The chance to evaluate the revolution more comprehensively and probe deeper into the causes of military politicization, using Cornell's vast Southeast Asian resources, was enough motivation to survive the sterility of the American political science and the dullness of American political life. My first seminar papers epitomized this concern — a short biography of Jose Ma. Sison, papers on peasant movements, and the AFP under Marcos.[52] Moreover, instead of taking the most popular path of complementing a difficult major (comparative politics) with an "easy" minor (political theory), I opted to make American politics my first minor, hoping that some knowledge on the empire's domestic history could shed light on the origins of Philippine politics. I was not disappointed: the Gilded Age of American political development brought echoes of Filipino cacique democracy (Anderson's), while the American imperial adventure century turned out to be motivated by reasons other than economic exploitation and colonial racism.

It was my dissertation, however, that altered my focus. Ben suggested I set aside my interest on Philippine communism and the AFP and instead explore the political histories of Mindanao where academic interest has so far been thin and intermittent.[53] The topic that immediately came to mind was the MNLF and the research proposal I submitted offered to explore the structural and institutional explanations behind its rebellion. But as has been the lore, fieldwork has a way of changing one's goals, and I gradually became more interested in the past. Ben's gentle prodding to explore alternative explanations also made me look for possible explanations as to why the Muslim community's opprobrium towards Manila and Filipino Christians remained embedded in the Philippine body politic.[54] Along the way I likewise discovered something that went against the grain of Filipino nationalist arguments: lingering positive memories of the U.S. colonial presence in the Muslim communities.[55] Finally, it was surprising to discover that for all the supposed academic interest in Mindanao, the sparse literature mainly concerned the Muslims. There was hardly anything on the "Christian" provinces of the island and no one seemed interested in exploring the reasons behind this void.[56] The finished dissertation was a comparative study of the political development of Cotabato and Davao provinces from the American colonial period to the eve of the declaration of martial law. It challenged orthodox and popular arguments about Muslim political history even as it tried to fill in the gap in the study of a similar history of settler/Christian communities.[57]

My post-Cornell work naturally elaborated on the arguments first presented in the dissertation. Approaching empire and nation "from below" they tried to provide new or alternative explanations for the remarkable resilience of pro-American sentiments among many Filipinos, and, more so, Muslims.[58] Careful review of the Philippine economic development experience and the role of international aid also revealed how critical Mindanao was to the endurance of a political economy that was perennially in crisis.[59] In its revised and published form, the dissertation and works that explored many of its themes, try to answer the question of why a weak state such as the Philippines seems able to withstand the stresses of several rebellions and constant patrimonial plunder of Filipino elites, by looking at the mechanisms of governance at the local level.[60] Even the return to Filipino communist studies began to look at Mindanao more closely, highlighting in particular the tensions and conflict that arose between Mindanao communists and their national leaderships.[61]

A book on state and social forces in the Philippines, which I co-authored with my wife Donna J. Amoroso, drew attention to overlapping histories of state formation, brought back the powerful effect of peripheries such as Mindanao on state centralization, and gave prominence to local community narratives, particularly those of the marginalized Chinese and Muslims.[62] Finally, the odd choices of major and minor disciplines in graduate school led to an essay that, by comparing American and Philippine political development in the early twentieth century in relation to the strengthening of central state capacities, placed empire and colony at the same level of inquiry, instead of the usual "uneven" approaches that privileges one over the other. It questions the prevailing academic myth in the United States that American politics is "exceptional" or, if comparable, only to Europe or Canada.[63] Current research continues to be guided by these perspectives.

CONCLUSION

Looking at national politics from the prisms of Mindanao and Southeast Asia radically altered the way I saw myself in relation to this testy relationship between Filipino intellectuals in the so-called "diaspora" and their comrades, colleagues, and protagonists in the Philippines. When faced with domestic criticism that they have become estranged from their "homeland", the former sometimes compensate by producing works with robust nationalist themes to show that absence or distance has not weakened their "love of country". This is a strong leitmotif that runs through some of the noted scholarship by Filipinos abroad which, while trying to conform to the criteria of originality in insight demanded and imposed by Western academia, are also written with a Filipino audience in mind.

The historian Reynaldo Ileto (see Chapter Four), for example, describes his work as dealing with a "subject matter ... determined by much of the same conditions that led the Filipino youth to question the nature of their society and politics during the late sixties and early seventies".[64] He sees this now classic book on peasant mindsets of the 1890s not simply as representative of a cohort of new historians trained under the so-called "Cornell school" of Southeast Asian Studies, but, more importantly, as a product of a historic postcolonial *revolutionary* struggle that mobilized the poor against an unjust political order.[65]

By associating himself with the generation that produced the "First Quarter Storm", Ileto has set a high bar upon which younger generations of Filipino intellectuals abroad must emulate or surpass. Ileto has also defined the diaspora's political line and has led the counter-offensive against Western (read: American) scholars of Filipino politics, including those whose works were — at certain times — extremely critical of the Marcos dictatorship.[66] Any attempt to interrogate nationalism, for example, has been rebuked as part of an orientalist conspiracy to devalue Filipino nationalism, as promoted by the communists, the bourgeoisie, or even the Marcos dictatorship. This near-occidentalist argument against non-Filipino scholarship has been picked up by a host of U.S.-based Philippine academics demanding that their home country be placed at the centre of American history — the brutal American imperial adventure in the Philippines; and by Japanese scholars who believed that the American empire's pall over Japan (the second largest economy of the world) and the Philippines (an underdeveloped society and one of Asia's poorest) have made these two dissimilar nations soul sisters.[67]

Yet, despite the strong evidence of intense love for the country and an unwavering commitment to an anti-imperialist position, the suspicion remains. Even the boost from international sympathizers is not enough to dispel domestic wariness. Colleagues back in the Philippines continue to treat the writings of those abroad with scepticism, and this comment by a young upstart on Ileto and others serves as a reminder that deep down they are already compromised simply because they are based abroad. C.S. Veric writes:

> When, then, in the minds of American-educated scholars whose bodies grow ashen in the climate of distant shores do we locate Philippine nationalism and the Filipino people and the unfinished revolution? Without a doubt, the question of nationalism is ultimately a national one. Recognition of such is a comprehension of the ineluctable primacy of the nameless multitudes that move History. The project of the coming times, then, is to examine the fictions that self-exiled scholars of nationalism have imagined, for themselves, as the necessity of our people and community.[68]

Yet if we counterpoise the "local" to this binary opposition between colonial-imperial-Western versus nationalist-radical-Filipino scholarships, a different portrait emerges. It is a picture that turns peripheries such as Mindanao into centres with connections that go beyond the nation. Roles become jumbled as colonizers are remembered with a certain fondness despite the brutality they inflicted on many communities, while representatives of the nation are blamed for their prejudices against, and repression of, minorities, despite their efforts to make integration a success. Weak states and national revolutions are preserved not by the compromises among central leaders or a factionalized politburo, but by mutual accommodation between local power and national authority, and the tense interaction between fiercely independent regional communist bodies and an imposing Party centre. Finally, the nation turns out not to be as cohesive and unified as it was thought to be, while local identities that pay homage to universal (extra-national) philosophies turn out to have a stronger resilience.

The multiple sites where I grew up and pursued my academic career, plus my views of a landscape that place the periphery and region at the centre and pushes the national capital to the role of "dependent variable", have insulated me from the bickering of nationalists.[69] The attachments are on the offside of these exchanges, a peculiar insider-outsider hue that the black and white world of these fraternal protagonists would find difficult to place. Instead of being pulled by either extreme ("orientalism" vs. "nationalism"), it looks at the national story as hemmed in by two more powerful histories — that of the home (is)land and the region. This displacement, this dislocation, probably explains my growing alienation to whatever nationalist initiative, because the Mindanao "periphery" has never benefited from any past and current schemes. And I doubt if this will be reversed in the near future.

Notes

The author is grateful to Donna Amoroso, Goh Beng-Lan, and the participants of the NUS workshop in which this essay was presented and discussed. All the shortcomings, however, are — as always — of his own making.

1. Born-again conservatives have a hard time explaining this position, but find a way to have their cake and eat it too by assigning themselves more important roles in the "movement" by way of covering up their relative insignificance.
2. Benedict Anderson, "Long-Distance Nationalism". In *Spectre of Comparisons: Nationalism, Southeast Asia, and the World* (London and New York: Verso, 1998), pp. 58–74.
3. But not transferring loyalties to another country, as in the case of thousands of Filipinos migrating to the United States and becoming Americans.
4. See Department of Education, "Guidelines for the Resumption of Classes under Martial Law", November 1972. The guidelines directed school administrations to set up "security measures" that included expelling students and firing faculty members identified with "subversive elements". The schools were also ordered to prevent "any acts of violence or any violation of existing laws as well as Proclamation 1081 [the martial law decree], and other orders, decrees and instructions issued as a consequence thereof". Schools that could not implement these orders would be subject to "immediate closure".
5. "AS students stage protest march anew". *Rebel Collegian* no. 4 (1973): 1–2. The *Rebel Collegian* was the underground version of the UP student paper, *The Philippine Collegian*.
6. I explored this rebuilding process in Patricio N. Abinales, "Fragments of History, Silhouettes of Resurgence: Student Radicalism in the Early Years of the Marcos Dictatorship", *Tonan Aijia Kenkyu* 42, no. 2 (2008).
7. P.N. Abinales, "The Left and the Philippine Student Movement: Random Historical Notes on Party Politics and Sectoral Struggles", in *Fellow Traveler:*

Essays on Filipino Communism (Quezon City: University of the Philippines Press, 2001), pp. 125–28.

8. Francisco Nemenzo, for example, noted: "NPA units were welcomed by peasants because they were not there only to fight. They also taught the peasants new agricultural skills, herbal medicine, acupuncture, makeshift irrigation, and so forth. More effective than the local governments and field agencies of national minorities, the NPA administered justice, maintained peace and order, organized small economic projects, ran adult education classes and, in the stable guerrilla fronts, even implemented a 'revolutionary land reform program.' [The] NPA thus projected a more positive image, they were not seen as parasites who fed on the meager products of the farmers." Francisco Nemenzo, "Rectification Process in the Philippine Communist Movement", in *Armed Communist Movements in Southeast Asia*, edited by Lim Joo-Jock and Vani S. (Singapore: Institute of Southeast Asian Studies, 1984), p. 32.

9. Patricio N. Abinales, "Radicals and Activists: Birth, Hegemony and the Crisis of the Philippine Student Movement". Unpublished manuscript (University of the Philippines Third World Studies Center Library, 1981), pp. 74–77.

10. Ibid., pp. 76–77.

11. Ibid.

12. The strongest advocate of this idea was the late Leandro Alejandro, who was the most intelligent, charismatic, and popular student leader that the CPP produced during the late martial law period. Alejandro, however, was also a constant headache for his political officers, with his penchant to maintain political and personal friendships with the academic critics of the Party, and, in 1980, his refusal to heed the order of his superiors to wage the student electoral campaign without the assistance of these "renegades". He was suspended for violating "democratic centralism", but the unanimous victory of the left wing student party immediately saw him reinstated to the roster. He was eventually promoted to national politics, taking over the position of secretary general of the CPP's legal coalition Bagong Alyansang Makabayan (New People's Alliance, or Bayan). I knew Alejandro personally and witnessed his transformation from an uncritical student activist to a critical and creative Party cadre.

13. I was personally involved in these particular tactical alliances and the campaigns to win Left control of the university student council and the major college councils of the UP.

14. This section is based on an introduction I wrote in a 2009 abridged version of the Third World Studies Center's *Marxism in the Philippines* series (see note 25), published by Anvil Publishing Incorporated.

15. These academics took advantage of Marcos' claims of being a leader of the "Third World" and saw an opportunity to reinsert left wing discourse in the UP. See the reminiscences of the staff and fellows of the centre in *Kasarinlan: Philippine Journal of Third World Studies* 12, no. 3 (1997).

16. Among many others, Tsuda Mamoru, "The Social Organization of Transnational

Business and Industry: A Study of Japanese Capital-affiliated Joint Ventures in the Philippines", *The Philippines in the Third World Papers Series*, no. 1 (1977); Rigoberto Tiglao, "Philippine Studies on Transnational Corporations: A Critique", *The Philippines in the Third World Papers Series*, no. 10 (1978); Rigoberto Tiglao, "Critique on Studies of Transnational Corporations", *Diliman Review* (January–March 1979); and "Non-Progress in the Periphery", *Diliman Review* (April–June 1979): 38–45; Third World Studies Center, *Political Economy of Philippine Commodities* (Quezon City: University of the Philippines Third World Studies Center, 1983); E.C. Tadem, "Japanese Interests in the Philippine Fishing Industry", *The Philippines in the Third World Papers Series*, Third World Studies Center, no. 6 (1978); Eduardo C. Tadem, *Grains and Radicalism: The Political Economy of the Rice Industry in the Philippines* (Quezon City: University of the Philippines Third World Studies Center, 1986).

17. Amado Guerrero, *Philippine Society and Revolution* (Hong Kong: *Ta Kung Pao*, 1971), p. 89. On the CPP's theoretical responses to Tiglao et al.; see Ricardo Ferrer, "The Semi-Feudal, Semi-Colonial Mode of Production: The Goals of Political Practice", *New Philippine Review* 1, no. 2 (1984); and Temario C. Rivera, "On the Contradictions of Rural Development", *Diliman Review* (September–October 1982), pp. 49–54.

18. A good overview of the debates is Virgilio Rojas, "The Mode of Production Controversy in the Philippines: Anatomy of a Lingering Theoretical Stalemate", *Philippine Left Review* no. 4 (September 1992): 3–43.

19. Ricardo Ferrer, "Theoretic and Programmatic Framework for the Development of Underdeveloped Countries", *New Progressive Review* 3, no. 2 (1987): 3–8. See also Joseph Lim, "The Agricultural Sector: Stagnation and Change", *New Progressive Review* 3, no. 2 (1987): 35–42.

20. See, for example, LUSSA Research Staff Countryside Report, *Focusing on Five Major Industries, Rice, Coconut, Sugar, Fishing and Abaca* (Quezon City: Luzon Secretariat for Social Action, 1982).

21. See Alternate Resource Centre staff, "A Theoretical Framework for Analysis of the Mode of Production and Social Formation in the Philippines: A Synopsis"; and "Steps in the Computation of the Mode of Exploitation and Determination of Social Classes", *Mindanao Focus*, no. 22 (1990).

22. For example, see Rigoberto Tiglao, *The Philippine Coconut Industry: Looking into Coconuts* (Davao City, Philippines: ARC Publications 1981).

23. As one former cadre put it to me, "While guerrillas could indeed wear down the state's armed capacities in the countryside, the handicap of protracted people's war is its very protractedness itself. No revolution has ever been won because of protracted people's war. Even in Vietnam, the success of their 'long tradition of resistance' owed much to quick victories in Dien Bien Phu and later the Tet offensive. It also had to do with the sudden collapse of the state apparatus, not its gradual weakening which the advocates of protracted people's

war want to happen." Interview with RR, former CPP Politburo member, April 1986. Other non-CPP groups welcomed the works of the Third World Studies Program. The programme became instrumental in helping a coalition of former members of the old Partido Komunista ng Pilipinas, a number of resigned CPP members, left-wing social democrats, "independent socialists", and some liberals define their ideological framework. The Bukluran sa Ikauunlad ng Sosyalistang Isip at Gawa (Alliance for the Advancement of Socialist Thought and Action, BISIG) made the *dependistas'* arguments the core ideology of their organization.

24. On the dictatorship as a Bonapartist regime, see Francisco Nemenzo, "Alternatives to Marcos", paper delivered at the Political Systems and Development workshop (Indian Council for the Social Sciences, 1980). On New Left-influenced arguments see, Alexander R. Magno, "The Marcos Regime: Crisis of Political Reproduction", in *Politics of Form: Essays on the Filipino State and Politics* (Quezon City: Kalikasan Press, 1991), pp. 70–92. See also Magno's "The Relative Autonomy Formulation and the Philippine Authoritarian State: A Critical Review" (MA dissertation, University of the Philippines, 1982).

25. *Marxism in the Philippines: Marx Centennial Lecture* (Quezon City: University of the Philippines Third World Studies Center, 1984); and *Marxism in the Philippines: Second Series* (Quezon City: University of the Philippines Third World Studies Center, 1988).

26. See, for example, a mimeographed document attacking BISIG and the Third World Studies Center, which was distributed all over the UP campus, "What the Recent Attacks against the Movement Amounts to", mimeographed (8 December 1992) (I was able to get a copy of this *ad hominine* [personal] attack on the staff of the Third World).

27. Kathleen Weekly, *The Communist Party of the Philippines, 1968–1993: A Story of its Theory and Practice* (Quezon City: University of the Philippines Press, 2001), p. 7.

28. Guerrero, *Philippine Society and Revolution*.

29. Benjamin Pimentel, U.G., *An Underground Tale: The Journey of Edgar Jopson and the First Quarter Storm Generation* (Pasig City, Philippines: Anvil, 2006).

30. Edicio de la Torre, *Touching Ground, Taking Root: Theological and Political Reflections on the Philippine Struggle* (Manila: Socio-Pastoral Institute, 1986). See in particular his essays, "The Challenge of Maoism and the Filipino Christian", pp. 61–77; and "The Passion, Death and Resurrection of the Petty Bourgeois Christian", pp. 87–96.

31. Together with Horacio Morales (who once headed the Party's National Democratic Front), De La Torre organized the Volunteers for Popular Democracy (VPD) after the People Power Revolution that overthrew President Marcos (which is alternately known as the EDSA revolution, the event having transpired in Manila's main throughfare — Epifanio de los Santos Avenue, EDSA) uprising to provide

a venue where the Left could dialogue with liberals and even some reactionary nationalists. VPD died a natural death, but one of its projects, the Institute for Popular Democracy (IPD) continues to thrive as a progressive research institute. See their website <http://ipd.org.ph/main/> (accessed 12 June 2008). On the first attempts to define popular democracy, see Edicio de la Torre and Horacio Morales, "Two Essays on Popular Democracy", Manila: Institute for Popular Democracy, 1986.

32. See the patronizing response of Roland G. Simbulan, "Yaong Pagsasamba sa mga Teoretistang Toreng-Garing [On the Veneration of Ivory-Tower Intellectuals]", *Diliman Review* (April–June 1979), pp. 46–47.

33. For example, A.R. Magno, "Agenda for Popular Democracy", in *Politics Without Form*, pp. 106–13.

34. Ma. Glenda Lopez-Wui and Chantana Banpasirichote, eds., *People's Initiatives: Engaging the State in Local Communities in the Philippines and Thailand* (Quezon City: Third World Studies Center, 2003); and Perlita M. Frago, Sharon M. Quinsaat, and Verna Dinah Q. Viajar, *Philippine Civil Society and the Globalization Discourse* (Quezon City: University of the Philippines Third World Studies Center, 2004).

35. See Maria Serena L. Diokno, ed., *Philippine Democracy Agenda, Volume 1, Democracy and Citizenship in Filipino Political Culture* (Quezon City: University of the Philippines Third World Studies Center, 1998); Marlon A. Wui and Ma. Glenda S. Lopez, eds., *Philippine Democracy Agenda, Volume 2, State-Civil Society Relations in Policy-Making* (Quezon City: University of the Philippines Third World Studies Center, 1998); and Miriam Coronel Ferrer, ed., *Philippine Democracy Agenda, Volume 3, Civil Society Making Civil Society* (Quezon City: University of the Philippines Third World Studies Center, 1998). See also the centre's "training programs", that include a "policy dialogue" series <http://www.upd.edu.ph/~twsc/training_PDS.html> (accessed 13 June 2008).

36. Concepcion Paez, "From Prison to Palace: The Long March of Bobi Tiglao", *Newsbreak* 2, no. 10 (1 April 2002): 19.

37. A sample of this pro-CPP, postmodernist influenced writing is Edel Garcellano, *Knife's Edge: Selected Essays* (Quezon City: University of the Philippines Press, 2001).

38. Rafael Salas, "Development Plan for Mindanao", *Sunday Times Magazine*, 2 February 1961, p. 3. Salas was Marcos' executive secretary during his first term and was largely responsible for setting up the president's team of loyal technocrats.

39. Among the classic works on the MNLF rebellion, see T.J.S. George, *Revolt in Mindanao: The Rise of Islam in Philippine Politics* (Kuala Lumpur: Oxford University Press, 1980); Eliseo R. Mercado, "Culture, Economics and Revolt in Mindanao: The Origins of the MNLF and the Politics of Moro Separatism", in *Armed Separatism in Southeast Asia*, edited by Lim Joo Jock and Vani S. (Singapore: Institute of Southeast Asian Studies, 1984); and Marites Vitug and

Glenda Gloria, *Under the Crescent Moon: Rebellion in Mindanao* (Quezon City: Ateneo de Manila University Centre for Social Policy and Public Affairs and the Institute for Popular Democracy, 2000).

40. B.R. Rodil, Kalinaw Mindanaw: *The Story of the GRP-MNLF Peace Process, 1975–1996* (Davao: Alternate Forum for Research in Mindanao, 2000).

41. According to the late historian, Peter Gowing, the MNLF war cost the dictatorship almost $1 million dollars a day, and left over 13,000 dead and 1.5 million refugees. Peter Gowing, *Muslim Filipinos: Heritage and Horizons* (Quezon City: New Day, 1979), pp. 234–35. Recently, the *Philippine Human Development Report 2005: Peace, Human Security and Human Development in the Philippines* (Manila: Human Development Network 2005), p. 72, came out with the following figures:

The Cost of the Protracted War in the Southern Philippines, 1969–96

Area/Province	Dead	Wounded	Displaced
Cotabato	20,000	8,000	100,000
Lanao	10,000	20,000	70,000
Sulu, Tawi-Tawi	10,000	8,000	100,000
Zamboanga	10,000	10,000	40,000
Basilan	10,000	8,000	40,000
Total	60,000	54,000	350,000

These figures must be treated guardedly, not simply because they seem to be oddly rounded out, but also because a set of statistics that covers the period up to 1996 failed to mention the various administrative subdivisions of the provinces mentioned.

42. On military politicization, see the various essays in *Kudeta: The Challenge to Philippine Democracy* (Manila: Philippine Centre for Investigative Journalism and Photojournalists' Guild of the Philippines, 1990); Francisco Nemenzo, "A Season of Coups", *Diliman Review* 34: 5–6 (November–December 1986): 1, 31–35; and Alfred W. McCoy, *Closer than Brothers: Manhood at the Philippine Military Academy* (New Haven: Yale University Press, 1999), pp. 183–221.

43. E.C. Tadem. *Mindanao Report: A Preliminary Study on the Economic Origins of Social Unrest* (Davao City, Philippines: AFRIM Resource Centre, 1980). See also Eugenio Demigillo, a former UP academic who went back to Mindanao and whose essay, "Mindanao: Development and Marginalization" in the *Third World Studies Center Philippines in the Third World Papers*, Series 20 (August 1979), laid out the basic features of the dictatorship's development projects.

44. Among some of the questions I faced in college were: Are you Muslim? Are you a criminal? Are you an exile? Are you a smuggler? And in the 1970s, of course, are you a rebel?

45. Abinales, *Fellow Traveller*, p. ii.

46. "Transnational Corporations and the Philippine Banana Export Industry", in *Political Economy of Philippine Commodities* (Quezon City: University of the Philippines Third World Studies Center, 1983), pp. 3–31.

47. The publication was *WHO Magazine*, which ended publication shortly before the fall of Marcos.

48. Ateneo de Manila University, Department of Economics, "The Socio-Political Nature of the Aquino Government", in *The Aquino Presidency and Administration, 1986–1992: Contemporary Assessments and the Judgement of History*, edited by Jose V. Abueva and Emerlinda R. Roman (Quezon City: University of the Philippines Press, 1993), pp. 28–29; Glenda M. Gloria, *We Were Soldiers: Military Men in Politics and Bureaucracy* (Quezon City: Friederich-Ebert Stiftung, 2003).

49. Patricio N. Abinales and Donna J. Amoroso, "The Withering of Philippine Democracy", *Current History: A Journal of Contemporary World Affairs 105* (September 2006): 290–95.

50. Dominique Caouette, "Persevering Revolutionaries: Armed Struggle in the 21st Century, Exploring the Revolution of the Communist Party of the Philippines" (PhD dissertation, Cornell University, 2004).

51. See Anderson's wonderful brief autobiography in the introduction to *Language and Power: Exploring Political Cultures in Indonesia* (Ithaca, NY: Cornell University Press, 1990), pp. 1–13. See also his explorations on his Scots-Irish ancestors in Benedict Anderson, "Selective Kinship", *The Dublin Review* 10 (Spring 2003): 5–29. Anderson's reminiscences would later be complemented by the investigations of his brother on the life of their father. See Perry Anderson, "An Anglo-Irishman in China: J.C. O'G Anderson" in *Spectrum: From Right to Left in the World of Ideas* (London and New York: Verso, 2005), pp. 343–88.

52. "Jose Maria Sison and the Philippine Revolution: A Critique of an Interface", *Kasarinlan: Journal of Third World Studies* 8, no. 1 (Third Quarter, 1992): 3–65. See also "State Leaders, Apparatuses and Local Strongmen: The Philippine Military under Marcos," and "State Building, Communist Insurgency and Cacique Politics in the Philippines", in *Images of State Power: Essays on Philippine Politics from the Margins* (Quezon City: University of the Philippines Press, 1998), pp. 100–36 and 137–65, respectively.

53. Samuel K. Tan, The Filipino Muslim Armed Struggle (Manila: Filipinas Foundation, 1977); Cesar A. Majul, *The Contemporary Muslim Movement in the Philippines* (Berkeley: Mizan, 1985); Peter Gowing, *Understanding Islam and the Muslims in the Philippines* (Quezon City: New Day, 1988); Jeremy Beckett, "The Defiant and the Compliant: The Datus of Magiundanao under Colonial Rule", in *Philippine Social History: Global Trade and Local Transformation*, edited by Alfred W. McCoy and Ed de Jesus (Quezon City: Ateneo de Manila University Press, 1982); George, T.J.S., *Revolt in Mindanao*; Thomas McKenna, *Muslim Rebels and Rulers: Everyday Resistance Politics and Armed Separatism in the Southern*

Philippines (Berkeley, Los Angeles and London: University of California Press, 1998); and Vitug and Gloria, *Under the Crescent Moon.*

54. This fondness for alternative explanations can be found most explicitly in Benedict Anderson, "Studies of the Thai State: The State of Thai Studies", in *The Study of Thailand: Analyses of Knowledge, Approaches and Prospects in Anthropology, Art History, Economics, History and Political Science*, edited by Eliezer B. Ayal (Athens, Ohio: Ohio University Centre for International Studies, 1978), pp. 193–233.

55. Even "Moro" historians have no clear answer for this.

56. Such that one of the pitfalls of many scholars is either to conflate the island's histories into one "Mindanao history", associate Mindanao with the Muslim zones, or worse, as in the case of one book reviewer, to refer to Mindanao as a mere province of the Philippines. See Dr Mina Roces, "Book Review of Patricio N. Abinales, ed. "The Revolution Falters: The Left in Philippine Politics After 1986", *Asian Studies Review* 22, no. 1 (March 1988).

57. Patricio N. Abinales, "State Authority and Local Power in Southern Philippines, 1900–1972" (PhD dissertation, Cornell University, August 1997). Among its conclusions were:

   a. The origins of Muslim separatism were pre-colonial as well as colonial, with the United States preserving anti-Filipino attitudes in the short one-decade of direct army rule of the Moro Province. This rule was exceptional for trying to apply some of the principles of the American Progressive Movement, specifically in terms of creating a "regime-within-a-regime" peopled by professional civil servants, and pushing a development project aimed at tapping the economic potentials of the "Moro Province".

   b. During most of the Spanish colonial period and the early years of American rule, "Moro Mindanao" had more affinities with the communities in maritime Southeast Asia than with the Philippine colony.

   c. Of the two provinces during the colonial period, "Christian" Davao — which came under the economic control of the Japanese — was able to exercise greater autonomy from Manila compared to "Muslim" Cotabato.

   d. Contrary to the popular explanation, it was not state-directed settlement programmes that created the conditions for land battles between settlers and indigenous communities, but rather the spontaneous, community-organized movement of families and individuals from the central and northern Philippines to Mindanao. Moreover, for the first twenty-five years of the Republic, there was remarkable stability in the frontier zones, due largely to the mutual accommodation between local strongmen and national state leaders.

   e. What kept the Muslim communities territorially integrated to the Philippines were the local strongmen who acted as Janus-faced brokers between a national state and a suspicious Muslim community. This "Muslim experience" was no different from the way local power interacted with Manila in other parts of the country. It was through these mechanisms also that most of Mindanao was kept peaceful for the next twenty years after the Philippines was granted independence.

f. Preserving local power need not necessarily be based on the proverbial use of "guns, goons [and] gold," but also in local strongmen making use of rituals of political mobilization like elections to legitimize their rule.

g. Finally, the breakdown of the Mindanao politics was the product of a more interventionist president (Marcos) breaking down networks of local strongmen opposed to him through the use of rival strongmen, the army, and paramilitary units. This also came at a time when young Muslim radicals were coming back from the universities in Manila and the Middle East to revive the cause of Muslim separatism, albeit on more ideological terms.

58. "American Rule and the Formation of Filipino 'Colonial Nationalism'", *Southeast Asian Studies* (Center for Southeast Asian Studies, Kyoto University) 39, no. 4 (March 2002): 604–21; and "The Good Imperialists? American Military Presence in the Southern Philippines in Historical Perspective", *Philippine Studies* 52 (2004): 179–207.

59. "Mindanao in the Developmentalist Fantasy of the Philippine State, 1900–2000", in *Checkpoints and Chokepoints: Learning from Peace and Development Paradigms and Practices in Mindanao* (Davao City: Mindanao Studies Consortium Foundation, 2007), pp. 79–100.

60. *Making Mindanao: Cotabato and Davao in the Formation of the Philippine Nation-State* (Quezon City: Ateneo de Manila University Press, 2000). Among works that drew much from the dissertation arguments are "Sancho Panza at Buliok Complex: The Paradoxes of Muslim Separatism", in *Whither the Philippines in the 21st Century*, edited by Rodolfo Severino and Lorraine Salazar, pp. 277–312 (Singapore: Institute of Southeast Asian Studies and Konrad Adenaeur Stiftung, 2007); "The Philippines: Weak State, Resilient President", *Southeast Asian Affairs 2008*, edited by Daljit Singh and Tin Maung Maung Than, pp. 293–312 (Singapore: Institute of Southeast Asian Studies, 2008).

61. "When a Revolution devours its Children ... before Victory: Operasyong Kampanyang Ahos and the Tragedy of Mindanao Communism", in *The Revolution Falters: The Left in the Philippines after 1986*, edited by Patricio N. Abinales (Ithaca, NY: Cornell University Southeast Asia Program, 1996); "Southeast Asia's Last People's War: The Communist Insurgency in the Post-Marcos Philippines", in *The Politics of Death: Political Violence in Southeast Asia*, edited by Aurel Croissant, Beate Martin, and Sascha Kneips (Berlin: Lit Verlag, 2006); and "Kahos Revisited: The Mindanao Commission and Its Narrative of a Tragedy", in *Brokering a Revolution: Cadres in a Philippine Insurgency*, edited by Rosanne Rutten (Quezon City: Ateneo de Manila University Press, 2008).

62. *State and Society in the Philippines*, with Donna J. Amoroso (Lapham, Maryland: Rowman and Littlefield, 2005).

63. "Progressive-Machine Conflicts in Early-Twentieth Century U.S. Politics and Colonial State Building in the Philippines", in *The American Colonial State in the Philippines: Global Perspectives*, edited by Julian Go and Anne Foster (Durham, North Carolina and London: Duke University Press, 2003). The main inspiration for atypical comparison was Anderson's *Imagined Communities: Reflections on the Origins and Spread of Nationalism* (London and New York: Verso, 1991).

64. Reynaldo Ileto, "Preface to Third Printing". In *Pasyon and Revolution: Popular Movements in the Philippines, 1840–1910* (Quezon City: Ateneo de Manila University Press, 1979), p. xi. Ileto, however, treads softly when engaging Filipino communists whose response to his work, so far, appears to be dismissive (peasants, after all, do educate themselves on the secular theories of Marx and Engels, and are not stuck with Catholic manuals as the ideological basis for their rebellion). On Ileto and the Left, see his "The 'Unfinished Revolution' in Political Discourse", in *Filipinos and their Revolution: Events, Discourse, and Historiography* (Quezon City: Ateneo de Manila University Press, 1998), p. 295.

65. Of Ileto's gratitude to his Cornell mentors, he writes: "I was fortunate in having mentors like Benedict Anderson, James Siegel, and Oliver Wolters [whose] scholarship on Southeast Asia is reflected in the questions I raise here concerning the Philippines." *Pasyon and Revolution*, p. xii.

66. Reynaldo Ileto, "Orientalism and the Study of Philippine Politics", in *Knowing America's Colony a Hundred Years from the Philippine War* (Hawaii: Centre for Philippine Studies, 1999), pp. 41–65. A prescient critique of Ileto's sweeping essay is Rommel Curaming, "Transcending Parochialism: Pitfalls and Promises of Postcolonial-Postmodern Approaches to the Study of Knowledge Production in Southeast Asia", paper presented at the Frontiers in Asian Studies Workshop, Old Canberra House, Australian National University, 2–3 October 2002 <http://arts.monash.edu/lcl/conferences/cultural-flows/cfpapers/cf-conf-paper-curaming.pdf> (accessed 17 June 2008).

67. See, among others, the essays in Luis Francia and Angel Shaw, eds., *Vestiges of War: The Philippine-American War and the Aftermath of an Imperial Dream, 1899–1999* (New York: New York University Press, 2002). On Japanese admiration for Ileto, see Yoshiko Nagano, "Transcultural Battlefield: Recent Japanese Translations of Philippine History", University of California, Los Angeles Center for Southeast Asian Studies Occasional Paper (2006) <http://repositories.cdlib.org/cgi/viewcontent.cgi?article=1008&context=international/ uclacseas> (accessed 18 June 2008). Nagano prefaces her English essay, delivered in California, with this plea to absent Japanese readers: "Please do not read it as their history, but read it as our history since both the Philippines and Japan are under the US shadow", p. 10. In one sentence the historical differences between the two societies, which include the brutal Japanese occupation of the Philippines, the turning of Japan into a receptacle for many an exploited Filipina "entertainer" and spouse, and finally the continued dominating presence of Japanese transnationals on the

commanding heights of the Philippine economy, are swept under the rug under the pretext of a dominating American hegemon.

68. Charlie Samuya Veric, "The Fictions of Necessity" in *Kritika Kultura: An Electronic Journal of Literary/Cultural and Language Studies* no. 1 (February 2002): 85 <http://www.ateneo.edu/kritikakultura/kk01.pdf> (accessed 17 June 2008). The occasion is Veric's review of Caroline S. Hau's attempt to problematize nationalism in her book, *Necessary Fictions* (Quezon City: Ateneo de Manila University Press, 2000). Veric is now a graduate student at the *American and elite* Yale University.

69. Like many dissertations which are subtle autobiographies, I wrote mine to try to explain my own perpetually marginalized story. Reflecting back, I now see it as having been inspired by the comments of historian Vicente Rafael that Anderson's now classic work, *Imagined Communities*, was thoroughly permeated with autobiography. Indeed Anderson reminisces: "As I look back now, it seems an odd book to be written by someone born in China, raised in three countries, speaking with an obsolete English accent, carrying an Irish passport, living in America, and devoted to Southeast Asia. Yet, perhaps it could only be written from various exiles, and with divided loyalties." *Language and Power*, p. 10.

References

Abinales, Patricio N. "Radicals and Activists: Birth, Hegemony and the Crisis of the Philippine Student Movement". Unpublished manuscript. University of the Philippines Third World Studies Center Library, 1981.

———. "Jose Maria Sison and the Philippine Revolution: A Critique of an Interface". *Kasarinlan: Journal of Third World Studies* 8, no. 1 (1992).

———. "When a Revolution Devours its Children … before Victory: Operasyong Kampanyang Ahos and the Tragedy of Mindanao Communism". In *The Revolution Falters: The Left in the Philippines after 1986*, edited by Patricio N. Abinales. Ithaca, NY: Cornell University Southeast Asia Program, 1996.

———. "State Authority and Local Power in Southern Philippines, 1900–1972". PhD dissertation, Cornell University, August, 1997.

———. *Images of State Power: Essays on Philippine Politics from the Margins.* Quezon City: University of the Philippines Press, 1998.

———. *Making Mindanao: Cotabato and Davao in the Formation of the Philippine Nation-State.* Quezon City: Ateneo de Manila University Press, 2000.

———. "The Left and the Philippine Student Movement: Random Historical Notes on Party Politics and Sectoral Struggles". In *Fellow Traveler: Essays on Filipino Communism.* Quezon City: University of the Philippines Press, 2001.

———. "American Rule and the Formation of Filipino 'Colonial Nationalism'". *Southeast Asian Studies* 39, no. 4 (March 2002).

————. "Progressive-Machine Conflicts in Early-Twentieth Century U.S. Politics and Colonial State Building in the Philippines". In *The American Colonial State in the Philippines: Global Perspectives*, edited by Julian Go and Anne Foster. Durham, North Carolina and London: Duke University Press, 2003.

————. "The Good Imperialists? American Military Presence in the Southern Philippines in Historical Perspective". *Philippine Studies* 52 (2004).

————. "Southeast Asia's Last People's War: The Communist Insurgency in the Post-Marcos Philippines". In *The Politics of Death: Political Violence in Southeast Asia*, edited by Aurel Croissant, Beate Martin, and Sascha Kneips. Berlin: Lit Verlag, 2006.

————. "Mindanao in the Developmentalist Fantasy of the Philippine State, 1900–2000". In *Checkpoints and Chokepoints: Learning from Peace and Development Paradigms and Practices in Mindanao*. Davao City: Mindanao Studies Consortium Foundation, 2007.

————. "Sancho Panza at Buliok Complex: The Paradoxes of Muslim Separatism". In *Whither the Philippines in the 21st Century*, edited by Rodolfo Severino and Lorraine Salazar. Singapore: Institute of Southeast Asian Studies and Konrad Adenaeur Stiftung, 2007.

————. "Fragments of History, Silhouettes of Resurgence: Student Radicalism in the Early Years of the Marcos Dictatorship". *Tonan Aijia Kenkyu* 46, no. 2 (2008).

————. "The Philippines: Weak State, Resilient President". *Southeast Asian Affairs 2008*, edited by Daljit Singh and Tin Maung Maung Than. Singapore: Institute of Southeast Asian Studies, 2008.

————. "Kahos Revisited: The Mindanao Commission and Its Narrative of a Tragedy". In *Brokering a Revolution: Cadres in a Philippine Insurgency*, edited by Rosanne Rutten. Quezon City: Ateneo de Manila University Press, 2008.

Abinales, Patricio N. and Donna J. Amoroso. *State and Society in the Philippines*. Lapham, Maryland: Rowman and Littlefield, 2005.

————. "The Withering of Philippine Democracy". *Current History: A Journal of Contemporary World Affairs 105* (September 2006).

Alternate Resource Centre Staff. "A Theoretical Framework for Analysis of the Mode of Production and Social Formation in the Philippines: A Synopsis". *Mindanao Focus*, no. 22 (1990).

————. "Steps in the Computation of the Mode of Exploitation and Determination of Social Classes". *Mindanao Focus*, no. 22 (1990).

Anderson, Benedict. "Studies of the Thai State: The State of Thai Studies". In *The Study of Thailand: Analyses of Knowledge, Approaches and Prospects in Anthropology, Art History, Economics, History and Political Science*, edited by Eliezer B. Ayal. Athens, Ohio: Ohio University Centre for International Studies, 1978.

————. *Language and Power: Exploring Political Cultures in Indonesia*. Ithaca, NY: Cornell University Press, 1990.

————. *Imagined Communities: Reflections on the Origins and Spread of Nationalism*. London and New York: Verso, 1991.

————. "Long-Distance Nationalism". In *Spectre of Comparison: Nationalism, Southeast Asia and the World*. London and New York: Verso, 1998.

————. "Selective Kinship". *Dublin Review* 10, Spring 2003.

Anderson, Perry . "An Anglo-Irishman in China: J.C. O'G Anderson". In *Spectrum: From Right to Left in the World of Ideas*. London and New York: Verso, 2005.

Anonymous. "AS Students Stage Protest March Anew". *Rebel Collegian*, no. 4 1-2 (1973).

————. "What the Recent Attacks against the Movement Amounts to". Unpublished manifesto, 8 December 1992.

Ateneo de Manila University, Department of Economics. "The Socio-Political Nature of the Aquino Government". In *The Aquino Presidency and Administration, 1986–1992: Contemporary Assessments and the Judgement of History*, edited by Jose V. Abueva and Emerlinda R. Roman. Quezon City: University of the Philippines Press, 1993.

Beckett, Jeremy. "The Defiant and the Compliant: The Datus of Magiundanao under Colonial Rule". In *Philippine Social History: Global Trade and Local Transformation*, edited by Alfred W. McCoy and Ed de Jesus. Quezon City: Ateneo de Manila University Press, 1982.

Caouette, Dominique. "Persevering Revolutionaries: Armed Struggle in the 21st Century: Exploring the Revolution of the Communist Party of the Philippines". PhD dissertation, Cornell University, 2004.

Curaming, Rommel. "Transcending Parochialism: Pitfalls and Promises of Postcolonial-Postmodern Approaches to the Study of Knowledge Production in Southeast Asia". Paper presented at the "Frontiers in Asian Studies Workshop", Old Canberra House, Australian National University, 2–3 October 2002 <http://arts. monash.edu/lcl/conferences/cultural-flows/cfpapers/cf-conf-paper-curaming.pdf> (accessed 17 June 2008).

De la Torre, Edicio. *Touching Ground, Taking Root: Theological and Political Reflections on the Philippine Struggle*. Manila: Socio-Pastoral Institute, 1986.

De la Torre, Edicio and Horacio Morales. "Two Essays on Popular Democracy". Manila: Institute for Popular Democracy, 1986.

Demigillo, Eugenio. "Mindanao: Development and Marginalization". *Third World Studies Center Philippines in the Third World Papers*, Series 20, August 1979.

Department of Education, the Republic of the Philippines. "Guidelines for the Resumption of Classes under Martial Law". November 1972.

Diokno, Maria Serena L., ed. *Philippine Democracy Agenda, Volume 1, Democracy and Citizenship in Filipino Political Culture*. Quezon City: University of the Philippines Third World Studies Center, 1998.

Ferrer, Miriam Coronel, ed. *Philippine Democracy Agenda*, vol. 3, *Civil Society Making*

Civil Society. Quezon City: University of the Philippines Third World Studies Center, 1998.

Ferrer, Ricardo. "The Semi-Feudal, Semi-Colonial Mode of Production: The Goals of Political Practice". *New Philippine Review* 1, no. 2 (1984).

——. "Theoretic and Programmatic Framework for the Development of Underdeveloped Countries". *New Progressive Review* 3, no. 2 (1987).

Frago, Perlita M., Sharon M. Quinsaat, and Verna Dinah Q. Viajar. "Philippine Civil Society and the Globalization Discourse". Quezon City: University of the Philippines Third World Studies Center, 2004.

Francia, Luis and Angel Shaw, eds. *Vestiges of War: The Philippine-American War and the Aftermath of an Imperial Dream, 1899–1999*. New York: New York University Press, 2002.

Garcellano, Edel. *Knife's Edge: Selected Essays*. Quezon City: University of the Philippines Press, 2001.

George, T.J.S. *Revolt in Mindanao: The Rise of Islam in Philippine Politics*. Kuala Lumpur: Oxford University Press, 1980.

Gloria, Glenda M. *We Were Soldiers: Military Men in Politics and Bureaucracy*. Quezon City: Friederich-Ebert Stiftung, 2003.

Gowing, Peter. *Muslim Filipinos: Heritage and Horizons*. Quezon City: New Day, 1979.

——. *Understanding Islam and the Muslims in the Philippines*. Quezon City: New Day, 1988.

Guerrero, Amado. *Philippine Society and Revolution*. Hong Kong: Ta Kung Pao, 1971.

Hau, Caroline S. *Necessary Fictions*. Quezon City: Ateneo de Manila University Press, 2000.

Ileto, Reynaldo. *Pasyon and Revolution: Popular Movements in the Philippines, 1840–1910*. Quezon City: Ateneo de Manila University Press, 1979.

——. "The 'Unfinished Revolution' in Political Discourse". In *Filipinos and Their Revolution: Events, Discourse, and Historiography*. Quezon City: Ateneo de Manila University Press, 1998.

——. "Orientalism and the Study of Philippine Politics". In *Knowing America's Colony a Hundred Years from the Philippine War*. Hawaii: Centre for Philippine Studies, 1999.

Kudeta: The Challenge to Philippine Democracy. Manila: Philippine Centre for Investigative Journalism and Photojournalists' Guild of the Philippines, 1990.

Lim, Joseph. "The Agricultural Sector: Stagnation and Change". *New Progressive Review* 3, no. 2 (1987).

Lopez-Wui Ma. Glenda and Chantana Banpasirichote, eds. *People's Initiatives: Engaging the State in Local Communities in the Philippines and Thailand*. Quezon City: University of the Philippines Third World Studies Center, 2003.

LUSSA Research Staff. *Countryside Report, Focusing on Five Major Industries, Rice, Coconut, Sugar, Fishing and Abaca*. Quezon City: Luzon Secretariat for Social Action, 1982.

Magno, Alexander R. "The Relative Autonomy Formulation and the Philippine Authoritarian State: A Critical Review". MA Thesis, University of the Philippines, 1982.

——. *Politics of Form: Essays on the Filipino State and Politics*. Quezon City: Kalikasan, 1991.

Majul, Cesar A. *The Contemporary Muslim Movement in the Philippines*. Berkeley: Mizan, 1985.

McCoy, Alfred W. *Closer than Brothers: Manhood at the Philippine Military Academy*. New Haven: Yale University Press, 1999.

McKenna, Thomas. *Muslim Rebels and Rulers: Everyday Resistance Politics and Armed Separatism in the Southern Philippines*. Berkeley, Los Angeles and London: University of California Press, 1998.

Mercado, Eliseo R. "Culture, Economics and Revolt in Mindanao: The Origins of the MNLF and the Politics of Moro Separatism". In *Armed Separatism in Southeast Asia*, edited by Lim Joo Jock and Vani S. Singapore: Institute of Southeast Asian Studies, 1984.

Nagano, Yoshiko. "Transcultural Battlefield: Recent Japanese Translations of Philippine History". University of California, Los Angeles Center for Southeast Asian Studies Occasional Paper, 2006 <http://repositories.cdlib.org/cgi/viewcontent. cgi?article=1008&context=international/ uclacseas> (accessed 18 June 2008).

Nemenzo, Francisco. "Alternatives to Marcos". Paper delivered at the "Political Systems and Development" workshop, Indian Council for the Social Sciences. Unpublished manuscript, 1980.

——. "Rectification Process in the Philippine Communist Movement". In *Armed Communist Movements in Southeast Asia*, edited by Lim Joo-Jock and Vani S. Singapore: Institute of Southeast Asian Studies, 1984.

——. "A Season of Coups". *Diliman Review* 34 (November–December 1986): 5–6.

Paez, Concepcion. "From Prison to Palace: The Long March of Bobi Tiglao". *Newsbreak* 2, no. 10 (April 2002).

Philippine Human Development Report. *Peace, Human Security and Human Development in the Philippines*. Manila: Human Development Network, 2005.

Pimentel, Benjamin. *U.G., An Underground Tale: The Journey of Edgar Jopson and the First Quarter Storm Generation*. Pasig City, Philippines: Anvil, 2006.

Rivera, Temario C. "On the Contradictions of Rural Development". *Diliman Review* (September–October 1982).

Roces, Mina. "Book Review of Patricio N. Abinales (ed.). The Revolution Falters:

The Left in Philippine Politics After 1986". *Asian Studies Review* 22, no. 1 (March 1988).

Rodil, B.R. *Kalinaw Mindanaw: The Story of the GRP-MNLF Peace Process, 1975–1996.* Davao: Alternate Forum for Research in Mindanao, 2000.

Rojas, Virgilio. "The Mode of Production Controversy in the Philippines: Anatomy of a Lingering Theoretical Stalemate". *Philippine Left Review*, no. 4 (September 1992).

Salas, Rafael. "Development Plan for Mindanao". *Sunday Times Magazine*, 2 February 1961.

Simbulan, Roland G. "Yaong Pagsasamba sa mga Teoretistang Toreng-Garing" [On the Veneration of Ivory-Tower Intellectuals]. *Diliman Review* (April–June 1979).

Tadem, E.C. "Japanese Interests in the Philippine Fishing Industry". In *The Philippines in the Third World Papers Series*, no. 6. University of the Philippines Third World Studies Center, 1978.

———. *Mindanao Report: A Preliminary Study on the Economic Origins of Social Unrest.* Davao City, Philippines: AFRIM Resource Centre, 1980.

———. *Grains and Radicalism: The Political Economy of the Rice Industry in the Philippines.* Quezon City: University of the Philippines Third World Studies Center, 1986.

Tan, Samuel K. *The Filipino Muslim Armed Struggle.* Manila: Filipinas Foundation, 1977.

Third World Studies Center. *Political Economy of Philippine Commodities.* Quezon City: University of the Philippines Third World Studies Center, 1983.

———. *Marxism in the Philippines: Marx Centennial Lecture.* Quezon City: University of the Philippines Third World Studies Centre, 1984.

———. *Marxism in the Philippines: Second Series.* Quezon City: University of the Philippines Third World Studies Center, 1988.

Tiglao, Rigoberto. "Philippine Studies on Transnational Corporations: A Critique". In *The Philippines in the Third World Papers Series*, no. 10. University of the Philippines Third World Studies Center, 1978.

———. "Critique on Studies of Transnational Corporations". *Diliman Review* (January–March 1979).

———. "Non-Progress in the Periphery". *Diliman Review* (April–June 1979).

———. *The Philippine Coconut Industry: Looking into Coconuts.* Davao City, Philippines: ARC, 1981.

Tsuda Mamoru. "The Social Organization of Transnational Business and Industry: A Study of Japanese Capital-affiliated Joint Ventures in the Philippines". In *The Philippines in the Third World Papers Series*, no. 1. University of the Philippines Third World Studies Center, 1977.

Veric, Charlie Samuya. "The Fictions of Necessity". In *Kritika Kultura: An Electronic Journal of Literary/Cultural and Language Studies*, no. 1, February 2002.

Vitug, Marites and Glenda Gloria. *Under the Crescent Moon: Rebellion in Mindanao.*

Quezon City: Ateneo de Manila University Centre for Social Policy and Public Affairs and the Institute for Popular Democracy, 2000.

Weekly, Kathleen. *The Communist Party of the Philippines, 1968–1993: A Story of its Theory and Practice.* Quezon City: University of the Philippines Press, 2001.

Wui, Marlon A., and Glenda S. Ma Lopez, eds. *Philippine Democracy Agenda*, vol. 2, *State-Civil Society Relations in Policy-Making.* Quezon City: University of the Philippines Third World Studies Center, 1998.

10

(UN)LEARNING HUMAN SCIENCES
The Journey of a Malaysian from
the "Look East" Generation

Goh Beng-Lan

Reflecting on one's intellectual journey can only be an enterprise coloured by one's current lens and disposition. Inevitably, such a project risks the conflation of manifold experiences of the self into a journey more coherent than what it had been in practice. After all, thinking is a transformative process not easily pinned down to any linearity of time, events, or thought. This chapter is no more than a caricature of my intellectual journey, with the hope that it may provide a glimpse into possible contexts, processes, and ethics under which Southeast Asian scholars of my generation, which is of the sixties, have come to think about Southeast Asia.

My arrival at a position to "think from" Southeast Asia is very much a product of a combination of history, geography, personal pursuit, and providence as I moved across various intellectual environments over time. Looking back, I realize how my journey has been shaped by the imprints of intellectual currents associated with emancipatory struggles emanating from Western human sciences as I began my undergraduate training in Malaysia, and then moved on to Japan, Australia, and New York for my graduate and postgraduate studies respectively. It was an initial education in the periphery where intellectuals were actively engaged in class and Third World struggles for self-determination that set in place a radical foundation. This foundation would lead to my eventual captivation with newer critical currents on feminism and postcolonialism, pushing my work beyond class analyses towards questions of gender, culture, and race. It was, however, as I struggled to live up to my role as an educator, observer, and resident of Southeast Asia, in an area study programme in Singapore, that I became aware of the debilitating effects the newer critical politics had had on an area study enterprise outside the West and political agency within the region. It was this realization that forced me to see Southeast Asia not just as a site of study, but also as a place from which to make known the nuances of critical thinking and action from the region, which while connected to Western progressive imaginations and politics, are also different from them. What follows is a narration of my experiences of the places where I came from, where I have been, and where I now am, as part and parcel of how my theoretical-political imaginings about Southeast Asia have taken shape.

THE WORLD I CAME FROM

I was born in 1960 in Penang, just three years after Malaysia's independence. As Catholic Missions had established some of the best schools in Penang, like the parents of many of my peers, mine sent me to a convent school[1] with the hope that an English-medium education would provide me with a better future. Nonetheless, the year I entered elementary school in 1967, Penang's worst racial riot in modern Malaysian history broke out, bringing to light the crisis of decolonization and nation making in the fledgling Malaysian nation state.[2] This was the 1967 *hartal* (economic boycott) riot.

This still understudied event in modern Malaysian history was an unintended result of an economic boycott (inspired by the Ghandian philosophy of civil or non-violent protests) organized by the Labour Party on 24 November 1967 to protest against the devaluation of the Straits dollar, given the introduction of the Malayan dollar, and the imminent loss of Penang's free port status.

Aged seven when this riot happened, I have recollections of this tragedy. I remember the chaos in my school as parents rushed to pick up their children when news of the riots broke out. One of my neighbours, the owner of the grocery store where my family shopped, was speared to death in the violence of this riot.[3] To this day, the sudden loud wailing I heard as a young girl emanating from the store, amidst a curfew which confined us to our home, as his family received news of his death, remains in my mind. As we returned to school, I remember the admonishments of teachers not to engage in rumour mongering.

In the third year of my primary school studies, the May 1969 ethnic riots happened, which were to change the course of Malaysia's political landscape and lives of its people. The only memory of this event that I hold is that when school reopened after the lifting of curfew, my classmates and I had to attend many *muhibbah* (goodwill) programmes where we visited neighbouring communal schools. This was part of a nationwide educational programme imposed after the event in order to foster inter-ethnic goodwill amongst school children.

The May 1969 riots changed the course of my education and eventually my career as the New Economic Policy (NEP),[4] which was implemented in response to this tragedy, saw ethnicity become a determining factor of the socio-economic and daily life of my country. In the year immediately after the 1969 riots, all my lessons, except for Science and Maths, were taught in Malay — Malaysia's national language. By the time I went to university, I was pursuing a social science degree entirely in the national language.

Educated under a heightened phase of nationalism, I internalized the nationalist ideology and grew up trying to be a good national subject, preferring to see myself as Malaysian rather than Chinese, and accepting the privileged position of Malays in the country. It took an unfortunate incident when I was studying in Japan to make me acknowledge my suppressed sentiments about my dislocation in my own country. I had procured a job as a part-time radio announcer and translator at the Malay Desk at NHK's Radio Japan[5] during my master's studies. When I began work, I was paired to work with a seasoned part-timer, an older Malay man who had studied, married, and lived in Japan since World War II. He behaved rather spitefully towards me and I was troubled by this. One day, I gathered enough courage to talk to the radio's news anchor, a fellow Malaysian on secondment from Radio Television Malaysia (RTM) in Kuala Lumpur. Through her I came to know that even before I had reported for work, this older Malay colleague had waged a campaign against my hire because I was the first non-Malay ever to be hired by the radio desk. I was abhorred by what I heard and when I returned to my dormitory that evening, to my shock, I found myself groaning on the floor out of sheer anger. I had experienced a catharsis as a result of this encounter with racism from a fellow Malaysian outside Malaysia.

Later as I felt a duty to return home to work in my own society, leaving a job as an urban planner in Singapore that I had landed after my master's, I experienced the exclusionary effects of the NEP on my career aspirations. Certain by then that I wanted to pursue an academic career in my country, I returned from Singapore to take up a tutor's position at my alma mater, the School of Social Sciences, Universiti Sains Malaysia (USM), in Penang. While on the job I discovered that other fellow tutors recruited around the same time as me, all of whom held similar master's qualifications but happened to be

Malays, were offered long-term contracts in contrast to my "month-to-month" contract. In fact, these tutors were sent off to pursue PhD degrees abroad with university sponsorship within a year or two of their service. I realized then how the NEP had made it difficult for non-Malays of my generation to have an academic career in Malaysia — which at that time was synonymous with civil service employment as there were only public universities. In part, this was because the ethnic quota for non-Malays had already been filled by scholars from previous generations, many of whom were non-Malays. Disappointed and disillusioned, I left two years later after securing from the Australian International Development Assistance Bureau (AIDAB), now replaced by the Australian International Australian Agency for International Development (AusAID) a "Merit" scholarship and went on to do my PhD at Monash University in Victoria, Australia. I returned to teach for a year at USM after my PhD where, not surprisingly, I could not get a position at the School of Social Sciences, but instead at the School of Long Distance Education — a mass education programme set-up via teleconferencing, with short, intensive face-to-face teaching sessions for mature/working students. I left a year later for a postdoctoral fellowship at New York University and then moved on to my current job in Singapore, and in so doing, joined the community of Malaysians living abroad.

Looking back, I realize my experience of dislocation within Malaysian society prompted me to start on a quest for knowledge, and it is to these beginnings which I next turn.

THE BEGINNINGS: CLASS AND THIRD WORLD POLITICS

I entered university in 1980, the same year that Dr Mahathir Mohamad came to power as prime minister. Enrolled at the School of Social Sciences, my four-year university education at USM coincided with the rapid economic transformations alongside growing socio-political and ethno-religious fragmentation in Malaysian society. It was a time when university campuses became hotbeds of religious fundamentalism and ethnic segregation as an Islamic revival, wrought by a global political Islam and inspired by the Iranian Revolution, led to other religious revivals, resulting in the widening of ethnic divides as everyday life became the site for the expression of ethno-religious differences.

Witnessing such transformations around me, I became attracted to anthropology and sociology — one of the majoring fields offered — believing that it would equip me with knowledge to understand events around me better. As it turned out, I learnt less about the fields of my majors than a hotchpotch of leftist political ideas in the social sciences — a legacy from my lecturers, not all of whom held PhDs, but all of whom were socially engaged intellectuals who had received part, if not all, of their education at universities in the West. Obviously influenced by ideas from the Old and New Left as they studied abroad during the 1970s and early 1980s, my lecturers were teaching ideas from social theorists such as Karl Marx, C. Wright Mills, Immanuel Wallerstein, Samir Amin, Andre Gundre Frank, Barbara M. Ward, Frantz Fanon, Paulo Freire, Edward Said, and the Iranian leftist sociologist of religion, Ali Shariati. It was a social science training heavily influenced by Marxist and other leftist perspectives, where class politics, world system theory, and Third World struggles for self-determination became the major theoretical-political paradigms for analysing socio-political transformation and the problem of ethnicity in Malaysian society. Local works I encountered also reflected these larger frameworks, and my undergraduate education introduced me to some of the major critical thinkers in the Malaysian academe such as Syed Hussein Alatas and his works on colonial exploitation and representation of the lazy native; Syed Husin Ali and the problem of unequal landownership amongst the Malays as a hindrance to Malay development; Chandra Muzaffar and his arguments of class, urban-rural, and global geopolitical divides in explaining Malaysian Islamic revivalism; and a host of New Left scholars whose works highlighted capitalist relations and exploitation in explaining Malaysian political economy, such as Jomo Sundaram, John Savaranamuttu, Heng Ai Yun (writing under the pseudonym of Fatima Halim), Fan Yew Teng, Lim Mah Hui, among others.

It was under this critical leftist influence that I chose to research the Malaysian labour movements for my honours thesis. I did a case study of the Malaysian Trade Union Congress, the original, nationwide umbrella body of trade unions in Malaysia. It was a thesis which adopted a predictably Marxist analysis where I studied the evolution of the trade union body alongside legislative changes, which gradually curbed the powers of trade unions in collective bargaining, and severed its links with the intellectual community.

Looking back, I realize it was a generic social science undergraduate education imbued with leftist political ideals. USM, where I studied, was a radical hub at the time and my lecturers' theoretical-politics played a major role in shaping the ideas that I came to know. Although I was taught to be aware of class politics and geopolitical relations between the First and Third Worlds, it was inevitably an education within the conventions of the day, whereby theory was presumed to come from the West and local research was used to empirically support these Western theoretical frameworks. The ideas I learnt were largely derived from the social sciences and disciplinary distinctions appeared not to have mattered, as I learnt very little about my supposed majors of anthropology and sociology. Overall it was a training which made me aware of the importance of politically engaged scholarship and the critical structural frameworks provided have continued to inform my work today, motivating me to seek a balance between constructive/materialist and hermeneutic/deconstructive approaches in my work.

"Conscientized" by my lecturers, I graduated with the idealism of wanting to help change society for the better. I decided that journalism was a career where I could do just that and got a job with the *National Echo* in Penang.[6] As a rookie reporter, I began covering everyday beats such as court hearings, press conferences by the various government departments, and everyday events such as evictions of urban squatters, road accidents, and so on. Encountering the microcosms of everyday life on the job made me acutely aware of the enormity and, at times, senselessness of the social problems of my society. For instance, covering road accidents — something which I hated — often exasperated me when I saw how apart from recklessness, deaths were often caused by negligence on the part of the relevant authorities to provide proper facilities, such as traffic lights at dangerous intersections, or clear road dividers, or the necessary traffic warning signs — which at this point in time were still lacking in Penang. Urban eviction was another common story due to a brief economic boom at this time. I covered several eviction cases and was disturbed by the incivility and mayhem witnessed at these scenes when residents scrambled to save what they could as bulldozers knocked down squatter houses. It was after covering several such stories that I came to hear about an urban kampong of Portuguese-Eurasians fighting eviction by their landlord, the Roman Catholic Church, and decided to investigate and ended up doing a feature story on their struggle — I would later return to this case for my PhD research.

A year and a half into my job, the Malaysian economy went into a terrible recession which affected the financial status of my newspaper. Soon, we reporters were carpooling to save costs, and helping one another out financially as our monthly pay cheques were delayed. It was a difficult time and it was at this time that I thought about furthering my studies. I had developed some interest in women's issues during my undergraduate studies and had, while on my job, written a few feature stories about women, work and society, besides participating in the Penang chapter of a nationwide lobby for the enactment of a "Domestic Violence Act", which had begun at this time in the mid-1980s.[7] Hence when I thought about a master's degree, women's issues became a logical research topic to pursue. This quest would lead me to Japan to research Japanese feminism.

PROGRESSING WITH FEMINIST PERSPECTIVES

Japan may seem a strange place for someone to pursue research on feminism, but my decision had as much to do with personal choice as with opportunities opened up by Malaysian history. Some six months into office, Dr Mahathir had launched a Look East Policy where Malaysia turned to Japanese development as an alternative to learning from the West. I became a beneficiary of this during my third year at university when I entered an essay writing competition on the Look East Policy, and won a Japan Airlines Scholarship to study at Sophia University for a summer course. My trip to Japan was my first encounter with a developed society and I was mesmerized by Japan's technological modernity and the seeming order and cleanliness of its society. It created a curiosity in me about Japanese society, which led to my application for a Monbusho (Japan's Education Ministry) scholarship in order to pursue a master's degree.

My initial interests in working on women's issues landed me at Ochanomizu Women's University in Tokyo, the first national women's university in Japan, established during the Meiji era. It was here that I had the opportunity to work with two leading experts on women's studies in Japan, Professors Hara Hiroko and Ehara Yumiko, the latter of whom became my thesis supervisor. It was through them that I got to know the history of Japanese feminism and the lives of Japanese feminist personalities, ranging from Hiratsuka Raicho and Ichikawa Fusae — who were members of Japan's first wave feminism — through to second wave feminists of the 1970s such as Tanaka Mitsu and Matsui Yayori (who passed away in 2002). From my two supervisors, as well as the work of the feminist scholar Ueno Chizuko, whom I had the opportunity to meet, I learnt about issues surrounding family, work, and gender relations in the feminist struggle in Japan.

On entering the master's programme,[8] I decided to research "feminist subjectivities" amongst members of the feminist networks formed from the splintering of the Japanese Women's Liberation Movement in 1970. It was a study of the social-biographies of feminists from a particular age cohort who had participated in the 1968 and 1970 student radical movements, the Zengakuren and Zenkyoto respectively, and who later joined the Women's Liberation movement before joining various feminist networks when the movement broke up. My research interest was in part facilitated by my leftist political training in my undergraduate studies. I was fascinated by the history of student radicalism in Japan, its anti-establishment, and anti-Anpo (US-Japan Security treaty) ideologies and, in particular, its links and tensions with the Japanese feminist struggle as, frustrated by what they saw as sexism, female members of these radical movements broke away to form their own separate Liberation Movement in 1970.

Incidentally, my encounter with Japanese feminism coincided with a time when post-structuralism was being debated in the Japanese academy. It was in Japan that I first heard about the "post-structural turn", when I was introduced to the works of Michel Foucault and Anthony Giddens during my master's seminars. In fact, for one full year, one of my graduate seminars was dedicated to translating Giddens' *Central Problems in Social Theory* from English into Japanese, as we tried to grasp his structuration theory. Given the limitations of my Japanese language and the newness of these ideas at that time, I could however not fully grasp the post-structural shift. Instead I turned to a combination of psychoanalytic and radical/activist feminist ideas found in the works of Nancy Chodorow, Juliet Mitchell, Julia Kristeva, Catherine Mackinnon, Adrienne Rich, among others, as I searched for a theoretical framework which could incorporate the realm of the personal in shaping feminist politics from my research findings. My readings led me to adopt a feminist interpretation of Herbert Marcuse's ideas in *Eros and Civilisation*, on the role of libidinal forces in driving feminist subjectivity in the face of totalitarian capitalist forces to frame my research findings. In retrospect, my turning to a combination of neo-Marxist and psychoanalytic feminist approaches marked a move away from my undergraduate training in classical Marxist analyses, which relegated cultural dimensions to mere epiphenomena. This attempt to incorporate dimensions of human subjectivity in my study on Japanese feminism was the beginning of a shift in my thinking to take culture seriously in explanations of social transformation.

On finishing my master's studies in Japan, I was in two minds about returning home to work. Landing a job as an urban planner with the Ministry of National Development in Singapore[9] made the decision for me, but a few months into the job, my guilt had taken over. So I returned to Malaysia only to realize that I was born a little too late and into the wrong ethnic group to pursue an academic career there. This realization motivated me to explore the potency of cultural politics in shaping Malaysian society, an interest that I had pursued in my PhD research.

TAKING CULTURE SERIOUSLY AND A POSTCOLONIAL TURN

I began my PhD studies at Monash University in Melbourne, Australia, in 1992, working under the supervision of Joel S. Kahn, a leading anthropologist working on Malaysia and Indonesia.[10] It was in Australia that I became a student of anthropology. However, my serious engagement with anthropology coincided with a reflexive turn in the field wrought by the crisis of representation. Encountering anthropology without a strong background in it at a juncture when the discipline's foundational ideas were being deconstructed placed me on precarious grounds during my first year of study as I struggled to follow the conversations around me. Much midnight oil was burnt as I frantically tried to catch up on ongoing as well as classical debates in the discipline. I have to admit that at this time of anxious confusion, I felt a little cheated by my undergraduate training as I had received almost no basic knowledge of anthropology, my supposed major.

Nevertheless, studying anthropology during this period provided me with a better overall picture of the post-structural/postmodern shift in the human sciences, as I learnt from the discipline's responses to the critiques of grand narratives, disciplinary boundaries, and the Western foundations of knowledge. It was also at this stage that I first heard the term "subaltern theory" from the sceptical murmurings of anthropologists critical of these ideas. Curious, I tried to read Gayatri Spivak and Homi Bhabha on my own, but could not at the time understand the gist of their ideas. Despite my ignorance, I was somewhat puzzled as to why some of the progressive/left-leaning scholars around me, who seemed open towards post-structuralism and cross-disciplinary approaches — which I had at least understood subaltern theory to have sprung from — appeared uneasy about subaltern ideas. Comprehension of the deep chasms within progressive thought created by subaltern theory would only come to me later when I was in New York, and insight into the complexities of its theoretical politics when practised from locations outside the West would first become evident when I became a practising academic in Singapore.

In preparing to define my PhD research, I became interested in the forces of Malaysian modernization, as the new National Vision 2020 was launched amidst a bustling economy a year before I went to Australia. As part of refining my research topic, I began with library research while in Australia, on the spate of economic liberalization during the late 1980s which lifted Malaysia out of a recession and into a bubbling economy by the early 1990s. My research efforts led me to read about changing investment and land law policies in Malaysia, alerting me in particular to the significant levels of capital flow into the real estate/construction sector from the late 1980s. Eventually, I began to narrow down my interests to the politics of urban development in the context of new economic and cultural dynamics fuelled by the nationalist visions of Mahathir's government. I decided to work on Penang, the city which I came from and knew best. It was then that I recalled the Kampong Serani struggle and when I returned home for my fieldwork, I eventually did an ethnographic study of this conflict as part of my investigations into urban transformations in Penang during the early 1990s. My initial writing in my PhD thesis had focused on cultural production as a field of power relations in which to understand the spatial transformations of a Malaysian city. My original thesis was aimed at contributing to a rethinking of Malaysian urbanism, one in which the power of cultural and ethnic politics in shaping urban struggles in modern Malaysia was highlighted.

It was only during a postdoctoral stint at the International Centre for Advanced Study at New York University in a year-long seminar series on the theme of Cities, Nation, and Modernity, organized by Tom Bender and Harry Harootunian, that I began to use my PhD research to think about cross-cultural comparative analyses of the experience of modernity. It was there, at the heart of the American intellectual world, that I began to see the relevance of subaltern theory to my own work and thinking as I learnt from different modern experiences all over the world. Already labelled a postcolonial discourse by this time, subaltern theory had also become more accessible as theorists aligned with this set of theories were reinterpreted and their analytical and political bases made clearer. These reinterpretations were opening up post-subaltern terrains which pushed theorizations beyond the fixation with the empire/colony binary and the inescapable power of Western thought. It was this newer theorizing which I found relevant to my work. In particular, I was drawn to use it in my attempts to redefine centre-periphery, global-local, and universal-particular relations by overturning linear and hierarchical conceptions instead to investigate simultaneous, coeval, interconnected, and dependent processes in structuring these relationships. Such theorizing provided an alternative to those invidious comparisons of Malaysian progress in terms of the Western experiences, which were not only found in scholarship, but also in popular discourses and state rhetoric. Post-subaltern theories were an antidote to my frustrations here as they offered useful analytical tools to reveal and overcome simultaneously the problem of hierarchical comparisons of social experiences and meanings.

It was in this year of learning about similarities, but also differences, of modern experiences across the world that I began to develop a vantage point using the Malaysian case to contribute to intellectual debates. It was therefore my encounter with an intellectual environment in New York, which searched for coeval comparisons between different social-historical experiences and meanings, that facilitated my consciousness about the role of theoretical interventions from regional perspectives. It was also during this stint that I witnessed the deep divides within progressive perspectives, between what could be loosely grouped as the political/Marxist left and the cultural left (comprising subaltern or postcolonial camps). Nevertheless, something which I developed great respect for was that while these scholars did not see eye to eye the majority of them at least listened to, and were well informed about, their opponents' theoretical-politics — a rarity in academic life, I later came to realize.

The ideas which I had learnt in New York were translated into a revision of my PhD thesis as I prepared it for publication when I moved to Singapore. While teaching and living in Singapore would further consolidate my conviction about making theoretical contributions from regional perspectives, it would also make me see some of the hindrances of the newer critical paradigms when applied to an intellectual enterprise of teaching in, and learning from, regions outside the West.

DEVELOPING A SOUTHEAST ASIAN PERSPECTIVE

Like any keen young PhD holder eager to impart one's knowledge, I soon introduced a graduate module on postcolonial perspectives on Southeast Asia when I arrived at the Southeast Asian Studies Programme, National University of Singapore (NUS), in 1999. In the first couple of years, my module was designed to evaluate contributions and limitations of critical procedures offered by postcolonial theory towards understanding contemporary subjectivities in Southeast Asian societies. This module initially introduced the works of pioneering scholars such as Edward Said, Homi Bhabha, Gayatri Spivak, Ranajit Guha, as well as other related works in anthropology, literary and cultural studies, and historiography. My location within a Southeast Asian Studies programme also compelled me to educate myself on intellectual debates within this field, and it was here that I began to realize how both area studies and postcolonial studies share similar concerns. In subsequent years I began to tweak my module to explore the epistemological entwinements, differences, and limitations between these two fields. In particular, I was interested in exploring how they could learn from each other in their common quest for alternative knowledge.

Nevertheless, trying to bring together these two fields at a time when theoretical politics was pulling them apart proved to be a difficult enterprise. I became aware of just how easily in-between spaces could be misunderstood when, a few years into teaching, I discovered that a colleague had prescribed readings to students as an "antidote" to my supposedly "postmodern" ideas, and that a leading senior scholar in my faculty had jibed in my absence that I was no "postcolonial" scholar during a meeting about cultural studies. Such polemics, I realized, were in step with the disciplinary and theoretical divides found in Western academic discourse which I had observed in New York. Encountering such polemics at a time when I was rethinking the assumptions of the newer critical perspectives, helped me see how the conceptual challenge to rethink non-Western societies when executed outside the West might require us to revise, complicate, and expand the critical and disciplinary registers of Western academic discourses.

Teaching and doing research on Southeast Asia from the region had begun to make me see both the virtues and limitations of the progressive critique of area studies. On the one hand, I saw how a reductive dismissal of area studies as mere Orientalist knowledge could unjustly invalidate all contributions from this field, while at the same time erase non-Western agency in knowledge production at a time when non-Western "locals" (both elites and non-elites) were just gaining a voice to talk about their "region" from local perspectives. On the other hand, I was disturbed by a blanket dismissal of postcolonial ideas by area study specialists as nothing more than "naval gazing" because such views overlooked postcolonial theory's useful epistemological arsenal, which could help overcome the persistence of colonial/Western power hierarchies and exclusions in knowledge production, without succumbing to essentializing and derivative comparisons of differences. Furthermore, pedagogical dilemmas encountered, as well as social realities observed as I lived in the region, convinced me that while thinking about Southeast Asia might benefit from the newer critical paradigms, it might also have to carve out its own progressive entelechies.

Let me begin with pedagogical concerns which motivated this thinking. When I first joined the Southeast Asian Studies Programme in NUS, I was asked to lecture for a section of an honours module on Theory and Practice in Southeast Asian Studies — a course which prepares honours students for their honours thesis research — where I had to introduce anthropological perspectives and ethnography as a research methodology. This module — taught by a colleague at that time — was partitioned into various disciplinary sections, introducing students to historical, political, cultural-linguistic, and anthropological approaches. The partitioning of this module into different humanities and social science approaches, I was told, had long been a practice at the programme. Its aim was to expose students to different disciplinary approaches and leave things open for them to choose whatever perspective they deemed best for their work.

I was tasked to teach this module the year after I joined the programme, with the departure of my colleague. Not wanting to rock the boat, I followed the established syllabus. From students' feedback at the end of the semester, it was obvious that students not only found it hard to decide on the appropriate disciplinary approach for their research, but they were also confused about the links between the disciplines and Southeast Asian Studies. It dawned upon me then that the module's structure was reflective of a post–World War II American imagination of area studies as an assemblage of different disciplines, but not an autonomous (post)discipline in itself.[11] Arguably, this could be because Singapore is more susceptible than its neighbours to the post–World War II North American construction of "area studies" because of the primacy of English in its human sciences. The prevalence of this American conception of area studies could in part explain why the Southeast Asian Studies Programme at NUS was accorded the status of a programme and not a department when it was established, despite the fact that, unlike the American model, it has been an autonomous department since its inception, first offering undergraduate and later graduate degrees, with its own full-time staff and students, just like other disciplinary departments in the faculty.[12] Inevitably, the influence of the American construction of area studies also meant that the theoretical and disciplinary baggage of Euro-American human sciences was automatically inherited, where area studies was seen as a quasi-discipline that lacked epistemological (theoretical-philosophical) and methodological coherence when compared with "real" disciplines. Since area studies was in the shadow of these mainstream imaginings, teaching its "Theory and Practice" in Southeast Asian Studies was no simple task as epistemological quandaries abound, for instance: Should area studies be a mere assembly of different but separate disciplinary approaches under one roof? Or should it endeavour to cross boundaries and forge interdisciplinary approaches? Even if interdisciplinary approaches were preferred, questions arose as to whether they should be anchored in one particular disciplinary influence, or should they be a true blend of disciplinary approaches, with no one single influence standing out? But then, could a truly cross- or interdisciplinary approach really be feasible?

Aware that existing debates provided no clear answers to these theoretical and methodological dilemmas, I decided to revise the "Theory and Practice" module according to what I could best offer my students. I began by using anthropological approaches — with which I was most familiar — as a base on which to build "interdisciplinary" perspectives on the study of Southeast Asia. My experimentation benefited when Professor Reynaldo Ileto joined my programme and jointly taught the module with me for two years. During this time, we experimented with historiography and anthropology together as bases on which to work towards "interdisciplinary" approaches in the study of social phenomena in Southeast Asia. I further redesigned the syllabus when I subsequently taught it on my own.[13] Here, the syllabus was divided into two main sections: the first provided students with an idea of how Southeast Asian Studies could be defined by exploring intellectual genealogies to this field from both Western and non-Western academies, as well as influences from theoretical-political and disciplinary debates in Western human sciences; and the second introduced selected texts/studies which displayed both "disciplinary" as well as more "interdisciplinary" approaches to the study of political-economy, history, and culture in Southeast Asia so as to enable students to identify and compare the effectiveness of different approaches.

I do not profess to know what constitutes a Southeast Asian Studies approach and have no answer as to what would be the best way to teach "Theory and Practice" in this field. But I do know that if I merely follow mainstream conceptions, the disciplinary versus interdisciplinary dilemmas will remain. In fact, if we were to follow the mainstream conceptions seriously, the existence of a Southeast Asian Studies degree programme could even be questionable. The question of whether the Southeast Asian Studies Department at NUS should just offer a graduate and not undergraduate degree has been raised within my department as there have been concerns that Southeast Asian Studies undergraduates would be disadvantaged, particularly if they would like to pursue graduate studies elsewhere, as they do not have "proper" disciplinary training. Even in terms of graduate education, differences abound over the kind of graduate training we envision, for instance, should PhD theses produced at our department be different from those written at the disciplinary departments, and if so, how? Evidently, both "disciplinary" and "area study" positions are found amongst members of my programme and it is unlikely that a consensus on how to distinguish an area studies from a disciplinary approach could be easily reached. While the human virtues of collegiality, respect, and civility will help in fostering dialogue, better understanding, and compromise when consensus is called for to resolve pedagogical differences, I would proffer that one way to lessen such dilemmas is to ask ourselves what role and direction could a Southeast Asian Studies set-up, located in the region of study, take. Beyond contributions to wider humanity, all knowledge academies everywhere have functions and ethical obligations to their immediate societies within which they are embedded. There are, therefore, justified grounds to suggest that a Southeast Asian Studies department which is located in Singapore — a country within the region of its study — has a foremost role and ethical obligation to both its immediate and regional communities. It is only by carving its own directions rather than being tied to any set of (inter)disciplinary or a priori assumptions that an area study institution can develop pedagogic directions which are responsive to local conditions and imperatives.

Beyond teaching concerns, witnessing the emergence of new orthodoxies arising from the postcolonial polemics of East/West oppositions in Southeast Asia, and its paralyzing effects on progressive agency in the region, alerted me to even more serious reasons for knowledge interventions from regional perspectives. That is, to help develop more capacity for progressive action and dialogic exchanges between political extremities. Coming from and working on Malaysian society, I have been concerned with how progressive agency has become increasingly incapacitated as it is quickly flattened by Western ideology, and rejected, as the issues of human rights, democracy, and cultural conceptions become increasingly defined in terms of the opposition between Islam/tradition versus neo-liberal Western frameworks in recent times.

Observers would know that since the late twentieth century, the Malaysian state, under the past leadership of Dr Mahathir, has successfully deployed history, political-economy, and racial-cultural difference as grounds for its marginalized location in global capitalism and turned this into an effective anti-West rhetoric. In this official postcolonial politics, tradition and Islam have been extolled to refute Western liberalism and its associated notion of universal human rights. As this counter-cultural politics becomes inevitably entwined with the vicissitudes of a global political Islam, a new tide of conservative Islamism has emerged as a moral-political high force in Malaysian society. By the new millennium, a new Islamic orthodoxy had spread into efforts to implement an Islamic state and Islamic criminal law, sparking divides between Islamists and progressives (comprising both Muslims and non-Muslims) over constitutional guarantees within the multiracial body politic of Malaysian society (Noor 2002; Othman and Hooker 2003; Martinez 2001; Mohamad 2001). This stage of Islamism is characterized by a struggle between groups advocating for Islamic conservatism and those advocating for secular spaces in Malaysian public life.

The immediate catalysts of this impasse were a series of controversial legal tussles over burial rites, rehabilitation, and forced separation of spouses and parents from their children, involving cases of Muslim converts and apostates, which became publicized in the mass media. These cases brought to light unresolved contradictions in the areas of jurisdictions between Malaysia's separate system of civil and shariah courts over religious freedoms as provided for in the Malaysian Constitution.[14] As contentions over whether Islamic or civil law reigns supreme in deciding matters of religious freedom escalated, overarching interests to protect both grounds led to hostilities never witnessed in Malaysian society before, including death threats, between coalitions of diverse groups advocating "Islamist" and "secularist" positions.[15] In this fight, Islamist groups argued for the unquestionable supremacy of the shariah courts in deciding Islamic matters and they wanted the powers of this religious court strengthened. For progressives, the supremacy of the Federal Constitution and the civil courts in adjudicating religious freedom was absolute and they wanted reassurance of this guarantee. The fundamentally opposed positions between the two camps have led to a deadlock, with Islamists vilifying their opponents as Western secularists while progressives disparage Islamists as demagogues. What is sinister in this scenario is that these contending politics appear to fall in tune with state and global postcolonial ideologies which posit Islamization and Western human rights conceptions in binary oppositions.

The touting of secularism by progressives to counter Islamic orthodoxy in the context of a pervasive ideology on East-West differences in Malaysia has seen their quick rejection as being influenced by Western ideology. This perception is compounded by the fact that the current definition of universal human rights is heavily underpinned by Western philosophical assumptions, given that Western countries have had stronger roles in the history of shaping universal human rights after World War II (An-Naim 1992, p. 428). Furthermore, the search for alternative conceptions of human rights have remained stuck in a fixation to reject Western philosophical assumptions without yielding effective results — perhaps not unlike the theoretical deadlock in the postcolonial critique of Eurocentric knowledge and attempts to recover alternative knowledge. It seems that at this moment in time, alternative arguments of human rights are caught in a limbo: between the peril of being lumped with unethical and elitist/state-driven cultural relativist agendas, on the one hand, and the lack of vocabularies/concepts to articulate alternative moral and ethical ideas on human rights, on the other.

The danger in this situation is that all progressive positions about human emancipation — regardless of whether they may or may not conform to dominant liberal assumptions — are quickly flattened by Western ideology and dismissed, and even if nuances are articulated, they are glossed over, and misunderstood. Against such an atmosphere, if following western (post)liberal assumptions, progressive factions continue to insist that the politics of emancipation must emanate from civic-secularist idioms, the current impasse over religious freedom will likely continue. Although what progressives may actually be advocating is more of a concept of a politics based on secularism,[16] which recognizes religious liberty rather than an anti-religious position, they must understand that a separation of these two conceptions of secularism is often difficult in the Malaysian context.

There is hence an urgent need for those of us studying the region to help find ways to articulate and make heard alternative/nuanced conceptions of "liberal" action/politics, which while different from Western critical discourses, are connected by the same belief in the ideals of human rights and freedom. This should be accomplished to help prevent the knee-jerk dismissals of progressive ideals as Western ideologues that we see, and establish dialogic spaces between fundamental extremes. A solution, I suggest, lies not in resorting to philosophical arguments on the universal entitlement of human rights, regardless of religion, race, and so on, since the idea of freely choosing individuals is an ideological construct in itself after all (see Ortner 1996; Abu-Lughod 2002; Mahmood 2005). Rather, the question of human agency is inevitably a project shaped by the precipitates of culture and history. It is by reflecting on how different ethno-religious groups, who had long lived side by side and shared common historical and material struggles, traversed and transcended differences, and forged respect, mutuality and unity, that we could find ways out of the ideological deadlock between Islamic and secularist perspectives on religious freedom. Holding on to either an extreme Islamism which refuses to recognize the rightful place of other ethno-religious viewpoints, or to a narrow secularist conception of human rights which refuses to recognize the place of ethno-religious difference in mediating notions of human emancipation, will lead nowhere. The questions that arise which both sides need to consider are: Is progressive action (or the pursuit of justice and liberty) only conceivable in secular-civic terms alone? Can there be progressivism within Islam? The resolution to these questions, I believe, lies not in the philosophical, but historical, in that the issues of rights and freedom can only be resolved at the level of social practice.

What is needed at this challenging juncture in Malaysian history, I suggest, is a radical change in the naturalized assumptions of religion and human emancipation in both Islamist and progressive traditions. Critical transformative spaces can only emerge if Islamists and progressives alike are able to realize their complicity with, and enact distance from, larger national, global, and postcolonial ideologies, to draw instead on alternative imaginings of religion and human coexistence in deeper Malaysian history as ways to resolve such conflicts. The challenge is to help find ways to learn from, and make known, the suppressed narratives forged from the long history of inter-ethnic mutuality and social practices in Malaysian history, in order to find viable alternatives to the extremes of a narrow Islamism, or a myopic conception of human rights in secularist terms alone.

CONCLUSION

Looking back, I realize how I think today is very much an outcome of how I became inspired, but also vexed, by the politics and ethics of Western knowledge archives as I learnt about these ideas from both outside and inside Western locales. Eventually circumstances and observations as I taught and lived in Southeast Asia were what forced me to see the constraints of, and enact distance from, the newer theoretical and disciplinary politics from which I had greatly learnt, as I tried to render knowledge responsive and relevant to the political and historical urgencies of the region.

Evidently, my intellectual journey is one which has been strongly shaped by Western imaginations and, perhaps precisely so, also haunted by their spectre as manifested in my initial mesmerization and eventual exasperation with postcolonial ideas. My journey is not unique if we were to draw analogies between the academic and sociopolitical realities. As Western imaginations so powerfully shaped intellectual currents about, and from, the non-Western worlds, the same domination is found in the global political-economy. The power of the West, both real and imagined, remains a structuring force in driving thinking and politics in Southeast Asia. From regional perspectives, the inequalities in knowledge production and modern colonization are real, which in part explain why they have been successfully employed for rhetorical purposes by the state.

Not surprisingly postcolonial politics have caught on in both academic and politics spheres in the region. Nevertheless, as politically correct and as beneficial as postcolonial politics may have been in pushing us towards hope for a more equal world, unfortunately the divides created have undermined the prospects for critical transformations, largely due to knee-jerk reactions from both conservative and progressive camps in both the academic and political worlds, as they become polarized by the varying theoretical-political/ disciplinary and geopolitical positions. Even more sinister, such polemical divisions have made it almost impossible for alternatives to, or nuances from, current dominant ethical imaginings, to be heard. Despite the call for the decentring of knowledge, ethical differences articulated have remained unheard, unrecognized, and misunderstood as they are quickly relegated to mere theoretical or geopolitical theatrics. Given this current scenario, as someone working on Southeast Asia, I see the need to intervene in the current debates to help make known the nuances of critical thinking and ethical politics from the region to enable the recognition of altered progressive imaginations and action so that bridges can be built across polemical differences both within the region and between the region and the rest of the world. Unless we find ways to make sensible cultural-historical differences and forge understanding and recognition of different ethical imaginations and action, the postcolonial politics of West/non-West oppositions so prevalent today will only escalate in the changing stakes of power balances in a post–Cold War world.

Notes

1. The convent schools I attended during my primary and secondary education were run by the Sisters of the Holy Infant Jesus order. I later attended Saint Xavier's school for my Sixth Form — which was run by the Jesuit Mission.
2. Penang was more or less spared the atrocities of the infamous May 1969 ethnic riots. The quick action by the local police force in preventing the killings in Kuala Lumpur from spreading to Penang was often attributed to lessons learnt from the previous violent incident of the 1967 *hartal* riots, which started in Penang and spread to the northern regions of mainland Peninsular Malaysia.
3. He died as his car was ambushed when he was taking a relative to the Penang General Hospital. Killings during the 1967 *hartal* riots in Penang were noted to have been largely caused from injuries by weapons such as axes and spears (see Chua 2008).
4. The New Economic Policy was a twenty-year long affirmative action policy from 1970–90, which was aimed at elevating the socio-economic status of the Malays and abolishing poverty in Malaysian society.
5. This is a shortwave radio broadcast run by the Nippon Hoso Kyokai, Japan's national broadcasting corporation.
6. The predecessor of the *National Echo* was the *Straits Echo*, the first English newspaper in the British Straits Settlements.
7. This lobby would lead to the eventual formation of the Women's Crisis Centre (later renamed Women's Centre for Change) in Penang, of which I was a committee member in charge of the Centre's *Herizon* magazine from 1990 to 1992, when I returned to Penang after my master's studies.
8. I had to take an entrance exam to enter the master's programme and spent my first one and a half years in Japan studying the Japanese language and preparing for this exam.
9. I was working at the Strategic Planning Department which was absorbed by the Urban Renewal Authority (URA) — the body in charge of urban planning in Singapore — during my employment.
10. Professor Kenneth Young later became a co-supervisor as Joel Kahn moved to La Trobe University and I remained at Monash University due to scholarship considerations.
11. As has been pointed out, area studies, which became established during the Cold War in America, was conceived as a multidisciplinary field where the social sciences with its theoretical-analytical paradigms were brought in to complement the humanities — a field originally associated with the study of Oriental languages, history, culture, ethnology, and so on which began in Western Europe (e.g., see Katzenstein 2001; Rafael 1994). In theory this had the potential to transform a North American model of area studies into a revolutionary, post-disciplinary frontier. Yet as we know, theoretical critiques have declared the interdisciplinary mission of area studies in America a failure,

while at the same time its institutional status has been eroded by a funding crisis brought on by the end of the Cold War.

12. It took twenty years since its inception for the Southeast Asian Studies Programme at NUS to be conferred a department status when an application for this conversion was approved by the university in 2011. See footnote 44 in Chapter 1.

13. Ileto's administrative duties as head of the programme prevented him from continuing to co-teach this module. Since 2007, I no longer teach this module as a younger colleague took over and its syllabus has again changed.

14. Malaysia's Federal Constitution provides for both civil law (based on British Common Law) and Islamic law (following Shariah law of the Shafie School within Sunni Islam). Shariah laws in Malaysia conventionally regulate family and property matters, as well as certain religious offences amongst Muslims in the various states. At present the shariah courts provided by the Federal Territories Act 505 is a system of three-tier Islamic courts parallel to the civil courts, that is, the Shariah Subordinate Courts, the Syariah High Courts, and the Shariah Appeal Court (Othman 1998, p. 5).

15. Ibid.

16. Heiner Bielefeldt has argued that the concept of "political secularism based on religious liberty" is not popular in most Muslim societies in the world. In part he attributes this as arising from an inability amongst Muslims to separate this political concept from "an ideological form of secularism that aims at banning religion from public space" (2005, p. 112).

References

Abu-Lughod, Lila. "Do Muslim Women Really Need Saving? Anthropological Reflection on Cultural Relativism and its Others". *American Anthropologist* 104, no. 3 (2002): 783–90.

An-Naim, Abdullahi Ahmed. "Conclusion". In *Human Rights in Cross-Cultural Perspectives: A Quest for Consensus*, edited by Abdullahi Ahmed An-Naim. Philadelphia: University of Pennsylvania Press, 1992.

Bielefeldt, Heiner. "Western versus 'Islamic' human rights conceptions? A critique of Cultural Essentialism in the Discussion on Human Rights". *Political Theory* 28, no. 1 (2000): 90–121.

Chua, Ching Poo, Norman. "The 1967 Penang Hartal Riots: The Forgotten Event in Malaysian History". Independent Study Module, Joint MA degree in Southeast Asian Studies, National University of Singapore and Australian National University.

Giddens, Anthony. *Central Problems in Social Theory: Action, Structure and Contradiction in Social Analysis*. Basingstoke, Hants: Macmillan, 1986.

Katzenstein, Peter J. "Area and Regional Studies in the United States". *PS: Political Science and Politics* 34, no. 4 (2001): 789–91.

Mahmood, Saba. *Politics of Piety: The Islamic Revival and the Feminist Subject*. Princeton, NJ: Princeton University Press, 2005.

Mohamad, Maznah. "Women in the UMNO and PAS Labyrinth". In *Risking Malaysia: Culture, Politics and Identity*, edited by Maznah Mohamad and Wong Soak Koon. Bangi: Penerbit Universiti Kebangsaan and Malaysian Social Science Association, 2001.

Martinez, Patricia. "The Islamic State or the State of Islam in Malaysia". *Contemporary Southeast Asia* 23, no. 3 (2001): 474–503.

Noor, Farish A. "PAS Post-Fazdil Noor: Future Directions and Prospects". ISEAS Working Paper on Forum on Regional Strategic and Political Developments no. 8. Singapore: Institute of Southeast Asian Studies, 2002.

Ortner, Sherry. "Resistance and the Problem of Ethnographic Refusal". In *The Historic Turn in the Human Sciences*, edited by Terrence J. McDonald. Ann Arbour: University of Michigan Press, 1996.

Othman, Noraini. "Islam and the State in Malaysia: A Problem of Democratization and Pluralism". Paper presented at the conference on "Constitution, Democracy and Islam", University of Hanover, 10–12 December 1998.

Othman, Noraini and Virginia Hooker, eds. *Islam, Society and Politics*. Singapore: Institute of Southeast Asian Studies, 2003.

Rafael, Vincente L. "The Culture of Area Studies in the United States". *Social Text* no. 41 (1994): 91–111.

11

ARCHITECTURE, INDONESIA AND MAKING SENSE OF THE NEW ORDER
Notes and Reflections from My Student Years

Abidin Kusno

More than twenty years ago, discussing the culture of Indonesian research in North America, Benedict Anderson pointed out that scholars are not only experts in their fields, but they are also members of their particular societies.[1] Anderson indicates the importance of the institutional contexts and socio-historical conditions within which knowledge is produced. Today, Anderson's point applies as much to American scholars as to us, students of Indonesia who are situated (to a certain degree) in the West, and yet are still part of the cultural order of the place we come from.

Indonesia is a product of both my experience as its national subject and my understanding of it through engaging with knowledge and ideas obtained largely from the Western academy. Yet Indonesia is also a place where we encounter the limits both of our concept and our subjectivity. In this sense, the country is not merely an object of analysis for scientific or theoretical inquiry, but also a place to engage with the question of how we have become who we are. For such an orientation, premises and theories are tools to be used, modified, and transformed. They are important in so far as they help us to engage with the place.

In the end, regardless of where we are from and currently at, through our work, we are involved in the appropriation of theories and the construction of ourselves and the places within which we are (or were once) located. In this mutual framing of knowledge, power, and subjectivity, few experiences are as difficult and as rewarding to reflect on as those from our student years. For it is then that we encountered the material place, the interdisciplinary field, and the institutions that, in my own case, shaped both my subjectivity and Indonesia.

TO ENTER: JAKARTA

I was born in Medan the same year Soeharto came into power.[2] My family moved to Surabaya when I was sixteen. After completing high school I entered an architecture school and, soon after graduation in 1989, went to work in the capital city as a junior designer for a major Japanese construction firm in Jakarta. For a youngster, a starting career in one of the most important Japanese construction companies was a glorious invitation to become a perfect middle-class citizen of the New Order. It gave a feeling that the city and the nation were doing just fine, on the way to fulfilling its aspiration to become a developed country. The proliferation of new buildings, highways, and new towns in the capital city could confirm nothing other than the achievement of "development".[3]

In the early 1990s, the march of "development" was already undeniably clear in Jakarta. The daily commute from my parents' house at the corner of northwest Jakarta to the office in the Golden Triangle of Central Jakarta offered a daily rite of confirmation that the city was rapidly moving upward and outward. There were many mega-constructions in the city of Jakarta. Several new towns had already grown rather uncontrollably, and shopping malls continued to pop up along the main streets and flyovers of the city. The several projects I encountered on my office's drawing board further confirmed a bright future for the city — if "development" is measured conveniently by the spectacular appearances of more and more skyscrapers of international stature.

In every respect, Jakarta was new to me. Perhaps this is what has made the city appear at once hopeful and terrifying, alienating and inspiring. I had never seen or experienced the effects of such a scale of development, the incredible volume of motor vehicles and new tall buildings, and the very visible sight of poverty in the city. This was a city that was clearly far more disorienting, and also far richer, as well as poorer, than Surabaya and Medan. The drawings in my office and the development of the cityscape outside the window were all absorbing, but the existence of police, thugs, vendors, and squatter settlements everywhere was also undeniably clear. Like thousands of others, I was a new migrant trying to find a place in the city without the capacity to make sense of it. Furthermore, I had inexplicable fears of the tension that existed in the materiality of the city.

As I was ignorant of the city and the nation's history and politics, my intellectual engagement was limited to attending workshops offered by schools of architecture in Jakarta. The favourite subjects were "urban heritage", preservation of especially the decaying Dutch colonial buildings, appreciation of "ethnic architecture" (for its traditional symbolism), and how to design buildings with a sense of "local and national identity". These architectural workshops, organized by universities and professional associations, did not, however, address the issues of urban poverty, politics, and violence that one could feel in the city, but they at least responded to the speed of development by reflecting on questions of identity and heritage.

Perhaps it was out of this "traumatic" encounter (for want of a better word) with the development of the capital city, combined with my disillusionment with the idea of becoming a "master builder", that after just a year, I quit my architecture job, and found refuge as an assistant lecturer in an architecture school close to where my parents lived. It was there that I put together a research proposal based largely on materials and sentiments I had gathered from the workshops. It must have looked like a naive but nevertheless genuine "architecture manifesto" on the importance of Indonesian identity and heritage in the age of "globalization" — a new exciting keyword I had just picked up from the metropolitan press. I submitted it to the American Indonesian Exchange Foundation (AMINEF) in Jakarta for consideration for a Fulbright Scholarship to support graduate studies on the history and theory of architecture.

Little did I realize that behind the façade of "architectural study", was an effort to come to terms with Jakarta and its frantic national development. I was not fully aware at the time that I was actually asking myself the following questions: How are we going to make sense of the rapid development in the cityscape of Jakarta? What do these changes mean to the inhabitants of the city? How should I situate my own professional discipline in this rapid transformation? What kind of intellectual position could I develop?

Urgent but vague, these kind of questions nevertheless caught the attention of the Art History Department at the State University of New York (SUNY) in Binghamton (perhaps via the generous eyes of its chair, Anthony D. King). Till then Binghamton was also the only university that had offered me a full tuition waiver. So, with the support of a Fulbright scholarship, I went abroad for the first time.

BINGHAMTON

I went to the United States under the sponsorship of the American Indonesian Exchange Foundation. The programme provided a memorable six-week language and cultural training programme at the University of Texas at Austin. Towards the end of this orientation programme, I was assigned a "mentor", a faculty member in the architecture department at UT Austin for advice related to my discipline. I showed my mentor the brochure of the Art History Department at SUNY Binghamton in order to discuss what I needed to prepare before going there. After looking through the list of the faculty members and their research interests, my mentor, noticing that I was from Indonesia, said: "I don't know what your ideological orientation is, but you need to be very open in this place."

In the 1990s, Binghamton's Art History department was indeed unique. It was not the kind of architectural department I had visualized in my mind. There were not many graduate students and faculty members, but each of them (including the international students) was committed to challenging traditional approaches to art history and encouraged to explore new theoretical perspectives. Little did I realize that they were then a minority in the large disciplinary field of art history. The faculty members assembled in the department had been engaged productively with various "new" scholarships generated by a great mix of neo-Marxism, Foucauldian post-structuralism, feminism, and postcolonial studies. For a "technical" youngster from Soeharto's New Order Indonesia who had zero knowledge of Marxism, the ride to post-Marxism was hard to explain. In many ways, the leap did not seem to be a matter for much concern, for the 1990s belonged to an era of the deconstruction of various intellectual establishments, including those that I had not yet had a chance to get to know.

Binghamton then, by various measures, was a great place for study. Perhaps because there was also still a lot of unused space in my brain (characteristic of the New Order subject), I was able to bury myself in literature, in new paradigms, and debates that were all absorbing and interesting without, however, knowing exactly how they might help me focus my research. For someone who had had insignificant exposure to the social sciences and humanities, all literature seemed to be relevant. I read as much as I could and attended as many talks as possible. I also took as many courses as I was allowed to in my first semester, but, just before the mid-term, I had run out of steam and had to drop all of them but one: "Issues in Colonial Culture" with Anthony King who then became my mentor. The comparative and interdisciplinary nature of Tony's course made me feel that I not only had whole schools of thought to worry about, but the entire world as well.[4]

Tony King's close association with the Fernand Braudel Centre at Binghamton had also brought together premises, questions, and theories from the humanities (art history) and social sciences to his students. His *Colonialism, Urbanism and the World-Economy* (1990), which came out just as I started my graduate studies, made it impossible to ignore the historical and contemporary political economy of global urban transformation. The works of Immanuel Wallerstein and the different implementations of dependency and network theories by urban sociologists were important to our class as they provided a coherent way of understanding the urban implications of the global circulation of capital. They allowed Jakarta to be on (and off) the map of "the world cities", even within the core-periphery hierarchy and (in some ironical ways) developmentally based perspectives. Through Tony King's courses, I also got in intellectual touch with the circle of students in the sociology department. We met regularly and informally (under the Braudel Centre's regional research working group) to discuss the meaning of shifting core-periphery relations, the "Asian miracle", and how best to characterize postcolonial cities, especially in relation to the nation, its politics, its people, and their experiences.

Tony King himself worked productively within the general framework of the world-system perspective, but he also challenged this paradigm by way of experimenting, selectively, with one form of theory after another to create an interdisciplinary and critical scholarship of architecture and the built environment.[5] The creative tension he maintained between different theoretical approaches had the effect of encouraging us to find our own path and to experiment with approaches from more than one discipline. However, in his openness to new social theories, Tony King (like many of his colleagues in the Braudel Centre) maintained an unambiguous critical position towards modernization theories.

Modernization theory assumes a transformation of "traditional" societies into modern nations under the benevolent programme of colonialism and postcolonial development aid. The practical aim of this theory is to promote political stability in postcolonial societies so as to provide a basis for the free market and democracy.[6] The theoretical assumption is policy-relevant and persuasive, but it is also "Eurocentric" (a perspective that could be traced back to the colonial politics of development) in the sense that the postcolonial societies need to fulfil a number of requirements to become a member of the "developed" countries. But it never quite asks the question of who speaks in whose terms and for which members of postcolonial societies? In many significant ways, both the world-system perspective and the postcolonial criticisms that I have come to read, seek to problematize the neocolonial ideology of modernization theory and its "Eurocentric" assumptions.[7]

However, it may be useful to acknowledge that while the world-system perspective and postcolonial criticism are helpful in deconstructing the hegemonic modernizing "voices from above", they do not immediately offer ways of approaching the reality on the ground. Various useful discussions came from subaltern studies on how a "post-national" historiography might be, but the immediate call for me was to understand how power actually operates in and through the materiality of urban space and how human subjects are formed and transformed. These questions both sustained and challenged modernization theories.[8]

FOUCAULT

For years, I had the opportunity to explore premises, questions, and theories with Anthony King and fellow graduate students who took his seminars,[9] but no less important for me were other faculty whom he worked with in the department. Charles Burroughs, the iconoclast of Italian Renaissance studies, later inspired me to think about the importance of rituals and symbolic expressions of the "ancient regimes" of Java. Barbara Abou-El-Haj, whose approach to the medieval cathedral revealed a fascinating narrative of power which helped to demythologize the sacred. And finally, John Tagg, whose institutional critique of art history, systematically exposed both the hegemony and the limit of the discipline of art history unambiguously.[10] With Tagg, one could learn instantly about what was wrong with art history as a discipline and then extrapolate his concern to other fields, including the history and historiography of architecture.

In the department, we were sensitized to the politics and effects of representation. A painting or a building is not just an expression of a context, but is part of an attempt to shape context which might or might not be successful. The attention paid to the social production, circulation, and reception of an "object" shifted the focus of conventional art history analysis which centred on the appreciation of the "significant form".[11] It is no longer the "truth" in the object that we are looking for, but rather how and why the object is understood in a particular way; and how it works and for whom in a particular context; and how these questions in turn shape the context itself.

The contribution of Foucauldian knowledge and power is undeniably clear in this form of analysis. This "method" allowed me to reflect on the effects of knowledge construction (including the narrative we decide to construct or exclude) and how they strengthen as well as challenge power relations. In the first half of my graduate studies in the department, I mostly read this type of theoretical text, though always with Indonesia somewhere lost at the back of my mind.

In addition, it is hard not to remember my own fascination with Foucault's "panopticism", and this may well be due to my own past training in architecture school.[12] Our school in Surabaya (and perhaps elsewhere) used to train us with the doctrine of "functionalism".[13] A simplified explanation of this doctrine is the assumption that the function of human life (as if this is an external existence) dictates the final form of a house, a building, or a town.[14] In other words, the organization of space can be expected to fulfil quantifiable functions of individual and social life. With form follows the prior existence of function, we do not need to take the trouble of critically looking at the rationale behind certain programmes and ask why certain functions become important for a building. We assumed that the functions of a house, a department store, or a hospital are more or less given. Our main task, as architects, is to turn the quantifiable functions into spaces and organize them in an economical way.

However, even though we adopted this "form-follows-function" paradigm, we knew that the cause-and-effect could be easily reversed into "function-follows-form". In other words, the form and space we designed can have the power to shape individual and social life. This also offers the opportunity for architects to imagine themselves as "master builders" capable of using spatial forms to control human behaviour. So we were already involved in the organization of behaviour and perhaps had even adopted "panopticism" in our school design of a house, for instance, through the placement of living room, kitchen, and bedrooms.

Two things were new to me after reading "panopticism". First, the presumably prior existence of "function" could be seen as a naturalization of a set of culturally and politically determined values. Second, the micropractices of space could be understood in macro-scale as both a symptom of and a discourse for societal change. For Foucault, the system of space represented by panopticon depicted an epistemic change in the way (Western) society has been disciplined from the spectacle method of punishment under the public gaze, to the reformation of the soul through an interiorized self-regulated "private" surveillance of personal behaviour. This gave me some ways to imagine Jakarta as if it were a field on which a structure of "panopticon" is imposed for the purpose of producing a self-regulated "national subject" intended by the nation state of Indonesia.

I was then trying to show how the panoptic paradigm of "the house of glass" is manifested in the new, concrete material structures of everyday life,[15] such as the flyovers, the new town, the offices, and the shopping malls, all under the name of modernity and national development. In the end, however, I realized that the model of self-regulation that I adopted from Foucault was also inadequate, for the case of Jakarta is predicated on many other disciplinary methods, ranging from the non-state governance by the community to the spectacle of violence, such as the exhibition of state-sponsored punishment and death in public, the criminalization of the street in advertisements, and the exposure of fear of the "underclass" in the media, among others.[16]

What I am pointing out here is that using Foucault's work (or any Western philosophy) is not just an instance of applying a theory with a principal concern on one place to illuminate the realities of other places. Instead, it is more a case of how theories, such as those of Foucault, have been adapted and reworked in order to both shape, and make sense of, local realities.

ART HISTORY

Despite Binghamton's commitment to deconstruct the assumptions and paradigms of mainstream art history, it is fair to say that materials from "non-Western" areas still pose a question for a discipline previously based on the study of the Western world, and whether they require a different approach in order to study them.

The dominant paradigms known to art and architectural history at that time included, most importantly, the formalist approach, a linear narrative of stylistic development where the identity of the artist and architect was paramount as the beholder of meaning.[17] These paradigms assumed an idea of "progress" in European art and architectural traditions and traced the development of ancient Egyptian culture to a higher form of Greek art; then from the Italian Renaissance to abstract impressionism and modernism. The evolutionary assumption of this framework, however, left out (or tried awkwardly to squeeze in) those that do not quite fit.

However, as indicated above, Binghamton's art history was critical in producing a developmental model of "art" and cultural artefacts, even though introductory classes and textbooks continue to operate within the dominant paradigm. The issue, however, was not only how to deconstruct, but rather where and how to place, say, Asian or African art and architecture in the predetermined passage of European time. Or should one formulate a comparable developmental model, but then still question what the value of the new comparable model is? Moreover, do we have enough histories of the artistic and cultural production of, say, Indonesia (leaving out for the moment the question of national coherence) to assess the possibility of formulating a developmental model? What insights would a different approach to, say, architecture in Southeast Asia bring, especially when names and specific dates are a rare luxury to the cultural history of that region. For us, students of Asia, influenced by the department's interests in what has come to be called "new art history",[18] we too were more concerned with framing questions in different ways that would allow us to escape the tyranny of a teleological narrative.

The approach highlighted by the "new art history" is centred on the issue of representation within the context of power relations and its implication for gender, sexual, class, race and ethnic specificities. Essentially a product of "multicultural-postcolonialism" in the West (both in reality as well as ideology), the premises and questions mobilized by the "new art history" could nevertheless include a concern over how to represent the "non-Western" world. In any case, this approach takes the spatial and temporal context of artefacts seriously, but it is less concerned with the date and personality of a particular work. Furthermore, the influence of the Foucauldian genealogical approach encourages us to deal with the politics of representation, the question of reception, and the production of meaning in our own era.

If by reception one spoke about the perception of Dutch colonial architecture by Indonesians in the post-independence era, it would be possible to produce a critical architectural history that addressed the problematics of the present. Such issues open up a space for us to understand the complex interweaving of culture, politics, and identity formation. Dutch, as well as Indonesian architects, are not just great artist-engineers producing impressive works, but are also members of particular social orders who work to maintain and perhaps also to challenge those orders. If by "issues in colonial culture", we could do away with the big names and identities of architects, we could come up with different questions to explore.

So the question now is what are my cases, objects, and sites for the grounding of new premises and theories? How can we create a space for Indonesia, or Southeast Asia, in the sphere of critical debates provided by the theoretically inclined interdisciplinary department of Binghamton?

CORNELL

My search for "Indonesia" brought me to Cornell University, the main centre for Indonesian studies in North America, reached in less than an hour's drive from Binghamton. This proximity helped me to re-encounter Indonesia in a different light. In many ways, my understanding of Indonesian politics and the position I took towards the country were profoundly shaped by the works of Indonesianists at Cornell. I never had the opportunity to take a course there, but I benefited from discussion with the scholars at the centre. The whole generation of what we know as the Cornell School of Indonesian studies was then still intact: Benedict Anderson, James Siegel, and Takashi Shiraishi, among others.

In my view, what is most at stake in their studies of Indonesia is the strong emphasis on social and individual agency, despite their occasional orientalizing interest in the power and wholeness of the Javanese cosmos. A lot of attention was also paid to the state's invention of traditions, and the real effect of such traditions for the cultural practices of everyday life. Lastly, and most profoundly, they acknowledge that Indonesia is, after all, a modern society with people interested in doing modern things and, at particular moments, willing to fight and die for modernity. These profiles developed, to a large extent, in response to the style of Soeharto's governance. In an ironic way, the more-than-thirty-year rule of Soeharto in Indonesia has helped these Cornell scholars to produce some of the most important and interesting works on the country's politics, history, and culture.

Soeharto's regime in some ways brought together premises and questions about modernity in Indonesia. I recall a conversation with Ben Anderson during one pleasant summer afternoon on the Kahin Centre's balcony. I was then pondering what to focus on in my research. During the conversation, I made every effort to suggest the potential of Indonesian "traditional architecture" for addressing the problems caused by modernization and globalization — whatever this might mean. I was interested in knowing how traditional architecture might play a role in shaping individual and collective identities, and how it might contribute to the formation of national identities at this time of globalization. Ben indicated, quite softly, that he didn't know exactly what I meant by "tradition" and nor did he know about the world of architecture. What struck him, however, was my interest in "traditional architecture" at a time when everyone else wanted to be "modern".

Perhaps I was not able to put my thoughts across clearly enough, but it was Ben's iconoclastic response that made me realize the importance of reframing what I saw in the urban landscape of Jakarta and the need to question the premise that, for better or worse, Indonesia was "modernizing". Before then, I saw "traditional culture" as carrying a potential to resist and an offer alternative to the domination of "westernization". And to criticize the homogenizing forces of the universalized West, I had my world-systemic framework to show the incorporation of Jakarta into the global network of urban hierarchy and the "peripheralization" of what seemed to be a "modernizing" Jakarta. But my encounter with the "state of culture" via Cornell changed my framing.[19]

The "state of culture" refers to the pervasive production of culture in New Order Indonesia both to displace and replace history and politics to achieve its legitimacy of rule. Yet such production remained unstable and thus needed to be continuously reproduced as something "authentic" and "traditional". In Pemberton's words, "this haunting sense of incompleteness so pervasive in New Order cultural discourse has the effect then, of motivating an almost endless production of offering, a constant rearticulation of things cultural, in an attempt to make up for what may have been left out in the process of recovering 'tradition' ".[20] In this sense, one could argue that under the "modern façade" of Soeharto's New Order, members of Indonesian society were being absorbed into the force of "tradition" (even if this was invented). This is more than just a classic binary game between modernity and tradition. Instead, the "state of culture" was due to the political rationalities of rule which could not be adequately understood under the evolutionary assumption of modernization, and in terms of the success or failure to modernize. With both "modernization" and "tradition" under the custody of the New Order state that I sought to criticize, I had to abandon their metaphysical standing by focusing instead on the "apparatus" that produced them. I had since then shifted my focus to chart the "state of culture" and to read against it to understand how my world of architecture and urban design (regardless of their appearances in modern or traditional form) had been constructed in and through the *effects* of the "state of culture".

By then, there were a sufficient number of studies that I could reflect on in order to turn Indonesian modernity under Soeharto's regime upside down. Besides Anderson's work, the contributions of Takashi Shiraishi, John Pemberton, and James Siegel, among others, brought home the importance of looking politically at the thin line between the invention of tradition and the persistence of past imageries even after their decline.[21] Their various works have brought to life the cultural dimensions of development, the Indonesian nation state, and its relation to the consciousness of the elites, the middle class, and the commoners. Their interest in the connection between politics and sites of representation in the production of "the state of culture" have also brought me back to the premises, questions, and theories I encountered in the Binghamton art history department. They also got me to see, not so much the market, the creativity, and professionalism that shape architectural imagination, but also the cultural politics of the state which affected my field of architecture and urban form. By the end of my coursework, therefore,

I had become interested in localizing the nation state through the study of its architecture and visual environment.[22]

In this sense Indonesia is not always a place where its prior existent content is to be discovered through hard archival and field research (although this certainly contributes to new information). It is, rather, a site formed through various encounters, experiences, and subjectivities of different researchers, each bringing with him or her their different premises, questions, and theories. It is also a product of political positioning as much as of knowledge based on data-filled research.

TO CLOSE AND OPEN AGAIN

In the end, when the question is about securing a space for national or regional identity, we are not only talking about some distinctive localized formations, but also how they are constructed as different formations, each with its particular "state of culture" and within the global setting of "intertwined histories and overlapping territories".[23] Through this series of encounters with theoretical constructs and historical realities, I wrote my dissertation with a tension between the political history of architecture on the one hand, and theories of representation on the other. When I look back, *Behind the Postcolonial* appears to be a political history of architecture, but it is not really based on in-depth historical or empirical fieldwork. Instead, it is more a product of various responses to different encounters to make sense of a place, a city, and a nation historically, and, through examining the cultural politics of Indonesia, to understand how my (professional, social, and cultural) subjectivity has been shaped.[24]

The result is a story of historical effects and political possibilities of architecture and urban space in constructing new times. Of how the postcolonial new times offered an opportunity for the ruling elites to both forget and reproduce the past, in the name of "tradition", by reconfiguring the material space of, say, the "modern" capital city of Jakarta. Of dialogue with various premises, different institutions of theories, and several teachers who worked both for and against them. After my study, my earlier images of linear development in the capital city of Jakarta appeared not so much as a progression, but rather as a series of attempts to represent progress by inventing both tradition and modernity in order to overcome tensions, gaps, and an unforgettable past. Such a story, I believe, cannot be told only by archival and field research, but rather by a dialogue with and a localization of theories, Western or otherwise.

Peering around the corner of different times, spaces, and institutions, I see my premises, frameworks, and questions are marked by social theories developed in the West as well as by the presence of the New Order of Indonesia. My notes reveal my debt not only to theories, but also to the problematics of Soeharto's rule, and the social and political environment of his Indonesia. Today, while the images of the Soeharto regime have merged with those of the pre-colonial and colonial past, they remain a case for deconstruction and reconstruction.

Yet, in some ways, we have also lost some common historical and theoretical adversaries. That is, unless we perhaps agree that in some fundamental way, the regime continues to live and haunt the present, along with the regaining of the power of modernization theory, now in new imperial clothes.[25] And this is perhaps what we need to do, that is, to deal with the return, the effects, and the possibilities for a new Indonesia. In my case, this does not mean a clearing of space, but a continuing assumption of interdisciplinary approaches, a cross-territorial framework to break up colonial and imperial compartments, and to keep alive the economy of reflection and action in Southeast Asian scholarship.[26] In the end, the notion of interdisciplinary studies brings back to me not so much a particular approach in the knowledge production of the social sciences and humanities, but more the urgency to make sense of the complexity of the world *politically*, an unsettling consciousness which has forced me to beneficially leave behind the compartmental view of my own discipline.

Notes

1. Benedict Anderson, "Perspective and Method in American Research on Indonesia", in *Interpreting Indonesian Politics: 13 Contributions to the Debate*, Interim Report Series. No. 62, edited by Benedict Anderson and Audrey Kahin (Cornell Modern Indonesian Project, Southeast Asian Program, 1982), pp. 69–83.
2. Soeharto officially came to power on 11 March 1966 after having manoeuvred President Sukarno to sign a document giving him full authority to restore order following the massacre of communist supporters and sympathizers.
3. For a discussion on discourses of Indonesian "development", see Ariel Heryanto, "The Development of 'Development'", translated by N. Lutz, *Indonesia*, 46, pp. 1–24.
4. The course description of Tony King's Fall 1991 Issues in Colonial Culture: "This course will explore recent critical literature on colonial cultures, on postcolonialism and postimperialism as modes of cultural critique. Attention will be paid to questions of cultural hegemony and the social production of knowledge. Imperial regimes considered will include the USA, Britain, France,

Spain and Japan and material illustrative of visual and spatial cultures will be taken from Africa, India, East Asia, Latin America as well as New York State."

5. Tony King's explorations can be found in his recently published *Spaces of Global Cultures: Architecture, Urbanism, Identity* (London and New York: Routledge, 2004). The Archi*text* book series that he has co-edited with Tom Markus since the mid 1990s, represents a profound challenge to the traditional scholarship of architecture, while opening up a path for a more "critical, comparative and interdisciplinary" scholarship in the field.

6. For a recent assessment of the state of modernization theory, see Harry Harootunian, *The Empire's New Clothes: Paradigm Lost, and Regained* (Chicago: Prickly Paradigm, 2004).

7. Like many other students, I followed postcolonial studies through the works of Edward Said, and moved from literary criticism to the disciplines of history and anthropology.

8. Just as I was wrapping up my dissertation, Brenda Yeoh's *Contesting Space: Power Relations and the Urban Built Environment in Colonial Singapore* (Kuala Lumpur: Oxford University Press, 1996) showed that meticulous, time consuming, archival research could offer not only new information, but also set a premise and theory of how to look at colonial space from the position of both the colonized and the colonizer.

9. Especially Greig Crysler, who gave me the links between the world of architecture and critical concepts we read inside, as well as outside, the class. Without the benefit of discussions with him, I would not have been able to use some of the theories that helped me represent Indonesia. There was also Nihal Perera, who first gave me Batavia's link to Sri Lanka's Colombo via his world-system analysis. Like Tony King, they were devoted to certain theoretical positions, but never to the exclusion of the world of practice.

10. See John Tagg, *Grounds of Disputes: Art History, Cultural Politics and the Discursive Field* (Minneapolis: Minnesota University Press, 1992), particularly his manifesto, "Should Art Historians Know their Place?"

11. "Significant form included combinations of lines and of colors (counting white and black as colors) ... is the only quality common and peculiar to all the works of art that move me ... we have only to consider our emotion and its object", thus declared Clive Bell in *Art* (New York: Stokes, 1928), pp. 10–12.

12. Michel Foucault, "Panopticism", in *Discipline and Punish: The Birth of the Prison*, translated by Alan Sheridan (New York: Vintage Books, 1977), pp. 195–230.

13. For a discussion on the training programme in architectural school, see Kazys Varnelis, "The Education of the Innocent Eye", *Journal of Architectural Education* 51 no. 4 (May 1998): 212–23; see also C. Greig Crysler, "Critical Pedagogy and Architectural Education", *Journal of Architectural Education (1984–)*, 48, no. 4 (May 1995): 208–17.

14. In the 1920s, architectural theorist Laszlo Moholy-Nagy defined more sophisticatedly: "The elements necessary to the fulfillment of a function of a building unite in a spatial creation that can become a spatial experience for us. The ordering of space in this case is not more than the most economical union of planning methods and human needs." As quoted in Reyner Banham, *Theory and Design in the First Machine Age* (London: Architectural Press, 1960), p. 317.

15. The "house of glass" is from Pramoedya Ananta Toer, "*House of Glass*", translated by Max Lane (New York: Penguin, 1992).

16. Especially after reading John Pemberton's *On the Subject of "Java"* (Ithaca, NY: Cornell University Press, 1994); James Siegel's *A New Criminal Type in Jakarta: Counter-Revolution Today* (Durham, NC: Duke University Press, 1998).

17. I am indebted to Hong Kal for sharing the notes she took from various art history courses in Binghamton. I have also benefited from reading Suzanne Preston Blier, "Truth and Seeing: Magic, Custom, and Fetish in Art History", in *Africa and the Disciplines*, edited by Robert H. Bates, V.Y. Mudimbe, and Jean O'Barr (Chicago: Chicago University Press, 1993), pp. 139–66.

18. Art historians defined New Art History as "the theoretically rigorous and 'politically correct' approach to the discipline, especially where certain issues of class, race and gender are concerned. As its name implies, the new art history was a reaction to the 'old art history,' 1980s' practitioners of the new art history introduced what they believed to be a more accountable approach to the discipline." See: Pam Meecham and Julie Sheldon, *Modern Art: A Critical Introduction* (London and New York: Routledge, 2000), p. 221.

19. For a discussion on the "state of culture", see Pemberton *On the Subject of "Java"* (Ithaca, NY: Cornell University Press, 1994); see also Mary Margaret Steedly, "The State of Culture Theory in the Anthropology of Southeast Asia", *Annual Reviews of Anthropology* 28 (1999): 431–54.

20. John Pemberton, *On the Subject of "Java"* (Ithaca, NY: Cornell University Press, 1994), p. 11.

21. Benedict Anderson, *Language and Power: Exploring Political Cultures in Indonesia* (Ithaca, NY: Cornell University Press, 1990); John Pemberton, *On the Subject of "Java"* (Ithaca, NY: Cornell University Press, 1994); James Siegel, *Solo in the New Order: Language and Hierarchy in an Indonesian City* (Princeton, NJ: Princeton University Press, 1986); Takashi Shiraishi, *An Age in Motion: Popular Radicalism in Java, 1912–1926* (Ithaca, NY: Cornell University Press, 1990).

22. Several books on the relations between the postcolonial state and architecture and urban design had then been published, among others: Lawrence Vale, *Architecture, Power and National Identity* (New Haven: Yale University Press, 1992); James Holston, *The Modernist City: An Anthropological Critique of Brasilia* (Chicago: University of Chicago Press, 1989).

23. The term "intertwined histories and overlapping territories" is from Edward Said, *Culture and Imperialism* (New York: Knopf, 1993).

24. The book version of my dissertation came out in 2000 as *Behind the Postcolonial: Architecture, Urban Space and Political Cultures in Indonesia* (London and New York: Routledge).
25. For a critique of the return of the developmentalist paradigm in the geopolitics of the world, see Harry Harootunian, *The Empire's New Clothes: Paradigm Lost, and Regained* (Chicago: Prickly Paradigm, 2004).
26. "Interdisciplinarity", "Cross-cultural framework", "the economy of reflection and action", and "provisional and open-ended investigation" are the mission statement of *Handbook of Architectural Theory*, currently in preparation for Sage under the editorship of Greig Crysler, Stephen Cairns, and Hilde Heynen.

References

Anderson, Benedict. "Perspective and Method in American Research on Indonesia". In *Interpreting Indonesian Politics: 13 Contributions to the Debate*, edited by Benedict Anderson and Audrey Kahin. Interim Report Series. No. 62, Cornell Modern Indonesian Project, Southeast Asian Program, 1982.

————. *Language and Power: Exploring Political Cultures in Indonesia*. Ithaca, NY: Cornell University Press, 1990.

Banham, Reyner. *Theory and Design in the First Machine Age*. London: Architectural Press, 1960.

Bell, Clive. *Art*. New York: Stokes, 1928.

Blier, Suzanne Preston. "Truth and Seeing: Magic, Custom, and Fetish in Art History". In *Africa and the Disciplines*, edited by Robert H. Bates, V.Y. Mudimbe, and Jean O'Barr. Chicago: Chicago University Press, 1993.

Crysler, C. Greig. "Critical Pedagogy and Architectural Education". *Journal of Architectural Education (1984–)* 48, no. 4 (May 1995): 208–17.

Foucault, Michel. "Panopticism". In *Discipline and Punish: The Birth of the Prison*. Translated by Alan Sheridan. New York: Vintage Books, 1977.

Harootunian, Harry. *The Empire's New Clothes: Paradigm Lost, and Regained*. Chicago: Prickly Paradigm, 2004.

Heryanto, Ariel. "The Development of 'Development'". Translated by N. Lutz *Indonesia* 46, pp. 1–24.

Holston, James. *The Modernist City: An Anthropological Critique of Brasilia*. Chicago: University of Chicago Press, 1989.

King, Tony. *Spaces of Global Cultures: Architecture, Urbanism, Identity*. London and New York: Routledge, 2004.

Kusno, Abidin. *Behind the Postcolonial: Architecture, Urban Space and Political Cultures in Indonesia*. London and New York: Routledge, 2000.

Meecham, Pam and Julie Sheldon. *Modern Art: A Critical Introduction*. London and New York: Routledge, 2000.

Pemberton, John. *On the Subject of "Java"*. Ithaca, NY: Cornell University Press, 1994.

Said, Edward. *Culture and Imperialism*. New York: Knopf, 1993.

Shiraishi, Takashi. *An Age in Motion: Popular Radicalism in Java, 1912–1926*. Ithaca, NY: Cornell University Press, 1990.

Siegel, James. *Solo in the New Order: Language and Hierarchy in an Indonesian City*. Princeton, NJ: Princeton University Press, 1986.

Siegel, James. *A New Criminal Type in Jakarta: Counter-Revolution Today*. Durham, NC: Duke University Press, 1998.

Steedly, Mary Margaret. "The State of Culture Theory in the Anthropology of Southeast Asia". *Annual Reviews of Anthropology* 28 (1999): 431–54.

Tagg, John. *Grounds of Disputes: Art History, Cultural Politics and the Discursive Field*. Minneapolis: Minnesota University Press, 1992.

Toer, Pramoedya Ananta. *House of Glass*. Translated by Max Lane. New York: Penguin, 1992.

Vale, Lawrence. *Architecture, Power and National Identity*. New Haven: Yale University Press, 1992.

Varnelis, Kazys. "The Education of the Innocent Eye". *Journal of Architectural Education* 51, no. 4 (May 1998): 212–23.

Yeoh, Brenda. *Contesting Space: Power Relations and the Urban Built Environment in Colonial Singapore*. Kuala Lumpur: Oxford University Press, 1996.

12

RIDING THE POSTMODERN CHAOS
A Reflection on Academic Subjectivity in Indonesia

Fadjar I. Thufail

Social science scholarship in Indonesia reflects three different generations: the pre-1970s and 1970s, the 1980s and 1990s, and the post-1998 generations. The pre-1970s and 1970s generation experienced limited opportunity and their intellectual work relied largely on the academic training they received abroad. The 1980s and 1990s generation had a greater chance to enjoy local training and only went abroad if they wanted to pursue advanced degrees. A more open political climate after the 1998 reformation has allowed more freedom for the younger generation of scholars to access centres of excellence in America and Europe, and to obtain English books and course materials. While those who grew up in the 1970s often had to overcome limited sources, scholars working in the late 1990s and in post-1998 were able to choose and manoeuvre among different, and often contradictory, theoretical approaches.

The most crucial time of my intellectual development was the period after I finished my *sarjana* (bachelor) degree in 1989. Therefore, I belong to the second generation of scholars who received local training and later enjoyed opportunities to harness this training abroad. The 1990s scholars also witnessed social science theory reaching its privileged position to explain social changes. As one of those working in the 1990s, I witnessed how analytical approaches converged into paradigms that directed scholarly work and illuminated scholarly subjectivity. In other words, my intellectual work took shape in a discursive context that structured the way Indonesian and foreign scholars perceived Indonesia as an object of intellectual exercise.

This chapter addresses an ambiguous discursive relationship that links the trajectory of my academic subjectivity to political and social opportunities and constraints in 1990s Indonesia. It highlights how ambiguity reflects different relations of professional calling to social or political imagination. Working as a professional researcher at the Indonesian Institute of Sciences hardly releases me from the demand to perform as a good citizen of the postcolonial republic. On the contrary, my academic subjectivity as a "professional researcher" reflects more the postcolonial desire of a modern subject than the calling of critical professional work. When critical work took precedence over the imagination of a modern subject during a particular moment of my intellectual history, I had to confront a condescending response that charged me and my work with failing to fulfil the "altruistic" role of social science in leading society towards development.

COLONIAL AND POSTCOLONIAL SUBJECTIVITIES

Social science scholars know that Indonesia has played an indispensable role in the development of many theoretical perspectives on culture, politics, and history. In the late nineteenth and early twentieth century, Dutch colonial scholars and Christian missionaries wrote accounts of societies mostly to serve the interests of the Dutch colonial government and Christian missions. The works of C. Snouck Hurgronje in Aceh and N. Graafland on Minahasan culture are a few examples of widely read colonial scholarship which, despite criticisms, still represent a quality of ethnographic work that is difficult to imitate. The arrival of Clifford and Hildred Geertz in the 1950s to carry out a Harvard-funded sociological project in the newly independent Indonesia, and their publications on comparative studies of Islam, introduced Indonesia to a wider academic audience across the world.

It would be necessary to learn how the colonial scholars in the Netherlands Indies influenced the work of postcolonial Indonesian scholars if one wanted to understand the genealogy of social science in Indonesia. While foreign observers, commonly called "Indonesianists", have been the focus of attention in recent critical reviews on area studies, the genealogical continuity between the colonial and postcolonial Indonesian scholars still awaits further exploration. Due to the lack of a careful study on this topic, comparing colonial and postcolonial work would oversimplify the matter.

However, it is nonetheless important to understand how the colonial and the postcolonial work could draw on a similar social imagination about the object of their writings.

Until the late 1980s, Indonesia appeared remote and exotic to most foreign observers, attesting to a legacy of colonial politics of knowledge. Colonial orientalists' work in Africa had crafted a space of "coeval time", framing how colonial scholarship perceived the "primitive" Africans (Fabian 1983). In Indonesia, however, a structure of "coeval time" can be found not only in the colonial writings on cultures and politics, but also in the postcolonial ones. For instance, the pre-1980s scholarship often exoticized the highly elaborate court cultures in Java and Bali to signify otherness that no longer exists in Europe or North America, the regions where most foreign observers come from. To these observers, many ethnic and linguistic groups in Indonesia came into the theoretical discourse because they represented categorizations missing from the discourse. This way of seeing the Other has shaped the knowledge about cultures and identities of the "exotic" Indonesians. The long period of the Orde Baru (New Order) regime, whose authority had partly relied on cultural essentialism, sustained the social imagination of otherness produced in the colonial and postcolonial scholarship (cf. Pemberton 1994).

We should not assume that the fascination with the exotic Other proliferates in all colonial and postcolonial work. At the same time, however, disregarding the fascination with the colonial imagination would risk neglecting how social imagination drives knowledge construction. We should, therefore, focus on the productive tension between social imagination and the contemporary politics of knowledge to understand how subjectivity works. Until the early twentieth century, the Dutch colonial government relied on reports and descriptions written by colonial officials and missionaries to facilitate their goal to exploit the colony. Interactions between the colonial officials and the missionaries took place through exchanges of reports and letters containing descriptions of customs, religions, and physical characteristics of the natives. Imagination and knowledge produced through this exchange illustrated colonial attitudes toward the natives, even though they ignored the agency of the native people except as colonial subjects.

The early twentieth century witnessed growing displeasure towards the way the Dutch colonial government handled the colony and treated the natives. The Dutch Government's Ethical Policy had produced more schools and educated more native people in the nineteenth-century Netherlands Indies. However, the policy was mostly aimed at creating as many local bureaucrats as possible instead of producing modern subjects, even though it is obvious that through the educational institutions, local natives had learned the modern way of life as well. From the Dutch colonial point of view, the change of attitude, from the traditional to the modern one, was an unintended effect, less desired, and therefore had to be controlled or re-domesticated.

On the other hand, some native people managed to seize the opportunity, opened up by the Ethical Policy, to liberate themselves from the constraints of tradition. The process was indeed ambiguous since the natives refused some traditional norms while maintaining others. Some of the traditional norms, such as harmony and respect for older people, in fact, helped them to domesticate Western lifestyles. It produced an ambiguous colonial subjectivity that was accommodative and at the same time confrontational towards tradition and modernity. The most evident representation of the ambiguous colonial subjectivity were the writings of early twentieth century writers. Their writings reflect the uncertainty they felt towards traditional norms and the role of customary leaders.

The late colonial period from the 1930s to 1940s produced a different kind of colonial subjectivity. In the earlier time, the educated elites in the colony perceived modernity and the western world as existing in a "coeval", shared time (cf. Fabian 1983). In so doing, the elites set them apart from the time of the natives. The transnational expansion of ideologies in the 1930s and the 1940s, and the increasing number of people studying in Europe, brought a new awareness among the elites and students on the role they could play in the worldly time. This new structure of awareness domesticated the discourses on nationalism, revolution, and class struggle that had driven anti-colonial resistances around the world, including in Indonesia.

The newly educated natives led the revolution against the Dutch colonial government and later against the Japanese occupying forces. Many leaders of the revolution had received training as engineers, legal scholars, medical doctors, and psychiatrists at professional schools established by the colonial government. However, their involvement in the revolution originated less in their professional calling as doctors, lawyers, or psychiatrists, than in their passion to take part in an anti-colonial spirit that had driven nationalist movements around the world. In other words, the education provided by the Dutch Government, and, to a certain extent, also by the missionaries, invoked a constricted professional subjectivity among the elite group. The elites learned to be modern subjects through imagining the passion of revolution more than through participating in professional work.

Mohammad Yamin was among the elites who received a Dutch education and later became an important figure in the revolution and in the postcolonial Indonesian Government. He went to a law school and earned the title of Meister in Rechten. Instead of practising as a lawyer,

Yamin joined an anti-colonial resistance movement, and later wrote a book introducing a controversial idea that traced the origin of the Indonesian nation to the fifteenth-century Hindu kingdom of Majapahit. His idea has failed to face historical examination, but it nevertheless strengthened the spirit of revolution as a symbolic root for the political concept of a postcolonial Indonesian nation and nationhood. Yamin's biographical history shows how a revolutionary leader found his subjectivity outside his professional calling, and many other leaders of revolution went through similar experiences. These include Mohammad Amir, a psychiatrist, and Sukarno, who was trained as an architect. Only after Sukarno become the first Indonesian president, for instance, did he practise his architectural knowledge by commissioning projects to build several national monuments.

Indonesia during post-1945 independence witnessed very turbulent years. The inflation rate was high and the political experiment for democratization faced strong resistance from military figures previously trained in the Dutch and Japanese armies. The popular jargon *politik adalah panglima* (politics command) had provoked violent ideological clashes. When the turbulent years culminated in the 1965–66 mass murder and the 1967 quasi-constitutional coup, Indonesia witnessed the making of a new kind of subjectivity that would later frame scholars' engagements with academic work.

When the New Order regime came to power in 1967, Indonesia had just experienced its most brutal historical episode. The country suffered from a violent ideological conflict that put the right-wing military faction against the leftist group. The military had sought to control politics and they managed to force a transfer of power in 1967. A new military regime started and since then a different political discourse gradually solidified. The political discourse crafted by the New Order military regime had at least three discursive components. It promised to correct the "political mistake" of the previous regime, which had failed to consolidate political institutions. In doing so, the New Order foregrounded the discourse on *pembangunan* (development) as an alternative to fix the mistake. In order to make the development work, the military regime promoted the discourse on *ketertiban* and *keamanan* (safety and security). Since the early 1970s, the New Order regime had invented and relied on linguistically framed political discourses to govern the state and curb resistance.

Many people have written about pre-1967 and post-1967 Indonesian politics, but only a few observers have paid attention to how people negotiate professional subjectivities in a chaotic or a "quiet" political environment. Kenneth George (2005) has written about the artistic subjectivity of an Indonesian Muslim painter who worked to find room to manoeuvre in, and cope with, the changing political landscape in Indonesia. George shows that painterly work mediates artistic and political subjectivity, and the paintings signify, not only the technical expertise of the painter, but also statements or commentaries on the painter's desires, expectations, anger, or frustration as he tried to craft room in a changing political situation. George's approach to artistic subjectivity highlights the cultural work involved in the professional practices of a painter.

Following his lead, I would argue that scholarly work also registers statements and commentaries that reflect the process of shaping the academic subjectivities of the scholars. Like the painter, A.D. Pirous, who develops, changes, and abandons his artistic style to manoeuvre within the restricted political climate of the New Order, postcolonial scholars draw on their knowledge and political passion to conduct research or teach. Therefore, the academic preference of a scholar does not merely emerge out of the scholar's expertise and training background. It signifies the passions and commentaries the scholar holds on the surrounding political climate and social life.

Academic subjectivity in postcolonial Indonesia mediates how scholars respond to social changes. While scholars in the United States often draw a clear line between professional and social life, their postcolonial Indonesian colleagues rarely separate their campus life from their social engagements. In 1966, student movements forced Sukarno to transfer his presidency to Soeharto, and helped the New Order regime to consolidate its power. In the early years of the New Order, once again students declared themselves a potential political force, staging a big demonstration to protest against Japanese Prime Minister Tanaka's visit to Jakarta. The activists and scholars in the 1990s often used the 1974 Malari — as the demonstration is called — and the 1966 movements to emphasize the blurred boundary between social engagement and academic work in Indonesia.

The New Order regime took power amid the deepening economic crisis in late 1960s Indonesia. Realizing that political stability was the only solution to prevent more crises, the New Order regime committed a strong effort to minimizing power struggles among conflicting political interests. To achieve the objective, the regime deployed hegemonic and militaristic control on society and invented the *pembangunan* discourse. The hegemonic control and the mobilization of the development discourse curtailed party politics, separated academic life from politics, and redefined the concept of social engagement. The introduction of Normalisasi Kehidupan Kampus (NKK), or Normalization of Campus Life by the Minister of Education and Culture in 1982 sealed campus life permanently from politics. Since then, the government has allowed no professors or students to get involved in politics beyond their mandatory support for GOLKAR, the state-controlled political party. Demonstrations and public expressions of political aspirations against state policy and state bureaucracy could face a swift and violent response from security apparatuses and local bureaucrats.

Ariel Heryanto (2005) and, in a similar tone, Hilmar Farid (2005) argued that the New Order's discourse on development turned into a hegemonic ideology, which no longer represented the actual need of development as a social transformation project. The New Order discourse stripped development of its social function and presented it as an empty signifier that can be manipulated by anyone. Farid has said implicitly that leftist scholars and activists have failed to take part in the discursive debate largely because the state has suppressed leftist political power since the failed 1965 movement.

The 1980s and the 1990s witnessed how the state's development discourse incorporated political projects. Development became a political objective and in doing so the discourse on development shaped an ideological framework that directed politics. In the 1980s and the 1990s the state worked hard to create "ideological state apparatuses" by transforming scholars teaching and working in the New Order academic institutions into the apparatuses of development. The government required state universities to develop undergraduate courses, mostly in social science departments, to prepare students as development practitioners. In the 1980s, the Ministry of Education and Culture launched a "link and match" policy, blatantly illustrating the connection between the state's political interest and the scholarly discourse on development. Universities and colleges should develop programmes and syllabuses to produce as many social workers as possible and meet the demand of the industrial workforce. Therefore, the New Order state managed to incorporate its political project into the academic realm, even though the regime always claimed that politics should be left out of the academic realm.

When postmodernism, critical theory, and post-structural approaches gained popularity in the late 1980s, Indonesian scholars remained less involved in the discussion. Scholars who recently returned from their education abroad were mainly the product of training which emphasized the legacy of social science theories in the 1970s and early 1980s, when functionalism and dependency theories still influenced perspectives to explain social change. Most fellowship holders left for their studies abroad in the 1970s, and at the time when postmodernism began to flourish, they returned to Indonesia or were at least at the latest stage of their education. On their return to Indonesia, they found that the theories they had learned abroad were perfectly suited to the interests of the New Order regime in privileging development and advancing modernity.

In various corners of the world, modernity appears in different guises and through different processes and trajectories. In 1990s Indonesia, modernity manifested itself in urban and elite lifestyles, and unlike in Europe or some other Asian countries, modernity in Indonesia was domesticated through the state and it reached the public as the New Order consolidated its power. Therefore, the critique against the state took the same form as the critique against capitalism. Like the conflation between development and politics in the 1980s, modernity and state politics merged in the 1990s in extending the discourse of development.

The obsession with "high development" in the 1980s shaped academic norms and practices. The contribution of social theory in fostering development practices became a norm for proper and socially acceptable academic work. As a consequence, scholars would face the challenge to produce work that met the strategies of social engineering drawn by state or transnational development agencies. Scholars should address development agencies and at the same time their professional colleagues. The important social science journal *PRISMA* often served as a venue where interests in development and scholarly work met. The journal became popular partly because it made discourse on development look scientific by highlighting structural analysis and cultural critique of the development. The journal set the standard for academic discourse, and many scholars would feel proud if *PRISMA* published their articles.

PRISMA gradually lost its prestige in the mid-1990s. The replacement of its editorial board, from those having a humanistic perspective to those having a scientific orientation, made the journal less responsive to a new trend in social science discourse that began to take hold in the mid-1990s. When postmodernism and post-structuralist approaches proliferated in Europe, America, Latin America, and in some Asian countries, the orientations of academic work in Indonesia had hardly changed. On the contrary, as the *PRISMA* editorship showed, Indonesian social science continued to emphasize the link between modernist thoughts and development practices. The collapse of *PRISMA* represents what I would call dislocated subjectivity among Indonesian scholars working in the mid and late 1990s when those interested in critical theory, postmodernism, and post-structuralism found little room to manoeuvre and express their work. This situation partly explains why Indonesian social scientists made little contribution, if any, to transnational theoretical exchanges, unlike their predecessors in the 1980s or their contemporary colleagues from India or Latin America.

This chapter hardly covers all Indonesian scholars. However, it is important to understand how scholars incorporate historical circumstances in the ways they define themselves as social scientists. In the last part of this short chapter, I will reflect on my experience to discuss how I mediated opportunities and constraints in the late 1990s and the early 2000s.

RIDING POSTMODERN CHAOS: A REFLECTION

I got my bachelor (*sarjana*) degree in 1989 from the Department of Archaeology of the Gadjah Mada University (UGM) in Yogyakarta.[1] After a short period of volunteering at the National Museum, I applied for a research position at the Indonesian Institute of Sciences (LIPI), a government research institution. State and private universities in the early 1990s still emphasized teaching and conducted less research or fieldwork. Only a few social science research centres at universities and state ministries carried out fieldwork regularly. LIPI, therefore, at that time acquired a status as the leading national research centre since it was the only institution that concentrated its work on research and fieldwork, even though as a government body its major clients were mainly government institutions. Due to the limited available research institutions in the early 1990s, my choice of LIPI had been the best path to pursue a career as a professional researcher. I was accepted as a junior LIPI researcher in 1990, and since then I have been working as a professional researcher.

During my undergraduate training at UGM's archaeology department, I hardly learned any social theory. The discipline of archaeology in Indonesia follows a scientific approach and pays more attention to artefacts than the social use of the artefacts. To fulfil my interest in social theory, I took courses offered in other departments in addition to reading books independently. These independent initiatives helped me when I later decided to pursue a career in social science instead of continuing with the scientifically oriented archaeology. I did not realize it at the time, and I only understood it after I reflected on my choice, that my decision to join LIPI was actually a commentary on the use of social theory. I did it because I was convinced that any theoretical knowledge always had practical application.

Since joining LIPI, I have been enjoying opportunities to conduct field research and learn social/cultural anthropology. I was involved in a research team headed by Professor Adrian B. Lapian, a respected maritime historian. The fieldwork assignments sent me every year to North Sulawesi to carry out research on marine resource management among fishing communities. Through this research project, I began to understand the realm of social imagination shared by many Indonesian social scientists, especially those working at and with LIPI.

LIPI researchers have double responsibilities. As part of a government institution, all LIPI researchers are state employees. During the New Order, all state employees were mandatory members of GOLKAR, the state's political party. Therefore, LIPI researchers must perform their function as a state apparatus and follow the state's political guidance. I should emphasize, however, that LIPI researchers have been less obedient than their colleagues at other state ministries or in local bureaucracies. As a matter of fact, some prominent LIPI researchers have been staunch critics of the New Order political regime. Besides performing duties as state employees, LIPI researchers must also be responsible to their academic peer groups since LIPI is basically an academic institution. LIPI incorporates academic responsibility into its standard of employee's evaluation. Every researcher should collect points (*kum*) to determine his or her administrative rank and as a criterion for promotion to a higher position. The points derive from published articles or books. Publication in a peer-reviewed journal and a single-authored book receive the highest points. This point system is similar to the criteria for tenure evaluation in most U.S. universities.

My experience tells me that one needs to be critical of LIPI's academic standard. By standard I do not mean the quality of academic work that LIPI produces, but the particular criteria most LIPI researchers and policymakers use in evaluating academic norms and research processes. As a nationally renowned research institution, LIPI's academic standard in social science research reflects the academic norms that Indonesian researchers hold to assess their knowledge. I would argue that the norms and products of LIPI's and other researchers' work mediate commentaries on the researchers' sense of professional self. LIPI's academic standard is a specific principle employed to ascertain what proper research should be, and, at the same time, signifies professional self shared by most of the research staff at the institution.

LIPI's research project should conform to the themes outlined by the National Planning Institution (Bappenas) and the Ministry of Science and Technology (Menristek). Although LIPI research staff may submit their own proposals, the theme of the proposal should meet the thematic guidelines from Bappenas. For LIPI researchers, the thematic preference for a research project is limited and should stay within the framework of government policy. I should say, however, that LIPI's research policy is hardly unique. Institutions in other countries follow a similar approach to research. However, the LIPI situation becomes critical because it produces a particular kind of professional subjectivity among Indonesian social science researchers.

During the first few years working at LIPI, I joined a team of researchers focusing on traditional marine resource tenure practices and conducted research on the fishing communities in North Sulawesi province. The North Sulawesi site was one of the field sites chosen by the team. The other sites were the Moluccas and Papua. This research project demonstrated how subjective interests meet larger demands and constraints linked to the state's policy on social science research. The topic of maritime community originally came from Profesor Adrian B. Lapian, who has said on many occasions that social science research in Indonesia has neglected maritime issues despite the fact that Indonesia is an archipelagic country. However, researchers are less encouraged to propose a project with the sole intention of filling a gap in academic knowledge on maritime issues when they are expected to situate it in the context of the government's projects on development and social engineering. Should the researchers insist on privileging the academic content and emphasizing the applied components of the research less, the research proposal would earn a very low mark from the internal review board of LIPI. This has been the common case over the last fifteen years. A few researchers have deployed a strategy to tailor their research projects to meet the review board's requirements without sacrificing the theoretical aspects of the topic, and this was the option chosen by Professor Lapian and our maritime research team. Other researchers, however, accept the presumption that privilege should be given to applied research topics. This perspective is not the consequence of the researchers' training background. It emerges from their conviction that academic work should first serve policymaking because only policy can direct development and advance modernity.

A five-year fieldwork experience provided me with sufficient data to develop my advanced interest in ecological anthropology. In 1995 I was awarded a Fulbright scholarship to pursue a master's degree in the United States. I selected the anthropology department at Rutgers University in New Jersey for its reputation in human ecology and maritime anthropology. The Fulbright experience has shaped my professional subjectivity in contradictory ways. On the one hand, it nurtured my conviction that scholarly knowledge drives social change. On the other hand, it introduced me to a realm of critical thinking less obsessed with the call to subject social science work to the need for development or social engineering. In other words, the Rutgers experience has enabled me to question my engagement with social science work.

Ironically, it began with departmental politics at Rutgers. Some professors at the Department of Anthropology also taught at the Department of Human Ecology, creating a nasty competition between those inclined towards the cultural approach, and those with a more scientific perspective. I was caught in the quarrel because my interest in ecological anthropology required me to take various courses at the human ecology department even though I was enrolled in the anthropology programme. While courses offered at the human ecology department were drawn on rigid social science approaches, courses at the anthropology department were mostly inspired by postmodernist thought and the post-structuralist approach. For instance, the concept of development gained different interpretations. On the one hand, study on human ecology perceives development in a more positive term as an inevitable process in social transformation. What remains is a policy question to formulate development's best strategy for social engineering. On the other hand, the critical approach to development brings to light the dark side of development as a cultural practice. Most of the time, the critical approach leaves no room for strategic thinking and delivers no recommendation that can be adopted by policymakers to minimize the effect of development. At Rutgers' anthropology department, however, what started out as a paradigmatic difference, ended up as a political quarrel.

I should acknowledge that at that time I was more attracted to critical thinking than the scientific perspective. The turning point happened during the two years of my graduate training at Rutgers, which shattered my conviction of the supremacy of practical knowledge in the social science discourse. My new encounter with works by Foucault, Bourdieu, Gramsci, Walter Benjamin, and with many other critical theorists and postmodernist figures, invited me to reflect on the sense of being a social science scholar. My new knowledge on discourse, reflexivity, and hegemony challenged the presumption that social science scholars enjoy a privilege by staying "objective". The reflexive moment, however, would run against the certainty many Indonesian scholars held regarding the practical role of social science.

Even though in the mid-1990s postmodernism had reached its peak in America and Europe, it had not yet been popular in the Indonesian artistic and academic scenes. Postmodernism's critical contribution to dislodging authority, history, and norms from their privileged positions evoked a new sense of resistance against capitalism and Western domination, and in doing so inspired civil and artistic movements in many African, Latin American, and Asian countries. The political use of postmodernist thought received a lukewarm acceptance in Indonesia, perceived cautiously by scholars and state apparatuses. They considered postmodernist thinking as a dangerous subversion to their conviction in the progress of the development they were trying to promote.

I wrote a master's thesis on the cultural politics of tradition in a small fishing community in North Sulawesi, and completed my master's degree at Rutgers University in 1997. In writing the thesis I had to struggle over choices to deploy critical theory and the post-structuralist approach, or follow the rigid analytical procedure of social science. This was not just a matter of choosing which approach suited the data I had collected. The ambiguity I felt during my writing reflected a very important moment when I had to decide which "label" of scholarly work I would give myself. This was a very important turning point in my scholarly career since it shaped the way I would pursue my research work. In other words, my academic subjectivity was rooted in a very specific moment, which would decide how my colleagues would "label" my work.

On my short return to Indonesia in 1997–98 and before going back to the United States to continue my PhD studies, I started to realize that Indonesian social science discourse remained reluctant to recognize critical and post-structuralist thinking. Most scholars would scorn it, arguing that it was an improper way to practise social science. A famous senior researcher at LIPI had accused me of falling into a postmodern trap and in doing so I had turned into a confused postmodernist. His reaction actually illustrates well how some Indonesian social science scholars found it difficult to differentiate the post-structural approach from postmodernism. The inability to take post-structuralism and postmodernism seriously reflects more than an indifference to the new approaches. It arose from a particular academic subjectivity that condemned post-structuralism and postmodernism for their inability to support social engineering and development practices.

POSTSCRIPT: ACADEMIC SUBJECTIVITY IN SOUTHEAST ASIA

In the aftermath of the Vietnam War, Southeast Asian scholarship appeared reluctant to pay more attention to themes of social conflict, violence, and political turmoil (Steedly 1999). Except for a few individual initiatives, Southeast Asianists preferred to devote more time to studying culture, religion, arts, or any other topic perceived to be less political. They avoided studies on conflict and violence because of different reasons. One of the reasons had to do with a restriction imposed on certain topics that a political regime thought to be dangerous or sensitive. Indonesia under the New Order, for instance, prohibited foreign researchers from carrying out research on topics that might incite *suku* (ethnicity), *ras* (race), *agama* (religion), and *antar-golongan* (group or class relation) sentiments. The regime also banned foreign researchers, and, to some extent, local researchers as well, from conducting fieldwork in sensitive areas such as Aceh, Papua (formerly Irian Jaya), and East Timor. Certainly this restriction would deter researchers from exploring the topics that were against the interests of the political regime.

Mary Steedly, in her thoughtful review on the state of the art of Southeast Asian studies (1999), has proposed a more interesting explanation to answer why few scholars have paid attention to violence and conflict in Southeast Asia. She argues that violence and conflict are situated out of the realm of cultural theory in Southeast Asian scholarship. In other words, violence and conflict are often not the focus of research on culture because they could help little with the understanding of normative and symbolic systems. As long as explaining cultural systems is the objective of any study, violence and conflict will always be relegated.

I have drawn on Steedly's critical review to suggest a different explanation, particularly in dealing with the work of local scholars instead of foreign researchers. In the aftermath of the Vietnam War, a new kind of academic subjectivity emerged among local Southeast Asian scholars. The war sent a strong message that political turmoil and conflict would solve nothing and, in fact, bring more suffering to people. Some Southeast Asian regimes, such as the Indonesian New Order, immediately seized the chance and drew on the message to consolidate its political power. The dawn of the "high development" era in the Southeast Asia of the 1980s was part of the emerging new academic subjectivity, shaping a proper norm for academic work and social science discourse. Scholars, especially those working in state institutions, would find more opportunities in this period to mediate their passion for development oriented research work. The regime's political interest and the scholars' sense of professional self have converged in the state's policy on teaching and research in some Southeast Asian countries.

Note

1. Indonesian universities differentiate the anthropology (social/cultural) department from the archaeology department, unlike the American system where archaeology is a subdiscipline in the department of anthropology.

References

Fabian, Johannes. *Time and the Other: How Anthropology Makes Its Object*. New York: Columbia University Press, 1983.

Farid, Hilmar. "The Class Question in Indonesian Social Sciences". In *Social Sciences and Power in Indonesia*, edited by Vedi R. Hadiz and Daniel Dhakidae. Jakarta: Equinox, 2005.

George, Kenneth M. *Politik Kebudayaan di Dunia Seni Rupa Kontemporer: A.D. Pirous dan Medan Seni Indonesia*. Yogyakarta: Yayasan Seni Cemeti, 2005.

Heryanto, Ariel. "Ideological Baggage and Orientations of the Social Sciences in Indonesia". In *Social Sciences and Power in Indonesia*, edited by Vedi R. Hadiz and Daniel Dhakidae. Jakarta: Equinox, 2005.

Pemberton, John. *On the Subject of "Java"*. Ithaca, NY: Cornell University Press, 1994.

Steedly, Mary Margaret. "The State of Culture Theory in the Anthropology of Southeast Asia". *Annual Review of Anthropology* 28 (1999): 431–54.

INDEX